Crime Without Borders
An Introduction to International Criminal Justice

❖

AARON FICHTELBERG

University of Delaware

Upper Saddle River, New Jersey 07458

Library of Congress Cataloging-in-Publication Data

Fichtelberg, Aaron.
  Crime without borders: an introduction to international criminal justice/
  Aaron Fichtelberg.
    p. cm.
  Includes bibliographical references and index.
  ISBN-13: 978-0-13-231992-8 (alk. paper)
  ISBN-10: 0-13-231992-6 (alk. paper)
  1. Criminal justice, Administration of—International cooperation.   2. Judicial
assistance—International cooperation.   3. Criminal jurisdiction—International
cooperation.   I. Title.
HV7419.F53 2008
364—dc22

                                                                2007031489

Editor-in-Chief: Vernon R. Anthony
Senior Acquisitions Editor: Tim Peyton
Associate Editor: Jillian Allison
Editorial Assistant: Alicia Kelly
Marketing Manager: Adam Kloza
Production Liaison: Joanne Riker
Cover Design Director: Jayne Conte

Cover Design: Bruce Kenselaar
Cover Illustration/Photo: Getty Images, Inc.
Full-Service Project Management/
  Composition: Integra Software
  Services Pvt. Ltd.
Printer/Binder: Courier Companies, Inc.

Credits and acknowledgments borrowed from other sources and reproduced, with permission,
in this textbook appear on appropriate page within text.

Pearson Education LTD.
Pearson Education Australia PTY, Limited
Pearson Education Singapore, Pte. Ltd.
Pearson Education North Asia Ltd.

Pearson Education, Canada, Ltd.
Pearson Educación de Mexico, S.A. de C.V.
Pearson Education–Japan
Pearson Education Malaysia, Pte. Ltd.

10 9 8 7 6 5 4 3 2 1
ISBN-13: 978-0-13-231992-8
ISBN-10:   0-13-231992-6

Dedication

For Oliver and Theodore. Thanks for making it all worth it.

Contents

❖

Contents

Preface

❖

The purpose of this book is to give the student a grip on this new and complex area of modern crime and criminal justice. It is written for a student who knows little about international crime, international law, and international law enforcement but wants to understand this complex and evolving field. This will make it useful for those who wish to go into international criminal justice or into more conventional criminal justice fields but expect to handle international issues. Thus, those who expect to work with European law enforcement or fight against international drug trafficking or international terrorism will (hopefully) find something useful here, as will law enforcement personnel, future lawyers, and corrections officers who may deal with international criminals.

However, this book is not solely practical in orientation. This is to say that it does not focus exclusively on the nuts and bolts of international crime and international law enforcement. It also raises abstract, theoretical issues for reflection, discussion, and debate by students. It asks critical questions about the best ways to think about international criminal justice problems. For example: Is terrorism a problem that should be treated like a criminal problem or is our fight against terrorism an all-out war? What is the difference? These questions don't have a single practical answer and the answers you arrive at probably won't impact on the work of criminal justice professionals in any concrete way. Nonetheless, this text spends a substantial amount of time on these and similar sorts of questions.

I've chosen to do this for three primary reasons: First, the distinction commonly made between "theory" on one hand and "practice" on the other is not a real one. Our practical policies toward crime are always informed by theories of criminology, psychology, sociology, and even moral philosophy. What we believe should be done to stop crime depends to a large degree on what we think causes criminal behavior. If we believe that many crimes are caused out of economic necessity, then we are more likely to search for economic solutions to these problems. However, if we look at crime as a moral failing of the criminal, then we are more likely to seek punitive solutions to crime problems, or possibly to make efforts to restore the moral values that bind a community together. Similarly, we may choose to revise our theories if they don't provide satisfactory results when put into practice. In the real world, theory and practice are never separate and distinct categories. Our theories shape our practice and our practices alter our theories.

Second, most of the problems of international criminal justice are new ones. Government policy makers are still struggling to understand the threats that international crime poses and to formulate solutions to them. This means that the criminal justice system's responses to international problems are likely to change as new threats and new theories of international crime develop to explain these threats. The more that criminal justice professionals working "on the ground" are able to reflect on the bigger issues, the better able they are to contribute to important debates about changes in international criminal justice. The policies that ultimately develop will be informed by new ideas that come from students, scholars, and criminal justice practitioners—all of whom have something to contribute to our understanding of international criminal justice. Theories help to make sense out of the chaos and uncertainty that changes like globalization give rise to.

Third, much of what will be discussed in this book will be controversial. Because international criminal justice is largely a new field, there is a good deal of disagreement and controversy surrounding it. The country has not yet settled on the appropriate ways to handle many issues of international criminal justice, and so a good deal of the topics discussed here are still "hot topics" in contemporary political debate. For example, many critics believe that international law doesn't really exist in any meaningful sense. Some scholars dispute the legitimacy of international courts and others reject America's approach in its fight against drug trafficking, which punishes suppliers rather than seeking to curb demand. A sharp student may find reasons to disagree with parts of the analysis given in this text. This is perfectly acceptable, and students are encouraged to look at this book (and all other textbooks for that matter) with a critical eye. A broad, theoretical discussion of the international criminal justice system can help the student understand some of these debates and participate in them, developing their own views on them and other related subjects.

Finally, theoretical discussions play an important role in sharpening the student's ability to think critically in general, a skill that is undoubtedly useful outside of the classroom. Many of the issues that we will discuss are not only important for a criminal justice professional to understand; they impact on all participants in modern society. Everyone has felt the effects of terrorism and drugs, either directly or indirectly, and many Americans have a good deal of concern about human rights throughout the world. For these reasons, I have sought to balance analyses of practical problems of criminal justice with a discussion of the "bigger picture," tracing some of the connections between globalization, politics, and criminal justice. To be a fully informed citizen requires that a student learn about the consequences of globalization.

This book isn't exclusively for the criminal justice student or professional. It is also written for those from other fields who wish to see how globalization is viewed within the criminal justice field. Globalization has impacted virtually all fields of study: Economists have examined the transformation of global markets and their influence on domestic economies. Political scientists have examined how transformations of political and economic power that resulted from globalization impact on the behavior of political actors (such as states or other organizations). Even scholars of literature map how the artistic and literary traditions of different cultures have impacted upon each other in modern societies. A student from any of these different backgrounds will find something useful here that they may be able to apply to their own fields of study.

While almost every academic discipline studies "globalization" in some form or other, they do not necessarily study the same thing. Each field looks at globalization in their own way, through their own conceptual lens, as it were. For example, political scientists and economists each examine international issues with very different questions in mind. They both might look at how the forces of political power affect the world, how wars are fought, how nations seek to influence each other, or how the United Nations works to settle disputes, and so on. What interests the political scientist in these processes is how political power shifts and changes across the globe over time. Economists, on the other hand, are likely to examine the impact of global trade on different parts of the world, seeking to determine why certain industries, regions, or states are economically successful and why others fail. What interests the economist about all of this is money (or "capital," to be more precise) and how these social and political changes influence the flow of capital throughout the world. But it is important to note that neither approach is comprehensive. That is to say that there is a lot more to globalization than power and money. Like the proverbial blind men studying an elephant, each discipline studies one facet of globalization, pointing out particular dimensions of it, but no single discipline can capture the whole thing. In fact, it is doubtful that any single approach could ever do justice to such a complex phenomenon.

Criminal justice, as we will see, is largely concerned with one specific part of the globalization phenomenon, the world of lawbreaking, crime, and deviance. This is the "lens" through which criminal justice studies globalization. Of course, crime cannot be studied in isolation. Economics and politics affect crime, and crime has political and economic consequences. This means that a study of globalized crime and the international criminal justice system cannot help discussing some of these broader issues. However, the narrow focus of criminal justice, coupled with the unique interests, methods, and skills that the criminal justice student brings to bear on the topic of globalization, can be useful to those who examine globalization from the standpoint of a different discipline. By examining some of the topics discussed here through the eyes of a criminal justice scholar, a student in a different field can learn some new and useful things about globalization and the international system.

Acknowledgments

A great number of people have helped me with this text and their assistance has been invaluable. Some have generously donated their time to look at chapters, others have provided me with specific information or they have suggested places to inquire further. I would like to thank Ronet Bachman, Joel Best, Eric Rise, Anne Bowler, Margaret Anderson, Aaron Kupchik, and Benjamin Fleury-Steiner at the University of Delaware for their guidance and advice. Tim Peyton, Margaret Lannaman, and Frank Mortimer at Prentice Hall have been very supportive of my efforts and have been an excellent resource for this novice textbook author. Among those who provided important "material support" are Ethan Nadelman, Nadia Gerspacher, Christoph Safferling, David Bederman, Jennifer Bodde, Bill McDonald, Roger S. Clark, Matthieu Deflem, Ellen Podgor, Harvey and Laurie Fichtelberg, and Wes and Annette Bowers. Students in my International Criminal Justice course here at the University of Delaware were gracious in helping me even out the "bumps" in the text. The anonymous reviewers of the manuscript also provided extremely helpful criticisms and suggestions, making this book much better than it would otherwise have been and I want to thank them for their constructive criticisms. Caroline Spangler and Nancy Quillen have been invaluable in providing administrative support and helping get the manuscript in "fighting shape." Most importantly, I'd like to thank my wife, Renee Bowers, for all of her love and support.

Of course, any errors in this book are strictly my own and all feedback is welcome.

1

Introduction

Globalization and Globalized Crime

The world is at your fingertips, almost literally. Your clothes were probably made somewhere in China; your computer was likely assembled in Japan. Some of the food sitting in your stomach was probably grown and processed in Europe, and the gasoline in your car was probably pulled out of the ground in either South America or the Middle East. Nearby, you can log on to the Internet and instantly access news and information from any possible part of the world, including audio and video clips from Asia and South America. You can quickly discover what issues politicians in Russia are discussing and what bothers the "person on the street" in Kuala Lumpur. When you call your computer manufacturer for technical support, chances are that you are talking to a person in a call center on the other side of the world. Manning these call centers are people who have been taught to mask their accents and have memorized details about American popular culture (including events on current television shows like *Desperate Housewives*) in order to mask their foreign nationality and convince you that they are really American. In some ways, we are more closely connected to people on the other side of the planet than we are with those people living next door to us.

Economists call this phenomenon "globalization": the linking of different national economies and local cultures into one global economic system. Developments in transportation and shipping mean that goods are exported across borders more quickly and more easily than ever before. New technology has allowed for global communication in a way never dreamed of even a few decades ago. These in turn have dramatically affected the way that capitalism functions. In the new global economy, Chinese manufacturers can compete with Americans for contracts from American businesses like Wal-Mart (and with their lower wages, it is usually cheaper to have goods manufactured overseas and shipped into America than it is to make them here!) and high-tech workers in India can compete for engineering and computing jobs with the rest of the world as the Internet allows them to send their finished product to the customers at the same speed with which it would arrive from the office next door. Developments in transportation, information technology, and trade relations have changed the nature of capitalism itself. We are now competing in a global marketplace. As one well-known political observer has described it, the world is now "flat" and all of the barriers that separated our national economies (and also protected them) have quickly disappeared.[1]

This global economic interdependence has had a tremendous effect on the rest of our lives, influencing the world's cultures in countless ways. American movies and television shows have found audiences around the globe, even in places where our more racy comedies are frowned upon by powerful religious authorities. *Will & Grace,* an American comedy about a gay man and his female friend plays daily over the airwaves in India, where homosexuality itself is strictly taboo. American food has appeared on street corners in Berlin and Santiago, where McDonald's and Burger King products are eagerly consumed by teenagers wearing Levi's jeans and shirts emblazoned with English-language slogans and American flags. American pop music pulses from radios in Cape Town and New Delhi, and Israeli teens, mimicking young people from American cities, write hip-hop tracks detailing their experiences (not to mention the middle-class youths in the American suburbs who seek to emulate their urban peers). Among some elements in many parts of the world, this American influence is welcome and its offerings are greedily consumed. Among others, in particular, the older, more conservative, and more religious sectors of the globe, the Americanization of cultures is observed with apprehension, anxiety, and in some cases, outright hostility.

Likewise, Americans have been exposed to foreign cultures in countless ways, consciously and unconsciously absorbing aspects of their lifestyles. Immigrants from Asia, Latin America, and Africa have filled American towns and cities with their own sights, sounds, tastes, and smells, giving even the smallest towns a dose of cosmopolitanism. Few American cities lack a *tienda* selling Latin American products, food, and music. Bigger cities have Chinatowns, Koreatowns, and Little Saigons, where immigrants have congregated and set up shops, cafes, and restaurants. Classroom discussions on almost any topic can gain benefits from the insights of all kinds of students from widely diverse backgrounds, each of whom can contribute a different set of experiences about an issue. "Diversity," a term that once only meant the inclusion of African Americans in American social and political life, has become much more complex as groups with different histories, different experiences, and different interests have woven themselves into the American experience. Globalization has made America a different country.

One dramatic change that globalization and modern communication have helped bring about has been the development of a sort of "global conscience." As we learn more about each other's lives and each other's troubles and suffering, some of the traditional barriers that separate "us" (members of one group) and "them" (those of another group) have begun to dissipate and something that affects one part of the world is considered to be relevant to the rest of the world. This is a process that has been ongoing for a long time, and was particularly strong in the horrified response of

---

[1] Friedman, Thomas (2005) *The World Is Flat; A Brief History of the Twenty-First Century.* New York: Farrar, Straus, and Giroux. See also Scholte, Jan Aart (2005) *Globalization: A Critical Introduction,* 2nd ed. New York: Palgrave.

many who observed the Nazi Holocaust of the Jews and others during the World War II. It has become particularly acute as mass communication media, and the "unfiltered" Internet, have shown graphic images and testimony of atrocities from the Balkans, Africa, and Asia. Organizations like Amnesty International and the Human Rights Watch based in Europe and in the United States monitor the behavior of governments across the world, and stars like Bono and Angelina Jolie work to fight poverty and disease around the globe. While this conscience has sometimes been manipulated by politicians and interest groups to distort complex conflicts, and while atrocities have often been ignored by powerful nations that do not want to put their own people at risk to help others, it is nonetheless true that the citizens of wealthy countries have become more aware of problems in the rest of the world and have been more willing to do something to help.

There are many uncertainties in globalization. Whether this process will benefit humanity by promoting diversity and understanding in the world, or it will destroy this very diversity by foisting junk food and junk culture on the ancient civilizations of the world is not clear. One thing is perfectly clear, however. The changes that globalization will cause are largely inevitable and will undoubtedly prove dramatic, affecting virtually everybody almost everywhere. The train cannot be turned back and nobody knows where it is headed.

With all of the benefits provided by the globalization of economies and cultures has come at least one important downside: Criminals have globalized themselves, too. Illegal drugs that are grown and manufactured in South America are quickly shipped across borders and over oceans, finding eager buyers in North America and Europe. Sometimes this happens in the holds of smuggling ships or airplanes and sometimes in the bodies of "mules"—people recruited to carry their deadly cargo by swallowing it. Humans are smuggled, too. Some seeking freedom or a chance at a better life in a more prosperous nation slip across borders. Others are brought as slaves to fulfill the sexual whims of the wealthy. Credit card numbers are illegally obtained in the United States and used to purchase goods in Hong Kong and Moscow. Computer hackers routinely cause havoc throughout the global computing world, while music and movie pirates routinely display bootlegged American movies and music stretched out on towels on street corners from Madrid to Jakarta. Real pirates, too, have resurfaced in parts of the world, stealing ships as large as oil tankers (frequently murdering their lawful occupants) and selling them and their cargo on the black market. The global economy is not only the arena for law-abiding companies seeking honest profit, but also for industries that prey on the vulnerable and cater to buyers with unwholesome tastes.

Other dangerous organizations have also globalized themselves, but they do it in order to spread or defend a political ideology or religious doctrine. While not motivated by the simple pursuit of wealth, terrorists and other guerilla organizations have worked alongside international criminal organizations to wage their wars against existing political and economic powers. Sometimes they have relied on a black market to obtain weapons to kill their opponents or forged documents that allow them to travel without arousing suspicion. In terms of their beliefs, they are not entrepreneurs like other organized criminals but rather are warriors with a fanatical agenda; in terms of their methods and the tools of their trade, they are criminals. Regardless of their different motives, terrorist organizations and other international criminal outfits have both relied on the mechanisms of modern international markets, the same tools used by the likes of Visa, Nike, and Guinness, to reach their consumers (and also their victims).

These dangers of the globalization of crime hit home for Americans in a particularly tragic way on September 11, 2001. Terrorists from all over the Middle East—Saudis, Yemenis, and Egyptians—who had lived and traveled throughout the globe (including prolonged stays in both Europe and the United States) hijacked four planes and flew two of them into the World Trade Center in New York City, killing nearly 3,000 people, crashing the third into the Pentagon and the fourth into the fields of central Pennsylvania. Their targets weren't strategic, but symbolic. They were not only attacking America and American power, but were seeking to bring down the globalized economy that the World Trade Center symbolized. A new era in American history had clearly begun, with a new, serious threat to the American way of life.

The U.S. government struggled (and still struggles) to understand this new enemy. Many saw the September 11 attacks as "another Pearl Harbor," the first salvo of a new world war. Others saw it as a dangerous threat, but one that could be handled by existing political institutions (including law enforcement). Shortly after the attacks, President George W. Bush declared that "The deliberate and deadly attacks which were carried out yesterday against our country were more than acts of terror. They were acts of war."[2] However, for the first time America was not at war against a country or a nation. Some countries may support terrorism, but defeating these countries would not mean the end of terrorism as such. Terrorism is first and foremost a tactic and terrorists cannot definitively surrender and end a conflict in the way that Germany did at the end of the World War II, or Iraq did after the United States and its allies invaded. This enemy is different.

Rather than declaring war against one particular country, the president declared war against a globalized enemy—a loose group of individuals funded surreptitiously by religious fanatics from every corner of the world. Many of these terrorists operated (and continue to operate) under the radar of traditional militaries, using false documentation such as phony passports and fake driver's licenses to slip across borders undetected and using the Internet to coordinate their attacks and spread their propaganda from continents away. They do not use uniforms or fight on battlefields, as do ordinarily combatants, but remain under "deep cover," operating in small cells and posing as ordinary citizens until their designated time to strike.

Despite the symbolic importance of figures like Osama bin Laden as leaders of Islamic terrorism, al-Qaeda does not have a structured hierarchy of commanders who pass orders down to subordinates. Rather, al-Qaeda functions as a loosely knit organization, working with people who have only a remote connection to bin Laden. Some, such as the bombers who killed 52 people in the London Underground in July 2005, or those arrested in Canada in June 2006, may only draw inspiration from September 11 and bin Laden. Scholars have begun to refer to al-Qaeda as a "brand" (like KFC or Honda) rather than as an organization. What links these terrorists is not a flag, an ethnicity, or an organizational structure. What holds al-Qaeda together is a fanatical

---

[2] Remarks by President Bush to Security Team, September 12, 2001, available at http://www.whitehouse.gov/news/releases/2001/09/20010912-4.html.

ideology and a loose network of Internet sites, mosques, and dark corners where they meet for sharing information, inspiration, training, and funding. Al-Qaeda is a set of beliefs and a set of tactics that they use to realize their goals, and is not a single unit. Globalization has found some of its most adept and most dangerous handlers in bin Laden and his followers.

Criminal justice institutions have responded to the rise of terrorism and other aspects of the globalization of crime in a number of important and novel ways—ways that have revolutionized modern criminal justice. New legal rules, some highly controversial, have been developed at both the national and international level, to deal with these new threats. States have come together to handle common problems and common enemies, negotiating treaties that have led to a new level of international cooperation, and at times, new reasons to disagree. New institutions have been developed to coordinate intelligence sharing between nations about suspected international criminals and their activities, and new courts have been formed to hold international criminals accountable for their acts. The idea of "international criminal justice," which once referred exclusively to cooperation in the investigation of criminals and their extradition from one state to another, now encompasses some dramatic and exciting new areas of policy, courts, and corrections. There is now an international "system" of sorts to deal with international crime problems, a system that has grown dramatically in the last two decades. With the rise of globalization, international criminal justice has become the cutting edge of modern criminal justice.

WHAT IS INTERNATIONAL CRIMINAL JUSTICE?

International criminal justice as an independent field of study is for the most part new, so before we can begin to analyze and discuss it in any sort of depth, we must first understand what it is, broadly speaking. While the international criminal justice system is new, the concept of an international crime is in some ways very old. Piracy on the high seas, for example, has been punished as an international crime for centuries (as we will see in the next chapter). Similarly, warriors were executed for allowing the soldiers under their command to rape and pillage a conquered city in violation of the laws of war. However, the concept of an international crime has been dramatically transformed and expanded by globalization as well as the development of the UN and other international institutions. Here I will try to explain what I think is the best way to go about understanding this concept. Like many other aspects of this text, this will be somewhat controversial (and might serve as a good issue for classroom discussion).

Rather than focus on a single definition of international crime or international criminal justice, it best to understand these entities as consisting of a number of different, but connected categories. There is not one single essence or definition that determines which crimes are properly labeled "international crime," and a crime can be "international" in a number of different senses. Many people interpret international criminal justice much more narrowly than I will here, but what combines these aspects of international crime and international criminal justice is that they each involve globalization: either the globalization of crime or the globalization of justice. Here are some of the main aspects of international crime and criminal justice that will be discussed in this book.

International Crime and International Criminal Law

The first and most obvious international crimes are those crimes that violate international criminal law and are punished by international courts and tribunals. International criminal law consists of a set of treaties and customary practices of states that have defined certain behaviors as international crimes. We will discuss some of the important areas of international criminal law in later chapters, but for now it should be clear that only a specific set of crimes are international crimes in this narrow sense of the term. These crimes rely on the unique international legal system of treaties and its own institutions such as the UN and the International Criminal Court (ICC).

While it is true that international criminal law has created a special category that it calls "international crimes," the focus of these laws is quite narrow and does not do justice to some of the most important crimes that have an international character. Crimes under international criminal law are largely limited to genocide, aggression, war crimes, and crimes against humanity. While there is no doubt that these are each important crimes in their own right (and will be discussed thoroughly in later chapters) this definition leaves out a number of important crimes that have an international character. This is simply because many important crimes that possess an international dimension are not criminalized by international law. International drug trafficking and human trafficking are only two examples of crimes with an international dimension that are not prosecuted by international courts or banned under international criminal law.

Thus, to do justice to the complexity of international crime and international criminal justice, we must go beyond this narrow legal definition. American law enforcement will occasionally deal with those types of crimes, but they frequently confront more "mundane" international crimes like cross-border drug smuggling or international credit card fraud. Also, noticeably missing from this list is terrorism (the reasons for this will be discussed in detail in the next chapter).

Transnational Crimes

This second category of international crimes are offenses that have a substantial effect across national borders. Sometimes these are referred to as *transnational crimes* because they are problems that transcend any local or national government. A crime may be international in this sense when it is a problem that affects people in states other than the one where the crime is perpetrated or when the crime is linked in a "chain" with other crimes that stretch from one state to another. The crime itself may not necessarily be defined by international criminal law or punished by international courts, but it is nonetheless international on the basis of the way that the criminals conduct their business. They usually operate across international borders. Traffickers ship their goods, be they drugs, people, or money, across international borders in order to make their profits, requiring that they elude law enforcement in both countries as well as naval forces like the U.S. Coast Guard. Terrorists work through a shadowy network of operatives that can stretch from Pakistan to London to the United States. In each of these cases, fighting transnational crime requires the cooperation of the law enforcement institutions of a number of different countries, making them a unique category of crime.

It may surprise you to know that there is no international court to try and punish international drug traffickers. While drug trafficking is illegal in every country, and states often have agreements to punish drug smugglers and to extradite them to states where they are wanted, these agreements do not explicitly state that trafficking is an international crime in the way that genocide is. However, despite this fact, we would be remiss if we didn't include cross-border drug smuggling as an international crime as it undoubtedly has a transnational character: A vast amount of the cocaine that is consumed in the United States and Europe, for example, is produced in Latin America (mostly Peru, Bolivia, and Columbia). American law enforcement and the American military work extensively with Latin American governments to help them combat drug production and smuggling. To say that the harvesting of coca plants is an issue only for Colombians and consumption is an issue solely for countries whose citizens purchase cocaine is to miss the obvious link between these problems. Solutions to the drug problem cannot be found solely on one end of the production–consumption chain. These sorts of issues need to be understood in their transnational context and so they will be featured prominently in this book.

Most of the crimes that we will discuss will be of this sort: crimes that have a global impact but don't necessarily violate international criminal law. Creating international laws is a slow, cumbersome process that is frequently caught up in the web of complex international politics and power struggles that continually structure the relations between states. What might be considered a problem for one country, such as the export of classified technology or scientific data that could be used to develop nuclear weapons, could be seen by another country as essential for its security and as a boost to its status in the world. While this second state may *say* that it is opposed to the spreading of nuclear technology, it will undoubtedly *act* in a very different manner. It may seek to slow down any attempt on the part of the international community to legally regulate the spread of nuclear technology and repudiate treaties that aim to limit the development of nuclear weapons. Similarly, environmental problems like global warming might hurt small states but are ignored by wealthy states that have no interest in creating laws that might harm their domestic economies. The same is true for criminal laws: Many states are jealous about their right to prosecute criminals and are often unwilling to surrender this power to other states or to an international court and thus have not pressed to develop treaties that would outlaw such crimes.

These ongoing (and undoubtedly endless) political conflicts mean that international law has yet to adequately confront a number of important global crime problems. This has left the domestic legal systems to pick up their slack. While it is extremely hard to hold a person criminally liable for an act that they commit in another state, some techniques have been developed to deal with criminals in other states when their home state refuses to prosecute them or when the criminal acts harm citizens of another state. Often different states work together on certain types of crimes in order to confront a shared problem. They will share information and work together across borders to deal with these crimes. In Columbia, for example, the U.S. military has provided training and support to Columbian forces fighting against cocaine producers in that country's rural areas. Organizations like Interpol allow national police systems to share information about criminals who they believe have gone abroad. Thus, drug trafficking is an international crime regardless of whether or not there exists a treaty to designate it as such or an international court to punish it. It is international by its very nature and the response to drug trafficking has been, to a certain extent at least, an international one.

Some transnational crimes appear to be domestic on their face but have important international elements to them. An Islamic terrorist with Israeli citizenship who purchases explosive materials and detonates them in a Tel Aviv marketplace has committed no international crime per se. In one sense, he is a common murderer, similar to an individual who burns down an occupied building to perpetrate insurance fraud. But it would be a mistake to describe the terrorist's crime as purely a domestic phenomenon—it would overlook many salient details of the crime that distinguish his actions from those of the conventional murderer. The bombing was likely to have been funded and supported by sources outside of Israel and was likewise inspired by a global Islamic terrorist movement. The arsonist's actions were not. This means that there may be no technical reason to describe the bombing as an international crime, but to do justice to the phenomenon one must place it in a broader international context.

The International Criminal Justice System

Along with these categories of crimes, this text will deal in depth with the international criminal justice system. However, like the concept of international crime, the international criminal justice system also is a complex and controversial subject. Strictly speaking, there is no international criminal justice system if we think of it as analogous to the system in the United States. Traditionally, a criminal justice system consists of four interconnected parts: A legal system to define criminal behavior, a police system to enforce these laws, a court system to apply the law to a particular case, and a corrections system to either punish or reform convicted criminals. In the United States all of these aspects of criminal justice fit together in one whole. Each of the 50 states has law, policing, courts, and corrections alongside the federal system, which is regulated by the Constitution, the supreme law of the land.

International criminal justice as a system is not as neatly or clearly defined as domestic criminal justice. Because each state is sovereign and independent, international law is much weaker than domestic law and international criminal justice consists in a number of different, overlapping legal systems and institutions. International law, local police systems, and national courts, along with governmental officials must interact if they are to adequately deal with transnational and international crimes. They may not all agree on the nature of a problem and they may not all agree on how to deal with it. Despite this, these various criminal justice institutions have increasingly found formal and informal ways to cooperate to deal with matters of common concern. This means that, although there is no international criminal justice system per se, we can describe international criminal justice as an evolving institution developing new tools to work together to counteract international crime. International and domestic institutions interact in some very specific and regular ways to fight international and transnational crime, so in this sense we can say that there is an international criminal justice system.

In general, we will discuss the international criminal justice system in three major forms:

1. *International law enforcement:* There is no international police force, but national law enforcement agencies have worked together in order to share information about international criminals and combat shared crime problems, creating organizations like INTERPOL and EUROPOL to help them quickly cooperate with each other. They have also developed legal tools, such as special treaties, that

allow investigators in one country to easily obtain evidence from abroad. Similarly, the various national governments have worked together to allow for the swift transfer of criminals from one state to the state where they committed their crimes. This process, known as *extradition,* along with these other investigatory matters, will be discussed in some depth in Chapter 5. Even without a world police force, the national governments have developed an effective system to handle international criminals.

2. *International criminal law and courts:* The first modern international criminal courts were created after the World War II to handle German and Japanese war criminals. Since then, three other international criminal courts have been created: two temporary courts to handle atrocities in Rwanda and Yugoslavia and a permanent court in The Hague (the capital city of The Netherlands). These courts apply international criminal law to a select group of particularly egregious cases that national courts are unable or unwilling to effectively prosecute. Though international criminal trials are rare, they have gone a long way toward helping develop the principles of international criminal law and the formation of the international criminal justice system. Many hope that these courts will expand to tackle international crimes beyond genocide, war crimes, and crimes against humanity and deal with crimes such as piracy, terrorism, and international drug trafficking.

3. *Domestic criminal justice goes abroad:* Much of what we will discuss here will be American criminal justice. That is, U.S. law enforcement has operated abroad and U.S. courts have had to deal with cross-border crimes, sometimes acting alone and at other times with the cooperation of foreign governments. While this is American justice, it is not removed from other aspects of international criminal justice, if for no other reason than that these agents must follow international procedures and international law to get their job done.

Since September 11, a novel field of law enforcement has developed to handle new threats to the American people. The federal Department of Homeland Security (DHS) functions on the border between international and domestic law enforcement and represents an effort to keep America safe from international terrorists. Thus it fits under the subject of this text. The DHS (discussed in depth later) plays a variety of domestic law enforcement roles, such as securing transportation and protecting high-ranking government officials, but always with an eye toward external threats.

I should note that there are other types of crimes that are sometimes labeled as "international crimes" that will not be discussed here. For example, there are many international lawyers who argue that states (and not individuals) may be held criminally liable for certain actions. This would mean that "Australia," as a state, could commit a crime. This is different from, say, the political leaders of Australia committing a crime. So-called "international crimes of state" are controversial and largely irrelevant to the work of criminal justice professionals, so they won't be discussed here. It is also important to note that states can be found to be in violation of a law, but this does not mean that the state has committed a crime. The word *crime* denotes a special part of the law with a lot of unique features, such as punishment, and due process that would be hard to apply to a country like Australia. The focus of this study will be crimes that are likely to be confronted by international criminal justice professionals, not diplomats or other foreign policy experts.

Some aspects of this typology of international crime may change as the international criminal justice system grows and changes. One of the things that makes international criminal justice unique and exciting is that as a field, it is in many ways still in its infancy. Like any infant, it can grow and develop in very different directions depending on how it is treated and nurtured by those who surround it and depending on the environment with which it interacts. As part of this text, particularly in the final chapter, I will try to suggest ways that the international criminal justice system will likely develop or should develop in order to effectively address international crimes.

INTERNATIONAL CRIMINAL JUSTICE AND INTERNATIONAL POLITICS

As you have probably already observed from the subjects that we have already touched upon, international criminal justice is closely bound up with international politics and a lot of international crimes have a political character. In fact, many of the issues that we will examine in this text are typically studied in political science or international relations courses. There is no doubt that many of these crimes (especially aggression and war crimes) will be political "hot potatoes" for the foreseeable future, constantly a subject of heated political debate. It is unlikely that terrorism would ever be treated similarly to more conventional sorts of crimes like street crime or armed robbery. Politicians and scholars will probably argue endlessly over who is properly labeled a terrorist and how best to eradicate the terrorist threat. It is nonetheless important for students of criminal justice to understand these issues through the lens of their own discipline, separate from the assumptions of political science. The fact that many international crimes are "political" should not lead us to overlook the fact that they are indeed crimes. Despite their obvious connections, the study of international criminal justice is not the same thing as the study of international politics and should be treated as distinct from it.

Not all international crimes are subject to the whims of international politics, and even highly politicized crimes are not politicized all of the time. Police units investigate most international crimes in the same manner as they do conventional murders, burglaries, or car thefts. Even international courts and war crimes trials have prosecutors who use detectives and other forensic experts to help build the cases against suspects. International trials are run in a manner similar to trials for common criminals, with prosecutors and defense attorneys presenting their respective cases and arguing over the introduction of evidence, and a judge (or a panel of judges in some cases) reaching a judgment on the guilt or innocence of the accused. All of this usually goes on with little interference from governments or other political bodies that are usually the primary actors in international politics. Most of the time international crimes are treated just like ordinary crimes, albeit crimes with great political, historical, and moral importance.

Second, criminal justice can provide insights into international criminal justice that are distinct from those that would be offered by political scientists. Political scientists look at international relations primarily as groups of countries either cooperating or alternatively seeking to dominate each other on the world stage. Certainly this approach can tell us a lot about the way that the world works, but it overlooks a lot of issues that are important in international *criminal justice*—issues that interest a criminal justice scholar and those who work in the field of criminal justice. Criminal justice scholars and criminologists ask very different questions than do other professionals—questions about gathering evidence, criminal psychology, or criminal procedures, to name only a few. Criminologists want to understand the nature and origins of crime, while criminal justice professionals want to use these tools toward the very practical goal of stopping crime. This means that contemporary criminal justice students may contribute some unique and valuable insights to this field.

Third, those who work in the field of criminal justice, either domestically or internationally, are not politicians, and the bigger questions about the political forces that shape international criminal justice aren't necessarily their professional concern. Of course, police officers, prosecutors, and others in the criminal justice system are citizens and should take part in political discussions about the role that America should play in the world. However, while they are on the job, this is not a part of what they do. Their job is to do their best to stop would-be lawbreakers from causing harm or to make sure that these criminals answer for their criminal behavior. This means that, although they should be aware of the broader policy questions and political debates that shape criminal justice, this does not mean that they should allow these issues to affect how they do their job. Thus, there is a big difference between a politician and a criminal justice professional.

While it is certainly true that politicians and diplomats play a strong role in the international criminal justice system, and we will look at some of the political influences on the field, any close examination of conventional criminal justice would reveal exactly the same thing. That is to say that *all* criminal justice issues are in some sense political. Lawmakers in Washington DC and in state capitals frequently choose what to criminalize and how to punish lawbreakers based on what will help them look "tough on crime" and help them garner votes in the next election. Likewise, politically savvy prosecutors will target those lawbreakers whose prosecution is likely to make them look good and get positive headlines to bolster their future political ambitions. Politically powerful lawbreakers frequently seek to influence criminal justice through back channels, using connections, influence, and sometimes simple bribery to avoid facing prosecution. Many criminologists have labored to show the hidden class and racial biases which make American criminal justice discriminatory against minorities and the poor.[3] This means that to a great extent domestic criminal justice is political in its own way. Even in America, the line between criminal justice and politics is not as clear or absolute as one would like.

THE UNITED STATES AND INTERNATIONAL CRIMINAL JUSTICE

One of the crucial differences, of course, between domestic criminal justice and international criminal justice is that Americans tend to be much more skeptical about international institutions in general and this attitude carries over into international criminal justice. American politicians frequently mock the UN and other international bodies, and the United States has often withheld funds from the UN for extended periods of time. The United States has cut aid to some states that have agreed to participate in

---

[3] Reiman, Jeffrey H. (1998) *The Rich Get Richer and the Poor Get Prison: Ideology, Class, and Criminal Justice.* Boston: Allyn and Bacon.

the ICC and has even threatened to use military force in order to rescue Americans held there! (We will discuss this further later.) This is surprising given the influential role that the United States played in constructing some of the main bodies of international society; the United States was one of the central forces behind the creation of the UN and its predecessor, the League of Nations, to name only two of many significant examples.

The roots of American hostility toward the international community are complex. Some scholars argue that without some sort of world government to enforce them, international laws are meaningless scraps of paper. These critics argue that force and power always predominate in international politics, and that any effort to apply laws and governance to international society is hopelessly naïve and will inevitably end in disaster. This view of the world is sometime referred to as *realism* or *realpolitik*. As an ancient realist, the Greek historian Thucydides described this view of global politics in his *History of the Peloponnesian War:* "The strong [countries] do what they have the power to do and the weak [ones] accept what they have to accept." [4] International law, the realists argue, cannot stop dictators bent on conquest and destruction and only the force of arms can keep peace in the world. They further assert that the American government should use international institutions and international law only when it is in its interest to do so. When there is no advantage in cooperating with the international community on criminal matters or other issues, the United States should ignore the opinions of the rest of the world and do what it must to ensure its strength, security, and prosperity. This view has remained a strong one in American political thought and (to some extent) inspired President George W. Bush to invade Iraq without authorization from the UN or the support of the vast majority of the international community.

At other times, however, American skepticism toward international law is rooted in what is sometimes referred to as *American exceptionalism.* American exceptionalism, a term first coined by the French philosopher Alexis de Tocqueville, is the belief that America, as the greatest free nation in the world (a "city on the hill" to use former President Ronald Reagan's phrase) occupies a unique position in the world and should not follow the rules that apply to other states. Because we are the most powerful nation in the world, we must do things that other nations will not do. Other nations are willing to condemn brutal dictators, but only the United States is able to act against them. This means that we must occasionally ignore UN declarations or violate treaties that we have made with other states in order to "get the job done." However, exceptionalists claim that when America acts unilaterally, it is not in pursuit of power or wealth, but rather in an effort to spread freedom and democracy to others. For a country as uniquely powerful as the United States, the ends of liberty justify the means of violating the norms of international institutions and the international community, or so the argument goes. From this perspective, the American invasion of Iraq, "Operation Iraqi Freedom," was motivated by the exceptionalists' sense that America should use its tremendous military power to spread freedom and human rights to a country that had been brutally oppressed.

---

[4] Thucydides translated by Warner, R. (1952) *History of the Peloponnesian War.* New York: Penguin Press, p. 402.

Both of these views are deeply entrenched in current American political debates and will indubitably be a part of your classroom discussions. Regardless of the political fights that underlie international criminal law and international politics more generally, there is nonetheless a desperate need for American criminal justice professionals to understand the ways that the international criminal justice system functions. The reality is that the world is shrinking and criminals have no real interest in respecting the boundaries that separate one country from another. Drugs flow into the United States from South America and Asia. Terrorists are trying to harm Americans from the four corners of the earth. This means that, like it or not, American law enforcement professionals and other criminal justice professionals will have to work beyond American borders to keep Americans safe and secure.

2

International Criminal Law

In many ways international law is quite different from American law or the law of other countries, but in some respects it is very similar. As a legal system, it has a long history, stretching back long before America was founded (some scholars even trace it back as far as ancient Babylonia[1]). However, international *criminal* law is a relatively new phenomenon. The first international criminal trials took place at the end of World War II for the leaders of the Axis powers, but more recently several tribunals have been set up around the globe that can be described as international criminal courts. We will deal with each of these courts and tribunals in the next chapter, reserving this chapter for the legal rules and principles that these court systems apply. It is important to note, however, that different criminal courts apply slightly different legal systems (depending on what their charter, or founding document, says) and that there is a good deal of ambiguity in parts of this legal field. Nonetheless, it is possible to talk about international criminal law as one legal system with some variations depending on context just as it is possible to talk about "American criminal law" while acknowledging that there are variations in law among California, Georgia, and other states, as well as differences between the laws in the 50 states and the federal criminal laws.

International criminal law developed out of what lawyers refer to as *public international law* and still uses many concepts from this legal system. Thus, international criminal law is a part of the broader international legal system, and cannot be understood completely independent from it. Most attorneys who work in international criminal law are not conventional criminal lawyers, but rather international lawyers trained in the analysis of treaties and other areas of the international legal system. Given this, it is best to begin this chapter with an introduction to international law proper and then turn to its criminal aspects. Once we have set out some of the basic elements of international criminal law, we

---

[1] Bederman, David (2001) *International Law in Antiquity.* Cambridge: Cambridge University Press.

will be in a better position to evaluate how crimes are dealt with in international courts—the subject of the next chapter. I will make some reference to international courts in this chapter, as it is sometimes necessary to refer to them in order to understand the law. If you get confused in this chapter, however, feel free to glance ahead to the next one as this might help you understand the subjects described here.

INTERNATIONAL LAW: SOME BASIC QUESTIONS

Many students who have never had experience studying international law may find this field a bit confusing when they compare it to the legal systems of their home countries. As we will see, international law is in many ways a very different kind of legal order with concepts and institutions that are quite different from those one would find in the United States, Germany, or China. Most traditional legal systems usually have a clear line of legislative authority (that is, a single "place" to look for laws and a single body that is empowered to create them) that usually stretches back to a founding document that one can point to and say, "This is the source of our laws." In the United States, we have a legislature at the federal level (Congress), legislatures at the state level, and courts that interpret the law and adjudicate legal disputes, all of which get their ultimate authority from the Constitution. Of course, at the top of our legal system is a Supreme Court that stands as the final arbiter of the meaning of the Constitution and an executive (the president) who enforces domestic laws. While the roles played by courts and legislatures differ in different governments of the world and scholars debate whether or not such a simple view about the constitution actually reflects the reality of law in most countries, for the most part finding a law in a domestic legal system is a relatively straightforward process.

However, in international law, matters are much more complicated than this. There is no global constitution, no international legislature, and no final arbiter of legal questions in the international realm. That means that international law is much "looser" in structure than traditional domestic legal systems, and there is usually a lot more ambiguity in interpreting what international laws require from states and other international actors. This means that to some extent you will have to "let go" of some of your traditional ideas about the nature of law and think about law differently in order to adequately understand international law. If you have already studied the law in some of your other classes (such as a class on criminal law or criminal procedure, for example), you have probably discovered that there is a big difference between what the layperson thinks the law is and what it really is. Likewise, there is a difference between how people believe international law should work and how it does in fact work. Just as European and Islamic law are very different from American law in many ways (that lead some to mistakenly assume that they aren't really law either), international criminal law is a unique legal system with its own ideas about the nature of law and its own way of dealing with complex issues.

One feature of international law that is difficult for many to grasp is that international law lacks any clear enforcement mechanism in many cases. There is no international government or international police force (we will discuss the role of the UN shortly and the International Police Service—Interpol—in Chapter 4). Because of this, it is sometimes difficult to get unwilling states to obey international law when they do not wish to. This is particularly true for powerful states such as the United States, which lacks any serious military rival that could force it to obey a law that it does not wish to. Some scholars have argued that international law works by "self-help"—that states are entitled to enforce the law for themselves. Other times such as the first Gulf War in 1991, a number of states can band together to force an uncooperative "rogue state" like Iraq to acquiesce to the demands of the international community. However, these cases are rare exceptions to the fact that much of international law lacks a way to assure that states will follow the law when they do not wish to.

On account of these important differences between international law and other legal systems, many legal scholars have argued that international law is not really law. John Austin, a 19-century legal scholar, famously argued that there is no such thing as international law, but only an "international morality," and H. L. A. Hart in the 20th century described international law as a "primitive" legal system.[2] Others (such as the "realists" whom I discussed in the previous chapter) have asserted that international law is simply a part of international politics and does nothing independent of the will and desire of particular states. They quickly point to instances where states, including the United States, have violated treaties, UN Security Council resolutions, and other international legal obligations without being condemned as outlaws, much less punished for their violations. International laws may also have some other purposes, they argue; for example, it might be used as a propaganda tool that international diplomats can use to try and embarrass their enemies by showing that they are violating international law, or it might be helpful to clarify points that everybody already agrees upon. Beyond these roles, however, they argue that international law is largely meaningless. Once there is a conflict between international laws and national interests, any political leader would violate a treaty without a second thought.

International law is certainly different from domestic legal. Whether or not it is "really law" or is "meaningless" is a much-debated question among scholars. Any fair-minded examination of international law, however, will reveal that it is good at doing some things, but in others, such as its attempts to prevent war by outlawing it, it is much less effective. Despite its lack of enforcement power, international law has in many cases proven surprisingly effective at countering the behavior of international actors. As one U.S. legal scholar observed, "almost all nations observe almost all principles of international law and almost all of their obligations almost all of the time."[3] Even those states that seek to ignore international law and heap scorn on the United Nations, the so-called "rogue states," expect that their borders be respected, their diplomats be granted immunity, and their nation's passports be honored by other nations. A stamped envelope can go virtually anywhere in the world because of international treaties regarding international postal practices, and similar laws structure global transportation, global trade, and global environmental concerns.

International law is evolving with the times and it is becoming a more effective way for handling different sorts of disputes in the international community. In 100 years, it will probably function even better than it does now. For studying international *criminal* law, we don't need to determine the issue of whether or not international law in general "matters" in international politics. Mercifully, we can be much more limited

---

[2] Hart, H. L. A. (1994) *The Concept of Law.* Oxford: Oxford University Press, p. 227.

[3] Henkin, Louis (1979) *How Nations Behave.* New York: Columbia University Press, p. 47.

in our considerations. What is important for us in examining international law is to determine how the ideas and rules of international law affect international criminal law and what the rules of contemporary international criminal law consist in.

CLASSICAL INTERNATIONAL LAW

Traditionally, international law dealt almost exclusively with the relations between states, not with individual people. The agreements between states were rules that bound them only in their relations with each other and had nothing to do with individual human beings. To put it technically, states were the *subjects of international law* (they could make laws and had to follow laws) and individual people were *objects of international law* (they did not have any say in international law and they were not punished for breaking it). For example, if a businessman from the United States has a complaint against a Chinese citizen who is living in China, they could not go to an international court as individuals to resolve their dispute. Instead, they would have to go to their respective countries and convince them to lodge a complaint and the case would be listed as *"United States* v. *China."* If the U.S. government had no interest in the case and there were no domestic forums where the unhappy American could lodge a complaint against his former associate, then there was nothing else that he could do to seek justice. Even heads of state, kings, presidents, and the like were not considered to be individuals from the standpoint of law; they were considered to be representatives of the state, the state in physical form as it were. States were like atoms, bouncing against each other, sometimes bonding with each other, but never breaking into the smaller bits that comprise them. This classical model of international law is still the way most international law works (although, as we will soon see, international criminal law is one important exception).

The fact that classical international law dealt entirely with the legal relations between states and not individuals means that *sovereignty* was the central principle of most international law. "Sovereignty" refers to the rights of states to conduct their affairs in any way that they see fit without interference from others. In fact, in the classical model of international law, the only international laws that exist are laws that sovereign states have consented to follow and there is no legal power superior to the state itself. There is no world government that could force a state to obey a set of laws that it does not consent to. (Imagine if you only had to follow the laws that you agreed to follow!) Thus, the origins of international law are always in the states that make up international society and it is to the behavior of these states that lawyers have traditionally turned to find the material that comprises international law. That is, in order to determine what international law says about an issue, they would look to the agreements that different states have made with each other rather than to the acts of a legislature.

Rather than looking to a single constitution and a single legislature to find the rules that make up international law, international lawyers turn to a variety of different source. While these sources are all different from one another, they are all taken to be manifestations of state sovereignty. These sources have developed over the years and have been recorded in some important documents that serve as a guide of sorts for researching international law. The most often cited list of the sources of law is the one used by the

International Court of Justice (ICJ or "World Court," an institution that we will discuss in some depth in the next chapter) in their founding statute. These sources are important for us insofar as they are not only the sources of general international law, but are also the ultimate sources of international criminal law. The following are the legal sources cited by the ICJ for international law:

1. *Treaties* (or "Conventions"). As mentioned above, a treaty is an explicit, written agreement between states to behave or not to behave in a particular way. The creation and interpretation of treaties is governed by a treaty known as the *Vienna Convention on the Law of Treaties.* Treaties can either be *bilateral* or *multilateral.* Bilateral treaties are agreements exclusively between two states. Multilateral treaties are agreements between a number of different states on a common issue. A great deal of international law comes from treaties. Treaties cover a wide range of topics from trade to environmental law to human rights.

   Usually a country or group of countries enter into prolonged negotiations, frequently for years, about the details and the wording of the agreement. Then, a country's ambassador or otherwise designated representative (called a "plenipotentiary") signs a treaty and then the appropriate power in the government ratifies it, marking the state's consent to be bound by it. In the United States, the executive branch (the president) signs a treaty and the Senate ratifies it. The treaty is then binding on the parties.

   Often, countries will enter *reservations* to a multilateral treaty. A reservation means that a state agrees to some of the treaty's requirements, but rejects others. As sovereign states, this is their right. Sometimes a treaty reservation will stipulate that a country does not accept *all* of the treaty, but only parts. Also, it may stipulate that it interprets a particular treaty requirement in a specific way. For example, if a treaty said that a country agrees not to torture prisoners, the country may state in a reservation that it interprets the word *torture* in a particular fashion. Usually, multilateral treaties are then deposited with the United Nations.

2. *Custom.* A customary law is a longstanding practice in international politics that possesses a legal quality to it. To determine the existence of a customary international law, one must find two features: A longstanding practice among states and *opinio juris,* that is, the recognition that this practice is a legal obligation. If states have behaved in a particular way for a long period of time and behaved in such a way because they believed that they were legally bound to do so, then there is customary law. (Without *opinio juris,* all that exists is a custom or etiquette—*opinio juris* gives the custom its "legal quality.")

3. *General Principles.* Frequently, when judges need to sort out a particularly thorny issue of international law, they turn to the legal practices of various states. A survey of domestic legal systems can show that there is one common way of looking at a particular question and the court will apply this in international law. This sometimes allows international judges to fill in gaps in treaties and customs in order to deal with a particular question.

4. *Equity.* Along with the general principles of law, international jurists may sometimes appeal to a principle of "equity" or fairness in order to render a decision in a particular case.

While each of these sources of international law is consistent with a notion of sovereignty, the final source of international law is an exception to this principle.

5. *Jus Cogens.* Recently a doctrine of international law has developed that asserts that there are "peremptory norms" in international law, that is, rules that are superior to any other international laws that might exist. Thus, unlike other international laws *jus cogens* laws cannot be changed (except, in theory by another *jus cogens* rule) and they do not require a custom or a treaty to be a law. These norms are controversial because they override the concept of sovereignty that I mentioned above—states must obey *jus cogens* laws even if they do not wish to.

For example, the law against genocide, the effort to destroy a racial, ethnic, or religious group, is taken to be a *jus cogens* norm. While there is a multilateral treaty that outlaws genocide, called the *Genocide Convention* (the treaty that bans the practice of genocide), countries that have not signed or ratified the Genocide Convention cannot commit genocide with impunity, nor could a state sign a treaty with another state agreeing to cooperate in genocide against a group as such a treaty would automatically be void. Scholars disagree about which norms are *jus cogens* norms, but commonly mentioned candidates are laws banning genocide, slavery, and the prohibition of the use of force except in self-defense.

THE UNITED NATIONS AND INTERNATIONAL LAW

Contrary to what many believe, the UN is not a "world government" and it does not have the power to make international law on its own. The UN does not have a legislature that can vote on laws that states must then follow. This would violate the principle of sovereignty mentioned above. However, this does not mean that the UN has no significance for international law, in fact it does influence international law in a number of indirect ways.

The UN was founded after the close of World War II, during an international conference in San Francisco. There, the international community hoped to create an organization that would serve as a forum for debating issues of global concern, but one that would also have the power to enforce its will when a state or group of states refuse to behave properly. The founders of the UN had learned lessons from the League of Nations, the UN's prewar predecessor that had proven unable to stop Germany and Japan from invading their neighbors. The UN's founders hoped to create a body that would have the power to enforce its will on such rogue governments, but simultaneously not step on the prerogatives of sovereign states that created it.

The result of the conference was the creation of the Charter of the United Nations, a multilateral treaty setting out the powers and structures of the new international body. As set out in the Charter, the UN, based in New York City, consists of four primary bodies: the General Assembly, the Security Council, the Secretariat, and the International Court of Justice (ICJ). The General Assembly consists of all states that are a part of the UN, that is, those states that have signed and ratified the UN Charter. The Assembly serves as the main deliberative body, discussing issues and passing resolutions on various topics. While these resolutions sometimes attract a great deal of attention and are sometimes the subject of intense political debate, they are not law. They only express the opinions of the states that vote for them. The Secretary General who is in charge of the day-to-day operations of the

UN and helps to carry out the wishes of the other bodies heads the Secretariat. He too is not empowered to make international law.

The Security Council's relation to international law is somewhat more complex than this, however. The Council consists of 15 members; ten members are chosen on a rotation basis from among different countries, and five are permanent members (the United States, China, the United Kingdom, France, and Russia). Under Chapters VI and VII of the UN Charter, the Security Council is primarily in charge of maintaining international peace and security, and in order to do this, it can pass resolutions that order states to behave in particular ways. If these Security Council resolutions are not followed, the Council can then authorize the use of force against noncompliant states that threaten international peace. This is what happened during the first Gulf War. When Iraq failed to withdraw from Kuwait (which it had invaded), the Security Council authorized the United States, along with its coalition allies, to forcibly eject Iraq from Kuwait. (The second Gulf War in 2003 did not have authorization from the UN Security Council.) Thus, while it is not a formally recognized source of international law, Security Council resolutions can require that states behave in a particular way whether they wish to or not. We will discuss the role of the Security Council and the American invasion of Iraq in more detail when we discuss the crime of aggression.

INTERNATIONAL CRIMINAL LAW

If all that there was to international law were this classical model based on the agreement of sovereign states, there would be no such thing as international criminal law. There would only be laws that hold between these states, binding them in their interactions with one another. An individual could violate the laws of a particular government, but there was no way for an individual to violate an international law *as an individual,* much less any expectation that he would be prosecuted for violating international law. International criminal law would be a self-contradiction.

However, this classical international legal system had a number of significant flaws that forced it to change and develop new doctrines. A number of individuals "slipped through the cracks" of domestic legal systems—escaping their reach by working beyond the boundaries of any single government or acting in ways that were horrifying but weren't necessarily criminal in the state where they occurred. These weaknesses caused various governments and the international lawyers who worked for them to develop a set of special legal rules in order to handle these people. Thus, they sought to formulate a set of international laws that held *individuals* accountable for their behavior. Individuals started to gain legal personality in international law; they were no longer only objects but also subjects of law. This, in turn, has led to a revolutionary transformation of the classical model of international law and the development of international criminal law as a separate legal system.

The most influential of these special international laws were the laws against piracy. When one thinks of pirates, quaint images of Blackbeard, parrots, and the Jolly Roger usually come to mind, but piracy on the high seas has been a serious problem for trading ships for thousands of years. Organized bands of pirates menaced the Roman Empire and continued to steal ships, killing their crew and devastating sea-based economies through much of human history. Just like terrorism in the contemporary world, piracy was a unique criminal problem because, strictly speaking, nobody owns the ocean and thus no national legal system applies there. If they committed murder on the high seas, where there was no established government, who could say that they committed a crime? Whose law applies? What gives somebody the right to punish a pirate, particularly if they seized a ship that belongs to a country that differs from that of their captors? While it is obvious that pirates *needed* to be punished, it is not at all clear whether there could be a legal justification for this punishment in the classical model of international law.

Slowly, a doctrine developed that made piracy a unique sort of crime. Pirates were no longer ordinary criminals, people who violated the laws of a government, but rather were considered to be enemies of humanity as such. Pirates became *international criminals* (*hostis humanis generis*—enemy of mankind), people who can be caught, tried, and punished by representatives of any country, regardless of the nationality of the pirates or the victims and regardless of where the crime took place. Originally this developed as a rule of customary international law, but later became codified (written) in international treaties. For example, the "Convention for the Suppression of Unlawful Acts against the Safety of Maritime Navigation" gives states jurisdiction over "any person [who] . . . unlawfully and intentionally . . . seizes or exercises control over a ship by force or threat thereof."[4] Pirates, then, were the first truly international criminals.

The end of World War II led to the next significant development in the history of international criminal law. Nazi Germany and imperial Japan had waged an aggressive war against the Allied powers, an effort that was stopped only after the deaths of millions. Even more shocking, however, were the acts that were inflicted on Jews, Poles, and others who did not fit in with Hitler's twisted vision for the future of humanity. The Nazis killed nearly 10 million people during the war, many of them women and children. However, much of the acts that were perpetrated by the Nazis were *legal* under German law at the time and there was no clear international law that made waging an aggressive war an international crime in the way that piracy was. At the end of the war, the surviving leadership believed that as long as they had followed German law, they were immune to criminal prosecution (which, of course, does not mean that most expected to be left alone by the victorious Allies; most expected to be shot on sight). Similarly, many accepted that Germany had done something wrong by invading Poland, France, and Russia, but they did not believe that this war was a *crime*. According to most experts, there was no legal way to punish these individuals for their behavior. Germany could be made to suffer and the Nazi

---

[4] Article 3(1). Article 6 of the treaty established the jurisdiction of the states over piracy:

Article 6

1. Each State Party shall take such measures as may be necessary to establish its jurisdiction over the offences set forth in article 3 when the offence is committed:
   (a) against or on board a ship flying the flag of the State at the time the offence is committed; or
   (b) in the territory of that State, including its territorial sea; or
   (c) by a national of that State.
2. A State Party may also establish its jurisdiction over any such offence when:
   (a) it is committed by a stateless person whose habitual residence is in that State; or
   (b) during its commission a national of that State is seized, threatened, injured or killed; or
   (c) it is committed in an attempt to compel that State to do or abstain from doing any act.

leadership could be punished summarily (outside of a trial), but there was nothing that could be done legally against these people.

As we will see in greater detail in the next chapter, many of the surviving leaders of the Third Reich and the Japanese military government were tried as war criminals before special international military tribunals created by the victorious Allied powers. Accused of waging an aggressive war, war crimes against enemy prisoners, and crimes against humanity, they were tried and many were executed for violating international laws, not for breaking German or Japanese laws. The Allies determined that, just as with pirates, there were certain criminal activities that required all of international society as a whole to respond. The fact that there was no world government that could enforce international laws against these individuals was no reason to allow them to escape punishment for their deeds.

However, there was a further twist to the Nuremberg trials that was not found in the international laws against piracy. In addition to punishing the German leadership as individuals for violating international law, many of the German defendants were punished for acts that were perfectly legal (even required) under Nazi law—wrongs that were committed against *their own people.* This was the biggest challenge yet to the concept of sovereignty, and one that had serious consequences for the classical conception of international law. Under international law, political leaders were no longer the absolute masters of their own lands.

The final development that transformed international law was similarly an outcome of World War II: the concept of universal human rights. While the concept of a right has been a centerpiece of Western governments for centuries (the American *Declaration of Independence* and the French *Declaration of the Rights of Man and Citizen* are the two most influential documents establishing individual rights), few believed that these rights were *universal.* Rather, most believed that citizens had the rights that their government gave them and that no rights existed if the government was unwilling to grant them to their citizens. The British philosopher Jeremy Bentham famously denounced universal rights as "nonsense on stilts."[5] However, many felt that the atrocities committed by the Nazis in Germany, while legal under German law, were violations of basic rights that were superior to any domestic laws. Basic rights such as the rights to life and liberty were *inalienable:* They could not legitimately be taken away by any government. Thus the concept of a universal, human right was born in international law.

Shortly after the end of the war, the United Nations and the international community crafted a number of important human rights documents in order to make this ideal a part of modern international law. The most famous of these documents was UN General Assembly Resolution 217(A): the Universal Declaration of Human Rights (UNDHR). However, as we've already discussed, UN General Assembly resolutions are *not* international law, thus while the UNDHR is an important political document, its legal power is limited. However, two treaties were written shortly after the UNDHR, the International Covenant on Civil and Political Rights and the International Covenant on Economic, Social, and Cultural Rights. Each of these treaties spelled out in further detail the rights belonging to everyone, regardless of his or her race, gender, or nationality. Along with these, a number of regional treaties, applying only to a select part of the globe, have been created, such as the European Convention for the Protection of Human Rights and

---

[5] Bentham, Jeremy, "Anarchical Fallacies," Reprinted in Hayden, Patrick (2001) *The Philosophy of Human Rights.* St. Paul: Paragon House.

Fundamental Freedoms, as well as specialized human rights treaties dealing with specific topics, such as the Convention on the Elimination of All Forms of Discrimination against Women. Along with these treaties, a number of nongovernmental organizations (or NGOs) were formed, such as Amnesty International and Human Rights Watch, in order to monitor world governments' respect for human rights to make sure that they were living up to their commitments.

International criminal law came into being as a result of these developments in classical international law. First, international criminal law was formulated to deal with individuals whose criminal deeds did not clearly fall under the jurisdiction of one particular state. A separate legal system was needed to hold individuals accountable for their acts when states are unable or unwilling to do so. Second, it allowed for individuals, not states, to be punished for what would otherwise be considered "acts of state" (actions of individuals in their capacity as a head of government) within their own borders, such as in the case of the Nazis. Finally, like human rights law, which developed alongside it, international criminal law allowed for a legal standard of human conduct that was higher than those laws passed by any particular state. International criminal law "cracked the shell" of state sovereignty, which was the foundation of classical international law, making individual persons a part of the international legal system for the first time. From then on, international law was not just about Germany, France, Japan, Argentina, and so on but also about people like you and I. International law dealt not just with states, abstract entities embodied in symbols such as flags or crowns, but also with real human beings.

The Sources of International Criminal Law

Like all other parts of international law, international criminal law relies on the traditional sources that we just discussed. Thus, it turns to custom, treaties, general principles, and other sources to find out what acts are criminal in the international context. Once we have set out the primary sources of international criminal law, we will then turn to the actual crimes that comprise this legal system.

To complicate matters, different international courts will deal with these legal sources in slightly different ways. There is no *single* international criminal law. As we will see in the next chapter, most international courts have a founding document or charter that specifies what laws the court may apply and what crimes it may prosecute. Like America, where each of the 50 different states has its own legal code with a slightly different list of crimes and different definitions of each crime (making murder a slightly different crime in Arkansas than it is in Maine), different international bodies apply slightly different criminal codes. Thus, the charter of one tribunal may assert that individuals can be prosecuted for a particular crime that another tribunal ignores. In addition, when international crimes are prosecuted in domestic courts, those crimes will blend with the domestic legal systems, further complicating an already complicated picture. Nonetheless, we can still sketch out a rough outline of some of the basic sources of international criminal law:

We can distinguish further between two different types of international criminal law. One type deals with, the so-called "core crimes," crimes that are relevant to the international courts that we will discuss in the next chapter. These include crimes against humanity, war crimes, aggression, and genocide. In these cases, he accused criminal is directly responsible for violations of criminal law. The other type are international criminal laws that are some-times considered to be a part of "transnational criminal law" and refer to what is known as "crimes of international concern" rather than international crimes in the strictest sense.[6] In these cases, multilateral treaties set out acts that individual states agree to criminalize in their own domestic law. Both types of crime rely on the mechanisms of international law, that is, both involve treaties and other sources of international law.

Treaties   A number of international agreements set out the central principles of interna-tional criminal law. There is no *single* treaty that sets out all of international criminal law like the penal code in the American legal system. Rather, many different treaties each have elements to them that spell out in greater or lesser detail a list of international crimes.

The most famous of these treaties are the Geneva Conventions of 1949, setting out the rules governing the treatment of wounded combatants, prisoners of war, and civilians in wartime, and the Hague Conventions of 1899 and 1907 which further regulate the conduct of war. These treaties set out much of what we know to be the laws of war (also known as "international humanitarian law"). The Genocide Convention of 1948 sets out genocide as an international crime and also requires that states prosecute individuals who commit this international crime in their own, domestic criminal justice systems. We will discuss each of these treaties in further depth when we discuss the individual crimes that they set out.

Along with treaties that lay out the substance of international criminal law, that is, treaties that tell states what sorts of things are international crimes, treaties can also serve to create international courts that can try international criminals or rule on matters relevant to international criminal law. As we will see in the next chapter, some international criminal courts are the creation of such treaties. Thus, the Rome Treaty established the International Criminal Court (ICC), the first permanent international criminal court, in 2003. Along with creating this court, the Rome Statute set out the crimes that the ICC is charged with prosecuting and thus serves as the primary source of international criminal law for the ICC.

As I already mentioned above, transnational crimes are set out in treaties, but they are not be tried by international courts. There are numerous treaties that spell out transnational crimes, each of which deals with a different subject. For example, the Council of Europe's Cybercrime Convention lays out some of the guidelines for prosecuting and punishing cybercrime, and all the states that have ratified the treaty agree to follow its guidelines.

Customary International Criminal Law   Along with the treaties, the customary practices of nations can serve as a foundation for international criminal law. Many laws that govern armed conflict are not in the Geneva Conventions, but rather are a part of international custom (sometimes referred to as "the customs of war"). This aspect of international law can help "fill in the gaps" of treaty law as many states may not be a part of the Geneva Conventions but nonetheless are bound by those parts that are human-itarian law that are customary.

---

[6] This distinction is taken from Boister, Neil (2005) "Transnational Criminal Law?" *European Journal of International Law,* 15: 953–976.

General Principles   As was mentioned above, international lawyers will often refer to the general legal principles found in the majority of states in order to fill in gaps in international law. Legal systems are complex affairs that usually develop over centuries as judges and legislators work to plug in any holes that develop out of unforeseen circumstances.

Security Council Resolutions   As mentioned above, the UN Security Council's resolutions are binding on the international community, which in turn can affect international criminal law in a number of different ways. Security Council resolutions have been used to create international courts for Rwanda and Yugoslavia, not only establishing these bodies, but also defining the specific crimes that individuals may be punished for by them. This gives the Council a vast amount of power when it comes to determining the nature of crimes that could be punished under international criminal law. For example, the Council may set out exactly what acts are international crimes for these tribunals. Further, as we will see when we discuss the crime of aggression, under certain interpretations of international law, the Security Council is entitled to determine when an act of aggression has taken place.

Erdemovic

The case of Drazen Erdemovic, who went before the International Criminal Tribunal for the former Yugoslavia (more on this tribunal in the next chapter), is an excellent study in how international criminal lawyers reason about law. Erdemovic, a Bosnian Serb, was accused of participating in the murder of several Bosnian Muslims during that country's civil war. Erdemovic admitted to participating in the killings at a place known as Pilica Farms outside of the city of Srebrenica; however, he asserted that he had participated in the killings only because he feared for his life. When Erdemovic appealed his case, he argued that his claim of duress was a *complete defense* for his acts, meaning that, even though he committed the murders, he was not guilty of any crime. The lower court, however, argued that his claim of duress was a *mitigating factor,* lowering the amount of punishment that he deserved for his acts, but not relieving him of guilt. This is a complex part of criminal law, and the court did not have an obvious answer that they could apply to Erdemovic. Thus, they looked to some of the sources of international criminal law that we have just set out. Here is an excerpt of the appeals court ruling:

Judgement

On or about 16 July 1995, buses containing Bosnian Muslim men arrived at the collective farm in Pilica. Each bus was full of Bosnian Muslim men, ranging from approximately 17 to 60 years of age. After each bus arrived at the farm, the Bosnian Muslim men were removed in groups of about 10, escorted by members of the 10th Sabotage Detachment to a field adjacent to farm buildings and lined up in a row with their backs facing DRAZEN ERDEMOVIC and members of his unit.

On or about 16 July 1995, DRAZEN ERDEMOVIC did shoot and kill and did participate with other members of his unit and soldiers from another brigade in the shooting and killing of unarmed Bosnian Muslim men at the Pilica collective farm. These summary executions resulted in the deaths of hundreds of Bosnian Muslim male civilians.

At his initial appearance on 31 May 1996, the Appellant pleaded guilty to the count of a crime against humanity. The Appellant added this explanation to his guilty plea:

> Your Honour, I had to do this. If I had refused, I would have been killed together with the victims. When I refused, they told me: If you are sorry for them, stand up, line up with them and we will kill you too. I am not sorry for myself but for my family, my wife and son who then had nine months, and I could not refuse because then they would have killed me. That is all I wish to add.

. . .

For the reasons set out in the Joint Separate Opinion of Judge McDonald and Judge Vohrah . . . the majority of the Appeals Chamber finds that duress does not afford a complete defence to a soldier charged with a crime against humanity and/or a war crime involving the killing of innocent human beings.

From the separate opinion of Judges McDonald and Vorah

. . .

There are different views as to whether even the most extreme duress can ever constitute a valid defence or extenuating circumstance with respect to a particularly heinous crime, such as killing an innocent human being.

    1. No customary international law rule can be derived on the question of duress as a defence to the killing of innocent persons

       . . .

       (b) No consistent and uniform state practice underpinned by opinio juris Not only is State practice on the question as to whether duress is a defence to murder far from consistent, this practice of States is not, in our view, underpinned by opinio juris. Again to the extent that state practice on the question of duress as a defence to murder may be evidenced by the opinions on this question in decisions of national military tribunals and national laws, we find quite unacceptable any proposition that States adopt this practice because they "feel that they are conforming to what amounts to a legal obligation" at an international level.

       In the present case, duress, either as a general notion or specifically as it applies to murder, is not contained in any international treaty or instrument subsequently recognised to have passed into custom.

C. General principles of law recognised by civilised nations

A number of considerations bear upon our analysis of the application of "general principles of law recognised by civilised nations" as a source of international law. First, although general principles of law are to be derived from existing legal systems, in particular, national systems of law, it is generally accepted that the distillation of a "general principle of law recognised by civilised nations" does not require the comprehensive survey of all legal systems of the world as this would involve a practical impossibility and has never been the practice of the International Court of Justice or other international tribunals which have had recourse to Article 38(1)(c) of the ICJ Statute.

    . . .

    In order to arrive at a general principle relating to duress, we have undertaken a limited survey of the treatment of duress in the world's legal systems. This survey is necessarily modest in its undertaking and is not a thorough comparative analysis. Its purpose is to derive, to the extent possible, a "general principle of law" as a source of international law.

1. Duress as a complete defence
   (a) Civil law systems
   The penal codes of civil law systems, with some exceptions, consistently recognise duress as a complete defence to all crimes. The criminal codes of civil law nations provide that an accused acting under duress "commits no crime" or "is not criminally responsible" or "shall not be punished." We would note that some civil law systems distinguish between the notion of necessity and that of duress. Necessity is taken to refer to situations of emergency arising from natural forces. Duress, however, is taken to refer to compulsion by threats of another human being. Where a civil law system makes this distinction, only the provision relating to duress will be referred to.

   France
   In the French Penal Code, promulgated on 22 July 1992, Article 122–2 provides that:

   No person is criminally responsible who acted under the influence of a force or compulsion which he could not resist.

   It is apparent from this article that French law recognises duress as a general defence which leads to acquittal. The effect of the application of this provision is, speaking figuratively, the destruction of the will of the person under compulsion.

   Chile
   In the Chilean Penal Code of 1874 (amended as at 1994), Article 10(9) provides that criminal liability shall be removed in respect of a person "who commits an offence due to an irresistible force or under the compulsion of an insuperable fear."

   (b) Common law systems

   England
   In England, duress is a complete defence to all crimes except murder, attempted murder and, it would appear, treason. Although there is no direct authority on whether duress is available in respect of attempted murder, the prevailing view is that there is no reason in logic, morality or law in granting the defence to a charge of attempted murder whilst withholding it in respect of a charge of murder.

   United States and Australia
   The English position that duress operates as a complete defence in respect of crimes generally is followed in the United States and Australia . . .

   India
   In the Indian Penal Code of 1960, amended as at March 1991, section 94 provides: Except murder, and offences against the State punishable with death, nothing is an offence which is done by a person who is compelled to do it by threats, which, at the time of doing it, reasonably cause the apprehension that instant death to that person will otherwise be the consequence: Provided the person doing the act did not of his own accord, or from a reasonable apprehension of harm to himself short of instant death, place himself in the situation by which he became subject to such constraint.

(c) Criminal Law of Other States

Japan

In the Japanese Penal Code of 1907 (amended as at 1968), Article 37(1) provides: An act unavoidably done to avert a present danger to the life, person, liberty, or property of oneself or any other person is not punishable only when the harm produced by such act does not exceed the harm which was sought to be averted. However, the punishment for an act causing excessive harm may be reduced or remitted in the light of the circumstances.

Somalia

Article 27 of the Somali Penal Code of 1962 provides:

1. No one shall be punished for committing his acts under the coercion of another person by means of physical violence which cannot be resisted or avoided.
2. The responsibility for such acts belongs to the person who coerced [their commission].

. . .

3. What is the general principle?

Having regard to the above survey relating to the treatment of duress in the various legal systems, it is, in our view, a general principle of law recognised by civilised nations that an accused person is less blameworthy and less deserving of the full punishment when he performs a certain prohibited act under duress. We would use the term "duress" in this context to mean "imminent threats to the life of an accused if he refuses to commit a crime" and do not refer to the legal terms of art which have the equivalent meaning of the English word "duress" in the languages of most civil law systems. This alleviation of blameworthiness is manifest in the different rules with differing content in the principal legal systems of the world as the above survey reveals. On the one hand, a large number of jurisdictions recognise duress as a complete defence absolving the accused from all criminal responsibility. On the other hand, in other jurisdictions, duress does not afford a complete defence to offences generally but serves merely as a factor which would mitigate the punishment to be imposed on a convicted person. Mitigation is also relevant in two other respects. Firstly, punishment may be mitigated in respect of offences which have been specifically excepted from the operation of the defence of duress by the legislatures of some jurisdictions. Secondly, courts have the power to mitigate sentences where the strict elements of a defence of duress are not made out on the facts.

. . .

4. What is the applicable rule?

The rules of the various legal systems of the world are, however, largely inconsistent regarding the specific question whether duress affords a complete defence to a combatant charged with a war crime or a crime against humanity involving the killing of innocent persons. As the general provisions of the numerous penal codes set out above show, the civil law systems in general would theoretically allow duress as a complete defence to all crimes including murder and unlawful killing. On the other hand, there are laws of other legal systems which categorically reject duress as a defence to murder. Firstly, specific laws relating to war crimes in Norway and Poland do not allow duress to operate as a complete defence but permit it to be taken into account only in mitigation of punishment. Secondly, the Ethiopian Penal Code of 1957 provides in Article 67 that only "absolute physical coercion" may constitute a complete defence to crimes in general. Where the coercion is "moral," which we would interpret as referring to duress by threats, the accused is only entitled to a reduction of penalty. This reduction of penalty may extend, where appropriate, even to a complete discharge of the offender from punishment. Thirdly, the common law systems throughout the world, with the exception of a small minority of jurisdictions of the United States which have adopted without reservation Section 2.09 of the United States Model Penal Code, reject duress as a defence to the killing of innocent persons.

(a) The case-law of certain civil law jurisdictions

We would add that although the penal codes of most civil law jurisdictions do not expressly except the operation of the defence of duress in respect of offences involving the killing of innocent persons, the penal codes of Italy, Norway, Sweden, Nicaragua, Japan, and the former Yugoslavia require proportionality between the harm caused by the accused's act and the harm with which the accused was threatened. The effect of this requirement is that it leaves for determination in the case law of these civil law jurisdictions the question whether killing an innocent person is ever proportional to a threat to the life of an accused. The determination of that question is not essential to the disposal of this case and it suffices to say that courts in certain civil law jurisdiction may well consistently reject duress as a defence to the killing of innocent persons on the ground that the proportionality requirement in the provisions governing duress is not met.

. . .

(b) The principle behind the rejection of duress as a defence to murder in the common law

Murder is invariably included in any list of offences excepted by legislation in common law systems from the operation of duress as a defence. The English common law rule is that duress is no defence to murder, either for a principal offender or a secondary party to the crime. . . . There are two aspects to this position. The first is a firm rejection of the view in English law that duress, generally, affects the voluntariness of the actus reus or the mens rea. In *R. v Howe*, Lord Hailsham stated at page 777:

the second unacceptable view is that, possibly owing to a misunderstanding which has been read into some judgements, duress as a defence affects only the existence or absence of mens rea. The true view is stated in Lynch's case [1975] 1 AC 653 at 703 by Lord Kilbrandon (of the minority) and by Lord Edmund-Davies (of the majority) in their analysis. Lord Kilbrandon said:

". . . the decision of the threatened man whose constancy is overborne so that he yields to the threat, is a calculated decision to do what he knows to be wrong, and therefore that of a man with, perhaps to some exceptionally limited extent, a 'guilty mind'. . ."

. . .

Given that duress has been held at common law not to negate mens rea, the availability of the defence turns on the question whether, in spite of the elements of the offence being strictly made out, the conduct of the defendant should be justified or excused. The second aspect of the common law stance against permitting duress as a defence to murder is the assertion in law of a moral absolute. This moral point has been pressed consistently in a long line of authorities in English law and is accepted by courts in other common law jurisdictions as the basis for the rejection of duress as a defence to murder . . . Indeed, it is also upon this assertion which the decisions of the British military tribunals in the Stalag Luft III case and the Feurstein case based their rejection of duress as a defence to murder.

It is clear from the differing positions of the principal legal systems of the world that there is no consistent concrete rule which answers the question whether or not duress is a defence to the killing of innocent persons. It is not possible to reconcile the opposing positions and, indeed, we do not believe that the issue should be reduced to a contest between common law and civil law.

We would therefore approach this problem bearing in mind the specific context in which the International Tribunal was established, the types of crimes over which it has jurisdiction, and the fact that the International Tribunal's mandate is expressed in the Statute as being in relation to "serious violations of international humanitarian law."

D. The Rule Applicable to this Case

We accept the submission of the Prosecution during the hearing of 26 May 1997 that even in . . . a scenario where the killing of one life may save ten . . . there may be sound reasons in law not to permit a complete defence but to compensate for the lack of moral choice through other means such as sentencing. I think this is exactly the thinking behind the Common Law position . . . there is no categorical reason for saying that duress must necessarily apply. It may or may not be based on one's expectations of what is reasonable under the circumstances, based on one's expectations of the harm which creation of such defence may create for such a society at large.
. . .

[L]aw should not be the product or slave of logic or intellectual hair-splitting, but must serve broader normative purposes in light of its social, political and economic role. It is noteworthy that the authorities we have just cited issued their cautionary words in respect of domestic society and in respect of a range of ordinary crimes including kidnapping, assault, robbery and murder. Whilst reserving our comments on the appropriate rule for domestic national contexts, we cannot but stress that we are not, in the International Tribunal, concerned with ordinary domestic crimes. The purview of the International Tribunal relates to war crimes and crimes against humanity committed in armed conflicts of extreme violence with egregious dimensions. We are not concerned with the actions of domestic terrorists, gang-leaders and kidnappers. We are concerned that, in relation to the most heinous crimes known to humankind, the principles of law to which we give credence have the appropriate normative effect upon soldiers bearing weapons of destruction and upon the commanders who control them in armed conflict situations. The facts of this particular case, for example, involved the cold-blooded slaughter of 1,200 men and boys by soldiers using automatic weapons. We must bear in mind that we are operating in the realm of international humanitarian law which has, as one of its prime objectives, the protection of the weak and vulnerable in such a situation where their lives and security are endangered. Concerns about the harm which could arise from admitting duress as a defence to murder were sufficient to persuade a majority of the House of Lords and the Privy Council to categorically deny the defence in the national context to prevent the growth of domestic crime and the impunity of miscreants. Are they now insufficient to persuade us to similarly reject duress as a complete defence in our application of laws designed to take account of humanitarian concerns in the arena of brutal war, to punish perpetrators of crimes against humanity and war crimes, and to deter the commission of such crimes in the future? If national law denies recognition of duress as a defence in respect of the killing of innocent persons, international criminal law can do no less than match that policy since it deals with murders often of far greater magnitude. If national law denies duress as a defence even in a case in which a single innocent life is extinguished due to action under duress, international law, in our view, cannot admit duress in cases which involve the slaughter of innocent human beings on a large scale. It must be our concern to facilitate the development and effectiveness of international humanitarian law and to promote its aims and application by recognising the normative effect which criminal law should have upon those subject to them. Indeed, Security Council resolution 827 (1993) establishes the International Tribunal expressly as a measure to "halt and effectively redress" the widespread and flagrant violations of international humanitarian law occurring in the territory of the former Yugoslavia and to contribute thereby to the restoration and maintenance of peace.

As you can see, international criminal law has a lot of different sources to turn to in order to figure out what rules ought to apply in a particular case. This makes the process of making a decision in international criminal courts a difficult and complex process. On the other hand, it is important to note that the Appeals Chamber here ruled that there was no *single* answer to the question of whether duress is a defense or a mitigating factor in international criminal law. Thus, the court made a decision based on "policy"—that is, they decided that they would not allow duress as a defense for war crimes because they did not wish others to use duress as an excuse for committing atrocities. The *Erdemovic* case shows precisely how complex international criminal law can be when lawyers and judges attempt to answer the difficult legal questions that international criminal courts must face.

CONCLUSION

The purpose of this chapter has been to introduce you to some of the basic elements of international criminal law as well as the international legal system of which it is a part. International criminal law is a unique legal field because it is in many ways a mix of two different types of law. Originally based on the agreement of sovereign states, international law only later developed a criminal law dimension, importing the concepts of domestic criminal law as well as its notion of individual responsibility. Nonetheless, like international law more generally, international criminal law lacks some of the basic elements that are found in most domestic legal systems, namely, a founding constitution to determine its structures and a police force to enforce its rules. This makes international criminal law one of the most unique, complex, and challenging domains of modern law.

It is important to note that there are crimes other than the ones that we've set out in this chapter that are found in international treaties. Although they are defined by such treaties, international courts do not investigate or prosecute them. At present, genocide, war crimes, aggression, and crimes against humanity are the only crimes that are prosecuted in the international courts. These other crimes (crimes like air hijacking and drug trafficking) are dealt with only in the courts of various states, usually with the cooperation of other states. Some of these other crimes may fall under the jurisdiction of international courts in the future, but not at present. We will discuss many of these types of crimes in the second half of the text when we examine international and transnational crimes in more detail. In the next chapter, we will turn to the international courts that prosecute the international crimes that we have discussed here. After that, we will turn to the American legal system to examine how American courts have dealt with international crimes.

QUESTIONS

1. Do you think that aggression should be an international crime? If so, what defines "aggression"? Would you include preemptive self-defense? Why or why not?
2. Given the need for strict military discipline in combat, should a soldier who commits a crime by following the orders of a superior officer be punished?
3. Are there other crimes that should be considered international crimes? What are they? Why should they be *international* crimes?

READING AND RESOURCES

One should be careful when researching international criminal law on the Internet. A number of sites that purport to give an unbiased account of the law and its relevance for modern issues are in fact biased descriptions of either the facts or of the law that relates to them. Usually, they do this in order to push a particular political agenda, masking it as an objective account of a situation. Sometimes these websites do their best to appear to be legitimate by mimicking respectable news sources or academic websites. It's usually best to compare the information that you find on the Internet with other sources such as books or newspapers before reaching any conclusions.

There are several introductory English-language books on international criminal law. One of the best recent texts on the subject is *International Criminal Law* by the Italian legal scholar and international judge Antonio Cassese, Oxford University Press, Oxford, 2003. A somewhat more technical book, but one with a great deal of references for further research is Werke, Gerhard, *Principles of International Criminal Law,* T.M.C. Asser Press, The Hague, 2005. For an introduction to international law more generally, there are a number of useful texts. The best and most accessible are Janis, Mark, *An Introduction to International Law,* Aspen Publishers, New York, 2003; Malanczuk, Peter, *Akehurst's Modern Introduction to International Law,* 7th ed., Routledge, Oxford, 1997; and Bederman, David, *International Law Frameworks,* West Publishing Company, Eagan, 2001.

3

International Justice

❖

International courts (or international tribunals) are courts that function independent of any national government. Rather than interpreting and applying the laws of one particular state or government, they represent the legal judgments of all of humanity, or to put it a little less dramatically, the legal opinions of the international community. This means that they do not apply American law or German law, but rather base their judgments upon the international legal system that we described in Chapter 2.

These courts are a relatively new phenomenon, only having existed for the last 60 years, and the origins of these courts differ from each other. Some of these courts were created by the UN Security Council, others were created out of military victory, and still others have been creations of independent multilateral treaties. This means that the legal and political basis for these courts is complex, simply because they cannot rely on a government to give them their legitimacy in the way that the Supreme Court gets its validity from the Constitution, or state courts get theirs from their own state constitutions. Despite the fact that these courts have many critics, some of which we will discuss later, they have so far proven to be, at least in part, an effective response to some of the worst violations of international criminal law.

In this chapter we will set out some of the basics of modern international courts, discussing their history, along with their various structures and functions. This will include analyzing some of their most significant strengths and weaknesses, their ability to provide justice for the victims of international crimes, as well as their ability to deter future international crimes. As there are a number of different international courts, all of which are very different from one another, we will have to carefully distinguish between the different types of courts and the law that they apply in order to do this topic justice.

There are four major categories of international courts that we will discuss here: First are the international courts that handle conflicts between states. Second are the international *criminal* courts and tribunals that prosecute individual defendants for alleged international crimes. Third are the *internationalized courts* that are partly international courts but use some of the aspects of a country's domestic legal system. Finally, there are non-criminal *commissions,* such as truth commissions that deal with international crimes but do not conduct criminal trials. To complicate matters even further, some courts are regional, only applying to one particular area (such as Europe) while others apply to all states or alternatively to all individuals. We will deal with each one of these in turn in this chapter.

Once we have discussed the roles that international courts play in international criminal law in this chapter, we will then turn to the roles that international criminal laws play in *domestic* courts, such as American courts, in the next chapter. While it is true that international tribunals receive a great deal of attention from politicians, and their proceedings are frequently covered in newspapers and on television, much of the impact of international criminal law is felt in domestic courts away from the public eye. These two chapters should give us a good grasp of the legal and institutional basis for international criminal justice, and will be useful when we turn to the specific international criminal problems of today in the second half of this text.

We should also note that we will only deal with international courts that deal with matters relevant to criminal law. This means that we will not discuss "courts" (or dispute-resolution institutions) like the World Trade Organization, the International Tribunal on the Law of the Sea, or the Permanent Court of Arbitration. While these bodies have an extremely important role to play in international law and in the international system, they do not bear any direct relation to criminal matters, so we will pass them over.

The "Alphabet Soup" of International Courts

The international court system, like the international system in general, tends to use initials to refer to the various institutions (such as "the UN" for the United Nations). This can be confusing if you're not familiar with each of the initials and can't immediately recognize them. In order to help you, here are a number of the most important ones for you to use as a reference guide in this chapter:

> *ICJ* – The International Court of Justice located in The Hague, the Netherlands
> *PCIJ* – Permanent Court of International Justice, located in The Hague, the Netherlands
> *ICC* – The International Criminal Court located in The Hague, the Netherlands
> *ICTY* – The International Criminal Tribunal for the Former Yugoslavia located in The Hague, the Netherlands
> *ICTR* – The International Criminal Tribunal for Rwanda, located in Arusha, Tanzania
> *UN* – The United Nations, based in New York City
> *ECJ* – The European Court of Justice, located in Luxembourg
> *ECHR* – The European Court of Human Rights, located in Strasbourg, France
> *IMT* – International Military Tribunal at Nuremberg, located in Nuremberg, Germany
> *IMTFE* – International Military Tribunal for the Far East, located in Tokyo, Japan
> *TRC* – South African Truth and Reconciliation Commission

INTERNATIONAL COURTS AND TRANSITIONAL JUSTICE

One of the central roles of international criminal courts is to help provide what scholars refer to as *transitional justice*—justice for states that are transforming from chaotic or oppressive societies to societies that are stable, democratic, and protect individual rights. Sometimes the goal of transitional justice is described as establishing the *rule of law,* a situation where courts and legal rules replace force and power as the primary means for settling disputes. Societies that are recovering from large-scale atrocities, civil wars, or brutal dictatorships are often in a politically precarious situation. Frequently, their new governments are unstable and many of the individuals who committed crimes remain politically powerful people in or out of the government. Attempts to hold individuals accountable before a court of law for the crimes committed in a past conflict can easily undermine the efforts to stabilize a fragile society after serious conflict. Supporters of accused criminals often resist such efforts and can destroy any political stability that has developed and thus some of the worst criminals in the world avoid accountability for their acts.

One of the central problems in transitional justice is that different groups involved in these types of conflicts usually see them from very different perspectives. In civil wars, both sides often commit crimes and many feel that the atrocities that their side commits are exceptions to their otherwise moral methods of fighting—while their enemy's crimes are inexcusable. What might seem like oppressive acts of a dictatorship to some members of a society may seem to be necessary (but unpleasant) policies during a state of emergency for others. In these situations, the truth is often difficult to discern and even when the truth is discovered, no party wishes to accept ultimate responsibility for any atrocities that have occurred, but often prefer to point a finger at some other group or individual. This is normal in human psychology. Nobody wants to see themselves or the people who represent them as complicit in terrible acts, instead preferring to see themselves and their compatriots as "the good guys." According to an old cliché in international politics, "One person's terrorist is another's freedom fighter."

Criminal courts in particular play an awkward but important role in transitional justice. Such courts are usually confrontational places where blame is placed on an individual or group, not a place where all sides of a complex conflict are explored. Similarly criminal prosecutions of members of one's own group, tribe, clan, or ethnicity can easily lead members of a society to feel bitter and unfairly blamed as scapegoats for criminal acts that were committed by both sides. After World War II, for example, many German citizens felt that their leaders were being unfairly punished when the Allied powers had committed many crimes against innocent German civilians. They quickly point out that the Soviet military executed almost 4,000 Polish prisoners of war at Katja, and then tried to pin the blame on the German military—a crime that nobody in the Soviet Union was punished for. Thus, in a transition from a chaotic, lawless society to a stable one, criminal prosecutions are risky affairs and even if they are successfully carried out, they can still engender a bitterness that can linger for generations.

On the other hand, watching known criminals escape accountability for their acts can also have a destabilizing effect on a country. Granting immunity for war criminals can create a great deal of bitterness from her victims. This, in turn, can lead these angry survivors to commit revenge killings and other violent acts in order to exact some kind of justice from their former tormentors. After the new Turkish government refused to cooperate with a

British effort to try members of its predecessor government for crimes against Armenian civilians during World War I (scholars believe that one million people were killed by the Ottoman Empire) a group of renegade Armenians, under the moniker "Operation Nemesis", hunted down and assassinated former leaders of the Ottoman government. While it is tempting to declare a general amnesty after wars and other mass atrocities and hope that time will heal the wounds and allow everybody to move on, giving immunity to murderers and war criminals can be as destructive as, or more destructive than, prosecuting them in a court of law. Frequently, the wounds that mass atrocities cause are deep and can linger for centuries, creating conflicts that never quite fade.

The international courts will likely be subjected to a great deal of scrutiny and criticism, particularly from those countries whose citizens are indicted by them. Any court requires that its opinions be respected by those who are subject to it, that citizens recognize its authority and legitimacy. While Americans tend to assume that courts should usually be respected even when they disagree with a decision, this is not common around the world. Many countries (particularly those where international crimes are likely to have been committed) often consider courts to be mere political agents of the state, protecting the interests of the powerful, and not impartial arbiters of justice. Further, most groups are likely to be highly skeptical of an outsider court composed of foreigners prosecuting one of their own. Few like to acknowledge that their people may be involved in war crimes or crimes against humanity and are likely to remain in denial about it regardless of the outcome of a trial. These circumstances will undoubtedly make the court's prosecutions very challenging affairs and real cooperation from member states at times difficult to obtain.

There is no simple answer to the problems raised in transitional justice. As we will see, criminal courts are only one way for societies to achieve peace and stability after wars or other mass atrocities. Criminal prosecutions may not be the best way to handle war crimes or crimes against humanity in some contexts. In domestic criminal justice, prosecution is only one of many ways to handle crime, and other approaches, such as diversion programs, rehabilitation, and administrative warnings, have proven effective there, and the same may go for international crimes. Some question to think about as you examine these different international courts is whether criminal trials and criminal sanctions are always the best way to achieve transitional justice? What is the point of criminal prosecution? Is it simply to punish criminals or are there other valuable reasons to prosecute criminals? How might international criminal courts help achieve these goals? When there is a conflict between peace and criminal justice, which should win out?

The International Court of Justice and the European Court of Human Rights

The most well established international court is not a criminal court at all. The International Court of Justice (ICJ), sometimes called "the world court," sits at the Peace Palace, in The Hague, the capital city of the Netherlands. This court was established as part of the UN and was developed from its predecessor, the Permanent Court of International Justice (or PCIJ) that existed between World War I and World War II alongside the short-lived League of Nations. The world court handles many complex political issues but is not a criminal court because individuals have no *legal standing*. The court only handles disputes between states and gives advisory opinions to the United Nations on legal matters, but it cannot deal with the concerns of individuals. The only chance individuals have of bringing a case before the ICJ is if their government chooses to pursue the case in the international courts, and even then the dispute is one between the respective governments. (Thus, a German national who wants to sue Cambodia must convince the German government to lodge a complaint against Cambodia and the case will be listed as *Germany* v. *Cambodia*.) Likewise, the ICJ is not a criminal court—it does not punish or imprison anybody. There is no prosecutor in the court, but only two countries resolving their disputes before a panel of 15 judges. In this sense, the ICJ functions more like a civil court in the United States where individuals sue each other for damages rather than a criminal trial where the criminal responsibility of individuals is determined and individuals are punished. While some of these disputes may involve criminal matters, they do not involve individuals—there are usually no witnesses and the court does not hand out sentences. Thus, the ICJ is an important part of international law but it doesn't function as a criminal court.

However, the ICJ does make decisions that influence criminal proceedings throughout the world, and thus it has an indirect influence on criminal justice. Most of the proceedings before the ICJ involve disputes about territorial borders or similar matters, but some involve treaty obligations that affect the treatment of criminals. In 2004, the ICJ ruled in an opinion entitled "Avena and Other Mexican Nationals" (*Mexico* v. *United States of America*) that the United States had violated its treaty obligations with Mexico by not allowing 54 Mexican nationals arrested in the United States and sentenced to death in American courts to access the Mexican consulate. (This right was spelled out in a treaty entitled "The Vienna Convention on Consular Relations.") As a remedy, the court required that the American government revisit these cases and determine whether the outcomes were unduly influenced by the inability of defendants to get access to consular assistance. Reluctantly, the American government sought to comply with the ruling. They reopened their cases to examine whether or not the lack of counsel is grounds for commuting their death sentences. While this case is currently unresolved, it shows how the ICJ can have an effect on both international and domestic criminal courts.

Similarly, the European Court of Human Rights (ECHR) deals with international criminal justice in an indirect fashion. Like the ICJ, the ECHR is not a criminal court. Rather, the ECHR is court where Europeans may bring complaints about human rights violations perpetrated against them by the various European governments. This means that they can complain about unacceptable laws, unfair trials, cruel punishment practices, and other aspects of the criminal justice system that relate to human rights. The courts test these complaints against a treaty entitled "The European Convention for the Protection of Human Rights and Fundamental Freedoms" to see whether the government is infringing upon an individual's human rights. They then determine whether or not these governments need to revisit the case and perhaps change their practices or their laws. In this sense, the ECHR functions like an American Court of Appeals or the US Supreme Court when they rule on criminal matters—they render judgments that may ultimately force the governments to change the way that they behave based on a set of rights and cause "lower courts" (that is, the courts of the various European states) to reinterpret the law. Thus, like the ICJ, the ECHR deals with criminal matters only indirectly. It does not introduce evidence, interrogate witnesses, or determine whether or not an individual is guilty of a particular crime.

Of the international courts that *do* deal directly with the criminal responsibility of individuals, and not the legal responsibilities of entire countries, there have been five in modern history. Four of these courts were temporary courts designed to handle crimes that occurred during particular conflicts and two of them finished their business over a half-century ago. The other three are currently in existence, but two of these courts are ad hoc tribunals, meaning that they are limited in their scope and will disappear when they have fulfilled their mandate. The final court, the International Criminal Court (ICC), is a permanent court that will continue to exist for the foreseeable future. This court, however, is currently in its infancy and its effectiveness is untested. We will approach these various courts by examining their history and then afterwards, we will look in more detail at their structure and functions.

International Ad Hoc Criminal Tribunals: Nuremberg, Tokyo, Rwanda, and Yugoslavia

The origins of modern international tribunals were not auspicious. The first international criminal courts were proposed for Napoleon after his defeat at Waterloo, for Kaiser Wilhelm, the German leader who lost World War I, and for the leaders of the Ottoman Empire (modern Turkey) for the attempted Armenian genocide. However, each of these proposed courts fell apart before they could conduct any trials. In these cases, the governments that supported the trials abandoned their efforts after they recognized that the defeated French, German, and Turkish governments would resist them. Napoleon was ultimately sent to exile on the island of St. Helena in the Mediterranean without a trial, where he eventually died. Kaiser Wilhelm, removed from power, spent the remainder of his life in neighboring Holland, which provided him with sanctuary from prosecution (he died there in 1941). The British government relented on its efforts to prosecute the Ottoman leaders when the new Turkish government took 29 British soldiers hostage and demanded the return of the Ottoman prisoners. Soon afterward, the Treaty of Sevres gave the leaders of the Ottoman government amnesty for their acts. Nobody was ever prosecuted for the murders of almost a million Armenians. For most of the 19th century and the first part of the 20th, the idea of international criminal trials remained a goal only for a small group of idealistic politicians and lawyers.

The end of World War II marked the true beginning of the international criminal courts. With the war coming to a close, the Allied powers (the United States, the Soviet Union, the UK, and France) met in London in 1945 to discuss the fate of the Nazi leadership. Many, including the English Prime Minister Winston Churchill and the Soviet leader Josef Stalin wanted a "drumhead trial" (a short, informal trial followed by a quick execution) for German leaders like Hitler, Himmler, and Goering. The Americans, however, pushed for a full-blown criminal trial, arguing that such proceedings would send a message to future generations and set a new standard for international justice. They believed that a formal trial would expose the history of German war crimes and Nazi aggression in an open and public manner, preventing future generations in Germany from denying what had happened before and during the war. After a prolonged political struggle between various groups, the Allies finally agreed to a formal trial in the London Agreement of August 1945 that specified the nature of the trials and the crimes that the German leadership were to be charged with.

By the time the German army formally surrendered in May 1945, many in the Nazi leadership were already dead. Hitler had committed suicide in his bunker in Berlin, as had Joseph Goebbels (the Nazi propaganda minister) and Heinrich Himmler (the commander of the brutal SS). However, on November 22, 1945, twenty-two surviving former leaders of Hitler's government went on trial before four judges, one representing each of the victorious Allied powers. They were charged with "crimes against the peace" (that is, waging an illegal, aggressive war), crimes of war, and crimes against humanity. The Allied powers settled on the city of Nuremberg (where Hitler had held some of his most-famous rallies and the birthplace of the so-called "Nuremberg Laws," which robbed German Jews of their citizenship and ultimately, their humanity) as the site for the trials. The prosecutors at Nuremberg were legal experts representing each of the victorious powers, including Supreme Court Justice Robert Jackson, who took a temporary leave of absence from the Court to participate, and the accused were each provided with an attorney of their choosing.

The trial by the International Military Tribunal (IMT) at Nuremberg lasted for 11 months and ended in the execution of 12 defendants, the imprisonment of seven, and the acquittal of three. A few of the accused confessed to their crimes, but most never acknowledged their guilt, asserting either that the trial was illegal and all of their acts were perfectly lawful or that they were merely "following orders." (In a dramatic turn of events, Goering, the highest-ranking Nazi on trial committed suicide shortly before he was to be hung.) The various Allied powers held their own, separate military trials for lesser war criminals. The American courts held 11 trials for other representative groups, including "the Doctors Trial," where a number of Nazi scientists who performed vicious experiments on concentration camp victims and prisoners of war, and the "Einsatzgruppen Case" ("Special Action Groups") for a special SS organization in charge of mass executions in Eastern Europe during the war.

The architects of the Nuremberg trials were experienced politicians, not naïve idealists. They knew it was unlikely that the trials would change the world forever, but nonetheless hoped that the trials could substantially change international relations in the future. As Supreme Court Justice Jackson said in his opening statement to the court,

> [The prosecution] does not expect that you can make war impossible. It does expect that your juridical action will put the forces of international law, its precepts, its prohibitions and, most of all, its sanctions, on the side of peace, so that men and women of good will, in all countries, may have leave to live by no man's leave, underneath the law.

The proponents of the court had hoped that Nuremberg would be the beginning of a new movement. They hoped that the founding of the United Nations would lead to the development of an international criminal court that would handle particularly horrible international crimes. Unfortunately, the Cold War between the communist states and the Western democracies that began shortly after the end of the war prevented these countries from cooperating on future trials (as each feared that a trial would become a political tool that could be turned on them). Regardless of whether or not the trials met some abstract standard of "legality," their impact was tremendous, if delayed for half a century.

The criminal prosecution of political leaders before an international court for acts committed during wartime was certainly greeted with surprise by many around the world, including the Nazi leadership themselves. The legal basis for the Nuremberg

Tribunals was suspect (victorious military powers claiming that their defeated enemies were criminals was largely unprecedented), and lawyers and politicians both inside and outside of Germany viewed its proceedings with suspicion. At the time there were no clear international laws or legal precedents for this sort of trial and the accused were unfamiliar with the sorts of proceedings that they were undergoing. Much of the trial was structured like an American criminal trial, which was substantially different from a German one. To make matters worse, the tribunal's rules of procedure eliminated the *tu quoque* defense, that is, the accused could not offer the defense that the other side had committed the same or similar sorts of crimes. Thus, the defendants could not cite the crimes allegedly committed by the Allied forces (including the British firebombing of the city of Dresden and the Hiroshima and Nagasaki bombings, each of which killed tens of thousands of civilians) as part of their defense. Some felt that this was mere "victor's justice"—meaning, an attempt on the part of a triumphant power to demonize and humiliate its opponent. As Goering wrote on a copy of the indictment that he autographed for the Nuremberg prison psychologist, "The victor will always be the judge, the vanquished the accused." Many still hold such a view about Nuremberg, and others hold it toward international courts in general.

Despite some of these problems, most historians consider the Nuremberg Tribunals to be a success and international criminal lawyers frequently cite its rulings as valuable legal precedents. The Tokyo Tribunal, more formally referred to as the International Military Tribunal for the Far East (IMTFE), set up for the wartime leaders of the Japanese government, was significantly less successful and remains less well known by historians and scholars. However, in Tokyo, the occupying American government (under General Douglas Macarthur) prosecuted a number of leaders of the Japanese military and civilian government for crimes against the Allied powers. Twenty-eight Japanese leaders were put on trial before a panel of 11 judges (representing the different nations that fought against Japan) and seven were executed, including Hideki Tojo, the commander of the Japanese attack on Pearl Harbor. Nonetheless, many view these trials as General Macarthur's personal revenge against the men who defeated him in the Philippines, and other critics see it as a racist, political trial. Many noted that Emperor Hirohito (who was revered as a god by the Japanese people) was not prosecuted despite his responsibility for helping plan and conduct the war. Similarly, many questioned the legitimacy of the trial, including the Dutch judge B. V. A. Röling, who disagreed with the tribunal's judgments, and the Indian judge Radhabinod Pal, who wrote a 1200-page dissenting opinion to the Tribunal's judgment.

After the Nuremberg and Tokyo trials ended, there were no significant international criminal trials for nearly a half-century. The only exception of sorts was the trial of Adolf Eichmann, one of the major planners of the Nazi Holocaust against Jews, Gypsies, and others during the war. After the war, Eichmann went into hiding in Argentina. He lived there in peace under an assumed name until he was discovered in 1960, kidnapped by Israeli intelligence officers, smuggled into Israel aboard a civilian plane, and then placed on trial in an Israeli court in Jerusalem for crimes against humanity. While it was an Israeli trial and not an international one, the Israeli government claimed the right to try Eichmann as his crimes "involve[d] the perpetration of an international crime which all of the nations of the world are interested in preventing." (We will discuss the concept of *universal jurisdiction* underlying this issue in a later chapter.) Eichmann's defense was similar to that of many others who participated in the Holocaust and is similar to that of those who committed crimes against humanity after World War II, he was simply following orders from his commanders and had no real choice in his actions. However, after a lengthy trial, Eichmann was found guilty and hung in 1961.

Justice Jackson's Opening Statement

Here is the beginning of Jackson's opening statement before the tribunal. It is worth studying both as a testimony of the beliefs that motivated the trial and as an attempt to address the critics of the IMT:

> May it please Your Honors:
>
> The privilege of opening the first trial in history for crimes against the peace of the world imposes a grave responsibility. The wrongs which we seek to condemn and punish have been so calculated, so malignant, and so devastating, that civilization cannot tolerate their being ignored, because it cannot survive their being repeated. That four great nations, flushed with victory and stung with injury stay the hand of vengeance and voluntarily submit their captive enemies to the judgment of the law is one of the most significant tributes that Power has ever paid to Reason.
>
> This Tribunal, while it is novel and experimental, is not the product of abstract speculations nor is it created to vindicate legalistic theories. This inquest represents the practical effort of four of the most mighty of nations, with the support of 17 more, to utilize international law to meet the greatest menace of our times—aggressive war. The common sense of mankind demands that law shall not stop with the punishment of petty crimes by little people. It must also reach men who possess themselves of great power and make deliberate and concerted use of it to set in motion evils which leave no home in the world untouched. It is a cause of that magnitude that the United Nations will lay before Your Honors.
>
> In the prisoners' dock sit twenty-odd broken men. Reproached by the humiliation of those they have led almost as bitterly as by the desolation of those they have attacked, their personal capacity for evil is forever past. It is hard now to perceive in these men as captives the power by which as Nazi leaders they once dominated much of the world and terrified most of it. Merely as individuals their fate is of little consequence to the world. What makes this inquest significant is that these prisoners represent sinister influences that will lurk in the world long after their bodies have returned to dust. We will show them to be living symbols of racial hatreds, of terrorism and violence, and of the arrogance and cruelty of power. . . . These men created in Germany, under the "Fuehrerprinzip," a National Socialist despotism equalled only by the dynasties of the ancient East. They took from the German people all those dignities and freedoms that we hold natural and inalienable rights in every human being. The people were compensated by inflaming and gratifying hatreds towards those who were marked as "scapegoats." Against their opponents, including Jews, Catholics, and free labor, the Nazis directed such a campaign of arrogance, brutality, and annihilation as the world has not witnessed since the pre-Christian ages. They excited the German ambition to be a "master race," which of course implies serfdom for others. They led their people on a mad gamble for domination. They diverted social energies and resources to the creation of what they thought to be an invincible war machine. They overran their neighbors. To sustain the "master race" in its war-making, they enslaved

millions of human beings and brought them into Germany, where these hapless creatures now wander as "displaced persons." At length bestiality and bad faith reached such excess that they aroused the sleeping strength of imperiled Civilization. Its united efforts have ground the German war machine to fragments. But the struggle has left Europe a liberated yet prostrate land where a demoralized society struggles to survive. These are the fruits of the sinister forces that sit with these defendants in the prisoners' dock.

. . .

    Before I discuss particulars of evidence, some general considerations which may affect the credit of this trial in the eyes of the world should be candidly faced. There is a dramatic disparity between the circumstances of the accusers and of the accused that might discredit our work if we should falter, in even minor matters, in being fair and temperate.

    Unfortunately the nature of these crimes is such that both prosecution and judgment must be by victor nations over vanquished foes. The worldwide scope of the aggressions carried out by these men has left but few real neutrals. Either the victors must judge the vanquished or we must leave the defeated to judge themselves. After the First World War, we learned the futility of the latter course. The former high station of these defendants, the notoriety of their acts, and the adaptability of their conduct to provoke retaliation make it hard to distinguish between the demand for a just and measured retribution, and the unthinking cry for vengeance which arises from the anguish of war. It is our task, so far as humanly possible, to draw the line between the two. We must never forget that the record on which we judge these defendants today is the record on which history will judge us tomorrow. To pass these defendants a poisoned chalice is to put it to our own lips as well. We must summon such detachment and intellectual integrity to our task that this Trial will commend itself to posterity as fulfilling humanity's aspirations to do justice.

To what extent do you find Jackson's reasoning convincing here? Do you think that he successfully responds to the critics of the Tribunal, including Goering?

After the Cold War   Throughout the Cold War, there was little enthusiasm for an international criminal court. Both the communist and the democratic states, led by the Soviet Union and the United States respectively, feared that they would open themselves up to damaging and embarrassing criticisms as each side sought to use such an international court as a tool for political propaganda. This fear put the idea of an international criminal court in the "deep freeze" until global politics changed in the 1990s as the USSR collapsed and the Eastern European states under its influence were given autonomy.

    While the fall of the Soviet Union meant the end of oppression for many people in Russia and Eastern Europe, it also unleashed some terribly destructive forces that evoked memories of the German Holocaust and resurrected the idea of an international criminal court. The collapse of the communist states in Eastern Europe freed many people from an oppressive political and economic system, but it also led to its own forms of political instability and a dramatic rise in ethnic conflict. Many of the formerly communist countries were comprised of a number of different ethnic groups, some of which held ancient grudges against each other. However, when they were under Soviet domination, these states were held together by powerful governments that crushed any attempts to develop a group identity based on their ethnicity. With the end of these communist governments, many turned back to their ethnicities to find a sense of identity. Cultivated by ambitious and ruthless politicians, ancient ethnic identities were openly celebrated, and equally ancient ethnic rivalries, rooted in Eastern Europe's tumultuous history, rapidly resurfaced. Nowhere was this conflict strongest than in the Yugoslavia, a nation comprised of four rival ethnic groups (Bosnians, Serbs, Kosovars, and Croats) and three different religions (Eastern Orthodox Christians, Roman Catholics, and Muslims) that was kept unified during the war by the communist dictator Marshall Tito and his successors. Later, a new generation of politicians, seeking to gain power and wealth for themselves and their cronies, fanned the flames of ethnic conflict until war broke out between the ethnic groups when some of them attempted to secede from Yugoslavia in the early 1990s.

The disintegration of Yugoslavia touched off several conflicts as members of the different ethnic groups fought for independence and political dominance. The ensuing wars in Slovenia (1991), Croatia (1991–1995), Bosnia (1992–1995), and Kosovo (1998–1999) were bloody and terrible as each group sought to attain as large and valuable a chunk of territory as possible. Frequently, civilian populations were caught in the middle of the fighting as forces representing the different ethnic groups treated others, whether soldiers or civilians, as enemies. The term *ethnic cleansing* was coined during this war to describe the efforts to forcibly remove all members of an ethnic group from a particular territory by all means necessary, and the practice was carried out frequently and brutally during these wars. Much (although not all) of the crimes that occurred in the Balkan region were committed by Serb forces, headed by the Serbian President Slobodan Milosevic and his Bosnian-Serb compatriots. The city of Sarajevo, Bosnia, for example, was subject to repeated sniper and artillery fire while filled with Muslim civilians and surrounded by Serb troops.

The second major post-Cold War catastrophe to shock the conscience of humankind took place in the tiny east African nation of Rwanda. Two ethnic groups, the Hutu and the Tutsi, held long-simmering grudges against each other, stretching back to before World War II when Rwanda was a Belgian colony. The Tutsis were an ethnic minority who were perceived as holding political power against the Hutu majority (Tutsis were given preference over the Hutus while under Belgian rule after World War I). In April 1994, these tensions exploded in an orgy of violence. Spurred on by the murder of Rwandan President Juvénal Habyarimana, and inspired by the radical government that quickly replaced him, packs of armed Hutu members of the *interahamwe* militia massacred Tutsi (and moderate Hutu) men, women, and children in an orgy of violence that lasted 10 weeks and left almost 900,000 people dead. The massacres, largely carried out with machetes, only ended when the rebel Tutsi Rwandese Patriotic Front (RPF) overthrew the Hutu regime and established a new government.

The international community's response to both of these conflicts was anemic. The UN Security Council, the body charged with maintaining peace and security in the world, refused to send significant amounts of peacekeepers into either region and quickly withdrew them when they were threatened. Much of the international community refused to provide assistance to the Tutsis and sought to avoid any international obligation to assist Rwanda. Many felt that these regions, the Balkans, and Sub-Saharan Africa were congenitally violent and believed that international intervention would not help the situation and only lead to the deaths of Westerners. Many echoed the 19th-century German leader Otto von Bismarck, who once said, "For me, all the Balkans are not worth the healthy bones of a single Pomeranian Grenadier." When a number of Belgian forces were killed in Rwanda, much of the UN peacekeeping force was evacuated from Kigali, the country's capital. Most Western nations sought only to rescue their own nationals and left the Tutsis and Bosnians to their grim fates.

Eventually, the international community did take some steps to deal with these crises. When the conflict in the former Yugoslavia spread to Kosovo in 1999, NATO (the North Atlantic Treaty Organization—a military organization consisting of the United States and its European allies) conducted a bombing campaign that forced the Yugoslavian government to relent. In addition, the Security Council authorized the formation of two criminal tribunals to handle the crimes that occurred during these conflicts. The International Criminal Tribunal for the former Yugoslavia (ICTY), in The Hague (not far from the ICJ), and the International Criminal Tribunal for Rwanda (ICTR) were both established by Security Council resolutions. While some have attacked these courts as an effort by the international community to cover over their significant failures in handling these crises, they have nonetheless proven important for the subsequent development of international courts and further expanding on the principles of international criminal law. These ad hoc (meaning temporary and limited) criminal tribunals are the first international criminal courts since the end of World War II and have served as a valuable tool for developing international criminal law.

Both courts were creations of separate UN Security Council resolutions and were issued narrow mandates, limiting their jurisdiction to these conflicts. The ICTY sits in The Hague and handles individuals who are accused of committing war crimes, crimes against humanity, and genocide in the former Yugoslavia, including Bosnia, Croatia, Slovenia, and Kosovo. Unlike the Nuremberg or Tokyo trials, the ICTY is not designed to prosecute only one side of the conflict but prosecutes Serbs, Croats, Bosnian Muslims, and others accused of such crimes in the former Yugoslavia. (The only exception is UN peacekeepers who are immune to prosecution before the court.) The ICTR is located in Arusha, Tanzania, just across the border from Rwanda and handles the crimes that took place in 1994 in Rwanda.

The ICTY has had a mixed history (the trials tend to be extremely long and expensive) but nonetheless it has had some notable successes. Initially, the tribunal's efforts were slow as funding and political support were scarce, but with the backing of key members of the U.S. government and the efforts of the tribunal's prosecutors, the court established itself as an important factor in postwar development in the Balkan region. The Tribunal has handled dozens of cases, successfully prosecuting a number of Serbs, Bosnians, and Croats. Many other suspected war criminals have been indicted by the tribunal, which actively pushes for their arrest. Most famously, the ICTY prosecuted Slobodan Milosevic, the former President of Yugoslavia for crimes in Bosnia, Kosovo, and Croatia during the breakup of the former Yugoslavia (in March 2006 Milosevic died in his cell in The Hague of a heart attack before his trial could conclude). Most infamously, however, two leaders of the Serbian forces in Bosnia—former Bosnian Serb President Radovan Karadic and Serbian General Ratko Mladic (who is accused of organizing the massacre of 7,000 Bosnian Muslims in Sarajevo in 1995)—remain in hiding, indicted by the ICTY but protected by Serbs in the region who remain sympathetic to their cause.

The ICTR has had less success than the ICTY. Despite the fact that many more people died in the Rwandan genocide than in all of the Balkan conflicts combined

(the official number of deaths in Rwanda is 937,000), the ICTR has received significantly less political and financial support from the UN and from other states. The
Rwandans themselves have not been entirely supportive of the ICTR, as many feel that
the court is too far removed from their current needs and they object to the court's lack
of a death penalty (neither tribunal may sentence defendants to death, regardless of the
crime). Nonetheless, at the time of writing, the ICTR has completed 14 cases (with
8 more currently under appeal), with 25 cases underway, and 16 more suspects currently
awaiting trial.

The International Criminal Court

The establishment of these ad hoc tribunals by the UN Security Council inspired a movement by certain states and NGOs to form a permanent international criminal court.
Supporters believed that the international community could use such a court to prosecute
nefarious international criminals without having to form a new ad hoc tribunal each time a
new humanitarian catastrophe arose. Further, such a court could fulfill the hope of the
architects of the Nuremberg Tribunals that international relations would be more law
governed and more humane. Critics see the ICC as a dangerous threat to the sovereignty
and independence of individual states and an institution that could easily lend itself to
abuse by individuals or states who use it for political ends. However, the court's supporters
see the opportunity to dramatically reshape international criminal justice and international
society for the better. They believe that the best way to protect human rights is to have a
court to hold accountable those who violate them.

After five weeks of negotiation in Rome in the summer of 1998, a surprisingly
short time for an agreement of this importance, the "Rome Treaty" (more technically, the
Rome Statute of the International Criminal Court) was finalized in July 1998 and was
ratified in 2002 by 126 independent nations. This represents one of the most significant
developments in international criminal justice since Nuremberg. The ICTY and the
ICTR are ad hoc tribunals, limited to the conflicts in the former Yugoslavia and in
Rwanda. Like the Nuremberg trial before them, these ad hoc tribunals will be disbanded
when they have finished their mission and will not deal with new conflicts that arise.
Unlike these predecessors, the ICC is a permanent court that will deal with *all* future
international crimes that fall under the jurisdiction of the court, regardless of when they
occur. The ICC will be forced to confront matters that are novel and unpredictable (and
potentially politically explosive)—which makes it a striking departure from its more
limited and more carefully controlled predecessors.

The Structure of the ICC   The ICC consists of four major sections. The most important are the courts themselves, referred to as the "Chambers." Altogether, the Chambers
are made up of 18 judges who are selected by a majority of the "Assembly of States
Parties" (that is, the states that are party to the Rome Treaty) for 9-year terms. No two
judges may be nationals of the same country and no judge may serve more than one term.
The court is broken into three different chambers: Pre-trial Chamber, a Trial Chamber,
and an Appeals Chamber. The Pre-trial Chamber, consisting of three judges, is in charge
of approving the initiation of a prosecution, keeping tabs on ongoing investigations in
order to determine whether or not the prosecutions are being properly conducted, and

approving arrest warrants, all of which take place prior to the actual trial. The two Trial Chambers have three judges each and are in charge of conducting the trial itself, hearing witnesses, evaluating evidence, and ultimately deciding on the guilt or innocence of the accused. Finally, the Appeals Chamber has a total of 5 members and handles cases that are appealed from the Trial Chamber. This latter body, along with the Trial Chamber, will formulate and write down legal opinions that will ultimately influence the future development of international criminal law, giving specificity to the very general legal prohibitions that we discussed in the previous chapter.

Along with the various judicial chambers, the prosecutor is also a part of the structure of the ICC. This differs from the American system, where the judges are part of a separate branch of government from the prosecutor and are isolated from him or her (in the United States, the prosecution is completely independent of the judiciary). The prosecutor of the ICC is appointed by a majority of the Assembly of States Parties and the deputies are appointed by a similar vote (although the deputy candidates are chosen from a list determined by the prosecutor). It is the prosecutor's job, under the supervision of the Pre-trial Chamber, to determine which crimes are to be investigated, to carry out the investigation, indict the accused criminals, and to oversee the trial of the accused in the Trial Chamber. While the prosecutor is a part of the ICC (being under the same budget, for example), he or she is independent of the influence of both the president and the judges. The first prosecutor for the ICC, Luis Moreno-Ocampo, an Argentinean human rights attorney, was appointed in 2003 by an anonymous vote of the member states, and like all future prosecutors, he will serve a (non-renewable) 9-year term.

The two major administrative bodies of the ICC are the president and the registrar. The president is the head administrator for the court. Also, the president serves as a judge on the Appeals Chamber. The registrar provides protection and counseling for the witnesses and handles other important logistical issues of the court such as assuring that evidence is gathered properly.

Jurisdiction of the ICC   While the ICC is described as an international court, this does not mean that it applies to all individuals who commit crimes anywhere in the world. Because the world is divided into different sovereign states, not all of whom consent to be under the ICC's jurisdiction, the court's reach is limited in some important ways. Here I will introduce some of the technical, Latin terms used to explain each aspect of the court's jurisdiction.

Jurisdiction ratio materiae (subject matter jurisdiction—the types of crimes that are prosecuted by the court): The ICC presently prosecutes only four crimes: genocide, crimes against humanity, war crimes, and aggression. These crimes will be discussed in detail in later chapters.

Jurisdiction ratio temporis (jurisdiction based on time that the crime occurred): The court has jurisdiction only over crimes that occurred after April 2002, the date when the ICC came into effect. If further countries join the ICC, then, *once they have ratified the Rome Statute,* their citizens are subject to the jurisdiction of the court.

Territorial Jurisdiction (jurisdiction based on the location where the crime was committed): The ICC only has jurisdiction over crimes that occur in states that have ratified the Rome Statute or crimes that take place on their ocean vessels or airlines.

Jurisdiction ratio personae (jurisdiction over people): Although the ICC is an international court, it does not necessarily have jurisdiction over everybody on the planet. As we've already discussed, some states (including the United States) have refused to participate in the ICC and thus do not accept that it has jurisdiction over their nationals. However, the ICC may assert jurisdiction over the citizens of states that are not party to the treaty if they commit crimes in the territory of a state that *is* a part of the treaty. This means that an American who committed a war crime in Canada (which ratified the Rome Treaty in 2000) could be brought before the ICC against the wishes of the U.S. government.

Complementary jurisdiction: Finally, the ICC has "complementary jurisdiction" over accused international criminals. This means that the ICC will only prosecute individuals if states with jurisdiction are "unwilling or unable genuinely to carry out the investigation or prosecution" of the suspect. This is different from the jurisdiction of the ICTY and the ICTR, which were allowed primacy over domestic courts. This primacy meant that these courts could intervene in a domestic prosecution at any time and decide to transfer the defendant to Arusha or The Hague for prosecution before the international tribunal. Complementarity makes the ICC a sort of court of "last resort," that is, a court that will usually defer their investigations and trials to individual nations. The ICC is meant as a supplement to domestic courts prosecuting individuals when the more conventional criminal justice systems fail, not as a replacement for domestic criminal justice.

The Referral Process   Cases are referred to the ICC's prosecutor, who then determines whether or not he or she wishes to investigate it. The prosecutor can begin investigating a case in four major ways, two of which apply to state parties and two that apply to nonstate parties. The first way that the ICC can begin investigating a crime committed by a citizen of a member state is by the independent judgment of the prosecutor. Hundreds of cases have already been referred to the prosecutor's attention by private citizens, and he or she must then sift through these different complaints in order to find candidates suitable for further investigation. If the prosecutor believes that there is a reasonable basis to proceed, the available evidence is presented by the prosecutor to the Pre-trial Chamber, who may then authorize a full-blown investigation. Alternatively, a state party (and not an individual citizen) may choose to refer a case to the prosecutor and request that he or she investigate it.

There are two ways that the prosecutor may initiate investigations against nonstate parties (that is, investigate citizens of states that have not ratified the Rome Treaty). The first is from a reference of a case by the non-state party itself. This is to say that a state that is not a part of the Rome Statute may request that the prosecutor investigate a particular case that involves its citizens or took place on its territory. Article 12(3) of the Rome Treaty says that, "If the acceptance of a State which is not a Party to this Statute is required [to initiate and investigation] . . . that State may, by declaration lodged with the Registrar, accept the exercise of jurisdiction by the Court with respect to the crime in question." The second manner is by a referral from the UN Security Council. As was discussed in the previous chapter, the Council has the power to compel states to follow their resolutions. Likewise, the Security Council can compel states that are not parties to the Rome Statute to cooperate with the ICC and request that the ICC investigate a particular case. One of the first cases that the ICC has investigated was the genocide in the Darfur region of southern Sudan. Sudan was not a state party to the Rome Statute but in

Resolution 1593 (of March 2005), the Security Council referred the case to the court and ordered that, "the Government of Sudan and all other parties to the conflict in Darfur, shall cooperate fully with and provide any necessary assistance to the Court and the Prosecutor pursuant to this resolution."

The ICC prosecutor has a good deal of discretion in deciding whether to investigate and prosecute individual crimes. According to the Rome Statute, the prosecutor may choose not to prosecute suspected criminals on two different grounds: If there is no "reasonable basis" to pursue the case, or "there are . . . substantial reasons to believe that an investigation would not serve the interests of justice" (Article 53(1)(c)). The UN Security Council may also decide to delay an investigation for 12 months through a resolution, but it may never permanently halt an investigation. While it may indefinitely delay an investigation, it must do so by passing separate resolutions each year. This would presumably be politically embarrassing for the states who seek to shelter suspected war criminals and ultimately shame these states into consenting to allow the ICC to start an investigation. Provided that, after reviewing the results of the prosecutor's investigation, the Pre-trial Chamber is convinced that there are reasonable grounds to believe that the suspect has committed the crime, the chamber will issue an arrest warrant for the suspect.

Three cases have been referred to the prosecutor by state parties: Uganda, the Central African Republic, and the Democratic Republic of Congo. As mentioned above, the Security Council has referred the case of the genocide in Darfur to the prosecutor, who has undertaken an investigation of it. As of this writing, the ICC has indicted six people and one case has commenced (Thomas Lubanga Dyilo, a leader of a guerilla militia in the Democratic Republic of Congo who is charged with war crimes, notably the conscription of children to fight.[1]) Additionally, in February 2007, the prosecutor initiated two cases for crimes against humanity and war crimes in Darfur. Whether these cases will result in any convictions and whether these prosecutions will provide justice for the victims of these crimes or lead to peace in these countries is an open question at this point.

America and the International Courts

The ICC is opposed by several important countries, most notably by the United States, but Israel and China have also not supported the court. However, American resistance to the ICC is significant for many reasons: America is the wealthiest, most powerful nation in the world and could be of great assistance to the ICC in obtaining and prosecuting suspected international criminals. Likewise, American economic and military strength could be useful in getting states to cooperate with the court by offering incentives to states that agree to work with the ICC and applying sanctions to those who don't. Further, as we have already seen in our brief history of international courts, it was the United States that was the biggest proponent of the Nuremberg Tribunals and the two ad hoc tribunals, often over the objections of countries that are now the strongest supporters of the ICC. Such moral authority would be a big boost to the ICC.

---

[1] *Prosecutor* v. *Thomas Lubanga Dyilo,* Warrant of Arrest, ICC-01/04-01/06, February 10, 2006. (Available at http://www.icc-cpi.int/library/cases/ICC-01-04-01-06-2_tEnglish.pdf.)

As we discussed in Chapter 1, the American government has recently been particularly hostile to the international criminal justice system. This hostility is especially strong in regard to the international courts. In 1986, in response to an unfavorable ruling by the ICJ, the United States withdrew from that court's compulsory jurisdiction.[2] While the United States was the primary force behind the creation of the ad hoc tribunals, the relation to the ICC has not been as supportive. President Clinton signed the Rome Treaty but declined to send it to Congress for ratification because of concerns about the structure of the ICC. Shortly after taking office, however, President George W. Bush "unsigned" the Rome Treaty and announced that it would not cooperate with the court. In 2001 Congress passed the "American Service Members Protection Act," which prohibits American cooperation with the ICC and authorizes the president to use military force against the ICC if the court attempts to prosecute an American citizen. Thus, resistance to the international courts has been a widespread phenomenon in modern American politics.

American critics of the ICC give several reasons for the American position. One primary concern voiced is that American servicemen will be unfairly singled out for prosecution by the ICC because of the unique status of the United States in the world. The fact that the United States is the sole remaining superpower on earth means that the U.S. military must be deployed in many different places around the world, at times working in hostile environments. Likewise, American actions are often singled out for global condemnation in a matter that those of other, less powerful states are not. Often, states that refuse to allow free elections or routinely ignore the human rights of their citizens (such as Cuba) are treated as respectable members of international society, while the United States, a functioning democracy, is not. The American critics charge that this double standard could be used by a rogue prosecutor to turn the ICC into a political tool for states that are jealous of American power and wealth. The fact that nobody can permanently halt an investigation that the prosecutor wishes to conduct only adds to this concern.

A second major objection to the ICC is the concern about the legal standards that the ICC will use to try defendants. As we've already seen, there are a number of ways that an international trial is different from an American criminal trial. There is no jury, for example, nor do the traditional rules of evidence apply in many cases. This has led some critics to assert that the ICC may not meet the standards for a fair trial set out in the American Constitution and its Bill of Rights. Thus, they argue, it would be unconstitutional to allow American citizens to be put on trial before the ICC.

Because of the limited jurisdiction of the ICC, it is unlikely that any American would go on trial there. However, as a way to circumvent even the remote possibility that an American citizen could go before the ICC, the United States has formulated numerous "Article 98 Agreements" (or "Bilateral Immunity Agreements") with different states around the world. Signing these agreements has been listed as a precondition for U.S. financial aid to many third-world governments. These agreements stipulate that the respective governments will not extradite American nationals to the ICC (and vice versa) without the express consent of the U.S. government. At present the United States has over 100 bilateral agreements with different states around the world. (As of this writing, no

---

[2] Military and Paramilitary Activities in and against Nicaragua (*Nicaragua* v. *US*), ICJ, Judgment of November 26, 1984. See also Gill, Terry, *Litigation Strategy at the International Criminal Court.*

western European nation, including the United Kingdom has given the United States such an assurance.) Many states, such as Costa Rica, have refused to sign the agreements and lost millions in U.S. aid in order to remain faithful to the ideals of the ICC.

Whether or not these claims have any validity, the United States' nonparticipation will have important repercussions for the ICC. The political, military, and economic power that the United States holds is unparalleled, and its support could have made it much easier for the court to obtain defendants and gather witnesses. Uncooperative states could have been threatened with sanctions from the United States and its allies, and the United States could have provided crucial logistical support for the court—providing criminal justice experts of all kinds (such as forensic scientists) to help with the trials. Without this support, the ICC is weakened, although it is clearly not down.

However, despite strong rhetoric, American actions against international courts have not been as negative as some of the political language might initially indicate. While it is true that the United States has been hostile to the development of the ICC, it was the key force behind the Nuremberg Tribunals as well as the two ad hoc tribunals. Similarly, when genocide began in Darfur, Sudan, in 2004, the United States was willing to allow for an international tribunal of some sort to put the instigators of the genocide on trial. The Bush administration opposed referring the Darfur crisis to the ICC (preferring instead that the Council create another limited, ad hoc tribunal), but eventually it caved in to pressure from its allies. In April 2005, the UN Security Council referred the Darfur crisis to the ICC for investigation and prosecution without a veto from the United States. Similarly, as was already mentioned, the Bush administration agreed to review the cases of Mexican nationals held on death row in the United States after an unfavorable ruling by the ICJ. Whether this ultimately means that the United States will be a reluctant partner in the international courts or has simply bowed to political pressure in a few isolated cases is unclear, but at a minimum the courts have showed a good deal of resilience against their most vehement and most powerful critic.

The American Service Members Protection Act

One September 26, 2001, Senator Jesse Helms (former Republican Senator from North Carolina, now retired) introduced the American Service Members Protection Act before the Senate. Here are his comments.

> Mr. President, after dastardly terrorists killed thousands of American citizens in New York, Washington and that plane crash in Pennsylvania, President Bush instructed our armed services to "be ready."
>
> And, this nation is at war with terrorism, and thousands in our armed forces are already risking their lives around the globe, prepared to fight that war. These are courageous men and women who are not afraid to face up to evil terrorists, and they are ready to risk their lives to preserve and protect the miracle of America.
>
> And that is why, Mr. President, I am among those of their fellow countrymen who insist that these men and women who are willing risk their lives to protect their country and fellow Americans should not have to face the persecution of the International Criminal Court—which ought to be called the International Kangaroo Court. This court will be empowered when 22 more nations ratify the Rome Treaty.
>
> Mr. President, instead of helping the United States go after real war criminals and terrorists, the International Criminal Court has the unbridled power to intimidate

our military people and other citizens with bogus, politicized prosecutions. Similar creations of the United Nations have shown that this is inevitable.

Earlier this year, the U.N. Human Rights Commission kicked off the United States—the world's foremost advocate of human rights—to the cheers of dictators around the globe.

The United Nation's conference on racism in Durban, South Africa, this past month, became an agent of hate rather than against hate. With this track record, it is not difficult to anticipate that the U.N.'s International Criminal Court will be in a position not merely to prosecute, but to persecute our soldiers and sailors for alleged war crimes as they risk their lives fighting the scourge of terrorism.

Therefore, Mr. President, now is the time for the Senate to move to protect those who are protecting us.

I have an amendment at the desk to serve as a sort of insurance policy for our troops. My amendment is supported by the Bush Administration and is based on the "American Service Members Protection Act," which I introduced this past May. It is cosponsored by Senators Miller, Shelby, Murkowski, Bond, and Allen. Mr. President, many Americans may not realize that the Rome Treaty can apply to Americans even without the U.S. ratifying the treaty. This bewildering threat to America's men and women in our armed forces must be stopped.

And that is precisely what my amendment proposes to do—it protects Americans in several ways:

(1) It will prohibit cooperation with this kangaroo court, including use of taxpayer funding or sharing of classified information.

(2) It will restrict a U.S. role in peacekeeping missions unless the U.N. specifically exempts U.S. troops from prosecution by this international court.

(3) It blocks U.S. aid to allies unless they too sign accords to shield U.S. troops on their soil from being turned over to the ICC.

And (4) It authorizes any necessary action to free U.S. soldiers improperly handed over to that Court.

My amendment to the Defense Authorization bill incorporates changes negotiated with the Executive Branch giving the President the flexibility and authority to delegate tasks in the bill to Cabinet Secretaries and their deputies in this time of national emergency.

The Bush Administration supports this slightly revised version of the "American Service Members Protection Act." I ask unanimous consent that a letter from the Administration in support of this amendment be included in the record. Mr. President, nothing is more important than the safety of our citizens, soldiers and public servants. The terrorist attacks of September 11 have made that fact all the more obvious.

Today, we can, we must, act to protect our military personnel from abuse by the International Criminal Court.

Here is a template for the Article 98 Agreements that the United States has made with over 100 countries around the world.

A. Reaffirming the importance of bringing to justice those who commit genocide, crimes against humanity and war crimes,

B. Recalling that the Rome Statute of the International Criminal Court done at Rome on July 17, 1998, by the United Nations Diplomatic Conference of Plenipotentiaries on the Establishment of an International Criminal Court is intended to complement and not supplant national criminal jurisdiction,

C. Considering that the Government of the United States of America has expressed its intention to investigate and to prosecute where appropriate acts within the jurisdiction of the International Criminal Court alleged to have been committed by its officials, employees, military personnel, or other nationals,

D. Bearing in mind Article 98 of the Rome Statute,

E. Hereby agree as follows:

For purposes of this agreement, "persons" are current or former Government officials, employees (including contractors), or military personnel or nationals of one Party. Persons of one Party present in the territory of the other shall not, absent the expressed consent of the first Party,

(a) be surrendered or transferred by any means to the International Criminal Court for any purpose, or

(b) be surrendered or transferred by any means to any other entity or third country, or expelled to a third country, for the purpose of surrender to or transfer to the International Criminal Court.

When the United States extradites, surrenders, or otherwise transfers a person of the other Party to a third country, the United States will not agree to the surrender or transfer of that person to the International Criminal Court by the third country, absent the expressed consent of the Government of X.

When the Government of X extradites, surrenders, or otherwise transfers a person of the United States of America to a third country, the Government of X will not agree to the surrender or transfer of that person to the International Criminal Court by a third country, absent the expressed consent of the Government of the United States.

This Agreement shall enter into force upon an exchange of notes confirming that each Party has completed the necessary domestic legal requirements to bring the Agreement into force. It will remain in force until one year after the date on which one Party notifies the other of its intent to terminate this Agreement. The provisions of this Agreement shall continue to apply with respect to any act occurring, or any allegation arising, before the effective date of termination.

Hybrid Criminal Courts

Alongside the ICC and the two ad hoc tribunals, several courts have developed over recent years that have mixed international criminal justice with local criminal law. Variously referred to as "third generation" international tribunals (the IMT and IMTFE are the first generation; the ICTY, ICTR, and ICC are the second), mixed tribunals, hybrid courts, or internationalized courts, these tribunals seek to combine the respective advantages of both local and international courts. Located in the country where the crimes occurred, they usually draw some of their judges from the international community and some from the country's domestic judiciary and apply both international criminal laws and the domestic laws of the country in question. However, despite the fact that they are lumped together under the same heading, there is no one single format for each of the different courts: While they combine international and domestic criminal justice, they have their own distinctive structures and face unique challenges.

Mixed courts have been created as a response to several different conflicts around the world. At present, there are five different mixed courts in operation. Internationalized courts are currently functioning in Sierra Leone (a small West African country that fought a brutal three-way civil war from 1991 to 1997), East Timor (a former Indonesian colony that achieved independence after a brief and bloody war), and Kosovo (the breakaway Yugoslavian region mentioned earlier). The Cambodian tribunal, created to prosecute those responsible for the millions of deaths perpetrated in the 1970s under the Khmer Rouge indicted its first suspect in August, 2007.

The Special Court for Sierra Leone has been one of the most successful of the four mixed courts. The court was created in 2002 by an agreement between the United Nations and the government of Sierra Leone and is based in the city of Freetown, the national capital. It is structured like the international courts (consisting of judges, a prosecutor, a defense office, and a registry) and is authorized to prosecute individuals for war crimes, crimes against humanity and, in a novel development, certain violations of the domestic law of Sierra Leone. Specifically, under the statute of the court, individuals may be prosecuted for certain crimes against children (including, abusing young girls and the "abduction of a girl for immoral purposes") and "Offences relating to the wanton destruction of property." Each trial has three judges, two of which are selected by the UN Secretary General and one from the government of Sierra Leone. In 2006, the Special Court began proceedings against former Liberian President Charles Taylor for war crimes in Sierra Leone—forcing the court to temporarily relocate to The Hague to conduct its proceedings safely.

Internationalized courts have a number of advantages over the other international courts we've discussed. On one hand, they're local, taking place in the country where the international crimes have occurred. This means that they allow local judges and attorneys, who are likely to have a better understanding of local customs and history, to participate in the trial proceedings. This helps prevent misunderstandings that result from foreign judges who are unfamiliar with the cultural, political, and historical issues that can play an important role in individual cases. Further, the fact that local judges are handling local criminals in local courts makes justice a local affair. This gives nationals a sense of "ownership" over their problems—the local people are capable of finding their own solutions to their crimes without relying upon outsiders to "rescue" them. However, the international presence on the court also can prevent the abuse of the tribunals by those in power and can help to keep the trial proceedings fair and objective. Finally, placing the trials close to the scene of the crime helps save the courts and the UN a good deal of time and money as witnesses and defendants are nearby and easily obtained. As one prominent international criminal lawyer has said, "In the long term, resorting to mixed or internationalized criminal courts and tribunals may prove to be one of the most effective societal and institutional devices of the many which are at present available to international law makers."[3]

However, these courts have had a few problems. Many who are currently in power in the countries where mixed courts are being developed are in some way tied to the previous atrocities and do not wish to see themselves or their allies prosecuted. In Cambodia, some of whose leaders remain linked to the Khmer Rouge, the government insisted that local

---

[3] Cassese, Antonio (2004) "The Role of Internationalized Courts and Tribunals in the Fight against International Criminality," in *Internationalized Criminal Courts* (Romano et al., eds), Oxford: Oxford University Press.

judges, appointed by the government, constitute the majority on the bench. Thus, the political powers in that country can exert influence over the trials. This has been a "black eye" in the Cambodia tribunal and has led human rights organizations like Amnesty International to criticize it publicly. (The Cambodian government and the international community ultimately compromised and allowed for a majority of judges to be Cambodian but required that rulings be made with a majority of judges, *plus one additional judge.*) Similarly, cases like Charles Taylor's show that sometimes local trials for highly controversial cases can create security problems. Nonetheless, many scholars have argued that these mixed courts, if conducted properly, can be much more effective and much less costly than the more properly international courts such as the ICC.

International Criminal Procedure

Because there are a number of different international courts with different structures and different founding documents, there is no *single* international criminal procedure that governs the conduct of all of the international courts. Each court is run in a slightly different fashion. However, there are a number of shared features of the different courts and some shared ideas about how courts should be run. All of these courts are limited by the various international human rights treaties, each of which has a good deal to say about the proper conduct of a criminal trial. For example, the International Covenant on Civil and Political Rights asserts that all criminal suspects are guaranteed a fair trial, are entitled to be considered innocent until proven guilty, and are guaranteed the right to defend themselves in court. The Geneva Convention likewise requires fair trials for accused war criminals.[4] Despite their differences then, the procedures of the various international treaties all aim at the same results: A fair trial for the accused and a chance for defendants to rebut the charges against him or her.

The international courts use a "mixed" procedure, combining aspects of the Anglo-American system (known as the *adversarial* approach) and the European civil law tradition (called the *inquisitorial* system). Like the American system, the international criminal courts have a prosecuting attorney who is independent from the judges and a defense attorney who is an advocate for the defendant and presents the defendant's side of the story to the court. Also like American criminal trials, each side presents their respective cases, subjecting each other's evidence to scrutiny and each other's witnesses to cross-examination. This is different from the inquisitorial model, where attorneys play a very small role in the trial, as an investigating judge examines the case and presents the facts. While the judges in international courts tend to be slightly more active than they would be in an American courtroom (they often ask questions about evidence or interrogate witnesses in a way that an American judge never would), in many ways an American criminal attorney would feel at home in the international courts.

However, unlike the American system, there is no jury that makes the ultimate decision about the guilt or innocence of the defendant. In the American system, judges are in most cases supposed to be neutral referees who only rule on matters of law, such as

---

[4] Common Article 3 of the Conventions prohibit "the passing of sentences and the carrying out of executions without previous judgment pronounced by a regularly constituted court affording all the judicial guarantees which are recognized as indispensable by civilized people."

whether or not a piece of evidence may be presented or should be excluded. American judges do not usually decide whether or not the accused is guilty or innocent, a "finding of fact" (unless the accused waives his or her right to a jury and elects to have a "bench trial"). This decision is usually left up to a jury of citizens. In the international courts these decisions are made by a majority of the presiding judges. At the ICC, for example, a head judge and two subordinate judges determine by a majority vote whether the accused is guilty. This makes international judges much more powerful than they would be in an American court (and has led some American critics of the ICC to suggest that the court would violate the constitutional rights of an American defendant).[5]

The international courts must work in a complex political environment which affects how they are run. They have no police force or marshal service of their own that might allow them to obtain suspected international criminals and they must rely upon the assistance of member states to bring indicted criminals to The Hague for trial. Further, there is no international police force that could help to protect witnesses who come to The Hague in order to testify against powerful defendants. This means that many witnesses will likely face retribution in their home states if they choose to return and the court is effectively helpless to do anything about it. (The author personally witnessed one account from a witness who returned to the former Yugoslavia after testifying, only to discover that his home had been confiscated by Serbian government officials using forged documents.) This fact has influenced how the courts process cases, requiring that they bend some of the traditional rules of evidence.

Both the IMT and the IMTFE refused to be bound by "technical rules of evidence" and frequently improvised in handling novel sorts of evidence such as the first films of the liberation of the German extermination camps. Under certain circumstances, the ICTY has allowed testimony from anonymous witnesses (which, in an American criminal trial, would usually be a violation of the Sixth Amendment right to face one's accuser) and hearsay (second-hand) evidence, which would usually be inadmissible in American criminal trials. It is likely that the novel circumstances that the ICC will be forced to work in will also require that new procedures and new rules of evidence in order to balance the rights of accused international criminals with the complex demands that are placed on the court because of its unique circumstances.

Truth Commissions

Along with criminal courts, a number of countries have created so-called truth commissions to deal with mass atrocities that have occurred within their borders. While they are not courts, strictly speaking, these commissions usually consist in a panel of respected citizens who are charged with discovering what happened in political conflicts and presenting an official report to both the government and the public. Some of these organizations, such as those used in Latin American countries emerging from military dictatorships, are simple truth commissions. Sometimes, such commissions "point fingers," attributing individual responsibility for criminal acts; other times, they don't, sufficing themselves with a general accounting of facts without blaming any individuals for what happened. The philosophy

---

[5] See R. Wedgewood, The Constitution of the ICC, in Sewell, *The United States and the International Court.*

behind these commissions is that a simple public accounting of what happened can help a society achieve transitional justice without the bitterness and expense that criminal prosecutions can often engender. Critics, however, often accuse such commissions of whitewashing atrocities and protecting politically powerful criminals under the noble guise of facilitating transitional justice and promoting national reconciliation.

Some commissions have been given broader authority than simple truth commissions and function in many ways similar to criminal courts. South Africa's Truth and Reconciliation Commission (TRC) not only sought to discover what happened under its previous racist apartheid government, but in addition, it was granted a wide array of powers that are traditionally given the power to subpoena witnesses, seize evidence, and protect individuals whose testimony puts them in danger. Most significantly, the commission was empowered under certain circumstances to give amnesty to individuals who told the complete truth about the crimes that they committed as part of their political efforts. In its three-year existence, the TRC reviewed over 7,000 applications for amnesty and received the testimony of 21,000 victims and witnesses before producing its final report in October 1998. While many credit the South African Commission with facilitating a smooth, peaceful transition from apartheid to a democracy that respected the rights of all citizens, some refused to accept that killers and torturers should be given amnesty for their crimes because of a perceived need to forgive their former oppressors.[6] Others were incensed that the Commission investigated the actions of black South Africans who were fighting for political equality along with that of their white oppressors. In the words of Thabo Mbeki (former anti-apartheid leader and current President of South Africa), "the net effect of [the TRC's] findings is to deligitimize or criminalize a significant part of the struggle of our people for liberation."[7]

The relationship between truth commissions and other tools of transitional justice, such as criminal prosecution, is a contentious issue in international criminal justice. Defenders of the TRC and similar commissions argue that criminal prosecutions are unnecessarily divisive and costly, and in some cases may undermine peace and stability in fragile parts of the world. South Africa simply lacked the facilities to prosecute and punish everybody who had committed crimes under the previous apartheid government. Further, they argue that in the long term, discovering the truth about what happened to individual victims of mass atrocities is more important than assigning blame to individuals. If suspected political criminals are tried in a court of law, they are unlikely to ever be forthcoming about the fates of their victims and the families of these victims will never learn the whole truth about what happened to their loved ones. Defenders of criminal prosecutions argue that such commissions send an inappropriate message to despotic regimes around the world: If you commit crimes as a part of your government's political policies, you can escape prosecution for your crimes if you arrange for an amnesty as a condition of abdicating power.

The ICC was in part created to hold individuals criminally accountable for their acts when their domestic governments do not. This means that the ICC could prosecute those individuals who commit international crimes but are given amnesty by domestic truth commissions. This places the ICC's emphasis on criminal punishment in direct conflict with these truth commissions. They each seek to help the process of transitional justice but

---

[6] See: Wilson, Richard (2006) *The Politics of Truth and Reconciliation in South Africa.* New York: Cambridge University Press.

[7] Hayner, Priscilla (2001) *Unspeakable Truths.* New York: Routledge, p. 45.

through different, and perhaps incompatible means. One emphasizes truth, reconciliation, and forgiveness, while the other emphasizes individual moral responsibility and punishment for lawbreakers. While in theory, the two processes can work together (individuals who refused to testify before the TRC could be prosecuted criminally, for example) it is difficult to see how the two are truly compatible. A truth commission whose amnesties were ignored by the ICC would find few people willing to cooperate. Likewise, a criminal court which allowed killers to escape criminal punishment because their own government chose to give them amnesty runs the risk of undermining the ideals that inspired the entire history of criminal courts: that nobody is above the law.

International lawyers have yet to arrive at a consensus as to whether or not the ICC should be allowed to overrule the amnesties granted by domestic truth commissions. However, it is worth noting that (as was previously mentioned) the ICC's prosecutor may choose not to pursue a case if the investigation "would not serve the interests of justice." Presumably, the prosecutor may use this discretion in order to allow a domestic truth commission's amnesties to stand. However, under certain circumstances, the prosecutor's choice not to investigate a case is not the final word and may be contested by various parties. This means that eventually the ICC itself may have to settle the matter of the international legal status of the amnesties offered by truth commissions. Underlying this technical legal point, however, is the fundamental question of transitional justice: Which is more important, the peace and reconciliation that amnesties and truth commissions offer or the justice provided by criminal courts?

QUESTIONS

1. What are the goals of transitional justice? What is more important for societies recovering from wars or other mass atrocities: peace and stability or justice? Are the two separate? Why or why not?
2. What are the unique problems that an international criminal court would face that a conventional criminal court wouldn't?
3. Do you think that international courts are a good idea? Why or why not?
4. What should the attitude of the American government be to the ICC and the other international criminal courts?

READING AND RESOURCES

The International Criminal Court has a website that keeps track of activities surrounding the court (http://www.icc-cpi.int/).

The two ad hoc tribunals each have their own website. (Because they are affiliated with the United Nations, their websites are part of the UN's: http://www.un.org/icty/ and http://www.un.org/ictr/.) They each do an excellent job in organizing the documents for these trials and provide video recordings of some of the proceedings.

The websites for the special tribunal in Sierra Leone is http://www.sc-sl.org/. The website includes documents relating to the court's proceedings as well as video and audio footage of their trials.

Both Yale and Harvard Universities have very good websites that have a lot of original documents and photos from the Nuremberg Tribunals (http://www.yale.edu/lawweb/avalon/imt/imt.htm and http://nuremberg.law.harvard.edu/view).

A number of very good studies of the international criminal courts have been written. A particularly good history of war crimes trials, which deals with the political process that led to the creation of these courts in the 20th century is Bass, Gary, *Stay the Hand of Vengeance,* Princeton University Press, Princeton, 2001. For an analysis of the American relation to the ICC, see Sewell, Sarah and Kaysen, Carl (eds), *The United States and the International Criminal Court,* Rowan and Littlefield, Lanham, 2000. The U.S. State Department (www.state.gov) has a webpage devoted to the Article 98 agreements, which includes a defense of the American policies toward the ICC.

A readable and comprehensive study of truth commissions is Hayner, Priscilla, *Unspeakable Truths,* Routledge, NY, 2001.

There are two very good videos that deal with the Nuremberg trials. One is the 1961 movie *Judgment at Nuremberg;* the other is a miniseries produced in 2000 (which deals with the trial of Goering et al. with a fairly high degree of historical accuracy) starring Alec Baldwin, which is simply titled *Nuremberg.*

4

International and Transnational Crimes in Domestic Courts

As we've seen in the last two chapters, international criminal justice has developed a great deal since the end of World War II. However, as you've probably also begun to realize, the trials that these courts oversee are complex, politically treacherous, and costly affairs. The international courts require hundreds of well-paid legal experts and other staffers to help them conduct their business, all of whom must be paid for by the international community. More importantly, however, these courts lack a lot of the elements of a national criminal justice system that help these domestic systems function, most notably, a police force. Because of this, they must rely on the goodwill of states in order to successfully carry out their duties, serving warrants, collecting witnesses, and incarcerating offenders. If states refuse to cooperate with the international courts, there is usually little that these courts can do about it. Moreover, the international courts are limited to only a few select international crimes, and other sorts of global crime are beyond their reach. All of this makes the international courts a challenging place to prosecute international criminals.

On the other hand, domestic criminal courts, particularly those in the democratic, industrialized world, are politically secure and are usually respected by the majority of their citizens. Not only do they have a great deal more resources and receive more funding than do international courts, they are also less likely to be politically controversial than the international courts. Even if citizens grumble about an unpopular ruling from a domestic court, people tend to respect their judgments and follow through on their rulings. This makes these courts a safer and more effective way to prosecute some, though not all, international criminals.

In the last chapter, we discussed the concept of "complementarity" at the ICC – stating that the court will pursue individuals only if governments are "unable or unwilling" to do so on their own. This means that the current international court system will only exist as a supplement to national criminal justice systems in most cases, standing in when the domestic courts fail to fulfill their duty to arrest and prosecute international criminals. Despite the development of the various international criminal courts over the last few years and despite the importance of the ICC for modern international criminal justice, much of the development of international criminal law will be in the domestic courts of various states around the world. International courts may receive public attention, but the front lines of international justice will be in domestic courts.

Already, in Chapters 2 and 3 we saw that there are some acts that are considered to be international crimes but nonetheless do not fall under the jurisdiction of the international courts. Piracy is one such crime that is not punished by the ICC or other international courts. This means that it must be handled at the "state level"—in the domestic courts of sovereign states.

In this chapter, we will discuss the ways that international crimes are prosecuted in domestic courts. We will focus on American courts, but will also discuss how other countries around the world deal with international criminal issues in their own legal systems. There have been some novel experiments in punishing international crimes in other states (in particular Belgium and the UK) that can be very instructive for thinking about trying and punishing international criminals. Similarly, the United States has developed some novel legal strategies on its own in order to handle international criminals. We should note, however, that every country has its own, unique legal system with different rules and procedures, so it is difficult to make too many broad generalizations across the international spectrum.

We will approach the role of domestic courts in international criminal justice from "two directions" as it were. On one hand, we will look at how international criminal law reaches "into" domestic courts, affecting who is prosecuted and on what legal grounds they are prosecuted. On the other hand, we will also look at the outward grasp of domestic criminal law, looking at how criminal laws of the United States and other countries can "reach out" beyond their borders and reach individuals who commit crimes overseas. We will also begin to discuss transnational crimes more directly—looking at how national courts prosecute international drug traffickers, terrorists, and others, alongside war criminals and other violators of international criminal law.

COMITY AND SOVEREIGNTY

There are two fundamental principles that affect how domestic courts deal with international crimes: *comity* and *sovereignty*. "Comity" is a slippery concept, but usually refers to the desire that states have to get along with one another. It usually consists in informal, reciprocal obligations between governments that may, after time, become a sort of customary international law. As one scholar defined comity, it is "the rules of politeness, convenience, and goodwill observed by States in their mutual intercourse without being bound by them."[1] Comity means that states are reluctant to encroach on

---

[1] Oppenheim, cited in Brownlie, Ian (2003) *Principles of Public International Law,* 6th ed. Oxford: Oxford University Press, p. 28.

the territory of other states or act against their citizens from a fear that the other state will do the same.

Another important thing to keep in mind is the significance of the concept of *sovereignty* that we discussed in Chapter 2. "Sovereignty" implies the right of states to handle their own domestic affairs as they see fit, including issues related to crime and criminal justice. This principle can make the prosecution of international crimes politically volatile matters. No state likes to see its nationals prosecuted in foreign courts before foreign judges, or to see them serving time in foreign prisons. There are often genuine concerns that foreigners will not get a fair hearing in court and that foreign juries and judges will be biased against outsiders. Often states will go to great lengths to shield their citizens from foreign prosecutions. In 1994, Michael Fay, an American teenager, was arrested in Singapore for vandalism and was quickly sentenced to a three-month prison term and six strokes of a cane, a common punishment for vandalism in Singapore. This sentence provoked a massive outcry from the American people as well as from the U.S. government, including an intercession by President Clinton (who was able to get the sentence reduced to 4 strokes). Warren Anderson, the former chairman of Union Carbide, has been indicted by an Indian court for negligently causing the disaster in Bhopal, India, that killed over 4,000 people, but the United States has refused to hand him over to the Indian courts. Sometimes political issues and public opinion can play a strong role in the outcome of efforts to prosecute international crimes in domestic courts. States jealously guard their sovereignty and are often unwilling to surrender it to other states or to international bodies like the ICC.

We will approach these issues in three parts: First, we will discuss the concept of jurisdiction in relation to international crimes, outlining some of its central tenets. These principles were a part of international law and thus apply to *all* states, not just to the United States. Then we will turn specifically to the case of the United States—examining the concept of *extraterritorial* jurisdiction in U.S. law. Finally, at the end, we will examine the twin concepts of *immunity* and *inviolability*—those legal principles that make some individuals, diplomatic personnel, and heads of state immune to criminal prosecution in many cases.

JURISDICTION IN GENERAL

Put simply, a state must have *jurisdiction* over a particular criminal act in order to lawfully prosecute it. The term *jurisdiction* simply means that a particular law applies in a particular place and time to a particular individual or case. In most domestic cases, jurisdiction isn't difficult to discern. A person who breaks a law in China is usually a Chinese citizen, is arrested on Chinese soil by Chinese police officials, and is then tried and punished under Chinese law. As long as crimes stay within the their own borders, there is little controversy. However, there are plenty of cases where criminal jurisdiction is not such a simple matter. Imagine a British citizen murders a Chinese citizen in Paris. Subsequently, the killer flees France for Morocco, where he is arrested by Moroccan authorities for an unrelated offense. Of course, all three countries (Britain, China, France) want custody of the suspect in order to bring him to trial, but who has the legal right to prosecute him? Does Morocco have to give him up to one of these other states? If so, which state gets him?

Jurisdiction isn't only an aspect of international law: there are frequently jurisdictional issues in American criminal law. There is not one single criminal law for the United States but rather there are 50 slightly different codes for the different states (along with a Criminal Code for the District of Columbia and a Federal Criminal Code). A law passed by the Tennessee legislature does not apply to people living in Arizona. The two states have different penal codes, which may have different sets of crimes or describe the same crimes in a slightly different fashion. In the United States, the federal government may also have jurisdiction over certain crimes regardless of which state they are committed in. This same concept applies in the international sphere: Each nation has its own criminal code and then, on top of this, are the international criminal laws that we discussed in the previous chapter.

The vast majority of a country's criminal laws only apply to acts that occur within that country's borders. However, there are some important exceptions to this rule. In certain cases, a crime may be prosecuted by a government other than the one within whose borders the crime occurred. This is usually referred to as *extraterritorial jurisdiction.* The murderous Englishman mentioned above may be just such a case—he could be prosecuted in China or England or France. However, other countries that held a grudge against the killer for other reasons could *not* do so, unless they could come up with some other jurisdictional claim.

Like much of the international criminal justice system, the laws of jurisdiction are currently undergoing a transformation in light of the September 11 terrorist attacks. There is no strict rule in international law about who may prosecute a particular offender, and governments have changed their views about this matter over time. Many of the international laws of jurisdiction depend upon which country is claiming jurisdiction over a particular individual. Often they will seek to interpret these principles charitably in their own case, and strictly when other states want to claim jurisdiction over their own nationals. Lawyers speak about the various forms of international jurisdiction as "principles," not rules, implying that they are less rigid and less defined than other aspects of international criminal law. As we will shortly see, the American attitude toward international jurisdiction has changed a good deal over the years, and politicians and lawyers are currently debating changing the laws of American criminal jurisdiction even further in order to more effectively deal with terrorists, cybercriminals, and other international threats. This means that it is important not only to understand the various forms or principles of jurisdiction, but also to see them in their proper political context.

Often, a state's right to prosecute an individual who committed a crime in another state can be perceived as an insult to the latter state. State B's perceived right to prosecute individuals who commit crimes in State A (regardless of the nationality of the individuals involved) may be perceived as an affront to A's autonomy and its sovereignty. By prosecuting an individual for a foreign crime, State B can be perceived as telling other states what to do within their own borders, and dictating what sorts of acts they ought to punish. (Imagine the response from the American people if a foreign judge started prosecuting American citizens for crimes that they committed within American borders!) Further, foreign prosecutions imply that State A cannot properly maintain law and order on its own territory and that A requires B's assistance in order to properly do its job. This means that states are sometimes hesitant to arrest people who commit crimes on foreign soil and that foreign prosecutions may, at times, lead to delicate political and diplomatic situations.

Under international law, there are typically four ways that a state may claim a right to prosecute a particular case, that is, crimes over which it may assert its jurisdiction: territoriality, effects (or "objective territoriality"), active personality, and passive personality. However, there is also an emerging principle of *universal jurisdiction* for certain crimes, which although somewhat novel, has become an important part of the modern international law. We will discuss each of these forms of jurisdiction in turn.

A) *Territoriality:* A state may claim jurisdiction over a crime when the crime occurred on that state's territory. Obviously, it is in every state's interest to prosecute a crime that is perpetrated within its borders—keeping the peace is one of the central jobs, if not *the* job, of any decent government. Thus, a Mexican court can prosecute a Canadian (or any other national) who robs a bank in Mexico City.

As straightforward as territorial jurisdiction may initially appear, with many modern crimes it is difficult to determine exactly where a crime has occurred. A person in Moscow who uses the Internet in order to hack into an American computer to steal credit card information and sell it to a Chinese gang may have committed a crime, but where? Russia? the United States? China?

Similarly, as we've already seen, many crimes are perpetrated across borders, and some acts that are part of the crime take place in one state, others in a different place. A group of people who conspire in Paris to murder a man living in Berlin, and then attempt to kill him in Germany have committed criminal acts in both states (conspiracy to commit murder in Paris, and attempted murder in Berlin). In most cases *either* state may prosecute the individual. Usually, a state may prosecute a crime if any part of the criminal act took place within its borders.

B) *Effects* or (*"objective territoriality"*): If the effects of a criminal act are felt in a particular country, that government may assert jurisdiction over a crime. As U.S. Supreme Court Justice Oliver Wendell Holmes asserted, "acts done outside a jurisdiction, but intended to produce and producing detrimental effects within it, justify a state in punishing the cause of the harm as if he had been present at the effect, if the State should succeed in getting him within its power."[2]

One of the most commonly cited cases in international law dealing with the issue of international criminal jurisdiction is known as the *Lotus Case*. This case involved a French steamer, *Lotus,* that collided with a Turkish ship in the Aegean Sea shortly after midnight in August 2, 1926, killing 8 Turkish sailors. When the *Lotus* stopped at a Turkish port shortly thereafter, members of its crew were arrested and charged with manslaughter by Turkish authorities. The French government protested the action and took the case to the PCIJ (the Permanent Court of International Justice, the international court that was the precursor to the ICJ).

In its opinion, the PCIJ set out some of the basic international laws of criminal jurisdiction. The court held that in most cases, governments had a right to prosecute individuals on the basis of the location where the crime occurred and that "in all systems of law the principle of the territorial character of criminal law is fundamental." Even though the criminal act occurred on a French ship, its effects were felt on a Turkish vessel, and the court held that "[T]here is no rule of

---

[2] *Strassheim* v. *Daily,* 221 U.S. 280 (1911).

international law prohibiting the State to which the ship on which the effects have taken place belongs, from regarding the offence as having been committed in its territory and prosecuting, accordingly, the delinquent."[3] Thus, the PCIJ established the effects principle as a definitive part of the international laws of criminal jurisdiction.

However, in a globalized economy and society, it is difficult to find an international crime that does not have *some* kind of effects on another country. Clearly a person who manufactures and processes drugs to be imported to the United States has committed a crime that has effects in the United States, but counterfeiting currency (especially U.S. currency, whose value influences economies throughout the world) can affect every nation in the world. Similarly, credit card fraud can affect buyers and sellers around the world, as well as international financial institutions like banks and other lending companies. The global links that bind together different peoples mean that many ordinary crimes produce results that can, under certain circumstances, make them international crimes.

C) *Active personality* (or *"nationality jurisdiction"*): An individual may be prosecuted by a government's criminal courts if he or she is a national of that state—even if the crime took place somewhere else. Thus, the Belgian government can usually prosecute a Belgian citizen for a crime, even if they committed the crime in Greece. Obviously, many states would prefer to handle their own citizens and punish them in their own prisons, even though they committed their crimes elsewhere. As we will see when we discuss the *Sheinbein* case later in this chapter, conducting trials abroad can be very difficult.

D) *Passive personality:* Somewhat more controversial than the active personality principle is the right to prosecute an individual based on the nationality of the *victim* of a crime. Under the passive personality principle, states claim a right to prosecute individuals whose acts harm their own citizens—regardless of where the victims are at the time of the act. Thus, under this principle, a South African court can prosecute an Indian citizen if he killed a South African citizen somewhere in India.

Jurisdiction based on active and passive personalities is controversial in the U.S. legal community. On one hand, the United States has opposed punishing Americans for violating the criminal laws of other states. One of the seminal cases dealing with the passive personality doctrine was the *Cutting* case of 1887. Here the Mexican government prosecuted a U.S. citizen after he had reportedly libeled a Mexican national in an article he had published in an American newspaper. The U.S. government angrily refuted Mexico's claim to jurisdiction, asserting that a citizen of the United States cannot be "held under rules of international law to answer in Mexico for an offense committed in the United States, simply because the object of that offense happens to be a Mexican national."[4]

On the other hand, the U.S. government has recently expanded its right to prosecute individuals for extraterritorial crimes based solely on the fact that Americans are the victims of the crime in question. For example, the United States has claimed a right to

---

[3] *The Lotus Case* (*France* v. *Turkey*), 1927 PCIJ, Ser. A, No. 10.

[4] See Geoffrey R. Watson (1993), "The Passive Personality Principle," 28 TEX. INT'L L.J. 1, 7.

prosecute foreign nationals who kill Americans overseas under the Omnibus Diplomatic Security and Antiterrorism Act of 1986, which asserted that "whoever kills a national of the United States, while such national is outside the United States, shall—(1) if the killing is murder . . . be fined under this title, punished by death or imprisonment for any term of years or for life, or both."[5] Also, this act gave the U.S. courts jurisdiction over individuals who conspire to kill Americans abroad and over those who engage in serious violence against Americans abroad. This act has been used to prosecute a number of terrorists who have killed Americans abroad, including Fawaz Younis, who was arrested by the FBI in 1988 for hijacking a Royal Jordanian airplane with American citizens on board.[6] The many anti–drug trafficking laws likewise assert jurisdiction over foreign criminals on similar grounds. (We will discuss some of these issues further in the next chapter when we discuss the expanding role played by U.S. law enforcement officers overseas in investigating crimes and arresting international criminals.)

A number of experts have expressed concern that the shift in American criminal law toward passive personality jurisdiction could expose Americans who travel abroad to unnecessary danger. By expanding the doctrine of passive personality, America runs the risk of setting precedents that other states might use to unfairly punish Americans in retaliation for acts of the U.S. government. Imagine a state hostile to the United States that punishes an American citizen for the crime of "supporting an aggressive government." Similarly, cases like *Cutting* could reemerge, and Americans could be prosecuted for exercising their free speech rights to criticize a foreign government that does not tolerate political dissent. An American critical of a foreign leader could be arrested while overseas for things he said while on American soil. Thus, critics argue, rather than prosecuting terrorists and other international criminals based on the passive personality principle, prosecutors should base their jurisdictional claims on other, more traditional grounds.[7]

UNIVERSAL JURISDICTION

In order to prosecute the vast majority of crimes, a state must have one of the four forms of jurisdiction outlined above. However, some governments and some criminal courts have gone further, claiming a right to prosecute individuals for certain crimes regardless of where these crimes were committed, and independent of the suspect's nationality or the nationality of the victims. These governments assert jurisdiction without any claims of territoriality, active or passive personality, and without arguing that the crime has had any effects on their own country. Thus, according to this theory of jurisdiction, an Indonesian who commits certain crimes on other Indonesians in Indonesian territory may be prosecuted in a foreign court (not an international one). This controversial doctrine, known as "universal jurisdiction," has become a subject of much debate in the international criminal justice community.

---

[5] 18 U.S.C. 2331.
[6] Robinson, Joshua (1998), "United States Practice Penalizing International Terrorists Needlessly Undercuts Its Opposition to the Passive Personality Principle," 16 B.U. Int'l L.J. 487.
[7] Scharf, Michael P. and Corrin, Melanie, K. (2002), "On Dangerous Ground: Passive Personality Jurisdiction and the Prohibition of Internet Gambling," *New Eng. Journal of Int'l & Comp. Law,* Vol. 8, No. 1.

Again, like much of international criminal law, piracy is the model for universal jurisdiction. As we've already discussed, piracy was one of the first truly international crimes and although it is not prosecuted by any international court (as we saw in the last chapter, it is not under the jurisdiction of the ICC) any country can prosecute pirates regardless of any of the principles of jurisdiction mentioned above. Countries that have claimed universal jurisdiction have sought to expand the laws against piracy to other international crimes, including torture, genocide, and crimes against humanity. Further, some of these universal jurisdiction states allow for trials *in absentia,* meaning that the accused individual does not need to be present to be tried, convicted, and sentenced. (The theory behind trials *in absentia* is that if the accused truly believed that he was innocent, he would show up to defend himself. American criminal courts do not allow for trials *in absentia,* but they are an important part of many other legal systems.) This legal principle is radical because under universal jurisdiction, *any* individual anywhere in the world may be prosecuted and sentenced in a criminal court without ever having any relationship with that country, and even without setting foot in the country that is trying and perhaps convicting them.

Not any crime can lead to a state claiming universal jurisdiction. Usually, these crimes have to be serious, international crimes. That is, these crimes must be violations of international criminal law (such as the ones that we described in Chapter 2) and in most cases the states that would traditionally have jurisdiction over the accused criminal must have refused to prosecute the accused. Like the ICC, universal jurisdiction is a matter of "last resort," functioning when criminal courts closer to the "scene of the crime" fail to prosecute alleged criminals. Only if these criteria are met would a state be willing to assert universal jurisdiction.

Universal jurisdiction has taken on slightly different forms in different states. The most dramatic experiment with it was in the tiny European country of Belgium. In 1993, Belgium passed an Anti-Atrocity Law, claiming the right to try individuals who commit grave breaches of the Geneva Conventions, genocide, and crimes against humanity, regardless of whether or not there is any connection between Belgium and the accused. Even further, Belgium claimed the right to try an international criminal *in absentia* and refused to acknowledge any immunity for individuals on account of their official capacity (thus, refusing to acknowledge the settled international laws of diplomatic or head-of-state immunity discussed below). Under this law, Belgian courts could effectively become another sort of international criminal court, prosecuting individuals for violating international criminal laws anywhere in the world. Only, unlike the ICC, Belgium did not require that the defendant be physically present for the trial.

Regardless of how well intentioned its authors were, the Belgian law was in many ways a political disaster. Not only were vicious international criminals indicted by the Belgian courts, but idealistic Belgian citizens started lobbying to have prominent heads of state prosecuted in Belgium for crimes they allegedly committed in their home states. Thus, Ariel Sharon, the prime minister of Israel, was indicted for his alleged role in a 1982 massacre of Palestinian civilians, Saddam Hussein was indicted for massacring Kurds in Iraq, the foreign minister of the Congo was indicted, and numerous other prominent heads of state were similarly indicted on the basis of universal jurisdiction. Some had even suggested that President Clinton be indicted for NATO's allegedly unlawful bombing of Serbia in the Kosovo conflict. What had started as a noble effort to prosecute notorious international criminals who would not face trials at home threatened to turn into a political free-for-all, with Belgian courts pronouncing judgment on political leaders throughout the world.

The end of the Belgian universal jurisdiction experiment resulted from an ICJ opinion entitled the "Case Concerning the Arrest Warrant of 11 April 2000" (*Democratic Republic of the Congo* v. *Belgium*). On that date, a Belgian judge issued an arrest warrant for Yerodia Ndombasi, the foreign minister of the African nation of the Congo, asserting that Ndombasi was guilty of grave breaches of the Geneva Conventions and crimes against humanity for inciting racial hatred in 1998 (which allegedly led to the massacre of several hundred Tutsi nationals). The court ruled that Belgium could not prosecute Ndombasi because of his diplomatic status.[8] The result of this case and the political fiasco that Belgium's criminal jurisdiction created caused the Belgian government to revise its universal jurisdiction law so that it could no longer prosecute *anybody* who commits an international crime, but rather limited potential targets to those with some connection with the state of Belgium.

Other countries have interpreted the "universality" of universal jurisdiction a little less strongly than Belgium.[9] Some states, for example Austria, Germany, and Switzerland, allow for universal jurisdiction but reject the idea of trials *in absentia,* insisting that the defendant must be present in the state before they investigate a crime. Presumably, an individual who is wanted for an international crime could avoid these states in order to evade prosecution. Other states have required that the crime, the victim, or the accused have some kind of connection with the prosecuting state. Thus, under this version of universal jurisdiction, either the accused must be present in the state for them to be put on trial or the victim must be present, though neither need be nationals of the prosecuting nations. These limitations have helped to eliminate the problems that plagued Belgium's experiment but do not quell the concern that many have about universal jurisdiction.[10]

INTERNATIONAL LAW IN DOMESTIC LAW

There is a connection between international law and domestic legal systems; however, this connection is different for different countries. Some countries, so-called "monistic" countries, make international law a part of domestic law automatically. When a government signs and ratifies a treaty, the legal rules spelled out in the treaty are incorporated into the domestic legal system.[11] The other view is called "dualist"— international law requires separate legislation from the national government in order

---

[8] "Case Concerning the Arrest Warrant of 11 April 2000" (*Democratic Republic of the Congo* v. *Belgium*) Judgment 14, February 2002.

[9] Spain has a similar law, and with some qualifications, as do Italy and Germany. See Cassese, Antonio, *International Criminal Law,* pp. 286–291.

[10] In 2003, the US House of Representatives introduced H. R. 2050, the "Universal Jurisdiction Rejection Act," which asserted that "it is the policy of the United States to reject any claim of universal jurisdiction made by foreign governments and to refuse to render any assistance or support to any foreign government pursuing an investigation or prosecution under a universal jurisdiction act." The bill also asserted that "The President may use all means necessary . . . to bring about the release form captivity of any person . . . who is being detained or imprisoned . . . under a universal jurisdiction act." This bill never became law, however.

[11] For example, Article 25 of the German Constitution says: "The general rules of public international law are an integral part of federal law. They shall take precedence over the laws and shall directly create rights and duties for the inhabitants of the federal territory."

to become a part of domestic law. So if a state signs and ratifies a treaty making a certain act a crime it automatically becomes a crime in a monistic country, but in a dualist country, their parliament or congress must pass their own set of laws. However, beyond these simple theories, the relation between international law and domestic law is much more complex. Here we will focus on international law in the American legal system.

"International law is part of our law, and must be ascertained and administered by the courts of justice of appropriate jurisdiction as often as questions of right depending upon it are duly presented for their determination,"[12] wrote U.S. Supreme Court Justice Horace Gray in 1900. While Justice Gray's maxim is clear and authoritative, it masks the reality that the U.S. court's application of international law is at times inconsistent and half-hearted, particularly in relation to criminal matters and human rights law. Only recently, with the development of the war on terrorism, has the United States' attitude toward international law begun to change significantly.

In some ways this ambivalence reflects the elements of American political culture that we discussed in the opening chapter. The twin doctrines of American exceptionalism and realism that we discussed there have had a profound impact on the American legal community's response to developments in international law. American presidents have been hesitant to sign treaties, the Senate has been hesitant to ratify them, and overall, the U.S. government has vehemently resisted international scrutiny in how it deals with its citizens (especially in criminal matters), much less foreign nationals being put on trial in American courts. Few American law students study international law or international criminal law as part of their training, which means that attorneys are hesitant to use it in their arguments and judges are unfamiliar with it.

Additionally, there is heated, ongoing debate in the American legal community about the relevance of non-U.S. law, including international law, for American courts. Many prominent judges (including Supreme Court Justice Anthony Scalia) have derided judges who make references to foreign or international rulings to arrive at their judgments. These judges and legal scholars argue that it undermines democracy when judges use non-American laws to decide the fate of Americans. When, in *Lawrence* v. *Texas* (a case involving the legality of sodomy under U.S. law), the majority opinion made reference to a ruling of the European Court of Human Rights, Justice Antonin Scalia attacked the reference as "meaningless" and "dangerous." Similarly, Justice Clarence Thomas has attacked the court's use of foreign and international law in making their rulings, asserting that "While Congress, as a legislature, may wish to consider the actions of other nations on any issue it likes," he argued, "this Court's Eighth Amendment jurisprudence should not impose foreign moods, fads, or fashions on Americans."[13] Many judges and politicians see the use of international and foreign laws in American courts as a dangerous threat to American sovereignty and view the American legal system as "hermetically sealed" and precluding any external influence.

---

[12] *The Paquete Habana,* 175 US 677, 20 S.Ct. 290, 44 L. Ed. 320 (1900).

[13] *Foster* v. *Florida* (Thomas, concurring).

Despite their concern about entering alliances with the warring European powers, the founding fathers believed that international law should play a significant role in the American legal system and the U.S. government actively fought international and transnational crime. Pirates were a continuing nuisance in the New World and President Jefferson sent an armada to the Barbary Coast (off the coast of northern Africa) to crush them in what some historians have described as America's first "war on terrorism." The Constitution gives Congress the power "To define and punish Piracies and Felonies committed on the high Seas, and Offences against the Law of Nations."[14] Similarly, it gives the Supreme Court power over, "All Cases, in Law and Equity, arising under . . . Treaties made, or which shall be made, under their Authority;—to all Cases affecting Ambassadors, other public Ministers and Consuls; [and] to all Cases of admiralty and maritime Jurisdiction."[15] While there has always been an isolationist streak in U.S. foreign policy, the American legal system incorporated international law (alongside the British common law that it inherited) into its legal system from the very beginning.

As the above constitutional passages show, treaties are a part of American law; however, there is more to this story. When the U.S. government signs and ratifies an international treaty, this can affect domestic law either directly or indirectly. Some treaties are called "self-executing" treaties, meaning that they directly become a part of U.S. law and American courts are required to apply it in individual cases. Non-self-executing treaties, on the other hand, require a separate act of the legislature to become a part of U.S. law. If Congress refuses to sanction the treaty by making the additional laws required by the treaty, the treaty is effectively useless in American courts. (Usually, judges will examine the wording of a treaty to determine whether or not that treaty is meant to be self-executing.) However, treaties are restricted by the "supremacy clause" of the Constitution, which makes the Constitution the supreme law in the United States, superior to any treaties or any state laws.[16] If there is a conflict between a federal law and a treaty, the most recent rule holds, but treaties are nonetheless superior to the laws of individual states.

Because of the fact that many important international criminal law treaties are not self-executing, the United States has also passed its own federal laws that are explicitly intended to incorporate some of their principles into the U.S. criminal code. Many of the laws of war, for example, were codified in treaties that were not self-executing and in order to remedy this, President Clinton signed the "War Crimes Act of 1996" giving the U.S. government the right to punish violations of the Geneva Conventions, provided that "the person committing such war crime or the victim of such war crime is a member of the Armed Forces of the United States or a national of the United

---

[14] Article 1, Section 8.

[15] Article 3, Section 2.

[16] Article VI of the U.S. Constitution says, "This Constitution, and the Laws of the United States which shall be made in Pursuance thereof; and all Treaties made, or which shall be made, under the Authority of the United States, shall be the supreme Law of the Land; and the Judges in every State shall be bound thereby, any Thing in the Constitution or Laws of any State to the Contrary notwithstanding."

States."[17] (Hence, the jurisdiction of the act was limited to either active or passive personality.) Similar provisions were incorporated into military law.[18]

One of the major, but unofficial statements of the relationship between U.S. law and international law is the *Restatement of the Law (Third), Foreign Relations Law of the United States,* which is put together by the American Law Institute (ALI). The ALI is an organization consisting of prominent American lawyers that seeks to influence U.S. legal practice and, where necessary, reform it. The *Restatement* is an ongoing ALI project to outline the international components of U.S. law, seeking to explain how an impartial judge would consider international law in their rulings (including rulings on criminal issues). Frequently, judges and legal scholars will refer to the *Restatement* when they analyze international law from the perspective of the American legal system and it is a useful study guide.

Extraterritorial Application of U.S. Criminal Law

While American judges and legislators have been hesitant to apply *international* laws in American courts, they have sometimes been more enthusiastic about applying *American* criminal laws overseas. That is to say that Congress has structured certain American laws so that they are applicable not only to criminal acts that are carried out in the United States, but also to acts committed in foreign countries (even if those acts are legal in that foreign country). One of the central ways that American laws do this is by having what is known as *extraterritorial application.*[19] If a criminal law is extraterritorial in nature, then

---

[17] 18 USCS § 2441. The section in its entirety reads as follows:
   (a) **Offense.—** Whoever, whether inside or outside the United States, commits a war crime, in any of the circumstances described in subsection (b), shall be fined under this title or imprisoned for life or any term of years, or both, and if death results to the victim, shall also be subject to the penalty of death.
   (b) **Circumstances.—**The circumstances referred to in subsection (a) are that the person committing such war crime or the victim of such war crime is a member of the Armed Forces of the United States or a national of the United States (as defined in section 101 of the Immigration and Nationality Act).
   (c) **Definition.—**As used in this section the term "war crime" means any conduct—
      (1) defined as a grave breach in any of the international conventions signed at Geneva 12 August 1949, or any protocol to such convention to which the United States is a party;
      (2) prohibited by Article 23, 25, 27, or 28 of the Annex to the Hague Convention IV, Respecting the Laws and Customs of War on Land, signed 18 October 1907;
      (3) which constitutes a violation of common Article 3 of the international conventions signed at Geneva, 12 August 1949, or any protocol to such convention to which the United States is a party and which deals with non-international armed conflict; or
      (4) of a person who, in relation to an armed conflict and contrary to the provisions of the Protocol on Prohibitions or Restrictions on the Use of Mines, Booby-Traps and Other Devices as amended at Geneva on 3 May 1996 (Protocol II as amended on 3 May 1996), when the United States is a party to such Protocol, willfully kills or causes serious injury to civilians.
[18] See 10 USCS § 818.
[19] This should not be confused with the concept of *territoriality,* which we will discuss shortly.

it can be used to punish individuals who commit these crimes, even if they commit them in other countries. However, only a select few laws are considered to have extraterritorial jurisdiction. Usually the extraterritorial reach of a particular law will be explicitly written into the statute but sometimes may be inferred from the language of the law or the intent of the legislators.

One of the most well known American criminal laws with explicit extraterritorial application is the Foreign Corrupt Practices Act (FCPA). Passed in 1977 (and Amended in 1988) the FCPA was meant to restore integrity to U.S. companies by preventing American businesses from bribing foreign officials while they are conducting business overseas. A voluntary disclosure to the U.S. government in the mid-1970s showed that over 400 companies admitted to making "Questionable or illegal payments in excess of $300 million to foreign government officials, politicians, and political parties."[20] As the vast majority of these bribes took place abroad, the FCPA would have to be applicable beyond American borders to be effective. The FCPA punishes businesses (by a fine of up to 2 million dollars) and individuals (by a fine of up to $100,000 and/or five years' imprisonment) who bribe foreign officials, but it does *not* claim a right to punish the foreign officials who take these bribes. (Some have objected that bribery or "greasing the wheels" is a standard part of doing business with government officials in much of the world and that this law puts American businesses at a disadvantage when compared to foreign businesses.) However, it can only apply to American corporations, not to foreign businesses or to affiliates of U.S. companies that are based overseas.

Some other laws explicitly mention that they apply overseas, such as the "Uniting and Strengthening America by Providing Appropriate Tools Required to Intercept and Obstruct Terrorism Act" (more commonly known by its acronym, USA Patriot Act), which, for purposes of prosecuting computer fraud, gives the federal government jurisdiction over "protected computers," "including a computer located outside of the United States."[21] (We will discuss the USA Patriot Act in more depth in Chapter 7 and cyber crime in Chapter 10.) Similar extraterritorial clauses exist in federal statutes that cover money laundering and perjury.

International Crimes and Civil Suits (the Alien Tort Claims Act)

In 1976, Dolly Filártiga, the daughter of Paraguayan political dissident Joel Filartiga, was awakened in her home in the middle of the night by members of the Paraguayan police. Rubbing the sleep out of her eyes, she was brought to the home of the head of the local police in the town, Americo Norberto Peña-Irala. There she was presented with the mutilated corpse of her 19-year-old brother Joelito, who prior to being murdered had been tortured with whips, knives, and electrical shocks as punishment for his father's political activities. After showing Dolly her grisly present, Peña-Irala reportedly chased Dolly as she fled in tears, yelling, "Here you have what you have been looking for for so long and what you deserve. Now shut up."

---

[20] H. R. 105–802. Cited in Podgor, Ellen (2004) *Understanding International Criminal Law.* Lexis-Nexis, Newark, p. 29.
[21] 18 U.S.C. 1621.

All of the Filártigas' efforts to find justice in Paraguay failed. Peña-Irala was simply too powerful and influential to be prosecuted in his home country. However, when Peña-Irala came to the United States in 1979, the Filártigas made their move. When Peña-Irala overstayed his visa, he was arrested by immigration authorities and scheduled for deportation back to Paraguay. Fearing trouble, he requested that he be sent home as soon as possible. But in a move that was unprecedented, a federal judge in New York intervened and granted Dolly and Joel Filártiga the right to sue Peña-Irala in U.S. Federal Court for killing Joelito three years earlier. This was new in U.S. courts: A U.S. federal judge was claiming the right to hear a civil suit regarding a criminal act committed by a foreign national on another foreign national while both were living in their home country.

The clever lawyers working for the Filártigas used an old and obscure law, the Alien Tort Claims Act (ATCA), to justify the suit. Written in 1789 and largely forgotten for nearly 200 years, the ATCA asserts that "The district courts shall have original jurisdiction of any civil action by an alien for a tort only, committed in violation of the law of nations or a treaty of the United States." What this means is that American federal courts ("district courts") can handle lawsuits ("torts") pressed by foreigners ("aliens") for violations of international law. The statute does not make any special reservations about where the crime occurred—only that the individual being sued, the "respondent," is present in the United States to answer for the charges against him. Thus, a foreigner can sue another foreigner in U.S. Federal Court for violating an international law, a powerful tool that victims may use in American courts to address international crimes. In a manner of speaking, the United States is taking on a form of "universal civil jurisdiction" under this act, in some ways akin to the criminal laws of Belgium that we discussed earlier. Over a hundred lawsuits have been filed under the ATCA after *Filártiga* first went to court.

In 1990, the U.S. Drug Enforcement Agency (DEA) hired a former Mexican police officer to kidnap a doctor who they believed was involved in the torture and murder of one of their agents. Unfortunately, Dr. Humberto Alvarez-Machain was acquitted of all charges in relation to the murdered agent and promptly sued the former DEA officer (Jose Francisco-Sosa) under the ATCA for the kidnapping. In *Sosa* v. *Alvarez-Machain* the U.S. Supreme Court reviewed this case and examined the status of the ATCA in American federal law. In its ruling, the court rejected Alvarez-Machain's suit, but did not completely reject the idea of allowing civil suits from foreigners for violations of international law (as the federal government requested). This ruling meant that the ATCA remained an established part of U.S. law.

Unfortunately, the ATCA only authorizes civil litigation, lawsuits for monetary damages, and not criminal prosecution. Nobody is imprisoned for their acts or even labeled a "criminal" by the government as a result of a civil suit. Additionally, obtaining compensation from international criminals for their misdeeds is nearly impossible in many cases as they may flee the country or lack the assets to appropriately compensate their victims. Of the 100+ rulings citing *Filartiga* that were handed down in federal courts, none resulted in the plaintiffs actually obtaining the compensation that they are due. (Peña-Irala himself fled the United States to Paraguay and then to Brazil, and to this date he has yet to give the Filártigas the money they were awarded by the court.) But a civil suit can provide a number of important benefits for the victims of international crimes: It can give them a public forum in which to tell their stories as well as official recognition of the crimes that occurred. Also, it can give victims a chance to confront their attackers—an experience that can be invaluable for victims of brutal crimes. Likewise, it can have a political effect: Shaming individuals and governments into reforming their behavior or pursuing those criminals like Peña-Irala who have never been punished at home for their misdeeds. In this sense, civil suits can function in a manner similar to the truth commissions that we discussed in the previous chapter, helping the victims of international crimes recover from their personal tragedies, even if their attackers are never criminally sanctioned for their behavior.

IMMUNITY AND INVIOLABILITY

Two of the most significant barriers that prevent more international criminals from being punished domestically are the concepts of immunity and invioloability. Immunity means that an individual cannot be prosecuted for criminal acts regardless of the amount of evidence against the suspect and regardless of whether a state has jurisdiction over a particular crime. This means that, for whatever reason, the government is forced to let killers, drug dealers, and other criminals go, in spite of their criminal deeds. (As you can imagine, immunity is a very controversial aspect of criminal law!) Inviolability means that law enforcement or other government officials may not harm or detain certain individuals and their property may not be searched or intruded upon without their permission. People are given immunity for a variety of reasons, and it is a part of almost all legal systems around the world (some immunities result from an agreement between a prosecutor and a suspect in order to secure his or her testimony for an important criminal trial), but under international law there are only two major sorts of immunity: *diplomatic immunity* and *head of state immunity*. We will discuss each of these in turn.

The most well known form of immunity is *diplomatic immunity*. Under international law diplomats may not be prosecuted in almost all cases. Additionally, their homes, property, and embassies are immune from searches by local law enforcement officials. Diplomatic pouches, used to transport objects and documents between an embassy and its home country, cannot be searched. This principle is taken to be one of the bedrock principles of modern international law and is likewise considered essential for the conduct of modern diplomacy.

Diplomats are given such broad immunity for a number of important reasons. Philosophically, the diplomat represents a foreign government (they are an "agent of state") and thus in most cases when they act, they do not do so as an individual. Even when they break local laws, they do so as the state, not in their capacity as a private citizen. Legally speaking, they *are* the country that they represent and since no government may enforce its law upon another, no diplomat may be prosecuted in a foreign court. More practically, while posted in a foreign country, diplomats can often be in a very dangerous position. Without legal immunity they could easily be used as pawns in a larger political conflict between states—arrested under some pretext and then forced to bear the brunt of any disputes that develop between the two nations. Without diplomatic immunity, a respected government representative can easily become a hostage (or punished as a scapegoat) when relations between the two states sour. (In 1979, inspired by Islamic fundamentalists, Iranian revolutionaries seized the U.S. embassy in Tehran, Iran, and held 66 American embassy personnel, including diplomats and a number of U.S. Marines, hostage for 444 days—an act that was condemned by the entire international community as a gross violation of international law and still poisons U.S.–Iranian relations.) Finally, states need to be able to conduct affairs with their embassies in secret, without being observed by the country that hosts them and without a fear that law enforcement will enter their embassies on a putatively criminal matter and end up spying on the embassy's activities or searching through secret documents. Thus, it is very important that diplomats be free to conduct their affairs without being subject to investigation and prosecution by local authorities.

The Vienna Convention on Diplomatic Relations set out the parameters of diplomatic immunity in contemporary international law:

Article 29

The person of a diplomatic agent shall be inviolable. He shall not be liable to any form of arrest or detention. The receiving State shall treat him with due respect and shall take all appropriate steps to prevent any attack on his person, freedom or dignity.

Article 31

A diplomatic agent shall enjoy immunity from the criminal jurisdiction of the receiving State. He shall also enjoy immunity from its civil and administrative jurisdiction, except in the case of:

  (a) a real action relating to private immovable property situated in the territory of the receiving State, unless he holds it on behalf of the sending State for the purposes of the mission;
  (b) an action relating to succession in which the diplomatic agent is involved as executor, administrator, heir or legatee as a private person and not on behalf of the sending State;
  (c) an action relating to any professional or commercial activity exercised by the diplomatic agent in the receiving State outside of his official functions.

(A diplomatic agent's family members are entitled to the same immunities unless they are United States nationals.)

While diplomatic immunity is an important right under international law, it is not an absolute right. Law enforcement authorities are usually entitled to act against diplomats in order to protect public safety as well as their own safety. Thus, a foreign diplomat who is driving while intoxicated may be pulled over and prevented from driving until he is sober. Likewise, a diplomat who poses a threat to a police officer by threatening physical violence may be restrained by the police using handcuffs and other restraining devices. The immediate threat to public safety presented in these cases usually overrides the need to protect the diplomat's immunity. However, even if they may be lawfully restrained in these cases, they cannot be arrested by the officer or charged with a crime.

Along with having immunity from criminal prosecution, most diplomatic residences, including embassies are inviolable. It is frequently, but falsely asserted that an embassy is "foreign soil" (meaning that the German embassy in Washington DC is in fact a little piece of German territory) and therefore domestic laws do not apply there. However, this is not true. American law still applies in foreign embassies in the United States; however, in most cases this is a moot point as embassies are considered inviolable by the Vienna Convention. The police cannot enter embassies to enforce the criminal laws that apply there. Article 23 of the convention asserts that, "The agents of the receiving State may not enter them, except with the consent of the head of the mission," and does not list any exceptions to this rule. It also provides the same inviolability to the private residence of the ambassador and all of his or her personal documents. While a foreign embassy is still standing on American soil and American law in some sense applies, what occurs inside the embassy remains effectively beyond the reach of law enforcement.

The only exceptions to the inviolability of embassies are cases where a government's law enforcement agency receives the permission of the minister of the embassy, usually, the ambassador, prior to entering the embassy. When gunshots opened from the Libyan embassy in London in December 1984, killing British police officer Yvonne Fletcher and wounding several anti-Libya protestors, the British police could not go inside the embassy to investigate the crime and arrest the killer. Many further suspect that embassy officials used the inviolability of diplomatic packages in order to smuggle the murder weapon out of the embassy and back to Libya. However, an individual without immunity who commits a crime in an embassy can still be arrested by local officials *if* the individual leaves the embassy, or if the embassy officials give the local law enforcement officials the right to enter the embassy and arrest the individual.[22] Diplomatic immunity and the inviolability of embassies are two of the oldest and most widely respected parts of international law and governments are *very* reluctant to violate them for the short-term gain of arresting a particular criminal, such as Fletcher's killer. Here is the chart given by the State Department regarding the nature and scope of diplomatic immunity.[23]

Category	May Be Arrested or Detained	Residence May Be Entered Subject to Ordinary Procedures	May Be Issued Traffic Citation	May Be Subpoenaed as Witness	May Be Prosecuted	Recognized Family Member
Diplomatic						
Diplomatic Agent	No[1]	No	Yes	No	No	Same as sponsor (full immunity and inviolability).
Member of Administrative and Technical Staff	No[1]	No	Yes	No	No	Same as sponsor (full immunity and inviolability).
Service Staff	Yes	Yes	Yes	Yes	Yes	No immunity or inviolability.[2]

(continued)

---

[22] Cf. *Fatemi* v. *United States* 192 A.2d 525; 1963 D.C. App.

[23] http://www.state.gov/m/ds/immunities/c9127.htm.

Consular					
Career Consular Officers[24]	Yes, if for a felony and pursuant to a warrant.[2]	Yes[4]	Yes	No—for official acts. Testimony may not be compelled in any case.	No—for official acts. Otherwise, yes.[2]	No immunity or inviolability.[2]
Honorary Consular Officers	Yes	Yes	Yes	No—for official acts. Yes, in all other cases.	No—for official acts. Otherwise, yes.	No immunity or inviolability.
Consular Employees	Yes[2]	Yes	Yes	No—for official acts. Yes, in all other cases.	No—for official acts. Otherwise, yes.[2]	No immunity or inviolability.[2]
International Organizations					
International Organizations Staff[3]	Yes[3]	Yes[3]	Yes	No—for official acts. Yes, in all other cases.	No—for official acts. Otherwise, yes.[3]	No immunity or inviolability.
Diplomatic-Level Staff of Missions to International Organizations	No[1]	No	Yes	No	No	Same as sponsor (full immunity and inviolability).
Support Staff of Missions to International Organizations	Yes	Yes	Yes	No—for official acts. Yes, in all other cases.	No—for official acts. Otherwise, yes.	No immunity or inviolability.

[1] Reasonable constraints, however, may be applied in emergency circumstances involving self-defense, public safety, or the prevention of serious criminal acts.

[2] This table presents general rules. Particularly in the cases indicated, the employees of certain foreign countries may enjoy higher levels of privileges and immunities on the basis of special bilateral agreements.

[3] A small number of senior officers are entitled to be treated identically to "diplomatic agents."

[4] Note that consular residences are sometimes located within the official consular premises. In such cases, only the official office space is protected from police entry.

---

[24] Unlike a diplomatic agent or ambassador, a consul is appointed to handle everyday interactions in a foreign country, including assisting their nationals who are abroad and issuing visas. They work in consulates, of which there may be several in a country.

The second major sort of immunity under international law is *head of state immunity*. Heads of state are generally immune from both civil and criminal liability while they serve as a head of state. Along with the reasons that were given for diplomatic immunity, these political leaders are given immunity in order to avoid embarrassing a foreign leader who is traveling overseas by involving him in some kind of local litigation with his political foes. Finally, this immunity is a holdover from the "classical model of international law" (discussed in Chapter 2) that assumed that there was no legal authority higher than the state itself, and thus the head of the state was his own ultimate legal authority. For these reasons, heads of state usually have the strongest form of immunity from criminal prosecution, although, as we will shortly see, even this immunity is not absolute. Generally speaking, no sitting head of state may be prosecuted in a foreign court, regardless of the crime that they are accused of committing.

For both heads of state and for other diplomatic personnel, international law makes a distinction between acts that are performed in their role *as a government official* and those that are committed as a private citizen. Immunity is much broader for official acts than it is for other sorts of acts—and immunity for official acts usually continues after the official has left his or her governmental position and remains in perpetuity. For unofficial acts, immunity usually ends after the head of state has left power. (When King Farouk of Egypt refused to pay for 11 Christian Dior outfits that he had acquired for his wife while in Paris, the French courts ruled that he could be sued by Dior, but only *after* he had abdicated power, as purchasing designer clothes was not an official act.[25]) As the Vienna Convention on Diplomatic Relations puts it:

> When the functions of a person enjoying privileges and immunities have come to an end, such privileges and immunities shall normally cease at the moment when he leaves the country, or on expiry of a reasonable period in which to do so, but shall subsist until that time, even in case of armed conflict. However, with respect to acts performed by such a person in the exercise of his functions as a member of the mission, immunity shall continue to subsist.

Thus, a diplomatic official or a head of state has complete immunity while they are in their diplomatic post, and up to the moment that they leave the country where they are posted. But once they leave their diplomatic position, when "their function . . . has come to an end," they only possess immunity for acts that they committed in their official capacity.[26]

Underlying this distinction between official acts and other acts is a difficult philosophical question about the legitimate roles of the state and its head. Which acts are perpetrated in one's official capacity and which acts are not depends to a great degree on what you think the role of the government should be. On one hand, it may seem ridiculous to suggest that a king who refused to pay for dresses for his wife did so as an government official, but what if the queen needed these dresses for official, royal events? The royal family is an important part of the cultural life of many societies and it is (arguably) imperative that the queen look her best

---

[25] *Ex-King Farouk of Egypt* v. *Christian Dior,* 84 Clunet 717, 24 I. L. R. 228, 229.

[26] When an official performs a crime in his official capacity, it is assumed that he is behaving as an "agent of state" and not an individual. Thus, if anyone is responsible for the criminal act, it is the state itself, not the individual who perpetrated it.

for an official event. Thus, so the argument goes, it should be a part of government policy to assure that her status and image be protected. In such a case, it isn't clear when an individual has acted in his private capacity and when he has acted as a head of state. Silly cases like this, however, mask the deeper question, What about a diplomat who ordered the assassination of one of his government's political opponents? the leaders of foreign governments? Would these be considered official acts or simple crimes? If you believe that such acts are not legitimate for *any* government, then this would affect the scope of the immunities given to former diplomats and deposed heads of state. As we will soon see in the *Pinochet* case, this is precisely what the British courts faced in handling a criminal charge against Chile's former dictator.

While most diplomats are conscientious professionals, immunity is sometimes abused by the diplomatic corps in the United States and elsewhere. Sometimes, diplomats have gone so far as to commit espionage while serving in foreign embassies. Others have committed lesser crimes such as speeding, drug smuggling, driving while intoxicated, or other similar offenses. A 1984 report by the British House of Commons reported 546 "serious offenses" committed by individuals possessing diplomatic immunity from 1974 to mid-1984 (most were shoplifting or drunk driving).[27] Each year, UN diplomats posted in New York City rack up millions of dollars in parking tickets that they refuse to pay. While diplomatic immunity is an important part of international law, it is frequently a nuisance for law enforcement officials as well as the community at large in capital cities around the world.

Despite the strict requirement that diplomats not be arrested or charged with a crime, law enforcement does possess a few options when dealing with criminal offenders who possess diplomatic immunity. An individual with diplomatic immunity may be charged if the offender's home government agrees to waive his immunity and thereby allows him to be prosecuted. Further, under the Vienna Convention, a diplomat can be declared *persona non grata* (meaning literally "an unwelcome person") by his host nation. In this case, the diplomat's home government must recall him back to his home state or risk the revocation of the offending diplomat's immunity.[28] The misbehavior of diplomats either in their personal life or in carrying out their professional duties may be addressed by governments if it becomes extreme, but generally speaking, this sort of misbehavior is the price that must be paid for the benefits that are gained by the practice of international diplomacy.

---

[27] Report of the Foreign Affairs Committee, House of Commons, December 12, 1984.

[28] Article 9 of the Vienna Convention states:

1. The receiving State may at any time and without having to explain its decision, notify the sending State that the head of the mission or any member of the diplomatic staff of the mission is *persona non grata* or that any other member of the staff of the mission is not acceptable. In any such case, the sending State shall, as appropriate, either recall the person concerned or terminate his functions with the mission. A person may be declared *non grata* or not acceptable before arriving in the territory of the receiving State.
2. If the sending State refuses or fails within a reasonable period to carry out its obligations under paragraph 1 of this Article, the receiving State may refuse to recognize the person concerned as a member of the mission.

The Kidnapping of Umaru Dikko

Among the more bizarre attempts to abuse the right of diplomatic immunity was the 1984 attempted kidnapping of the former Nigerian transportation minister Umaru Dikko in London. Dikko, a member of the former Nigerian government, had fled to London the previous year when a coup removed his brother-in-law, the president of Nigeria, from power. The new Nigerian government considered Dikko to be a wanted criminal, accusing him of embezzling millions of dollars from the Nigerian government before leaving Africa. However, they had no success finding and extraditing him. Dikko hid from his former country, settling in a quiet part of London and keeping a low profile until he was discovered by Nigerian officials.

In early July 1984, a van pulled up next to Dikko outside of his home and several men leapt out, forcing him into the van, and quickly speeding off. Several of Dikko's neighbors saw the kidnapping and alerted London's metropolitan police. Shortly thereafter, British customs officials at London's Stansted Airport stumbled upon a suspicious piece of allegedly diplomatic cargo being boarded onto a Nigerian Airways jet. The crate was labeled "Diplomatic Property" and addressed to the Ministry of External Affairs in Lagos, the capital of Nigeria. However, customs officials in London were suspicious about the package: It was very big and light for a diplomatic parcel, was not properly labeled, and was not with any other similar material. Airport officials decided to open it in the presence of a Nigerian official and discovered inside a drugged Dikko accompanied by another man with a kit of syringes and other tools to keep Dikko unconscious until they arrived in Lagos. They opened a second, similar box and discovered two more men with Israeli nationality.

A diplomatic fiasco quickly unfolded. The British government prevented the Nigerian Airways plane from taking off, which then prompted the Nigerian government to hold a British Airways flight hostage in Lagos in retaliation. The Israeli government quickly denied any involvement in the affair and speculation arose that the Israelis were mercenaries, professional soldiers, hired to carry out questionable missions. It later turned out that a private Israeli citizen with close connections to the Nigerian government had been hired by Nigeria to kidnap Dikko and return him to his homeland to stand trial. Three Israeli citizens were sentenced to prison terms for the crime, as was a Nigerian military officer who was also involved in the kidnapping. But, in an effort to salvage Nigerian–British trade relations, the British government declined to prosecute the case any further. Dikko eventually returned to Nigeria to become a prominent attorney.[29]

The Dikko affair shows some of the challenges surrounding the practices of diplomatic immunity and diplomatic inviolability under international law. The London police officers were able to inspect the crates and examine their contents only because of a technicality in the Vienna Convention on Diplomatic Relations. The Convention does indeed say that diplomatic bags are inviolable, but it also requires that such bags be accompanied by a courier carrying the proper documentation. As there was none accompanying the questionable "packages," the London police were able to lawfully open the crate. However, had the Nigerian embassy carried out the proper procedures in labeling and transporting them, there may have been little that the airport officials could have done lawfully to stop the abduction of Dikko. Of course they might have chosen to disregard the inviolability of the diplomatic baggage and opened it nonetheless, just as the Iranian government violated the immunity of

---

[29] *Haaretz* (newspaper), 01/10/2001.

the American diplomats in Tehran in 1979, but the diplomatic, political, and legal consequences of such an act could have proven to be very damaging for the British government and for British–Nigerian relations.

The Trial of Augusto Pinochet

Nowhere was the promise and the perils of universal jurisdiction and head of state immunity more brightly highlighted than in a Spanish judge's 1998 attempt to prosecute the former Chilean dictator Augusto Pinochet. Pinochet seized power from the democratically elected socialist government in a 1973 *coup d'etat* and served as Chile's dictator until 1990. Before abdicating power, Pinochet declared himself a "Senator for life," thereby guaranteeing his immunity from prosecution in Chile. Under his regime, democracy was suspended and enemies of the state were ruthlessly pursued. Leftists and other perceived agitators were kidnapped, tortured, and many were brutally murdered by agents of Pinochet's government. Some of these victims simply "disappeared," their bodies dumped at sea from military helicopters without anyone ever acknowledging that they had been held in custody. In one particularly spectacular case, Pinochet's agents carried out the assassination of Orlando Letelier, an official of the former Chilean government, by planting a bomb in his car in downtown Washington DC, an attack that also killed his American assistant. By the time he left office, Pinochet's government was suspected in the deaths of hundreds, if not thousands of Chileans and other political opponents of his government.

After leaving political office, Pinochet was fond of visiting the United Kingdom, where he would shop and visit with his old friend and anticommunist ally former British Prime Minister Margaret Thatcher. Unbeknownst to the general, during a 1998 trip to the UK, a Spanish judge had requested that Pinochet be apprehended by the British government and extradited to Spain to be put on trial for torture. The Spanish judge argued that Spain had the right to prosecute as he had "intentionally inflicted severe pain or suffering on another in the purported performance of his official duties." Specifically, the judge cited the International Convention Against Torture as the legal grounds for the warrant, which required that Britain either prosecute Pinochet or send him to Spain, where he could be put on trial.

The effort to prosecute a former head of state of a foreign country in a British court for acts he had perpetrated while in office, particularly acts that had no substantial effects on England itself, was unprecedented. The defense argued that, as a former head of state, Pinochet had immunity for anything that he may have done while he was the leader of Chile. Similarly, they argued that the amnesty that Pinochet had been given when leaving office eliminated any legal grounds for prosecuting him in any court, Chilean or otherwise.

Eventually, the *Pinochet* case went before the British Law Lords, the highest court in the UK. In his opinion, Lord Browne-Wilkinson saw the significance of the case: "If Senator Pinochet is not entitled to immunity in relation to the acts of torture alleged to have occurred [under his authority], it will be the first time so far as counsel have discovered when a local domestic court has refused to afford immunity to a head of state or former head of state on the grounds that there can be no immunity against prosecution for certain international crimes." This is to say that this would be the first crime for which there was absolutely no immunity. After a first ruling was voided due to a conflict of interest (one of the judges was affiliated with Amnesty International, the human rights organization that zealously advocated sending Pinochet to Spain), the court finally ruled that Pinochet could be extradited to Spain and that his status as a former head of state did not provide immunity for ordering acts of torture during his rule. The precedent set out by the IMT at Nuremberg, that powerful individuals could not escape accountability for criminal acts that they committed while in government, had received one of its most significant new legal confirmations in a British court.

In reaching this conclusion in the *Pinochet* case, Lord Browne-Wilkinson offered an important insight into the Torture Convention that affected Pinochet's claims to immunity. Torture, he noticed, is defined in the Convention as "Any act by which severe pain or suffering is intentionally inflicted on a person . . . when [it] is inflicted by or at the instigation of or with the consent or acquiescence of a public official or other person acting in an official capacity." Because the convention restricts "torture" to public officials acting in their official capacity, Lord Brown-Wilkinson observed, "All defendants in torture cases will be state officials." This means that, if Pinochet is considered to be immune for acts of torture committed under his orders, *every official but the head of state* will be criminally liable for this act of torture—which would be both illogical and unacceptable. "[I]f the former head of state has immunity, the man most responsible will escape liability while his inferiors (the chiefs of police, junior army officers) who carried out his orders will be liable. I find it impossible to accept this." Thus, he argued, "The implementation of torture as defined by the Torture Convention cannot be a state function." And because the legal immunity provided to former heads of state is not immunity *tout court,* but rather only immunity for official acts or "state functions," Pinochet cannot use this immunity to escape criminal liability.

However, as is sometimes the case in international criminal justice, political expediency won out over the rule of law in the *Pinochet* case. After a thorough medical exam, British doctors determined that Pinochet was mentally unfit for trial. The British government determined that, because of his mental state, it would be inhumane to send the former leader to Spain for trial. Before its decision could be challenged in a courtroom, the UK government quickly bundled Pinochet onto a private plane and returned the general to Chile without his ever having to face the Spanish judge. Initially it appeared that Pinochet had escaped any accountability for what had occurred under his rule. However, shortly after he returned to Chile, Pinochet was stripped of his immunity the democratic government that had replaced him and charges were pressed against its former leader. Pinochet died in December, 2006, never facing a trial for any act of torture or official murder that took place under his government. Nevertheless, many Chileans give the British Law Lords and the Spanish judge who requested Pinochet's extradition credit for knocking down a dictator who was once widely feared in Chile and considered by many Chileans to be above the law.

Despite the disappointing outcome of the *Pinochet* trial, many consider it to be a landmark case for international criminal law. First and foremost, it undermined a centuries-old principle that heads of state were completely immune from prosecution for what they did while in charge of a government. Further, many give the *Pinochet* case credit for setting a precedent that government-sponsored torture is never acceptable, no matter what the cause. Likewise, it showed that with a good deal of patience and skill, clever attorneys and judges can hold even the most politically powerful individuals accountable for international crimes. The *Pinochet* precedent has been cited in a number of cases to facilitate the prosecution of politicians who commit international crimes while behind the shield of legal immunity.

CONCLUSION

In this chapter we have discussed the different ways that international crimes may be handled in domestic courts. Some of this has involved international law "seeping into" the domestic criminal justice systems of countries around the world, and in particular, the American system. Other parts have involved domestic legal systems "reaching out" beyond their borders and into the global sphere as certain states have asserted extraterritorial jurisdiction for their criminal law.

As you might have begun to realize, in many cases there is no hard distinction between domestic criminal law and international criminal law. An international crime, such as torture, can have an international form in a treaty such as the Convention Against Torture and can be prosecuted in international courts such as the ICC. On the other hand, this same crime can be a part of the domestic legal system either because the treaty is self-executing or because the domestic legislature has passed a criminal law that mirrors the international treaty. This conclusion should make sense if we take seriously the idea of globalization: As countries become linked together, where the legal borders of one country end and another begin becomes increasingly hard to discern. Like the various economies of the world, the separations between the various legal systems of the world have become blurred.

Of course, the law is useful only if there is somebody empowered and able to enforce the law. Otherwise it is all mere words on paper. In the next chapter we will examine the various organizations and tactics that have developed both internationally and domestically in order to effectively investigate international crimes and arrest wanted international criminals. Here too we will see that the borders that traditionally separated nations, governments, and people have begun to blur in the age of globalization. Here also, we will see, the U.S. government has played a crucial role, at times leading the way in the development of institutions of international criminal justice, at other times stubbornly hindering its progress.

QUESTIONS

1. What are some of the dangers of each of these different forms of jurisdiction? How might they be exploited by reckless governments with a "score to settle" with the United States or another country?

2. Are the benefits of diplomatic immunity worth the trouble that it causes? If not, what other options are there?

3. On your view, what are the advantages and disadvantages of prosecuting international criminals in domestic courts in comparison to the international courts that we discussed in the previous chapter?

READING AND RESOURCES

The following are two excellent books that deal with the application of international criminal law in U.S. courts. Although they are designed for law students and may deal in matters in more depth than most undergraduates would care for, they are nonetheless helpful guides to understanding this field:

1. Wise, Edward M., Podgor, Ellen S., and Clark, Roger S., *International Criminal Law: Cases and Materials,* 2nd ed., Lexis Nexis, Newark, 2004.
2. Pogdor, Ellen, *Understanding International Criminal Law,* Lexis-Nexis, Newark, 2004, which is a companion book to the casebook and provides additional useful information for the student of international criminal law.

Professor Podgor has also written numerous useful pieces on international laws of jurisdiction as well as on U.S. laws on extraterritorial jurisdiction. Some of which are:

- "Cybercrime: National, Transnational, or International?" *The Wayne Law Review,* Vol. 50.
- " 'Defensive Territoriality': A New Paradigm for the Prosecution of Extraterritorial Business Crimes," *The Georgia Journal of International and Comparative Law,* Vol. 31.

Brownlie, Ian, *Principles of Public International Law,* 6th ed., Oxford University Press, Oxford, UK, 2003.

Ratner, Steven, and Abrams, Jason, *Accountability for Human Rights Atrocities in International Law: Beyond the Nuremberg Precedent,* Oxford University Press, Oxford, UK, 2001. (See especially Chapters 7 and 8.)

The website for the U.S. State Department's Office of Foreign Missions is http://www.state.gov/ofm/.

The website for the Department of Justice dealing with the Foreign Corrupt Practices Act is http://www.usdoj.gov/criminal/fraud/fcpa/intagmt.htm.

The American Law Institute website is http://www.ali.org.

The American Society of International Law has a website that keeps track of international law in the news, with a particular interest in its impact for America. Their website is http://www.asil.org.

5

International Law Enforcement

❖

There is no "world police force" empowered to investigate international crimes or arrest criminals throughout the globe. This puts international lawbreakers at an advantage compared to criminals who operate within the borders of a single state. Criminals have historically enjoyed the benefits of knowing that it is substantially less likely that they will be discovered by law enforcement if they leave their home country and reside elsewhere. Even if they were discovered by law enforcement officials while overseas, it was unlikely that they would be prosecuted for their crimes. The political difficulties and expense involved with arresting a criminal abroad and transferring him back home were high enough for it to not be worth anybody's while. Butch Cassidy and Harry Longabaugh (aka "the Sundance Kid") escaped from the United States and hid out in Bolivia until they were (according to most modern historians) killed by government forces after carrying out a streak of armed robberies there. Had they not been so foolish, they could probably have lived a comfortable life in their new home. Historically, international boundaries have provided a great deal of freedom for criminals. "Running for the border," a movie cliché of old westerns, once meant a life of freedom and impunity for a wanted criminal.

That view of the cross-border reach of law enforcement has changed dramatically over the last century. In order to counter international and transnational crimes and to apprehend those who commit them, governments and their law enforcement agencies have developed a number of tools to investigate crimes that have an international or transnational character. They have also developed ways to share helpful information regarding crimes that take place in each other's countries, and the means to apprehend and transfer criminals who either flee from a country where they have broken the law or who participate in a criminal enterprise from the other side of an international boundary.

In this chapter, we will discuss law enforcement in a world of globalized crime, examining some of its central institutions and its most powerful tools. Like the last chapter, we will approach this issue from "two directions": On one hand, we will discuss the international institutions that have been developed to deal with international and transnational criminal problems. Specifically, we will look at Interpol (the International Criminal Police Organization), Europol, the World Customs Organization (WCO) (along with its European counterpart), and the United Nations Office on Drugs and Crime (UNODC). Then, we will look at how domestic law enforcement, in particular American law enforcement, has worked overseas, investigating crimes in other countries (including terrorist crimes), apprehending foreign criminals, and bringing them to the United States for trial. Finally, we will look at the legal questions that develop from the activities of American law enforcement overseas, in particular, examining the admissibility of evidence gathered overseas in American courts.

One thing to keep in mind throughout this chapter is that law enforcement activities can be performed by any number of different groups in any number of different ways. In America, the FBI and the state police can enforce the law. But so do the DEA and municipal police forces. Local building inspectors enforce municipal codes, and although they are not formally authorized by governments, neighborhood watch committees help to keep the peace and enforce the law in many American communities. We may not use the term *cop* to describe many of these people, and they may not carry guns or wear uniforms, but they are engaged in enforcing laws nonetheless. In order to do justice to international law enforcement, we will have to look at a number of different organizations that function as international law enforcement bodies, only some of which we would immediately recognize as "police organizations."

INTERPOL AND EUROPOL

Interpol

The International Criminal Police Organization (known either by its abbreviation, ICPC, or simply as Interpol) was founded in 1923 to facilitate greater cooperation among law enforcement officials in the different nations of the world. One of the unique aspects of this organization is that it was founded by the world's police bodies working largely on their own and has functioned relatively independently. Governments of course have had a say in the functions of Interpol, but law enforcement agencies have played the lead in developing its structures and using its services, which makes it in many ways less political than the UN or other international bodies. While Interpol has a reputation as a dashing James Bond sort of organization that tracks down and confronts dangerous criminals in exotic locations, it (rather unfortunately) does none of these things. Interpol is *not* an international police force. It doesn't have the power to investigate crimes, arrest individuals, or interrogate suspects. Rather, Interpol is an information clearinghouse for law enforcement—it helps domestic police forces share data about particular crimes or about wanted criminals who are at large in any of the 182 states that comprise its membership. It also helps to coordinate investigations and share important information that domestic law enforcement agencies may then use. This may make Interpol seem less exciting and dramatic than it is often imagined to be, but this does not mean that it is not an extremely important part of the international criminal justice system.

Interpol works with the various governmental police forces who funnel their information through their own national centers. Individuals have no power to request information from Interpol, nor can they post notices regarding international fugitives. Even state, local, and federal law enforcement agencies cannot request any information from Interpol on their own. Rather, each country has a National Central Bureau or NCB that maintains contact with Interpol, receiving information from the organization regarding wanted criminals or criminal behavior and passing on requests for information to and from local law enforcement authorities. The USNCB is located in Washington DC and currently has about 100 employees. Each state has representatives who help coordinate local requests for information with the NCB and Interpol, as well as do several major cities that are "hubs" of international crime. Along with these, 18 federal agencies, ranging from the FBI, to the Food and Drug Administration (FDA), to the Secret Service, have representatives at the USNCB.

Interpol fulfills a number of different roles in the international criminal justice system. Primarily, it helps national law enforcement agencies keep track of international criminals and provides a database of international criminal activity—recording the types of crimes that are committed and keeping tabs on criminal suspects who travel abroad. A state will either submit requests for information to Interpol about a particular individual or provide an important piece of evidence (such as a fingerprint, a photograph, or a

---

Some of the forms of assistance provided by the USNCB are as follows (taken from the USNCB website):[1]

- General investigative services, non-compulsory nature (compulsory process will be coordinated with the Office of International Affairs at the U.S. Department of Justice)
- Law enforcement intelligence information
- Address verifications
- All points bulletins
- Criminal record checks
- Disaster victim identification
- Humanitarian requests (death notifications, serious illness)
- Interview witnesses
- Trace and locate fugitives wanted for extradition
- Trace and locate missing person
- Trace and locate abducted children
- Locate stolen art and artifacts
- Telephone subscriber information
- Weapons and vehicle traces

---

[1] http://www.usdoj.gov/usncb/usncborg/pointinterlaw.html.

particular aspect of a criminal's *modus operandi*) in order to find out what other governments know about that particular criminal or crime. Alternatively, the national police forces may respond to notices sent out by Interpol—requests for information by other member states. Local law enforcement may enter certain features of a crime into the Interpol database, such as a license plate number or an alias; these features are then compared with other bits of data from crimes that have occurred around the world. Interpol may then help the law enforcement agencies tie together the evidence of diverse crimes to find a pattern of criminal activity that stretches across borders. When local police forces seek information about a case, such as an unidentified body or a suspect that they believe has gone abroad, they will contact their NCB, who will then send a request to Interpol with all the relevant information. The organization will then send out notices to the NCBs around the world who will then keep an eye out for pertinent information. Finally, Interpol will share information about stolen goods, such as artwork, with some private groups (such as art dealers and auction houses) to prevent the trafficking of stolen goods.[2]

While it is true that states may share their information directly with each other, thereby circumventing the Interpol process, the organization is nonetheless useful to national police officers for a number of reasons. A national police system may not know the nature or the full extent of the criminal enterprise that they are investigating, how large the criminal operation is, and what country's nationals are involved, and so they may not know exactly who to share information with. Possessing around 182 member states, Interpol allows domestic law enforcement to amplify their local investigations and cast their net very widely when they are investigating a crime. A carefully constructed search through the Interpol database can show that a seemingly isolated crime is actually connected to similar acts around the world. This allows small countries, or seemingly small-scale investigations in large countries, to see how the crimes that they investigate are linked to other crimes around the world.

Interpol can also be useful because some countries do not have political or diplomatic relations with each other but may still face shared problems of international crime. As one scholar observed, "Given Interpol's near global membership . . . the NCB has often provided the only means of communicating with police agencies whose governments are not on friendly terms with the United States," adding, "During the 1980s, routine requests were exchanged with Soviet-bloc states and with Qadaffi's Libya"[3]—states that the United States was bitterly opposed to and who did not possess formal diplomatic relations with America. Interpol helps a large number of states to cooperate on shared international crime issues without having to deal with political differences between their governments. Governments may not get along, but Interpol allows their police officers to share information nonetheless. All of this makes Interpol a valuable tool for law enforcement bodies in both large and small states.

Cooperation with Interpol is completely voluntary. States may choose to assist each other through Interpol, or they may choose to ignore the notices that they receive. The reason for this is sovereignty: Interpol does not seek to undermine the sovereignty of states by requiring that they share information or request it. Since Interpol is not a world police force, states should be left free to pursue their own criminal justice policies in any way that

---

[2] "The Man from Interpol" (Interview: *CIO Magazine,* June 15, 2000).

[3] *Cops across Borders,* p. 184.

they see fit, even if this means ignoring problems of international crime. Likewise, there are other means through which states may request information from each other (often the U.S. DEA will be asked by other countries to provide information about international drug dealers) that do not require going through Interpol. This feature of the organization has led some scholars to refer to Interpol as an "international police cooperation organization" as opposed to a traditional international organization like the UN that can require that states behave in a particular way. Nonetheless, despite the voluntary nature of Interpol, states often share a great deal of information about international crime through the organization and the activity of Interpol has grown steadily since its creation.

Political Issues   There are some limits to the sorts of crimes about which Interpol will share information. Specifically, its constitution seeks to limit the cooperation of police agencies to nonpolitical sorts of crimes. Additionally, while Interpol is committed to aiding the various national police forces, it has pledged to do so, "within the limits of the laws existing in the different countries and in the spirit of the 'Universal Declaration of Human Rights,' " [4] meaning that it will not assist oppressive governments carry out their policies under the guise of "law enforcement." Likewise, Article 3 of Interpol's constitution asserts that "It is strictly forbidden for the Organization to undertake any intervention or activities of a political, military, religious or racial character." These limits help the organization avoid being used as a tool by governments who want to track down and suppress their critics or enemies working overseas. In 2002, the government of Kazakhstan requested that Interpol issue an arrest warrant for Akezhan Kazhegeldin, a Kazakh dissident. Interpol initially withdrew the warrant, citing the political nature of the crime, only later to reinstate the warrant when it was shown that Kazhegeldin had committed some non-political crimes for which he had been convicted *in absentia*. Nonetheless, at other times this can create friction between the organization and its member states when a government rejects the organization's classification of certain crimes as being political or nonpolitical in nature.

The United States has had a tumultuous relationship with Interpol through much of the organization's history. Longtime FBI director J. Edgar Hoover kept the organization under close supervision in the United States. Instead of creating an actual NCB for the United States, Hoover insisted throughout his tenure at the FBI that all Interpol material go directly through him, choking off any meaningful cooperation between the organization and American law enforcement. Even more dramatically, Hoover temporarily withdrew the United States from the organization in 1950 because of efforts by communist Czechoslovakia to extradite political fugitives who had hijacked airplanes in order to escape to the West (the United States opposed Interpol's ruling that the hijackers were not political criminals). To make matters even worse, in the 1970s, L. Ron Hubbard, the science fiction writer and founder of the Church of Scientology began a series of bitter attacks on the organization, alleging that the organization was a sort of "secret government" that had worked with the KGB and the Nazis against the U.S. government. Though most of Hubbard's charges were ridiculous, his well-organized and well-funded campaign led some American politicians to launch investigations into Interpol that further tainted the organization's reputation in American political circles. Nonetheless, since the end of

---

[4] Interpol Constitution, Article 2(1).

Hoover's tenure at the FBI the United States has developed a strong relation with the organization, particularly in its fight against terrorism, and Interpol's current Secretary General, Ronald Noble, is an American former federal prosecutor.

Notices   One of the central ways that Interpol helps keep track of international criminals is by sending out "notices" to police forces around the world. These notices are to warn national law enforcement officials about particular criminals or other issues that are relevant to the global law enforcement community. According to Interpol, in 2004, there were over 13,000 different notices in circulation, dealing with everything from war crimes and terrorism to missing persons and lottery fraud. These notices are color-coded according to their subject matter. The color codes are as follows:

> *Red Notices:* The vast majority of notices issued by Interpol are red notices (or "red corner notices"—so called because the Interpol symbol in the corner of the notice is set against a red background). Red notices refer to individuals who are wanted by particular states because they are suspected criminals or have already been convicted *in absentia* by a government. The country that receives the notice and arrests the suspect then prepares to extradite the individual according to the procedures of their extradition treaty (more on this later). Some countries, those that do not recognize the red notice as grounds for arrest and extradition, may either ignore the notice or place the suspect under *provisional arrest* until the requesting state can issue their own request for arrest and extradition.
>
> In order to issue a red notice, the requesting state must provide the relevant information to Interpol so that they can provide this to the international community and ensure that the notice does not violate the Article 3 requirements mentioned above. This information may include a photo of the suspect, a physical description of him, as DNA sample DNA, or any other data that would help police officers recognize the suspect.
>
> *Blue Notices:* Collecting information about criminal activity or regarding a particular individual.
>
> *Green Notices:* Warnings about individuals who have committed crimes and are likely to commit further crimes in other states.
>
> *Yellow Notices:* Notices for assistance locating missing persons or to uncover the identity of people who cannot identify themselves (such as small children).
>
> *Black Notices:* Requesting assistance identifying dead bodies.
>
> *Orange Notices:* Warning national law enforcement agencies of threats such as hidden explosives or parcel explosives.

Europol

Over the past several decades, Europe, a continent of independent, sovereign states, has participated in a bold and novel political experiment. These different countries, long plagued by wars and cultural rivalries, have undergone a process of integration, linking together their economies, their legal and political systems, and their citizens to an unprecedented degree. In many ways, Europe is becoming a single nation, articulating a set of shared values and ideals, such as a common respect for human rights and democracy, along with a set of more concrete institutions such as a common currency (the *Euro*) and efforts to develop a European constitution. The European Union (EU) has created a political system which handles economic and political issues that arise between the states. Likewise, the political and economic barriers that once separated these countries have begun to be lowered and the European states have allowed most of their citizens to travel freely through Europe with no preauthorization and very little paperwork. One aspect of this integration has been the partial integration of the European criminal justice system.

Because of the close integration of the European Union, many European politicians felt that the continent required its own, special police intelligence organization. *Europol* was created in 1999 to function in a manner akin to Interpol, sharing information about crime problems that affect all EU members. Europol is in many ways similar to Interpol, but with a more limited mandate and scope. Whereas Interpol has around 182 member states across the world, Europol has only 27 European members and focuses on pan-European crime problems. Thus, Europol helps to stop the counterfeiting of the euro and helps provide information about war criminals from the former Yugoslavia who are wanted by the ICTY and remain hidden in European nations. Like Interpol, Europol does not have any law enforcement powers, but rather serves to maintain a database for information regarding international and transnational criminal activity and the transmission of international arrest warrants. It also assists domestic law enforcement to develop, investigate, and prosecute transnational criminal enterprises, such as organized criminal gangs that work across the European borders. Like Interpol, Europol is limited in its powers, but unlike its international predecessor, Europol must deal with the open borders between its various member countries, which allow people to pass between them with very little difficulty and minimal record keeping.

THE UNITED NATIONS OFFICE OF DRUGS AND CRIME

The UNODC is the branch of the United Nations that helps states to fight international and transnational crime. It was founded in 1997, has about 500 employees, and works out of Vienna, Austria, along with a number of field offices around the globe. It has several different suborganizations, each focusing on one specific aspect of international crime. The main subgroups are the United Nations Drug Control Program, the Center for International Crime Prevention (CIPC), the Global Program on Money Laundering, the Terrorism Prevention Branch, as well as programs that deal with corruption, human trafficking, and international organized crime.

The UNODC has three main functions: First and foremost, the organization provides research and data analysis regarding international and transnational crime. Each year, for example, it publishes a lengthy report, collecting and analyzing social scientific data about drug abuse globally, keeping track of where illicit drugs are used, which kinds of drugs are abused, and in what quantities.[5] Second, the organization

---

[5] We will discuss the UNODC World Report in more depth when we analyze international drug trafficking.

promotes the development of national laws that help curb international crimes, including promoting the ratification of international treaties designed to confront drug trafficking and money laundering. Finally, the UNODC provides assistance to local law enforcement at the "ground level" in dealing with international crimes. Like Interpol and Europol, the UNODC is a police intelligence agency, restricted to providing information and promoting policies, and does not perform "executive tasks" such as gathering evidence or arresting international criminals.

The UNODC has been active throughout the world providing information to nations about drugs and other international crimes, as well as helping nations develop anti-crime programs. They frequently host international conferences that give national criminal justice experts opportunities to share information as well as outline shared agenda for fighting international crime. Since the U.S.-led invasion of Afghanistan in 2001, the organization has been working in that country to monitor the cultivation of opium poppies (used to make heroin), and in Columbia, they have worked to help coca farmers convert their land to legal crops. Thus, while the UNODC is limited in its role in international criminal justice, it is nonetheless a valuable tool for the international community.

THE WORLD CUSTOMS ORGANIZATION

The WCO was established in 1952 to help deal with international customs issues. It has over 140 members and helps domestic law enforcement synchronize and strengthen their customs systems.[6] Like Interpol and Europol, its primary job is to facilitate the exchange of information between domestic systems and to help standardize and improve the customs practices of member states. Like the UNODC, the WCO is also involved in collecting data and it has numerous offices in countries where the trafficking in illicit goods is widespread, where officials collect data.[7] In 2005, the WCO members voted to standardize international shipping practices, to enhance security and prevent terrorists from smuggling dangerous goods across borders, including electronic security measures and provisions for X-ray or radiation testing of high risk cargo.[8]

JURISDICTION AND LAW ENFORCEMENT

We have already discussed the concept of jurisdiction in Chapters 4 and 5. In this chapter, however, we are interested in a slightly different notion of jurisdiction. In the previous chapters, for a law to have jurisdiction meant that the courts could apply a law to a certain type of crime that happened in a particular place at a particular time. Thus, the ICC only has jurisdiction over specific crimes that are committed by specific people in specific places. Likewise, American laws against drug trafficking and bribery have extraterritorial

---

[6] Nordegren, Thomas (2002) *The A-Z Encyclopedia of Alcohol and Drug Abuse*. Parkland: Brown Walker Press, pp. 686–687. See also Burnham, R. W. (2005) "The World Customs Organization," in Natarajan, Mangai, San Francisco: McGraw Hill, pp. 201–208.

[7] Their website is http://www.wcoomd.org/.

[8] Lipton, Eric (2005) "Global Group Backs Antiterror Customs Standards," *New York Times,* June 24.

jurisdiction—they apply to acts committed beyond American borders. In this chapter, we are interested in the jurisdiction of law enforcement personnel, their authority to investigate crimes overseas and to arrest criminals abroad. This is usually referred to as "jurisdiction to enforce."

There are some cases where a person may violate an American law overseas, but because they are operating abroad when they commit the crimes, U.S. law enforcement has no authority to arrest them. To use an example from the last chapter, an American citizen may bribe an Egyptian government official while working in Cairo (thereby violating the Foreign Corrupt Practices Act), but American law enforcement would be powerless to do anything about it, so long as the individual remained in Cairo and the Egyptian government refuses to extradite him. (We will discuss the international rules governing the acquisition of suspected criminals later in this chapter.) Only if the American returned to the United States would he or she fall under the jurisdiction of American law enforcement and thus could be arrested by them. Thus, here we are examining jurisdiction in terms of the authority of law enforcement bodies, not in terms of applicability of a particular criminal law.

In most cases, law enforcement organizations require the permission of the local governments to function within the territory of a particular state. Many states have strict laws that govern the behavior of foreign law enforcement personnel while they are operating within their borders. In some states, it may even be crime for them to conduct operations without government approval. However, when official permission is not forthcoming, U.S. and foreign law enforcement will sometimes work "undercover," investigating crimes and seeking intelligence about criminal activities in places where they are unwanted and unwelcome. This means at times that the line between police work and spying can be difficult to determine. The Central Intelligence Agency (CIA), ostensibly an intelligence organization, may investigate drug smugglers or terrorists, providing information or evidence that can be used in an investigation or in a courtroom or it may help to determine threats that more conventional law enforcement agencies like the FBI may then act upon. The CIA, of course, often operates in places where an American presence is not wanted and so they must work undercover. (Though virtually every country gathers intelligence through spies, it is nonetheless illegal everywhere.) Again, domestic law enforcement does undercover work in the United States, too, using agents to infiltrate criminal gangs, but the crucial difference is that American law enforcement agents working overseas do not have jurisdiction, and are not legally authorized to enforce the law in these places. (One exception to this rule, however, is the U.S. Army Criminal Investigation Division or CID which sometimes operates abroad on the basis of special agreements with host countries.[9]) This means that undercover detective work carried out by American law enforcement personnel overseas is at times a very different and, in many ways, significantly more risky sort of activity than it would be here in the United States.

---

[9] The CID's website is http://www.cid.army.mil/.

International Law Enforcement: The U.S. Experience

Clearly, international organizations like Interpol and the UNODC are helpful aides for national police forces that must tackle international crime. Nonetheless, these organizations are severely limited in what they can do. They are not law enforcement bodies; they do not have the authority to arrest suspects or conduct independent surveillance operations. Rather, they provide resources for domestic law enforcement to use. Most of the real police work that must be done to stop international criminals is still performed by the conventional local and national police forces of the countries around the world.

Along with the international organizations that help domestic agencies investigating crimes, a good deal of international law enforcement happens through the policing agencies of different governments or their respective court systems working together to share information and develop collaborative investigations. For American law enforcement, this means that either American police officers must go abroad to acquire evidence for a case being investigated or prosecuted in U.S. courts or they must get agents of the foreign governments to provide the necessary information themselves. Other times, Americans have to obtain suspects who are currently living abroad but are wanted in the United States by seeking their extradition. These two aspects of international law enforcement require the cooperation of foreign governments, foreign courts, and foreign law enforcement personnel, which is not always guaranteed. We will now discuss each of these aspects of extraterritorial law enforcement.

There are two major challenges that American agents must face overseas. The first is sovereignty. As we've already discussed, most governments jealously protect their right to control what happens on their own lands and sometimes view the presence of foreign law enforcement officials in their countries as a threat to this right. This means that foreign government officials are often unwilling to cooperate with American law enforcement personnel and they may refuse to allow them to operate in their country. Some may even go so far as to consider American law enforcement personnel to be criminals when they try to conduct investigations on their territory. Another problem is *cultural:* Other societies may not share our ideas about law enforcement, proper courtroom procedure, or the appropriate types of evidence to gather or the correct means to gather it. Likewise, different societies have dissimilar ideas about police procedures and the role of police in a society, and even different ideas about appropriate police behavior on topics like the use of force and police corruption. In many countries, police officers are as much agents of the state, seeking to preserve the power of those in charge against their critics, as they are crime fighters or defenders of community order. In some cases, local police officers are corrupt and are more inclined to help criminals than to assist American law enforcement. All of these differences make investigating crimes abroad and international cooperation in criminal matters very challenging prospects for any American law enforcement officer.

While it is certainly true that American police officers working overseas are sometimes distrusted by foreign governments and there may be substantial cultural differences that impede cooperation, this does not *always* go for the officers at the lower levels of foreign police agencies. Frequently, foreign police officers share a bond with American officers that develops from a sense of common purpose and the possession of a common enemy. Sometimes these officers are more willing to share information or participate in joint operations with American police officers than would be allowed by the higher-level government officials of either country. As one scholar describes this, "Police tend to place a higher priority than most politicians on going after criminals, and a lower priority on political considerations and sensitivities of national sovereignty. The common sentiment that a cop is a cop no matter whose badge he or she wears, and that a criminal is a criminal no matter what his or her citizenship is or where the crime was committed, serves as a kind of transgovernmental value system overriding political conflicts between governments."[10] Higher-level government officials can often be more sensitive to issues of national sovereignty and are more likely to resist efforts of American police officers to work abroad. Lower-level police officials do not necessarily share these concerns. Provided that they are able to avoid public attention or the ire of their political superiors, American police officers can sometimes be free to work extensively with foreign officers on overseas investigations. This means that, at times, American police officers abroad can be more successful than their diplomatic peers in the State Department or higher-level government officials.[11]

American law enforcement organizations have a strong presence overseas, but the reverse is not necessarily the case. It is true that a number of embassies in Washington DC have legal attachés who can perform some law enforcement in the United States. Europol also has had a liaison office in Washington since 2002. However, cooperation is limited, especially in terrorist cases. In one notable case in Germany, a suspected al-Qaeda member named Mounir El Motassadeq had his conviction overturned because the FBI refused to provide crucial evidence to the German court.[12] Moreover, many countries lack the resources to have effective representation abroad, as it would cost too much to put teams of police in foreign embassies. Thus, there are a number of legal, political, and financial limitations that prevent foreign governments from working in the United States.

Investigating Crimes Overseas I: Letters Rogatory and MLATs

While investigating international crimes, law enforcement officers will frequently require evidence that is located in a foreign country for use in an American trial. Sometimes this will be physical evidence such as a weapon used in a crime, other times it will be documentary evidence, like financial records from a foreign bank, and still other times, it might be a witness statement taken by someone abroad who observed criminal activity. In American criminal law there are strict rules of evidence that control how such proof may be properly obtained by law enforcement personnel so that it can be used in a court of law. For example, the Sixth Amendment to the Constitution requires that an accused criminal be given the right to confront his or her accusers. To make matters more complex, the *exclusionary rule* of U.S. criminal law says that evidence that is improperly obtained may

---

[10] *Cops across Borders,* p. 201.

[11] See also Deflem, Mathieu (2000) "Bureaucratization and Social Control: Historical Foundations of International Police Cooperation," *Law and Society Review,* Vol. 34, No. 3, 739–778.

[12] Safferling, Christoph J. M. (2004) "Terror and Law Is the German Legal System Able to Deal with Terrorism?—The *Bundesgerichtshof* (Federal Court of Justice) decision in the case against *El Motassadeq" German Law Journal,* Vol. 5, No. 5, 515–524. See also Winer, Jonathan M. (2004) "Cops across Borders: The Evolution of Transatlantic Law Enforcement and Judicial Cooperation," Council on Foreign Relations, September 1 (available at http://www.cfr.org/publication/7393/cops_across_borders.html).

not be used in court. Of course, this could be extremely difficult if the defendant is in New York and his accuser is a Jamaican citizen living in Kingston who refuses to come to the United States to testify. If it is improperly obtained, the Jamaican's testimony may be excluded from the New York trial. All of this means that governments have a great deal of interest in ensuring that they can have proper access to evidence from abroad.

There are two different ways that American law enforcement officials can get information from foreign nations. The first is to request information from a foreign government. This can be done through two different legal mechanisms. The first is called a *letter rogatory* and the second is called a *Mutual Legal Assistance Treaty* or MLAT. A letter rogatory (sometimes called a "letter of rogatory") is a formal request from one court to another court for evidence relating to a particular case. If there is no treaty between the requesting state and the state that holds the sought-after evidence, then cooperation is usually on the basis of comity, not out of a legal obligation. Such letters are typically used when there is no treaty or other international agreement that standardizes how governments may obtain evidence. (Letters rogatory may be used in either civil or criminal matters.) Letters rogatory may be requests for specific documents or a list of questions that the authorities would like to ask a particular witness. Usually the list must be exhaustive and most countries require that it be extremely detailed. As the U.S. State Department warns, "Letters rogatory are a time consuming, cumbersome process and should not be utilized unless there are no other options available."[13] Additionally, letters rogatory are slow—they must go through the State Department to the U.S. embassy abroad, which in turn transfers the letter to the foreign ministry of the state, which transfers it to their justice department, which passes it on to a prosecutor and the relevant law enforcement organization. The evidence comes back through the same process and the entire transaction usually takes six months or longer.[14]

MLATs, on the other hand, are not specific requests from one court to another, but rather are treaties between various states that are designed to insure cooperation on legal matters. Unlike letters rogatory, which are ad hoc agreements that work through diplomatic channels, MLATs are permanent arrangements between two countries and may include obligations to compel foreigners to produce evidence, or to summon witnesses for interrogation. The advantage of an MLAT is that a treaty may rely on more than the goodwill of a foreign court to obtain evidence abroad and likewise it can standardize and streamline the process of gathering evidence overseas. In most cases, only prosecutors may use MLATs, while defense attorneys and attorneys in private law suits must rely upon letters rogatory.[15] The United States negotiated its first MLAT with Switzerland in order to assist in American efforts to prosecute mobsters who stashed their profits in the legendarily secretive Swiss banking system. It currently has assistance treaties with 59 different countries with several more signed by the states parties, but not yet entered into force.[16] All

---

[13] http://travel.state.gov/law/info/judicial/judicial_683.html.

[14] Culter, Stephan F. (1999) "Building International Cases: Tools for Successful Investigations," FBI Law Enforcement Bulletin, December 12, p. 5.

[15] There is also a multilateral treaty on obtaining evidence in civil cases, entitled the *Hague Convention on Obtaining Evidence Abroad in Civil and Commercial Matters.*

[16] http://travel.state.gov/law/info/judicial/judicial_690.html.

requests for evidence from abroad are handled by the Department of Justice's Office of International Affairs (OIA).

One of the problems with letters rogatory and MLATs is that "evidence" is not thought of the same way in different legal systems and evidence is not usually obtained in the same way in different courts around the world. In the American legal system, defendants have the right to confront their accusers and to scrutinize evidence. This is not the case in many other legal systems where judges, not attorneys, investigate crimes and evaluate evidence (without the interference of lawyers from the prosecution or the defense). Similarly, many rights that are provided to criminal defendants and witnesses in the United States may not apply overseas. Finally, American prosecutors may not be sure about the exact evidence that they are seeking and so their requests may be somewhat vague, an issue that has raised problems in the past.[17] This can create a good deal of confusion when foreign judges set about gathering requested evidence, and as we will soon see, it raises a number of questions about the admissibility of evidence obtained overseas under the American Constitution. Some courts have found American procedures for obtaining evidence to be either cumbersome or silly and have therefore resisted following their guidelines to the detriment of American investigations.

Investigating Crimes Overseas II: U.S. Investigators Abroad

The second way for American officials to get information regarding crimes that occur abroad is by sending American investigators overseas to investigate the crimes where they occur. Sometimes they will do this because they are invited by the host country. Other times they do it specifically because Americans are involved in a crime, either as perpetrators or as victims. Nonetheless, for many states, the presence of any foreign official or even private foreign attorneys seeking to obtain evidence there may be considered an encroachment on their national sovereignty. As the U.S. State Department sternly warns on its website, "Attempting to obtain evidence without following the requirements of the foreign country may result in the arrest, detention, deportation or imprisonment of participants, including American counsel."[18] This means that American law enforcement operatives abroad are often in delicate political situations, and any misstep can have serious diplomatic consequences for relations between the countries involved.

The United States has had a long history of working overseas to fight crimes that impact upon Americans. For the first 150 years of American history U.S. agents, largely working under the Federal Customs Service, operated abroad in various ways. They rooted out smugglers, sought runaway slaves, or (during prohibition) fought the illegal importation of bootleg whisky. Nonetheless, for much of early American history, there were no systematic efforts to formulate a permanent policy for conducting extraterritorial law enforcement operations. Some of the investigation work done overseas was even carried out by private detectives such as the Pinkerton Detective Agency,[19] operating on the federal government's payroll. In the twentieth century, however, particularly after World War II, these international efforts expanded dramatically as the United States shed

---

[17] Cane, Alan (1985) "U.S. Court's Request for Documents Refused," *Financial Times,* March 7.

[18] http://travel.state.gov/law/info/judicial/judicial_684.html.

[19] *Cops across Borders,* pp. 55–60.

its isolationist foreign policy and sought to address the rapidly expanding problem of international and transnational crime. While many federal agencies developed an international presence in the years following World War II, the organizations that played the largest role in the internationalization of American law enforcement are the DEA, the CIA, and the FBI. The New York City Police Department has even begun to go abroad to investigate terrorist cases.[20]

As we saw in Chapter 4, the application of U.S. power overseas generates a number of distinct legal, diplomatic, and political problems. In particular, the U.S. government does not have jurisdiction in foreign countries and American law enforcement officers cannot act as government agents while overseas. While U.S. law may have formal jurisdiction over crimes that happen overseas (such as violations of Foreign Corrupt Practices Act), they may not be able to do anything about such criminal violations without the permission of the relevant foreign government. Were a U.S. agent to arrest an individual and take him into custody while not on American soil, they would be kidnapping him. At times, U.S. agents may work with foreign law enforcement personnel in obtaining suspects, but very rarely can they do so without such cooperation.

In some cases, U.S. investigators will travel overseas at the behest of foreign governments to assist with investigations on criminal matters. American investigators provide advanced equipment and training that can help less sophisticated police forces evaluate evidence or interrogate suspects. Often, American investigators will be brought in when the issue is of concern to the U.S. government—such as terrorist attacks—or as a show of goodwill between governments. When the *USS Cole,* an American naval vessel was damaged in a 2000 terrorist attack, nearly 100 FBI investigators flew to Yemen, the sight of the bombing, to examine the ship, sift through the evidence, and transport any crucial material back to the United States for further testing. Then FBI director Louis Freeh was clear that the agents were responding to an invitation from the Yemeni government. "The investigation is being run by the Yemeni police and security authorities," Freeh said, "we are there as a partner, which is the word that the president used, but we are the junior partner, as we are in every country outside the United States where we participate in support investigations."[21] Though American investigators provide a great deal of expertise in these operations, they can never officially run an overseas operation—such a claim would be an affront to their host's sovereignty.

Many U.S. embassies overseas have an FBI agent who serves as a legal attaché or "legat" to facilitate this process.[22] The legat's job is to serve as a liaison between American law enforcement and foreign governments, to help coordinate law enforcement overseas, and most generally, "to keep foreign crime as far from American shores as possible and to help solve as rapidly as possible those international crimes that do occur."[23] The legat's office is usually not an "operational" one. That is, the legat does not conduct investigations on their own but may help to follow up on international leads for domestic investigations or coordinate between American law enforcement and their partners overseas. (They can be

---

[20] Finnegan, William (2005) "The Terrorism Beat: How is the N.Y.P.D. defending the city?" *New Yorker,* July 25.

[21] October 19, 2000, press conference.

[22] As of this writing, there are 51 legats working in the world (a sharp rise from the 32 that existed in 1998).

[23] http://www.fbi.gov/contact/legat/legat.htm.

essential in following through on requests for evidence from the United States through MLATs or letters rogatory, for example.) When Natalee Holloway, a young American citizen disappeared in the small Caribbean island nation of Aruba in May 2005, the government there requested assistance from the legat in neighboring Barbados. The legat then contacted FBI agents in Birmingham, Alabama, who flew there to aid in the search. In many ways, the legat has a "catchall" position that involves dealing with any number of criminal issues that may arise between the United States and a foreign country.

Along with the development and expansion of the legat system, the FBI has sought to build closer connections with foreign law enforcement agencies by helping train foreign police officers in American methods of crime fighting. Federal officials, usually through the legat's office, may train foreign officers in American police methods, either by holding courses overseas (there are FBI International Law Enforcement Academies in Budapest, Hungary, and Bangkok, Thailand) or by inviting promising foreign police officers to FBI's Academy in Quantico, Virginia. Here, law enforcement officers from around the world work alongside American trainees, taking courses in law, forensic science, leadership development, and physical fitness. Not only can such classes introduce foreigners to the crime fighting techniques used by American law enforcement, but also, they help build strong personal connections between American police officials and foreign officers. Such experiences can prove helpful later when these graduates rise to important positions in their own police agencies, and American officials may rely on these connections for future assistance in overseas investigations.

THE DEA

Along with the FBI, one of the U.S. law enforcement organizations that has a large presence overseas is the Drug Enforcement Agency (DEA). The DEA was formed in the 1970s as an outgrowth of the Federal Bureau of Narcotics (FBN), which served for many years to track down and arrest individuals involved in smuggling drugs into the United States from abroad. Like the FBI, it is currently part of the Department of Justice and serves under the attorney general (who in turn answers to the president).

The DEA has a very large international presence and has an enormous influence on the drug control policies of other many states. It has offices in over a hundred countries around the world, helping foreign states deal with their domestic drug trafficking problems. It does this in numerous ways: First it seeks to develop anti-drug strategies for local law enforcement, helping their governments more effectively counter drug criminals and prevent the exporting of drugs into the United States. This can include educating foreign police forces about tactics that Americans have found to be effective against drug traffickers. Other times, the DEA will promote bureaucratic or legal changes in a country in order to make the country more effective in stopping drug production or drug smuggling. For example, prior to intervention on the part of the DEA, many countries did not have special anti-drug divisions in their local or national police forces, nor did they conduct sting operations to catch drug traffickers. Some countries even considered such practices (common in U.S. law enforcement) to be unlawful. Also, like the FBI, the DEA runs a special training facility for foreign law enforcement personnel in Quantico, Virginia. All of this has dramatically changed the nature of the global war on drugs: The efforts of the DEA have led to the "Americanization" of the international war on drugs, leading foreign states to modify their drug policies in ways that make them look much more like the DEA's own practices.

More conventionally, the DEA helps local police units investigate and arrest drug manufacturers who operate abroad. They often work independent of their host country, developing their sources and their information independent of local law enforcement and only later sharing this with the local officials. Sometimes, the relationship with local law enforcement may even be minimal, particularly in countries where police and government officials are incompetent or corrupt. In such countries, DEA officials must sometimes work around local law enforcement, finding ways to force the government to extradite the suspect to the United States or lure him or her into American jurisdiction without the interference of local police.

The DEA has also taken on a role as a sort of rival to Interpol, developing a comprehensive database for law enforcement agencies around the world to utilize in their investigations of international drug criminals. Since it is the job of the DEA to fight drug trafficking worldwide, they have a vested interest in providing foreign police agencies (at least the reliable ones) with the appropriate tools to fight drugs in their home countries. This means that many foreign law enforcement organizations can rely on the DEA to get timely relevant information about drug activity within their borders. The organization has two primary research institutes that study and monitor illegal drug activity in the United States and elsewhere: The El Paso Intelligence Center (EPIC) and the National Drug Pointer Index (NDPIX). Consisting of over 300 analysts who monitor international crime data, EPIC is of particular interest to international criminal justice professionals as it keeps track of drug movements and immigration throughout the western hemisphere (it is conducted in partnership with the federal immigration services located in the Department of Homeland Security). Additionally, the various DEA field offices around the world can provide foreign police officers with useful information about the locations and activities of the drug traffickers around the world that they may then investigate on their own.

One of the other ways that the DEA helps fight drug trafficking is through an anti-drug certification process. Each year, the president is required to certify that each country around the world is cooperating in the fight against drug trafficking and the withdrawal of this certification can trigger economic sanctions against that country. Since it is in many ways the front line in the global war against drugs, the DEA plays an important role in advising the President in regard to whether or not to certify a country. However, despite its strong influence on the certification process, the agency's decisions are not final: In 1998, President Clinton certified Mexico over objections of the DEA, who felt that widespread and persistent corruption in the Mexican government's war on drugs merited condemnation by the U.S. government. (The president felt that, despite persistent problems, cooperation with Mexico would be more productive than sanctions in America's fight against drugs.) Despite the fact that it does not take the final in these decision in these cases, the DEA can play an important political role in the international fight against drugs by working closely with foreign law enforcement agencies and monitoring their conduct.

We will discuss the functions of the DEA further in Chapter 8 when we discuss international drug trafficking.

Gathering Evidence Abroad: Constitutional Questions

Along with the political and legal problems that arise when conducting police work overseas, the evidence that is gathered through these investigations presents a number of additional constitutional issues for American courts. Could an individual in a foreign country be interrogated either by American officers or by police agents of that country without being informed of his or her rights (that is, without being *Mirandized*) and then have this evidence used against them in an American criminal trial? Could evidence gained by a warrantless search conducted in a foreign country (by either American or foreign law enforcement officials) be used in an American trial? What about evidence gathered by torture carried out by foreign officials on individuals who are later brought to trial in U.S. courts? In most cases, the U.S. Constitution only applies within U.S. borders, but when individuals (foreign citizens or Americans) are brought into American courts for crimes committed on foreign lands or investigated overseas, this simple principle belies a much more complex reality.

One of the central questions that the Supreme Court has had to address in determining which rights belong to whom in extraterritorial crimes is the meaning of the term *the people*. The Constitution and the Bill of Rights give "the people" certain rights in relation to criminal investigations and criminal trials, but it does not explicitly state *who* these people are, and there is no discussion in the text of the Constitution about treating foreign citizens different from U.S. citizens during criminal trials. The task of making subtle distinctions over which rights belong to which people has been left to U.S. courts. We can break down the rights issues along two dimensions: First, we can analyze the issue in terms of types of people involved in the allegedly criminal behavior. U.S. citizens abroad, foreign citizens abroad, or foreign citizens in the United States are all going to be treated differently under constitutional law. Second, we can examine which rights are under scrutiny. A defendant's Sixth Amendment right to confront a witness may be treated different from his or her Fifth Amendment right to avoid self-incrimination. All of these issues make the application of constitutional principles to international criminal prosecutions an intricate affair.

In *United States* v. *Verdugo-Urquidez* the Supreme Court asserted that the term *the people* as used in the Constitution does not apply to everyone, everywhere in the world. " . . . 'The people' seems to have been a term of art employed in select parts of the Constitution. The Preamble declares that the Constitution is ordained and established by 'the People of the United States.' The Second Amendment protects 'the right of the people to keep and Bear arms,' and the Ninth and Tenth Amendments provide that certain rights and powers are retained by and reserved to 'the people.' " [24] To gain the protections of the Bill of Rights it is not enough that one simply be a person, but rather one must be a person with some "sufficient connection" with the United States:

> "the people" protected by the Fourth Amendment, and by the First and Second Amendments, and to whom rights and powers are reserved in the Ninth and Tenth Amendments, refers to a class of persons who are part of a national community or who have otherwise developed sufficient connection with this country to be considered part of that community.

---

[24] *United States* v. *Verdugo-Urquidez,* 58 USLW 4263, U.S., 108 L.Ed. 2d 222, 110 S.Ct. 1056 (1990).

As the defendant in the case was a Mexican national who had no (voluntary) relation with the United States, never coming to America of his own free will, he did not have such a connection and thus he could not claim the protections given to the people of the United States. Nonetheless, the "sufficient connection" doctrine spelled out in *Verdugo-Urquidez* has come under substantial criticism from many legal scholars, including Supreme Court Justice Brennan, who penned a strong dissenting opinion in the case.

U.S. Citizens   In *Reid* v. *Covert,* the Supreme Court ruled that the U.S. Government may not evade an American citizen's constitutional protections by prosecuting them overseas. In *Reid,* the court dealt with two women who murdered their husbands while they were both stationed at U.S. military bases abroad (Clarice Reid was stationed in England, Dorothy Smith was in Japan). Both defendants were civilians and there was ample evidence that they were both insane at the time that they committed their crimes. Nonetheless, they were tried under military law, which does not require a trial by jury as provided by the Sixth Amendment. The Court overturned the ruling, asserting that in this case, the defendants were entitled to the same constitutional protections regardless of where the crime occurred. As the Court put it,

> we reject the idea that when the United States acts against citizens abroad it can do so free of the Bill of Rights. The United States is entirely a creature of the Constitution. Its power and authority have no other source. It can only act in accordance with all the limitations imposed by the Constitution. When the Government reaches out to punish a citizen who is abroad, the shield which the Bill of Rights and other parts of the Constitution provide to protect his life and liberty should not be stripped away just because he happens to be in another land.[25]

Thus, Americans punished abroad for violating American laws are still given all of the protections that belong to any U.S. citizen accused of a crime within its borders.

In most cases, the Fourth Amendment prevents warrantless searches without showing probable cause, and any evidence gained from an inappropriate search is inadmissible in court. However, when the investigation is carried out by foreign law enforcement agencies, the rules are somewhat different. Normally, evidence obtained by foreign law enforcement *can* be used against American citizens in U.S. courts, regardless of whether or not the foreign officers had a judicially authorized warrant. However, if foreign police officials are involved in a "joint venture" with U.S. law enforcement such that, "the conduct of foreign law enforcement officials rendered them agents or virtual agents, of United States law enforcement officials," the evidence may be considered inadmissible if is was improperly obtained.[26] Given the strong role that U.S. law enforcement plays overseas (particularly the DEA) in investigating drug traffickers and other international criminals, one can understand the concern that U.S. law enforcement could use foreign police agencies as a tool to escape their constitutional obligations.

An important exception to this rule that is relevant to international crimes applies to searches conducted along the U.S. border or other points of entry onto U.S. territory. In *US* v. *Ramsey,* the court articulated a "Border Search Exception" to the Fourth Amendment,

---

[25] *Reid* v. *Covert,* 354 U.S. 1, 6 (1957).

[26] *United States* v. *Maturo,* 982 F.2d 57 (2d Cir. 1992). Cited in Podgor, Ellen, *Understanding International Criminal Law,* p. 72.

asserting that such searches were fundamentally different from other types of searches and that national security justified warrantless searches at points of entry into the United States. The case involved three men who were involved in a "mail order heroin" business, importing the drugs into the United States through international mail. The appellants argued that their mail was searched (and thus, the drugs discovered) without probable cause. However, the court ruled that, "[S]earches made at the border, pursuant to the long-standing right of the sovereign to protect itself by stopping and examining persons and property crossing into this country, are reasonable simply by virtue of the fact that they occur at the border, should, by now, require no extended demonstration."[27] Searches at entry points into the United States are different from other police searches. Because such searches are commonplace and thus do not stigmatize an individual the way that more conventional police searches do, they are usually considered reasonable by the courts.

Non–U.S. Citizens Abroad   While Americans abroad are given virtually all of the constitutional protections that are provided for Americans living in the United States, it is not the same for non-citizens who commit crimes abroad, but who are prosecuted in U.S. courts. In *Verdugo-Urquidez,* the Supreme Court ruled that in many cases, constitutional rights do not apply to foreigners overseas. Verdugo-Urquidez, a Mexican national, was suspected of being a powerful member of a large narcotics operation that smuggled drugs into the United States and was responsible for the torture and murder of a U.S. DEA agent. In 1986, he was arrested by Mexican authorities at the request of the DEA and transferred to U.S. Marshals in California. After his arrest, however, DEA agents in Mexico searched the home of Verdugo-Urquidez without a judicially authorized warrant and prosecutors sought to use the evidence that they found in his truck. On appeal, the Supreme Court ruled that the evidence found in the search could be used against the defendant as, "the purpose of the Fourth Amendment was to protect the people of the United States against arbitrary action by their own Government; it was never suggested that the provision was intended to restrain the actions of the Federal Government against aliens outside of the United States territory." Thus, foreign nationals may be searched by foreign police officers in a manner inconsistent with U.S. constitutional safeguards provided that the search is not part of a joint venture between U.S. and foreign law enforcement.

The only other exception to the rule set out by *Verdugo-Urquidez* refers to evidence obtained by acts that "shock the conscience." Evidence gathered through acts of torture carried out by foreign law enforcement officials will be excluded in a trial. In *United States* v. *Fernandez-Caro,*[28] a defendant's confession was excluded because Mexican police officers beat a suspect, tortured him with electricity, and threatened to murder him.

Non–U.S. Citizens in the United States   A number of Supreme Court opinions (including *Verdugo-Urquidez* and *Colvert*) have asserted that non-citizens who live with

---

[27] 431 U.S. 606 (1977). See also: *Boyd* v. *United States,* 116 U.S. 616 (1886). Arnold, G. T. (1995) Bordering on Unreasonableness?: The Third Circuit Again Expands the Border Search Exception in United *States* v. *Hyde,* 40 Vill. L. Rev. 835.

[28] 677 F. Supp. 893 (S.D. Tex. 1987).

the United States or who commit crimes in the United States have all of the same rights that are given to American citizens.

OBTAINING SUSPECTS ABROAD

Since the U.S. courts do not allow for trials *in absentia,* the American government must physically possess an individual in order to put them on trial. There are three ways that the American government may obtain criminals who are overseas: The traditional (and usually unproblematic) manner is through a legal process known as *extradition.* The other, somewhat more odious and controversial methods to obtain criminals from abroad are by either luring an individual into American jurisdiction and then arresting them or, in extreme situations, by abducting a suspect and then forcibly transferring them to the United States to be put on trial.

Extradition

When an individual who is wanted for a particular crime, or one who has already been convicted of a crime is apprehended in a state other than the one where he or she violated the law, he or she may be transferred or *extradited* back to the original country in order to be tried for his crime or to serve out his remaining sentence. Extradition is different from *deportation,* where an individual is forcibly removed from a particular country (such as an undocumented or "illegal" alien), and *repatriation,* which involves returning an individual to their home state without criminal prosecution. Extradition has a long history in international law, and is usually a relatively simple bureaucratic process. Sometimes, however, the decision whether or not to extradite an individual raises passions on both sides of a border and an extradition case can quickly become a controversial political issue (as we already in Chapter 4 in relation to the *Pinochet* case in England).

The international law of extradition consists of a vast number of treaties between different states around the world. The majority of these treaties are bilateral treaties between two individual states; a few are multilateral. The European Convention on Extradition has 46 states has parties to it, all of which agree to extradite criminals from one European country to another. Many extradition treaties accept the principle known as *aut dedere aut judicare* ("either extradite or prosecute"), which obliges states either to put an accused criminal on trial for a crime (if that state can legitimately claim jurisdiction over the accused), or to extradite them to a state that is willing to put them on trial. Such laws prevent criminals who have fled overseas from escaping the prosecutor's net.

A further element of international extradition is the principle of *double criminality.* Many extradition treaties specify that the acts that the individual is alleged to have committed must be crimes that are punished by a term of imprisonment up to one year in both countries. (Other treaties, so-called "list treaties," set out the specific crimes for which an individual may be extradited.) This prevents states from having to extradite an individual who would not be considered a criminal in that state, and thus detaining and punishing an individual without an obvious crime having been committed. This also prevents political dissidents who criticize oppressive regimes from being extradited for their politics. In addition, extradition procedures are prevented from being bogged down by attempts to extradite those who commit trivial crimes.

Extradition can be a tricky matter when the cases are controversial or the criminals are well known, and adverse public attention can easily complicate the extradition process. Because many states (particularly European states) consider the death penalty to be immoral and a violation of human rights, these states often will refuse to extradite criminals to the United States or to other countries when they may face execution. This has led a number of extradition treaties to include provisions that allow states to prevent such extraditions, unless the government "gives assurances satisfactory to the requested Party that the death penalty will not be carried out."[29] Also, most states will not extradite individuals for "political crimes," that is, crimes that are part of the political conflict in the state that seeks custody of them. Like Interpol's Article 3, this prevents a nondemocratic government from seeking to gain custody and punish a person who opposes their regime. Also like Interpol, most terrorists have not been considered political criminals for purposes of extradition.

The practical affairs of most extraditions are straightforward: The Department of Justice's Office of International Affairs (OIA) usually upon the request of the prosecutor of a particular state or a federal prosecutor issues a request for the individual to be extradited. This request is either transmitted through Interpol as a red notice or transmitted directly to the American embassy abroad, which passes it on to the relevant foreign authority. The individual is then placed under provisional arrest by local authorities to ensure that they do not leave the country to evade extradition. In some countries, an individual under provisional arrest may be released on bail, although this is rare. They are then presented to an extradition judge who rules as to whether or not the individual may be extradited. If the extradition is allowed, the individual is then sent to the United States for trial. (The U.S. Marshal Service has a special Justice Prisoner and Alien Transport System, or JPATS, that runs a fleet of vehicles and airplanes used to transport criminals around the country and the world.)

There are other ways for governments to gain access to indicted criminals who are overseas without having to deal with the bureaucracy or uncertainty involved in a formal extradition proceeding. One way is to have the state that possesses the accused thrown out of their country and then surrendered to the state that wants possession of him. In these cases, a person is "escorted" out of the country and into the hands of waiting U.S. Marshals who promptly arrest the individual. This transforms deportation into a sort of de facto extradition.[30] Still other police agencies may feel the need to resort to more drastic methods to obtain suspects abroad. "Extraordinary rendition" involves the president sending a suspected criminal abroad without any of the safeguards that are set up in the extradition process. Usually, the suspect is simply "handed over" to a foreign government. Critics have charged that extraordinary renditions have resulted in suspects being tortured by these governments. We will discuss them in greater detail in a later chapter when we look at the war on terrorism in greater depth.

---

[29] US–UK Extradition Treaty. Cited in, Martin, Mary K., "A One-Way Ticket Back to the United States: The Collision of International Extradition Law and the Death Penalty," 11 Cap. Def. J. 243 at 248.

[30] Paust, *International Criminal Law,* pp. 413–436.

The Soering and Sheinbein Affairs

Most cases of extradition are straightforward. A criminal is apprehended and they are transferred to the custody of the requesting state, from which they are escorted home for prosecution by U.S. Marshals. However, some cases can become much more complicated, especially when they involve delicate political matters or when a nation does not wish to surrender the accused for other reasons. The cases of Jens Soering and Samuel Sheinbein show how tricky the issue of extradition may become in cases where either national identity is at stake (that is, where a citizen of one state is wanted by another state) or controversial punishments like the death penalty are involved.

Soering was an 18-year-old German national who was accused of killing both of his girlfriend's parents (in collusion with his girlfriend Elizabeth Haysom) in Virginia in May 1985. After the killing, he fled to the United Kingdom, where he was ultimately apprehended by British authorities. The state of Virginia then sought to have him extradited to the United States, hoping eventually to execute him for the killings. Soering appealed his case to the European Court of Human Rights, arguing that extradition would violate the European Convention on Human Rights and Fundamental Freedoms. Though the UK was not a party to the sections of the Convention that forbade the death penalty, Soering's attorneys argued that the extradition would nonetheless violate the defendant's rights. Rather than arguing that his extradition to the United States would violate his human right to not be executed, Soering's attorneys argued that the "death row phenomenon" would be a form of "inhuman or degrading treatment," and thus a violation of Article 3 of the Convention. "In particular the delays in the appeal and review procedures following a death sentence, during which time he would be subject to increasing tension and psychological trauma," would be so harmful that it could be construed as a form of torture. This opinion was shared by Germany, who wished to extradite him there under the objective personality jurisdiction (see Chapter 4) to try him for the Virginia murders.

The court agreed with Soering's attorneys and refused to allow his extradition to the United States without assurances from the prosecuting attorney that they would not seek the death penalty against him. The Virginia prosecutor gave this promise and Soering was sent back into U.S. custody. After a trial in the United States, Soering was found guilty and sentenced to life in prison in Virginia, where he remains to this day. (Haysom was found guilty of being an accessory to her parents' murders and is also serving a 90-year sentence in Virginia.)

While the *Soering* case raises issues regarding the different penal philosophies of the United States and Europe, the *Sheinbein* case raises issues about nationalism, citizenship, and criminal justice. Samuel Sheinbein, an American, was 17 years old when he and his accomplice, Aaron Needle, murdered a mutual friend, Alfredo Tello, in 1997 in Rockville, Maryland. Prosecutors alleged that Sheinbein and Needle strangled, tortured, and beat Tello to death, hiding the corpse in an abandoned house. Two days later, Sheinbein and Tello returned to dismember and incinerate the corpse but they failed to completely destroy the evidence and the body was soon discovered by the local authorities. Upon discovery of the body, Needle was quickly arrested (he committed suicide while in jail awaiting trial). When he heard of the discovery of Tello's corpse, however, Sheinbein's father put his son on a plane to Israel, where he hoped that his son would be protected by the Israeli government. Once in Israel, Sheinbein claimed to be an Israeli citizen (his father was an Israeli citizen, and by Israeli law, the child of a citizen is a citizen) and requested that he not be returned to face trial in the United States. Instead, he proposed to answer for the crime in an Israeli court.

Like *Soering*, the legal issues surrounding the *Sheinbein* extradition case are complex and highly technical. Sheinbein's defense counsel recognized that prosecuting Sheinbein thousands of miles away from the site of the crime would make mounting an effective prosecution very difficult—Israeli prosecutors could not force witnesses to travel to Israel to testify and other evidence would likewise be very difficult to present at trial. The Israeli courts ultimately agreed that Sheinbein was an Israeli citizen by law, but also understood that Sheinbein should answer for his crimes. As a minor he would not face the death penalty in Maryland, but many Israelis were concerned that he would not receive a fair trial or would be punished much more harshly than he might otherwise be. Since Israel's founding in the wake of the Holocaust, there has been a good deal of concern among Israeli Jews that Jews will always be treated unfairly in non-Jewish countries. Israel has seen itself as a homeland for the Jewish people, promising to protect them from persecution. Many (including the Sheinbeins) hoped that he would receive a lighter, "more reasonable" sentence in Israel than he would receive in the United States. However, many Israelis and Jewish Americans decried the court's opinion and accused the Sheinbeins of cynically manipulating their ethnic identity to thwart justice.

Sheinbein's case was ultimately prosecuted in an Israeli court. There, he pled guilty for the murder and received a sentence of 24 years. As Israeli criminal justice is more lenient than that in the United States, it is likely that he will be released much earlier than this and will probably be treated much better in an Israeli prison than he would be in an American penitentiary.

Extradition and criminal punishment raise a host of complex moral and political issues for international law enforcement. Regardless of whether or not one thinks that the death penalty is moral or is justified, it will continue to be problematic for the American criminal justice system's attempts to extradite accused capital offenders who leave our borders. Many countries in the world, and particularly those in Europe, believe the death penalty to be a gross violation of human rights and wonder how a civilized country like the United States could practice it. Also, the belief that the criminal courts of foreign countries are incapable of fairly prosecuting foreigners can affect public opinion as can the related belief that each country should "take care of its own." Of course, the issues that are raised in cases like *Soering* and *Sheinbein* are not only issues that apply to conventional criminals like these. The terrorists who organized the September 11 attacks or other strikes against the United States could be apprehended overseas, and those who are fighting against their extradition will pay close attention to the precedents that cases like *Soering* and *Sheinbein* have set.

Luring and Abduction

Frequently, when law enforcement officials wish to obtain suspects who are overseas, and more conventional means to obtain them such as extradition or deportation are unavailable, they will resort to illegal, or at least questionable methods to get the suspects. Other times, it may be possible to extradite the suspect by lawful means but nonetheless U.S. agents may wish to avoid the hassle and red tape (as well as the public attention) that a lawful extradition may create. Luring or abduction are not always legal tools of law enforcement, at least under international law and according to the national laws of some countries, but they are nonetheless often used by various police organizations in order to obtain international criminals. However, because such tactics often involve deceit or even force to obtain suspects, they are controversial for moral, legal, and political reasons.

Sometimes, law enforcement officers will lure an individual outside of a certain territory in order to arrest them in international waters or in a more extradition-friendly state. Usually, this involves law enforcement officials (or their proxies) developing an elaborate scheme in order to convince the wanted individual to leave a country where they are immune from extradition, and then, once beyond its borders, arresting them and transporting them to the United States for trial. The United States has practiced this in numerous cases over the years. In one well-known case, when they were unable to obtain a suspected terrorist from the island nation of Cyprus, a group of FBI agents posing as drug smugglers lured Fawaz Yunis onto a yacht off of its coast in the Mediterranean Sea. When he was on board the ship he was arrested by the agents, handcuffed and quickly shipped off to the United States for trial. Despite Yunis' protests, a federal appeals court ruled that his arrest was lawful, asserting that (citing an earlier opinion), "There is nothing in the Constitution that requires a court to permit a guilty person rightfully convicted to escape justice because he was brought to trial against his will."[31] Yunis, a participant in the 1985 hijacking of a Royal Jordanian Airlines flight (which included 3 U.S. citizens), was sentenced to 30 years' imprisonment in US Federal Court.

Other times, when luring a suspect to America is impossible, law enforcement officers will resort to forcibly abducting suspects from foreign countries, by having them captured and then secretly transported to the United States for trial. Usually, this is done by foreigners or other private citizens working independently or under the employ of the U.S. government. In the case of *Sosa* v. *Alvarez-Machain* (discussed in the previous chapter), DEA agents paid a group of Mexican nationals, including Sosa, to bring a suspected cop killer into the United States for trial after attempts to have the suspect lawfully extradited proved fruitless. The party kidnapped the suspect from his medical office in Guadalajara, Mexico, and flew him to El Paso, Texas, by private plane, where he was then arrested and charged by the DEA. (However, when Humberto Alvarez-Machain was acquitted for the crime, he sued his abductor under the Alien Tort Claims Act.) Of course, this practice is not followed solely by American law enforcement—other governments do it, too. Amaru Dikko's (also discussed in the previous chapter) was such an attempted abduction on the part of Nigeria, carried out by paid foreign operatives from Israel. By carrying out abductions through private parties, law enforcement officials can avoid "getting their hands dirty" in the abduction and likewise avoid serious political damage if the abduction fails by denying any relation to the deed.

Abductions directly carried out by government agents of a foreign state are still more controversial. In these cases, states cannot deny their involvement with kidnappings and thus the political fallout may be much greater if the mission fails and the kidnappers are caught. When, in 1960, Israeli intelligence located Adolph Eichmann, one of the master planners of the Nazi Holocaust, living peacefully in Argentina under an assumed name, the Israeli intelligence service, Mossad, kidnapped him and brought him to Israel for prosecution. Significantly, the Israeli government initially denied carrying out the kidnapping, asserting

---

[31] *United States* v. *Yunis,* 681 F. Supp. 909 (D.C. Cir. 1988). Cited in Paust, Jordan et al., *International Criminal Law: Cases and Material,* p. 439.

that Eichmann had been brought to them by overenthusiastic Jewish volunteers, but later confessed to the deed. However, despite some protests from international lawyers and diplomats who were concerned about the precedent that the abduction set, Eichmann was ultimately placed on trial and executed by Israel in 1962 for his crimes. In February 2007, an Italian judge indicted 27 Americans, including a number of CIA agents, for abducting radical Muslim cleric Hassan Mustafa Osama Nasr (aka Abu Omar) from Milan in 2003 and sending him to Egypt for interrogation.[32] Abductions carried out by U.S. agents abroad have reportedly become significantly more common than before the war on terrorism commenced.

There is a controversial principle in the international criminal law on abduction and luring, commonly referred to as *mala captus bene detentus* (meaning literally, "bad capture, good imprisonment"). This principle says that, even though a country has obtained an individual through unlawful means or in violation of an extradition treaty, it may nonetheless legitimately prosecute them. In the *Alvarez-Machain* case, the abduction had been carried out in violation of an extradition treaty between the United States and Mexico. As a result of this, the lower courts initially ruled that the U.S. courts could not proceed with the case. However, in one of the many legal opinions surrounding this affair, the Supreme Court ruled that, in certain circumstances, international abduction could be lawful, despite a general rule against abduction in international law. Here, it ruled that "The fact of respondent's forcible abduction does not therefore prohibit his trial in a court in the United States for violations of the criminal laws of the United States."[33] Nonetheless, many scholars believe that abductions are a violation of international law, even if they are acceptable under American criminal law.

Some experts have suggested that luring and abduction are imprudent or even immoral and should not be supported by the American government or its criminal justice system. On one hand, many governments maintain that by either directly or indirectly using American police powers on foreign soil without a nation's permission such policies violate state sovereignty. As we've already discussed, most countries carefully guard their right to enforce their own laws within their own borders and frown on foreign officials working there without their permission. Further, most states do not allow their own police officers to lure suspects and consider abduction to be a form of low-level aggression. (Imagine the response from the American people if a foreign country's intelligence operatives came to the United States and kidnapped an American citizen for criminal trial elsewhere.) Frequently, diplomats have protested to the American government regarding such behavior.[34] Others have suggested that luring suspects may violate their human rights, amounting to a sort of governmental kidnapping. Despite the fact that such extraordinary means of obtaining international criminals may be unpopular and considered dishonest by their critics, they have largely been accepted under American criminal law. The underlying lesson of *Sosa* v. *Alvarez-Machain* and these other abduction cases is that when there is no clear extradition treaty or when states are unwilling to cooperate with each other on criminal matters, it is virtually inevitable that practices like luring or abduction of wanted criminals will occur.

---

[32] Fisher, Ian and Manzetti, Mark (2007) "Italians Indict C.I.A. Operatives in '03 Abduction," *New York Times,* February 17.

[33] *United States* v. *Alvarez-Machain* (91–172), 504 U.S. 655 (1992).

[34] Paust, Jordan et al., *International Criminal Law: Cases and Materials,* pp. 443–446.

CONCLUSION

In this chapter we have seen how the various national law enforcement organizations have worked together to deal with international crime, as well as how American police organizations have gone abroad in order to deal with crimes that harm American citizens. The mobility of international criminals has required that new laws are written and new institutions developed in order to effectively investigate transnational crimes and obtain their perpetrators. Further, the globalization of crime and the political animosities that have developed between states has required that, at times, American law enforcement work secretly, capturing international criminals by "tricking" them into entering American jurisdiction or by forcibly bringing them to the United States, where they can be arrested against the wishes of uncooperative governments.

One of the unique things about organizations like Interpol is that they developed through the efforts of the various law-enforcement bodies around the world, working in some ways independent of their own governments. Most other international organizations such as the UN developed from government leaders and foreign ministers meeting together to advance their shared interests. This makes Interpol a sort of "grassroots" international organization, developing from the collective efforts of the international law enforcement community, who to some extent share a common agenda as crime fighters. Like their enemies, drug dealers, terrorists, and transnational organized criminal enterprises, the law enforcement community has learned to act independently and to adapt to new circumstances. Just as many modern terrorists wage their wars subnationally without the direct support of any country or government, Interpol fights crime by coordinating the efforts of law enforcement sub-nationally, using their common enemies as basis for their cooperation. In some ways, this makes Interpol a globalized police force: it has changed and transformed as society, technology, and its opponents have changed.

The remaining chapters of this text will shift the focus away from the nascent international criminal justice system and toward the various crimes that this system has been designed to confront. One thing to keep in mind, however, is that much of what we've examined in the preceding five chapters is still emerging and developing. The international criminal justice system will no doubt evolve as it responds to changes in international crime as well as to changes in international politics. After it has prosecuted a few international criminals the ICC may look very different than it does now, which may alter the opinions of its supporters as well as its critics. Similarly, Europol and the UNODC are both less than a decade old and will likely undergo a good deal of "growing pains" as they adapt to new crime threats. New international criminal law treaties will be written in order to counter the new dangers that are sure to emerge in the coming years and states will further develop new means to share information about international crime and international criminals. What the international criminal justice system will look like in a few years is impossible to predict. One thing that is sure, however, is that, despite political disagreements between states, *some* sort of international criminal justice system will continue to exist to counter the endeavors of international criminals. As long as international criminals show no regard for national boundaries, and as long as weak states give international criminals legal impunity, there will be a need for an international criminal justice system.

READING AND RESOURCES

Abbell, Michael (2001) *Obtaining Evidence Abroad in Criminal Cases, Extradition to and From the United States, International Prisoner Transfer,* Ardsley: Transnational Publishers—An exhaustive study of the legal issues involved in international law enforcement.

Bresler, Fenton (1992) *Interpol,* London: Sinclair Stevenson.—A nice inside account of Interpol at work.

Deflem, Mathieu (2002) *Policing World Society: Historical Foundations of International Police Cooperation,* Oxford: Oxford University Press—A useful history of international policing with a focus on U.S.–German relations.

Fooner, Michael (1989) *Interpol,* New York: Plenum Publishing Company.—A somewhat dated, but interesting analysis of the functions of Interpol.

Gyandoh, Mark K. (2001) "Notes & Comments: Foreign Evidence Gathering: What Obstacles Stand in the Way of Justice?" *Temple International and Comparative Law Journal,* Vol. 15, pp. 81–100.—A nice, short introduction to the issues surrounding letters rogatory and MLATs.

Nadelman, Ethan (1993) *Cops Across Borders: The Internationalization of U.S. Criminal Law Enforcement,* University Park: Penn State Press.—An excellent study of the internationalization of the various institutions of American law enforcement; somewhat technical, but very highly recommended.

The website for Interpol is http://www.interpol.int.

The website for Europol is http://www.europol.europa.eu/.

The website for the U.S. National Central Bureau of Interpol is http://www.usdoj.gov/usncb/.

The website of the UNODC is http://www.unodc.org/.

The U.S. State Department website for obtaining evidence abroad is http://travel.state.gov/law/info/judicial/judicial_2514.html.

The website for the International Law Enforcement Academy in Budapest, Hungary, is http://www.ilea.hu/.

Information regarding the FBI's legat offices is available at http://www.fbi.gov/contact/legat/legat.htm.

6

War Crimes and Aggression

❖

In the opening chapter of this book, I said that there are different types of "international crimes" and that crime can be international in different ways. By that I meant that some crimes are international in the sense that they are prosecuted and punished by international courts. Other crimes like international drug trafficking are international in that they are outlawed by international treaties or have effects that spill over across international borders. In this chapter and the next, we will discuss the major crimes that are punished by the ICC and the other international tribunals, international crimes in the strictest sense of the term. Some scholars consider these to be the only international crimes, and others to be "transnational crimes." Be that as it may, there are different crimes that criminal justice professionals will have to confront in one form or another and there is no need to limit our analysis to just one category of international crime. In this chapter we will discuss the crimes that are most commonly committed in times of armed conflict, that is, we will discuss war crimes and the crime of international aggression. In the next chapter we will look at two crimes that may be committed during war, but are not always so: genocide and crimes against humanity.

JUSTICE AND WAR?

Anybody who has ever been in a stressful, dangerous situation knows how difficult it is to think clearly. People who commit "hit and run" offenses often leave the scene of the accident not because they are bad people, but because the heat of the moment causes them to panic and their instincts tell them to flee from danger. People do all sorts of terrible things when they are under extreme pressure and can't think straight.

War is the ultimate stressful situation. While many war movies show soldiers heroically facing enemy fire, risking their lives for the sake of their brothers in arms or in the name of a cause they passionately believe in, very often this is not the case. When bullets fly, people, especially the young people who serve in the world's armed forces, fear for their lives and will do anything to anyone in order to assure their safety. It is not cowardice that makes these people flee, but a healthy desire to survive.

Additionally, war is fundamentally about what most people would consider an immoral activity: killing another human being. It is the most barbaric activity that humanity engages in, a sign of utter failure for human civilization. Even if war may be necessary at certain times, it is surely a necessary evil.

For these reasons many people have been skeptical about the idea of a "law of war," as well as talk about "war crimes." If war is indeed necessary, it is better to get through it as soon as possible without pretending that there is a right and wrong to it: one should not talk about justice or injustice in warfare, only success or failure. Such views have often been attributed to the realists discussed in the opening chapter and many famous military and political leaders have held such an opinion. During the Civil War, Union General William Tecumseh Sherman famously said that "War is hell," and felt that it should be ended quickly, even if it meant that a lot of innocent blood must be spilled. (Sherman knew what he was talking about. He is infamous for his "march to the sea" which devastated the Southern economy, leaving it in tatters for over a century.) As the famous Roman politician and orator Cicero once said, *Inter arma silent leges*— "In times of war, the law is silent." To realists like Sherman and Cicero, talk about war crimes is either naïve or just plain stupid. Better to leave talk of law for civilized times.

Realists believe that there is no law or justice to war because there are no rules in armed combat: "All's fair in love and war," to use a cliché. However, on the other extreme are people who reject all sorts of violence and, consequently, believe that any warfare is inherently evil. Usually labeled pacifists, leaders like Mahatma Gandhi, the Dalai Lama, and Martin Luther King, Jr., along with religious groups like the Quakers and Buddhists, have advocated complete nonviolence, saying that any military force, regardless of how necessary it may seem at the time, is unacceptable. Peaceful solutions to conflicts are always possible and nonviolent tactics like civil disobedience and passive resistance are the only permissible way to change an intolerable situation. The decision to commence warfare is always wrong, and once you have decided to start a war, there is no right way to fight it. Hence, both the realists and the pacifists have maintained that justice and war have nothing to do with each other. Realists believe that all war is acceptable because war is "beyond justice"; pacifists believe that it is always inherently unjust. They may fundamentally disagree about the nature of war, but both realists and pacifists agree that in war there is no law and no justice.

However, throughout the history of civilization and in a striking variety of different cultures, lawyers, philosophers, and theologians have sought to articulate a middle ground, distinguishing between legitimate and illegitimate wars and attempting to limit the excessive use of force in combat. These thinkers are part of a tradition commonly known as "just war theory," a line of thought that has adherents among philosophers and theologians of different faiths, perspectives, and cultures. The central claim that just-war theorists make is that both realists and pacifists have a point, but both go too far. War is usually a bad thing but under certain circumstances, it may be justified or even obligatory. And when war does happen, not everything is permitted—there must be some constraints on the conduct of war. These restraints of just-war theory in turn have led to the creation of what we now know as the laws of war.

There have always been codes of war to regulate the behavior of soldiers on the battlefield. While a great deal of these came from Christian and in particular Catholic thinkers,[1] Islam and other traditions have also had a long history of thinking about justice in warfare.[2] The laws of Manu, an ancient Hindu religious text, set out limitations on the use of force for Hindu kings (including a rule that weapons that cause excess pain should note be used).[3] The code of chivalry was used by medieval knights to control certain forms of conduct on the battlefield. Universally, it seems that people have believed war should be limited by some sort of moral principles.

Similarly, laws regulating the conduct of war pre-date the modern religions and modern moral thinking. Rome, for example, had some very strict legal controls on when an army could engage an enemy. Julius Caesar among others was charged by the Roman Senate with engaging in an illegal war in Germany. One rule of ancient warfare was the principle that a city under siege was able to surrender until its defensive walls were breached, after which there was no mercy. While many of these laws were not terribly humane by modern standards (most citizens of a besieged city were either murdered or sold into slavery and their property was taken as plunder by the invading forces), and they were often breached in practice, they nonetheless limited some of the cruelest excesses of ancient warfare. Thus in many places at many different times, the use of force was regulated by certain legal rules.

Just Cause and Just Means

Most just-war theorists distinguish between what they call *just cause* and *just means,* both of which are important for understanding modern war crimes law and the international crime of aggression. Just cause, sometimes referred to by its Latin name *jus ad bellum,* refers to the possible justifications for going to war—when political leaders may legitimately fight each other. Just means, *jus in bello* in Latin, refers to the limits of what soldiers and commanders may do in conducting war. That is, what are the acceptable ways militaries may attempt to win a conflict once it has commenced? For most just war thinkers, these two are disconnected. That is to say that one can fight in an unjust war in a just way and one can fight a just war in an unjust way. Even if a country's leaders began a war illegally (say, to conquer a rival territory), a foot soldier who had nothing to do with this decision is not guilty of violating principles of *jus ad bellum.* It was not illegal in and of itself to fight in the German military during World War II regardless of the fact that Germany was clearly the aggressor in that conflict. Similarly, one can fight for the "good guys" and still commit war crimes. (Allied forces committed many war crimes during the same war.) "Just cause" usually refers to the decisions of political leaders to begin a war. "Just means" usually refers to the tactical decisions of military commanders in battle as well as to the actions of infantrymen and others on the ground.

These moral principles of *jus ad bellum* and *jus in bello* eventually developed into the laws of war that were then enforced by military and civilian courts. Prior to the military tribunal at Nuremberg, there were a number of significant war crimes trials, both domestically and internationally. In 1268, Conradin von Hohenstaufen was executed by Charles of

---

[1] See: Ramsey, Paul (1985) *War and the Christian Conscience. How Shall Modern War Be Conducted Justly?* Durham: Duke University Press.

[2] Kelsay, John (1993) *Islam and War.* Louisville: Westminster/John Knox Press.

[3] Clooney, Francis X. (2003) "Pain but Not Harm: Some Classical Resources toward a Hindu Just War Theory," in Robinson, Paul (ed.) (2003) *Just War in Comparative Perspective.* Burlington: Ashgate.

Anjou (a Sicilian king) for waging an unjust war.[4] In 1474 Peter von Hagenbach was tried by judges representing the states of the Holy Roman Emperor for rape, murder, perjury, and other crimes committed during the course of a military occupation.[5] As was mentioned in Chapter 3, international courts were also proposed for Napoleon, the Ottoman leadership, and Kaiser Wilhelm for either aggression or war crimes. Similarly, the United States and many other states have set up various military tribunals to try prisoners accused of violating the laws of war during various military conflicts. Thus, along with the development of just-war theory and the laws of war, there have been a number of different tribunals charged with punishing those who violate them.

A further significant development related to the laws of war was the creation of the International Committee of the Red Cross (ICRC) in 1859.[6] The ICRC is the principle international nongovernmental organization responsible for helping to uphold the laws of war and to monitor the actions of combatants during wartime. It is famous for remaining neutral in all international conflicts and quietly lobbying governments behind the scenes to change their behavior or policies. (The American Red Cross, the organization that responds to natural disasters around the country, is affiliated with the ICRC but is a separate entity.) The ICRC was founded by Henry Dunant, a Swiss banker who while traveling through northern Italy in 1859, stumbled onto the aftermath of the Battle of Solferino (a military engagement between Austrian and French forces). Dunant was deeply moved by the sight of the wounded and dying, lying in the field abandoned by their compatriots. He organized a group of volunteers to tend to the wounded, wrote of his experiences in a book entitled *A Memory of Solferino* and used it to campaign for the creation of an international organization that would remain strictly neutral but would help care for the sick and wounded on all sides of a conflict. He also campaigned for the first Geneva Convention ("The 1864 Geneva Convention for the Amelioration of the Condition of the Wounded in Armies in the Field")—the first treaty creating norms of international humanitarian law. Through Dunant's work, the ICRC along with the first significant laws of war were created.

The 1864 Geneva Convention was followed by a number of different treaties creating new legal obligations for states engaging in an armed conflict. In 1868, "St. Petersburg Declaration Renouncing the Use . . . of Explosive Projectiles Under 400 Grammes Weight" outlawed the so-called "dum dum bullets" that expand upon contact with the target (thereby grossly magnifying the damage that they cause to their victim). Following this treaty were the 13 Hague Conventions of 1907. Some of these banned certain weapons like asphyxiating gasses. Others set out the rights and duties of neutral states during war, including rules like "Belligerents are forbidden to move troops or convoys of either munitions of war or supplies across the territory of a neutral power (Article 2)," and, "The neutral Power shall supply the interned with the food, clothing, and relief required by humanity (Article 12)." After World War II, the international community created the 1949 Geneva Conventions, which are discussed in detail below, and they serve as the final major source of humanitarian law.

---

[4] Cryer, Robert (2005) *Prosecuting International Crimes: Selectivity and the International Criminal Law Regime.* Cambridge: Cambridge University Press.

[5] Bassiouni, M. Cherif (1999) *Crimes Against Humanity in International Criminal Law.* The Hague: Kluwer Law International.

[6] In the Islamic world, the ICRC is known as the "International Committee of the Red Crescent" and uses the Islamic crescent symbol in lieu of the cross.

While the Geneva Conventions and the other sources of international humanitarian law played a role in turning the moral principles of just-war theory into a legal code, they were largely concerned with *just means*. They had little to say about *just cause,* about when a state could go to war against a perceived enemy. Because the ability to wage war has always been considered one of the basic prerogatives of running a country, states have been less willing to submit this practice to legal scrutiny. It was always a custom of war to denounce the other side as an aggressor, but few people actually believed that it really mattered who started a conflict. War was just a part of power politics: something governments used when other means of getting what they wanted weren't available. This means that the history of the laws around military aggression is much different from that regarding the limits of force within war.

Historically, it was the right of every sovereign state to wage war as it saw fit, and wars were considered a normal part of international relations (the nineteenth-century Prussian military philosopher Carl von Clausewitz famously observed that, "war is simply politics by other means"). However, over the last 100 years or so, a number of different treaties and other developments have banned the waging of aggressive war, and some of these even imposed criminal sanctions on those who initiate such wars. The 1928 General Treaty for the Renunciation of War (more commonly known as the "Kellogg–Briand Pact" or the "Pact of Paris") renounced war as a tool of foreign policy. The signers of the pact "Solemnly declare[d] in the names of their respective peoples that they condemn recourse to war for the solution of international controversies, and renounce it, as an instrument of national policy in their relations with one another." This became the basis for the international prohibition on the use of force in armed conflicts, effectively making aggression no longer an acceptable part of state policy.

The other major sources for principles of just means are the two international organizations that were created after each of the two world wars. The League of Nations, mentioned in Chapter 2, and the UN both have been important for developing the modern laws governing armed conflicts. The framers of both of these international bodies believed that, by setting up political institutions to help resolve conflicts between states, they could replace war with negotiation and political compromise as the means to solve international disputes. As part of this goal, the UN Charter bans war, unless it is committed in self-defense or under the authorization of the UN Security Council (more on this a little later). While the UN has (obviously) not ended war in the modern world, it has been helpful in preventing some major armed conflicts as well as in limiting the scope and intensity of many of the wars that do take place. Most importantly, however, is that it ended the idea that war was a normal, acceptable instrument of international politics.

While it is sounds noble to talk about making war less frequent and less brutal, anybody who studies the laws of war must understand that is also something a little absurd about it. Expecting people to worry about violating a law when their lives or the lives of their families are at stake is a lot to ask. Expecting an army to withhold some of its forces or risking the lives of its troops when they are under enemy fire because of some purported fear of killing enemy civilians or excessively damaging property seems to be naïve. Moreover, many governments openly or secretly break these laws while accusing the others of doing the same thing. In World War I, both sides violated the Hague Conventions and used poison gas against each other. In World War II, many countries developed biological and chemical weapons to use against their enemies. (Ironically, the country with the smallest chemical and biological weapons program during that conflict was Germany.

Hitler had been wounded in a chemical attack during World War I and refused to allow Germany to develop an offensive chemical/biological weapons program.[7]) Terrorist groups, one of America's most dangerous foes, ignore the laws of war and indiscriminately target civilians and soldiers alike and would probably use any weapon they could get their hands on. Many groups use the protective emblems of the Red Cross to conduct secret military operations and otherwise abuse the protections granted by international law. Realities such as these have always given the laws of war and those of aggression an idealistic air.

On the other hand, the laws of war can help prevent *unnecessary* suffering in warfare. That is, when they are followed by all sides of a conflict, they can prevent excesses that do not serve the purposes that war is intended to serve. It is hard to believe that civilians must be made to suffer for the sake of a military conquest, or that weapons should be made more painful than necessary to disable or kill an opponent. Similarly, all sides of a conflict have an interest in making sure that their own prisoners are treated humanely, and one good way to do this is to treat one's own prisoners in a civil way. (At least if one side of a conflict brutalizes and murders their prisoners, they have no reason to complain when their enemies do.) Whether such rules make war more "civilized," or only give it the false appearance of civility, they have become an important part of modern warfare. Moreover, the laws of war have led to numerous prosecutions around the world of those who violate them.

AGGRESSION

While modern international law outlaws aggressive war, and everyone agrees that aggression should not be allowed, the issues surrounding the *crime* of aggression are much more complex than they may initially appear. There are a number of reasons for this: In the real world, determining the aggressor in a particular case often turns out to be very tricky. Few states are completely neutral and international politics often require states to wrestle with each other over the finite amounts of power, territory, and resources. Even countries that are allies can have conflicting political or economic interests that can lead them into conflicts with each other. While governments are quick to denounce the acts of other states as aggression and portray themselves as innocent victims, this is very rarely the case. In most military conflicts, there is plenty of blame on both sides. Second, political leaders (who play a very important role in defining international crimes) are hesitant to allow their decisions to use military force scrutinized by others and fear prosecution for their decisions. This means that political leaders do not have an interest in a clearly defined and enforceable crime of aggression. Finally, there is a distinction between an act of international aggression and the *crime* of aggression that for which a political leader could be prosecuted. A state can be an aggressor without its leaders being criminally liable for it. All of these facts make the international crime of aggression a politically and legally tricky issue.

There are some of the same problems in defining aggression in more mundane situations. In everyday life, we are always confronted with mildly threatening behavior.

---

[7] See Muller, Rolf-Dieter (2003) "Albert Speer and Armaments Policy in Total War," in Muller, Rolf-Dieter, Umbreit, Hans, and Cook-Radmore, Derry (eds) *Germany and the Second World War, Volume 5/II.* Oxford: Oxford University Press. See also the PBS Documentary "The Living Weapon." Available at http://www.pbs.org/wgbh/amex/weapon/.

A person driving by makes an obscene gesture. A person yells an insult at you as you walk across campus. Somebody you don't like makes a vague threat: "Someday I'm going to take care of you." A person gives you a slight push in line. Each of these is in some ways "aggression," but clearly not all of them allow you to use force to defend yourself. Even if you do choose to defend yourself, the border between mere self-defense and criminal assault is a blurry one.

At the international level, this becomes even more complicated. States are always fighting for scarce resources and are constantly challenging each other for influence around the world. Sometimes a state must "throw a few elbows" to get what it wants, and at times this requires skirting the line of aggression. This means that states will sometimes engage in hostile actions that may fall short of a full-scale war, raising further questions about the crime of aggression. Must a state deploy a large military force, or can small-scale military actions be considered aggression? Could economic sanctions or blockades be considered a form of aggression? What about a state funding a rebel organization seeking to undermine the government of another state? Where do you draw the line between aggression and mere hard-nosed politics?

Finding the appropriate description of aggression is a complex legal issue and a number of suggestions have been put forward in order to define it. The matter has been debated for a long time in a number of different contexts and, presently, there is no single international legal definition of aggression or the crime of aggression.[8] Here we will discuss a few of the most significant sources for the law.

UN Charter[9]

As we discussed in Chapter 2, the UN plays an important role in maintaining peace and security around the world. Its founding document, the UN Charter, lays out some of the basic elements of international aggression. One of the UN's central jobs, according to the very first article of the Charter is "To maintain international peace and security, and to that end: to take effective collective measures for the prevention and removal of threats to the peace, and for the suppression of acts of aggression or other breaches of the peace . . ."[10] While its aim is to find peaceful solutions, the UN also recognizes that there are limits to its power to prevent sovereign states from using their militaries—it is not a "world government" with any kind of monopoly over the use of force. For example, Article 51 of the Charter allows states to use force in self-defense ("Nothing in the present Charter shall impair the inherent right of individual or collective self-defence if an armed attack occurs against a Member of the United Nations.") but it says little about which wars are defensive and which aren't. Specifically, the concept of self-defense is ambiguous and hard to apply in real-world situations. Frequently, leaders believe that they are under direct threat from

---

[8] See Politi, Mauro and Nesi, Giuseppe (eds) (2004) *The International Criminal Court and the Crime of Aggression.* Burlington: Ashgate Publishing and Thomas, Ann Van Wynen (1972) *The Concept of Aggression in International Law.* Dallas: Southern Methodist University Press.

[9] For a more in-depth account of the UN Charter and the use of force, see Arend, Anthony Clark and Beck, Robert J. (1993) *International Law & the Use of Force.* New York: Routledge Press, pp. 29–68.

[10] UN Charter, Article 1(1).

another state and therefore feel compelled to strike first in what is sometimes called *anticipatory self-defense.*[11] Alternatively, states could strike before a threat develops, seeking to stop a potential problem before it can manifest itself. This is often called *preemptive self-defense,* and it was used by the United States to justify its invasion of Iraq in 2003 (more on this later). Under some definitions of aggression, both of these could be considered a crime.[12] Alternatively, "humanitarian intervention," the use of force by one state in order to rescue people who are being brutally murdered by the government of another state, could be considered aggression under some circumstances.[13] Once you look beneath the surface, then, the crime of aggression becomes a significantly more complex matter than it would seem at first glance.

UN General Assembly

The United Nations General Assembly (which, as we saw in Chapter 2, is not an international legislature, but can nonetheless be a useful guide on certain legal matters) sought to define aggression in 1974 through General Assembly Resolution 3314. This resolution defines aggression as "The use of armed force by a State against the sovereignty, territorial integrity or political independence of another State, or in any other manner inconsistent with the Charter of the United Nations, as set out in this Definition." In Article 3 of the resolution, the General Assembly goes into further detail about the specific acts that constitute aggression:

   a. The invasion or attack by the armed forces of a State of the territory of another State, or any military occupation, however temporary, resulting from such invasion or attack, or any annexation by the use of force of the territory of another State or part thereof;

---

[11] The most well-known example of this is the *Caroline* case of 1837. In order to stop a rebel movement in Canada, British forces snuck into the United States to attack a rebel ship anchored there. British troops set the ship *The Caroline* on fire and sent it over Niagara falls, prompting US retaliation. The matter was resolved, and the correspondence surrounding the case established that states may only resort to anticipatory self-defense if the threat is, "instant, overwhelming, leaving no choice of means, and no moment for deliberation" (See Arend and Beck, *International Law and the Use of Force,* pp. 71–80.)

[12] Arend, Anthony Clark (2003) "International Law and the Preemptive Use of Military Force," *The Washington Quarterly,* Spring, Vol. 26, No. 2, 89–103.

[13] The legality of humanitarian intervention under international law is a very controversial issue and the subject of a great deal of debate. In 1999, the United States and its NATO allies began a targeted bombing campaign against the government of Yugoslavia in order to force an end to violence in the Yugoslav territory of Kosovo. As they did this without authorization of the Security Council or without being attacked themselves, it was denounced by many as a form of aggression. This is just one of numerous examples of countries using force, either unilaterally (by themselves) or multilaterally (with others) to stop atrocities in another country. For more on humanitarian intervention, see Brownlie, Ian (1973) "Thoughts on Kind-Hearted Gunmen," in Lillich, Richard B. (ed.) *Humanitarian Intervention and the United Nations.* Richmond: University of Virginia Press. For a more detailed discussion of the NATO intervention in Kosovo, see a special issue of *The American Journal of International Law* devoted to the topic: Vol. 93, No. 4, October. 1999.

b. Bombardment by the armed forces of a State against the territory of another State or the use of any weapons by a State against the territory of another State;

c. The blockade of the ports or coasts of a State by the armed forces of another State;

d. An attack by the armed forces of a State on the land, sea or air forces, or marine and air fleets of another State;

e. The use of armed forces of one State which are within the territory of another State with the agreement of the receiving State, in contravention of the conditions provided for in the agreement or any extension of their presence in such territory beyond the termination of the agreement;

f. The action of a State in allowing its territory, which it has placed at the disposal of another State, to be used by that other State for perpetrating an act of aggression against a third State;

g. The sending by or on behalf of a State of armed bands, groups, irregulars or mercenaries, which carry out acts of armed force against another State of such gravity as to amount to the acts listed above, or its substantial involvement therein.

This definition would presumably exclude economic sanctions or any non-military forms of aggression.[14] Again, however, this resolution is not a law, although in a case involving American support of Nicaraguan anti-communist guerillas the ICJ found that parts of this resolution are customary international law.

UN Security Council

The UN Security Council is authorized under Article 39 of its own Charter to determine "The existence of any threat to the peace, breach of the peace, or act of aggression and shall make recommendations, or decide what measures shall be taken . . . to maintain or restore international peace and security." The Council can also authorize states to use military force or other means in order to counter the aggression. This means that a political body (the Council), not a legal one, can determine when an act of aggression has been committed. The fact that it is a political body means that it need not concern itself with being consistent or impartial in its findings regarding aggression. Aggressive acts by states that are friendly to Security Council members may find their behavior ignored while unfriendly states will not be so lucky. As we discussed in Chapter 2, the Security Council can impose obligations over states, but it is a fractious body where the world's most powerful states are often more interested in protecting their interests than in upholding the rule of law in the international sphere or punishing aggressive states. The Security Council has authorized the use of force in response to aggression only twice: The North Korean invasion of South Korea in 1948 and the Iraqi invasion of Kuwait in 1991. This means that it is an unreliable means to determine aggression.

---

[14] However, it should be noted that states can still legally use force in self-defense or under the authority of the Security Council. For a criticism of the General Assembly's definition, see Stone, Julius (1977) "Hopes and Loopholes in the 1974 Definition of Aggression," *The American Journal of International Law,* Vol. 71, No. 2, 224–246.

CRIMINAL AGGRESSION

As I said above, there is a difference between an act of aggression and the *crime* of aggression, although the two are obviously connected. To add to the confusion, alongside the ambiguity regarding the definition of acts of aggression, there is likewise no settled definition of the crime of aggression. As was mentioned in Chapter 3, the international criminal court may only prosecute individuals for criminal aggression, "Once a provision is adopted . . . defining the crime and setting out the conditions under which the Court shall exercise jurisdiction with respect to this [it]."[15] A great number of legal scholars have labored to give further definition of the crime so that the court can eventually prosecute offenders, but there is no final answer at this point.

The International Law Commission (a body that is responsible for helping clarify some of the more obscure parts of international law) defined the crime of aggression in 1996. There they defined an "aggressor" as

> An individual who, as leader or organizer, actively participates in or orders the planning, preparation, initiation or waging of aggression committed by a State, shall be responsible for a crime of aggression.

While this definition is not very helpful (if only because it includes the term that is supposed to be defined within the definition), it does link the *crime* of aggression with the other definitions of aggression that we've discussed above. More helpful than this, however, are the various international tribunals that have been forced to define the crime for the purposes of prosecution.

Nuremberg

As of the present, the only people to be prosecuted for the crime of military aggression were the Nazi leaders at Nuremberg and the Japanese leaders in Tokyo at the end of the World War II. In Nuremberg and Tokyo, the definitions of aggression used were basically the same. The defendants in these cases were charged with the "planning, preparation, initiation or waging of a war of aggression, which were also wars in violation of international treaties, agreements, and assurances."[16] (Notice that this definition criminalizes not only the act of aggression, but also the *planning* of such an act even if it is not carried out.) This charge was in part justified by reference to the Kellogg–Briand Pact, but nonetheless many people were skeptical about it, maintaining that it was unfair to prosecute somebody for something that was not clearly criminal at the time that the act was committed.[17] However problematic this charge was in these courts, the prosecutions set a precedent that aggressive wars could be considered a criminal offense in international law and violators could be punished. (We should also note that this definition is specific to the Nuremberg Tribunal but could be considered a part of customary international law by future courts.)

---

[15] Article 5(2).

[16] Nuremberg Trial Proceedings Indictment. Through the Avalon Project at Yale Law School. Available at http://www.yale.edu/lawweb/avalon/imt/proc/count1.htm.

[17] For an extended study of the crime of aggression at Nuremberg, see Harris, Whitney (1954) *Tyranny on Trial.* Dallas: Southern Methodist University Press.

When the ICC statute went into effect in 2002, the court established the "Working Group on the Crime of Aggression," which was meant to further discussion on the matter, and in 2009, the ICC will hold a review conference that will help give the crime a more specific definition. Until then the court cannot prosecute anybody for the crime of aggression.

The U.S. Invasion of Iraq: Aggression, Self-Defense, or Something Else?

"Operation Iraqi Freedom," the American-led invasion of Iraq in 2003 was one of the most controversial acts of American foreign policy in the country's history. Many in the United States as well as in the international community claimed that President Bush's decision to invade had undermined the foundations of the post-World War II international order, replacing law with military force as the primary means for settling international disputes. Some critics went even further, suggesting that the invasion was illegal and claiming that President Bush and his main ally, British Prime Minister Tony Blair, were "war criminals."[18] On the other side, the defenders of the president and of the war asserted not only that the war was legal and justified, but further suggested that the president's decision to invade ultimately helped to strengthen the international order. Saddam Hussein was a threat to global peace, they charged, and had to be removed for the sake of national and international security as well as for the sake of the oppressed Iraqi people. Since the invasion, the ensuing insurgency and low level civil war have only heightened the controversy surrounding the decision to invade Iraq.

Whatever the political issues that the war in Iraq raised, we can see that *legally*, the question of whether or not President Bush is a war criminal is a more complicated issue than the rhetoric might lead one to believe. More importantly for us, it provides a useful case to look at the complexities of the use of force and the crime of aggression in international criminal law. As I suggested above, these laws are both controversial and undeveloped in international law in general and international criminal law in particular. Briefly, here, I will evaluate Operation Iraqi Freedom, focusing on the legal issues regarding the use of force, the crime of aggression, and war crimes that we have discussed above.

The legal bases asserted by the U.S. government for the invasion of Iraq were threefold: First, the administration argued that the Security Council authorized the use of force in Security Council Resolution 1441, which ordered that if the Iraqi government did not comply with the requests of UN weapons inspectors, they would "face serious consequences." Thus, the United States and its allies were entitled to use force as part of the Security Council's Chapter VII powers—its duty to maintain international peace and security. However, the Security Council uses specific phrases in its resolutions when it authorizes forces. A resolution will authorize states to use "any means necessary" in a particular context if the Council wishes to allow the legal use of force. This phrase was not used in Resolution 1441.

The second justification for the use of force in Iraq reached back to the 1991 Gulf War and is sometimes called the "revival argument." There, in two separate resolutions, the Security Council authorized the use of force against Iraq in relation to its invasion of Kuwait. The U.S. government argued that these resolutions continued to authorize force against Iraq and thus they justified Operation Iraqi Freedom. However, this is a highly controversial reading of these resolutions and the only governments that accepted this claim were the United

---

[18] See, for example, the so-called "World Tribunal on Iraq."

States and the UK. Resolution 678 did authorize the use of force against Iraq, but it was limited by a previous resolution, Resolution 660, to the goal of removing Iraq from Kuwait. (It was Iraq's invasion of neighboring Kuwait in August, 1990 that touched off the first Gulf War.) Thus, even if Resolution 678 was still valid, this did not entail that the invasion of Iraq in 2003 was legal. Whatever problems the government of Saddam Hussein was creating, Iraq was no longer in Kuwait, and thus force was no longer necessary to remove it.

The final legal argument for the use of force in Iraq was the inherent right of states to defend themselves. That is, the invasion of Iraq was justified because it possessed weapons of mass destruction that required the United States to defend itself by invading that nation. Article 51 of the UN Charter does not require that a state receive permission from the UN Security Council in order to defend itself—it says that this is an "inherent" right of the states. This means that the United States could argue that the threat Iraq posed justified the use of force. However, it is clear that in 2003 Iraq had neither commenced an armed attack against the United States nor planned to commence one any time in the immediate future. Further, the concept of preemptive self-defense—the claim that a government may use force against a nation that *could* pose a threat in the future, but does not pose one now—is not looked upon favorably in contemporary international law. Such arguments were used by the German leaders at Nuremberg to justify their invasion of Norway (to preempt a British invasion) and by Israel in attacking the Iraqi nuclear power plant at Osirak in 1981. The Security Council, including the generally pro-Israel United States, rebuked Israel for the attack in the Osirak case by passing Resolution 487 which condemned the attack, and in the case of Germany, the Nuremberg Tribunal rejected the defense argument because no such attack was imminent.[19] The traditional rule of international law is that a threat must be imminent for a state to have a right to use force in self-defense and there is no acceptance of preemptive self-defense.

However, even if the war in Iraq was not legal under the UN Charter, this does not mean that President Bush is a war criminal or that he is guilty of the crime of aggression. As we will soon see, a war criminal is somebody who commits a grave breach of the laws of war, *not* somebody who commits the crime of aggression. What one would have to show in order to prove that the president was a war criminal was that some grave breaches of international humanitarian law were committed in Iraq and that the president bears responsibility for them. Thus, if the president had authorized the use of unlawful weapons (such as biological weapons) against insurgents or authorized the torture of prisoners of war, he could rightly be considered a war criminal. On the other hand, to show that he committed aggression, a lawyer would have to show that Operation Iraqi Freedom was aggression according to the definitions of this crime that were discussed in the previous section. It may be aggression according to General Assembly Resolution 3314, but as we've already seen, this resolution itself isn't law. If the Security Council is the only body capable of determining that an act of aggression has taken place, then it is up to this body to determine whether Operation Iraqi Freedom was an act of aggression. Until they do that, an unlikely possibility given the fact that the United States can veto any Security Council Resolution, it is difficult to say that this conflict was *criminal* aggression even if it was an unlawful use of force, much less a war crime.

Operation Iraqi Freedom and the ensuing occupation of Iraq lay bare the complexities of international criminal law and their relation to international law more generally. Just

---

[19] Drumbl, Mark A. (2003) "Self-Defense and the Use of Force: Breaking the Rules, Making the Rules, or Both?" *International Studies Perspectives,* 4, 409–431, at 422.

because some act violates international law does not mean that it is a crime (just like a violation of a contract is not a crime in American law). Second, an act may be unlawful but not necessarily unjust or undesirable. Removing Saddam Hussein from power *may* have been the best thing for Iraqis, even if the invasion was illegal. (It will probably be a long time before this issue can be settled.) Third, it shows how, at the international level, law and politics are often intertwined: Any attempt to argue that the war was unlawful is sure to be branded "political" in American public debate regardless of the legal merits of the argument. Finally, it shows how casually terms such as *war criminal* may be used in heated political debate, but how these terms in their legal context are much more complex and their use requires a good deal more care than they are usually given on television news or on angry web pages. Whether or not the U.S.-led invasion of Iraq was an imprudent or unjust decision is an important question for American public discussion. However, it is a significantly different matter to determine that the war was illegal and even more complex to determine whether or not this putative illegality act makes President Bush a *criminal*.

WAR CRIMES

A *war crime* is defined as a grave breach of the laws of war. While war has always been a violent and unpleasant experience, over the centuries a set of rules and principles have developed to regulate the behavior of soldiers and civilians both on and off the battlefield. These rules governing the conduct of warfare are commonly known as the laws of war (or more technically, *international humanitarian law*). The most celebrated source of the laws of war are the four Geneva Conventions of 1949, but there are other important sources of international humanitarian law that are not as well known. For example, the laws of war have a long tradition as customary international law.[20] During the Civil War, Abraham Lincoln commissioned the first major code of military conduct on the battlefield. Known as the "Lieber Code" after the Columbia University Professor who wrote it, this was the first effort to write down what were previously the customary rules governing the laws of war. Through the twentieth century, progressively more aspects of the laws of war were developed by scholars and written into texts of treaties. These laws not only touch upon the treatment of civilians, soldiers, and the sick and wounded, but also restrict the types of arms that may be used in armed conflict and the types of tactics that can be used on the battlefield—banning the use of chemical and biological weapons, for example.

The Geneva and Hague Conventions

There are many treaties that contribute to international humanitarian law. The primary treaties, however, are the Hague Conventions of 1899 and 1907 and the Geneva Conventions of 1949. The Hague Conventions limit the types of weapons that may be used in warfare (banning exploding bullets and asphyxiating gasses) and outline some of the limits of naval warfare. The Geneva Conventions are much more comprehensive, limiting the

---

[20] See: Alvermann, Carolin, et al. (2005) *Customary International Humanitarian Law.* Cambridge: Cambridge University Press.

conduct of combatants on the battlefield toward each other and toward civilians. There are four different Geneva Conventions, each detailing one aspect of the laws of war. They are:

1. The Amelioration of the Condition of the Wounded and Sick in Armed Forces in the Field.
2. The Amelioration of the Condition of Wounded, Sick and Shipwrecked Members of Armed Forces at Sea.
3. Relative to the Treatment of Prisoners of War.
4. Relative to the Protection of Civilian Persons in Time of War.

Along with these treaties, there are two "Optional Protocols" to the Geneva Conventions that were formulated in 1977 that help further detail the laws of war. One sets out the rules that limit the conduct of *non-international* conflicts such as civil wars and the other expands on the rules governing international conflicts, including special rules to help protect journalists, women, and children in wartime.

There are two important points to make about war crimes: First, though it may seem trivial to point this out, war crimes require that there be an actual war happening at the time that they are committed, that is, there must be an armed conflict taking place. These same acts are not war crimes when committed in times of peace. (As we will see in the next chapter, many of these acts would be considered crimes against humanity if they were committed in peacetime.) Second, not every violation of the laws of war is a war crime. A soldier who steals a loaf of bread from a civilian is not a war criminal although they have violated the laws of war. For a violation to constitute a war crime, the violation must be a "grave breach" of the laws of war—a severe violation of the standards of human decency.

While each Geneva Convention deals with different aspects of the laws of war, they all share one article: the third. "Common Article 3" as it is known deals with noninternational conflicts, such as civil wars. In this article, the states that are a party to the treaty agree that

> Persons taking no active part in the hostilities, including members of armed forces who have laid down their arms and those placed hors de combat ("out of the fight"-ed) by sickness, wounds, detention, or any other cause, shall in all circumstances be treated humanely, without any adverse distinction founded on race, colour, religion or faith, sex, birth or wealth, or any other similar criteria.[21]

Military lawyers have referred to Common Article 3 as a "mini treaty" setting out the core principles of international humanitarian law and making them applicable in every

---

[21] Common Article 3 goes further:
1. To this end, the following acts are and shall remain prohibited at any time and in any place whatsoever with respect to the above-mentioned persons:
   (a) violence to life and person, in particular murder of all kinds, mutilation, cruel treatment and torture;
   (b) taking of hostages;
   (c) outrages upon personal dignity, in particular humiliating and degrading treatment;
   (d) the passing of sentences and the carrying out of executions without previous judgement pronounced by a regularly constituted court, affording all the judicial guarantees which are recognized as indispensable by civilized peoples.
2. The wounded and sick shall be collected and cared for. An impartial humanitarian body, such as the International Committee of the Red Cross, may offer its services to the Parties to the conflict.

armed conflict. This article became significant in relation to the war on terror when the Supreme Court relied on it to rule against the legitimacy of military tribunals for alleged terrorists at Guantanamo Bay, Cuba in *Hamdan* v. *Rumsfeld*. (We will discuss this case when we examine the war on terror in later chapters.)

In their texts, the Geneva Conventions specifically label certain acts as grave breaches of the laws of war and thus, war crimes. Here is a list of some of the most common war crimes set out in the Geneva Conventions[22]:

Geneva Convention I, Article 50

. . . wilful killing, torture or inhuman treatment [of enemy wounded], including biological experiments, wilfully causing great suffering or serious injury to body or health, and extensive destruction and appropriation of property, not justified by military necessity and carried out unlawfully and wantonly.[23]

Geneva Convention III, Article 130

. . . wilful killing, torture or inhuman treatment, including biological experiments [of prisoners of war], wilfully causing great suffering or serious injury to body or health, compelling a prisoner of war to serve in the forces of the hostile Power,[24] or wilfully depriving a prisoner of war of the rights of fair and regular trial prescribed in this Convention.

Geneva Convention IV, Article 147

. . . wilful killing, torture or inhuman treatment [of civilians], including biological experiments, wilfully causing great suffering or serious injury to body or health, unlawful deportation or transfer or unlawful confinement of a protected person,[25] compelling a protected person to serve in the forces of a hostile Power, or wilfully depriving a protected person of the rights of fair and regular trial prescribed in the present Convention, taking of hostages and extensive destruction and appropriation of property, not justified by military necessity and carried out unlawfully and wantonly.

Additional Protocol 1, Article 85

. . . The following acts shall be regarded as grave breaches of this Protocol, when committed wilfully, in violation of the relevant provisions of this Protocol, and causing death or serious injury to body or health:

a. making the civilian population or individual civilians the object of attack;
b. launching an indiscriminate attack affecting the civilian population or civilian objects in the knowledge that such attack will cause excessive loss of life, injury to civilians or damage to civilian objects . . .
c. launching an attack against works or installations containing dangerous forces in the knowledge that such attack will cause excessive loss of life, injury to civilians or damage to civilian objects . . .

---

[22] This list is taken from the ICRC. (Available at http://www.icrc.org/Web/Eng/siteeng0.nsf/html/5ZMGF9.)

[23] Geneva Convention II includes an identical Article applying to wounded or shipwrecked combatants.

[24] That is, in the military of the state that is engaged in war.

[25] In this context, a civilian.

d. making non-defended localities and demilitarized zones the object of attack;

e. making a person the object of attack in the knowledge that he is hors de combat;

f. the perfidious use...of the distinctive emblem of the red cross, red crescent or red lion and sun or of other protective signs recognized by the Conventions or this Protocol.

Additionally . . .

a. the transfer by the occupying Power of parts of its own civilian population into the territory it occupies, or the deportation or transfer of all or parts of the population of the occupied territory within or outside this territory, in violation of Article 49 of the Fourth Convention;

b. unjustifiable delay in the repatriation of prisoners of war or civilians;

c. practices of apartheid and other inhuman and degrading practices involving outrages upon personal dignity, based on racial discrimination;

d. making the clearly-recognized historic monuments, works of art or places of worship which constitute the cultural or spiritual heritage of peoples and to which special protection has been given by special arrangement, for example, within the framework of a competent international organization, the object of attack, causing as a result extensive destruction thereof, where there is no evidence of the violation by the adverse Party of Article 53, subparagraph (b), and when such historic monuments, works of art and places of worship are not located in the immediate proximity of military objectives;

e. depriving a person protected by the Conventions or referred to in paragraph 2 of this Article of the rights of fair and regular trial.

There are others listed in the Geneva Conventions, but these are the most significant ones. Some, you may notice, are quite vague (such as the crime of "unlawful confinement") and lack the detail and clarity that one finds in domestic criminal law. To a certain extent, the international and domestic courts that apply the Geneva Conventions can give these laws greater specificity through their rulings.

The International Criminal Court   Along with incorporating the two sets of Geneva Conventions into its definition of war crimes, the statute of the International Criminal Court expands and greatly enhances the definition of such crimes. Article 8(2) of the Rome Statute includes 26 different war crimes, some of which are mentioned in other places, but many of which are novel to the court. Here is a list of these crimes that the ICC labels "war crimes":

i. Intentionally directing attacks against the civilian population as such or against individual civilians not taking direct part in hostilities;

ii. Intentionally directing attacks against civilian objects, that is, objects which are not military objectives;

iii. Intentionally directing attacks against personnel, installations, material, units or vehicles involved in a humanitarian assistance or peacekeeping mission in accordance with the Charter of the United Nations, as long as they are entitled to the protection given to civilians or civilian objects under the international law of armed conflict;

iv. Intentionally launching an attack in the knowledge that such attack will cause incidental loss of life or injury to civilians or damage to civilian objects or widespread, long-term and severe damage to the natural environment which would be clearly excessive in relation to the concrete and direct overall military advantage anticipated;

v. Attacking or bombarding, by whatever means, towns, villages, dwellings or buildings which are undefended and which are not military objectives;

vi. Killing or wounding a combatant who, having laid down his arms or having no longer means of defence, has surrendered at discretion;

vii. Making improper use of a flag of truce, of the flag or of the military insignia and uniform of the enemy or of the United Nations, as well as of the distinctive emblems of the Geneva Conventions, resulting in death or serious personal injury;

viii. The transfer, directly or indirectly, by the Occupying Power of parts of its own civilian population into the territory it occupies, or the deportation or transfer of all or parts of the population of the occupied territory within or outside this territory;

ix. Intentionally directing attacks against buildings dedicated to religion, education, art, science or charitable purposes, historic monuments, hospitals and places where the sick and wounded are collected, provided they are not military objectives;

x. Subjecting persons who are in the power of an adverse party to physical mutilation or to medical or scientific experiments of any kind which are neither justified by the medical, dental or hospital treatment of the person concerned nor carried out in his or her interest, and which cause death to or seriously endanger the health of such person or persons;

xi. Killing or wounding treacherously individuals belonging to the hostile nation or army;

xii. Declaring that no quarter[26] will be given;

xiii. Destroying or seizing the enemy's property unless such destruction or seizure be imperatively demanded by the necessities of war;

xiv. Declaring abolished, suspended or inadmissible in a court of law the rights and actions of the nationals of the hostile party;

xv. Compelling the nationals of the hostile party to take part in the operations of war directed against their own country, even if they were in the belligerent's service before the commencement of the war;

xvi. Pillaging a town or place, even when taken by assault;

xvii. Employing poison or poisoned weapons;

xviii. Employing asphyxiating, poisonous or other gases, and all analogous liquids, materials or devices;

xix. Employing bullets which expand or flatten easily in the human body, such as bullets with a hard envelope which does not entirely cover the core or is pierced with incisions;

xx. Employing weapons, projectiles and material and methods of warfare which are of a nature to cause superfluous injury or unnecessary suffering or which are inherently indiscriminate in violation of the international law of armed conflict, provided that such weapons, projectiles and material and methods of warfare are the subject of a comprehensive prohibition and are included in an annex to this Statute, by an amendment in accordance with the relevant provisions set forth in articles 121 and 123;

---

[26] "No quarter" means that no prisoners will be taken in combat.

xxi. Committing outrages upon personal dignity, in particular humiliating and degrading treatment;

xxii. Committing rape, sexual slavery, enforced prostitution, forced pregnancy, . . . enforced sterilization, or any other form of sexual violence also constituting a grave breach of the Geneva Conventions;

xxiii. Utilizing the presence of a civilian or other protected person to render certain points, areas or military forces immune from military operations;

xxiv. Intentionally directing attacks against buildings, material, medical units and transport, and personnel using the distinctive emblems of the Geneva Conventions in conformity with international law;

xxv. Intentionally using starvation of civilians as a method of warfare by depriving them of objects indispensable to their survival, including wilfully impeding relief supplies as provided for under the Geneva Conventions;

xxvi. Conscripting or enlisting children under the age of fifteen years into the national armed forces or using them to participate actively in hostilities.

Along with these international definitions of war crimes, the Uniform Code of Military Justice (UCMJ), the set of laws that apply to members of the U.S. military, lists several of these acts as punishable by court martial. These include rape, murder, theft, arson, and "cruelty and maltreatment." Any American soldier who violates these laws can be prosecuted and punished by the U.S. military with punishments that include the death penalty for the most extreme violations. Moreover, most modern military forces have specific "Rules of Engagement" (ROE) that determine when a soldier should use force and when he should refrain from doing so. These are often encapsulated in small cards that soldiers may carry with them into battle.

Why Do People Commit War Crimes?

Of course, this is a difficult question to answer. As we've already discussed, the stress of combat and the fog of war mean that people aren't always thinking clearly when they murder civilians or commit other vile acts in the heat of battle—they are often acting from rage or fear more than from deliberation or reason. Similarly, war to some extent requires that soldiers demonize or dehumanize their enemy, making it seem like enemy lives don't matter and you can do anything you'd like to them. In order to kill another person, particularly a stranger, you have to have a different attitude toward them than you would toward somebody you know. Their feelings and their fear of death must be irrelevant for you to get the job done. (In order to foster this view of the enemy, they are often referred to by degrading nicknames and robbed of their essential humanity.) It's only natural then that this view of the enemy would not stop when they have surrendered and would likewise extend to innocent civilians. When soldiers are frequently exposed to killing and bloodshed, they are bound to become desensitized to violence and to the suffering of others and not recognize the traditional limits of acceptable conduct. This anger and propensity to violence can be magnified when a comrade has been wounded or killed in combat. Finally, many military commanders regard the laws of war as essentially meaningless and thus don't feel inclined to order their troops to follow them and many soldiers on the ground feel similarly. All of these forces work together to make warfare one of the most dangerous places to be for both combatants and noncombatants alike.

One additional key to the puzzle was detailed in the famous obedience study conducted by Stanley Milgram in the early 1960s. Milgram conducted an experiment where he duped his subjects into giving others what they believed were lethal amounts of electricity simply because they had been ordered to by someone reportedly in charge. The subject of the experiment believed that he was an assistant to a study on memory when he was in fact the person being studied. He was instructed by the "researcher" to shock the "subject" (actually, an actor)—to administer electric shocks (again, not real) to the actor. Under orders from the researcher, the subjects were willing to administer doses of electricity that were labeled "Danger: Severe Shock." Few of the subjects of the experiment refused to administer the allegedly dangerous dosage of electricity.[27] The point of Milgram's study is that when they are ordered to do so by somebody who they accept as their superior, many otherwise normal people are willing to kill another human being. Add to Milgram's finding regarding obedience the chaos, fear, and stress of combat (along with the military's emphasis on obedience) and it is easy to see how civilians and other innocents are often deliberately killed in warfare.

The German social philosopher Hannah Arendt was an observer at the trial, in Israel, of Adolph Eichmann, one of the primary officials responsible for the annihilation of the Jews during the Holocaust. She published her observations on Eichmann, his prosecution, and ultimate execution in a now famous book entitled *Eichmann in Jerusalem: On the Banality of Evil*. What surprised Arendt about Eichmann was that he was not an obviously evil, insane, or fanatical individual, the type of person one would expect to be willing to order the murder of millions. Rather, he was in many ways an ordinary person living an ordinary life. As Arendt herself describes it:

> Eichmann was no Iago or no Macbeth . . . Except for an extraordinary diligence in looking out for his personal advancement, he had no motives at all . . . He *merely,* to put the matter colloquially, *never realized what he was doing. . . .* He was not stupid. It was sheer thoughtlessness—something by no means identical with stupidity—that predisposed him to become one of the greatest criminals of that period. . . . That such remoteness from reality and such thoughtlessness can wreak more havoc than all the evil instincts taken together which, perhaps, are inherent in man—that was, in fact, the lesson one could learn in Jerusalem.[28]

His evil is "banal" because he was an ordinary, unthinking person who simply went about his day doing what he was supposed to do. It just so happened that what he was supposed to do was mass murder. Like Milgram's subjects, Arendt's study of Eichmann shows that a great many otherwise ordinary people are capable of committing incomprehensible atrocities.

Clearly, war crimes are a unique type of crime committed in unique circumstances, although the people who commit them are often otherwise quite ordinary. However, despite its obvious importance, at present the criminological study of war crimes still remains largely undeveloped.[29]

---

[27] The results of Milgram's experiment were originally published in *Journal of Abnormal and Social Psychology,* 1963, Vol. 67, No. 4, 371–378.

[28] Arendt, Hannah (1994) *Eichmann in Jerusalem: A Report on the Banality of Evil.* New York: Penguin. For a similar study on the *Einsatzgruppen,* see Browning, Christopher (1998) *Ordinary Men: Reserve Police Battalion 101 and the Final Solution in Poland.* New York: Harper Perennial.

[29] Hagan, John, Schoenfeld, Heather, and Palloni Alberto (2006) "The Science of Human Rights, War Crimes, and Humanitarian Emergencies," *Annual Review of Sociology,* Vol. 32, 329–349.

COMMAND RESPONSIBILITY AND SUPERIOR ORDERS: THE CASE OF MY LAI

On March 16, 1968, First Lieutenant William Calley and C Company of the 11th Infantry Brigade (Task Force Barker) of the U.S. Army entered the village of My Lai in southern Vietnam. They had been taking sniper fire from this area and several members of their unit had been killed recently, including a beloved officer who died in a Viet Cong booby trap a few days earlier. Calley and his unit had been told by their commanding officer Captain Ernest Medina that the village was clear of civilians and that they were to completely destroy the village, which they believed was being used by the Viet Cong as a base to conduct operations against American troops. The details of C Company's orders were unclear. They were to destroy the village, but, "You must use common sense," Medina warned. "If they have a weapon and are trying to engage you, then you can shoot back, but you must use common sense." However, according to Calley's later testimony, Medina said that they were to kill everyone in the village and leave no survivors.

C Company entered the village of My Lai at approximately 9 AM. By the time they took a lunch break at 11:00, the company had killed approximately 500 unarmed men, women, and children. As they rounded up civilians, Calley claimed that he received two radio messages from Medina (who was in an operations center outside of the village) making sure that the company killed everyone in the village. They began shooting the civilians shortly thereafter, and many American troops reportedly took great pleasure in their work. Some of the women had been raped, sodomized, and had their vaginas ripped open with knives. Infants were bayoneted. Many of the civilians were lined up in a ditch and shot so that their bodies fell into piles. Calley himself unloaded on a group of villagers and when the dust cleared and there were still children standing, he walked over to the children and shot them dead with his pistol. According to reports, no shots were ever fired on American forces that day.

Despite a military effort to cover up the massacre at My Lai, eventually word leaked to the public about the murdered villagers and Calley and Medina were ultimately court marshaled. In his defense, Calley asserted that he was only following orders as the army had trained him to do. Similarly, Medina's defense was that he was not aware of what was being done under his command and that he did not authorize the atrocities.

The infamous "My Lai Massacre" raises a number of important issues in relation to the laws of war and the laws of war crimes. War crimes are almost always committed by a member of the armed forces working within a military hierarchy: There is somebody superior allegedly ordering some crime to be committed and there is somebody who is following these orders and carrying out the criminal act. Under the stress of normal combat it is essential that soldiers follow their commanding officers without question. It is also essential that soldiers show a certain degree of independent initiative, not expecting their commanding officers to direct their every single movement on and off the battlefield. When officers order their troops to massacre civilians or soldiers independently commit atrocities under the noses of their commanding officers (or with their tacit consent), determining criminal liability is sometimes an extremely difficult task.

Calley's defense that he was only carrying out the orders of a superior officer is frequently referred to as the *superior orders* defense and it has often been used by individuals accused of war crimes. Many Germans made a similar argument after World War II when they sought to evade responsibility for their war crimes claiming that they were only following the orders of their leader. In most cases, following superior orders is not an acceptable defense in international criminal law unless the order is not clearly illegal. As the Military Court of Appeals ruled in Calley's case:

> The acts of a subordinate done in compliance with an unlawful order given him by his superior are excused and impose no criminal liability upon him unless the superior's order is one which a man of *ordinary sense and understanding* would, under the circumstances, know to be unlawful, or if the order in question is actually known to the accused to be unlawful.

Because anybody "of ordinary sense and understanding" would recognize that an order to murder unarmed women and children was unlawful, Calley could not claim that he was merely following orders.

Medina claimed that he did not order the killings and he did not know what happened in the village, despite the fact that he was positioned just outside of it. However, in many cases, officers bear legal responsibility for the behavior of those they command regardless of whether they ordered it directly. This is known as *command responsibility* (or sometimes "superior responsibility"). Different courts have interpreted this form of criminal liability in different ways. For example, some courts have said that a commanding officer is only responsible for those criminal acts that he explicitly ordered his troops to commit. Others have maintained that a commanding officer is responsible for *everything* that happens under their command. Some rulings have landed somewhere in the middle: arguing that commanders bear responsibility either for what they knew was happening under their command (but may not have explicitly ordered) or what they didn't know about but, as a commanding officer, they should have been aware of. There is no clear, uniform standard for command responsibility, but given that individuals serving in the military will perpetrate the vast majority of international crimes, there is an important need to clearly define the limits of command responsibility in international criminal law.

One strong version of command responsibility was set out by the American Supreme Court in the post-World War II case of the Japanese general Tomoyuki Yamashita. The general had been sentenced to death for crimes committed under his command while the Japanese occupied the Philippine Islands. After a trial in Manila, Yamashita was sentenced to death but appealed his case, arguing that he neither committed the war crimes committed by Japanese forces himself nor ordered them. Nonetheless, in its opinion on the case (entitled *In Re Yamashita*) the U.S. Supreme Court denied Yamashita's appeal and ruled that he was responsible for the acts of those committed under his command regardless of whether or not he ordered them. In its opinion, the court ruled that military commanders have, "An affirmative duty to take such measures as were within his power and appropriate in the circumstances to protect prisoners of war and the civilian population." This formula became known as the "Yamashita standard of command responsibility" and became very influential in the laws of war. The general was executed in Manila in 1946.

The military court acquitted Medina of any responsibility for the massacre at My Lai. Calley was found guilty and sentenced to life in prison. However, a few days after he was sentenced, President Nixon removed Calley from prison and placed him under house arrest. Calley was released on bond in 1974. He spent a total of 3 days in prison for participating in the murder of hundreds of innocent Vietnamese civilians.

Since My Lai, another massacre of civilians reportedly committed by American soldiers has shocked the nation. In November 2005, 24 civilians were killed by American Marines in the town of Haditha, in central Iraq. Initially, the Marines claimed that 15 Iraqi civilians and one American had been killed by a roadside bomb, but after video footage of the aftermath of the killings was presented to the public through a *Time* magazine story,[30] the U.S. military opened a criminal investigation into the matter.[31] As in My Lai, the massacre was prompted by the death of a fellow soldier, Miguel "TJ" Terrazas, who was killed by an improvised explosive device (or IED) shortly before the Marines went on a rampage. Among their alleged victims was an elderly couple, a man confined to a wheelchair, and a four-year-old child.[32] Some of the Marines claim that they were being fired upon from inside the house and that the killings were a part of the confusion that always results in combat. However, in December 2006, four Marines were charged with murder and four senior officers were charged with covering up the crime.[33] As of this writing, these cases are awaiting trial in U.S. military courts.

NUCLEAR WEAPONS AND THE LAWS OF WAR

Most weapons of war are discriminate to greater or lesser degrees. That is to say that they allow their users to destroy specific targets and not hit others nearby. A rifle can kill one person and leave the person next to him untouched. A carefully targeted bomb can destroy one building and not significantly damage others nearby. Weapons are usually labeled as "smart" or "dumb" depending upon their ability to distinguish between enemy combatants and innocent civilians. (Hence the term *smart bombs* for laser-guided munitions.) Of course, there can be *collateral damage* in a strike, the unintended killing of innocents, but as weapons have become more accurate, more discriminatory, and thus "smarter," civilian casualties have become less and less frequent and less and less acceptable.

Nuclear weapons are the ultimate "dumb weapon." Their blasts are massive and incapable of distinguishing between civilians and soldiers. Even after the blast has subsided, radiation lingers and spreads in the form of "fallout"—radioactive dust that travels along with the winds, affecting those in other places, causing radiation sickness and increasing the risk of cancer deaths. This means that even "tactical" or small-scale nuclear weapons can kill thousands or tens of thousands of people over the long term.

Lawyers and politicians have debated whether or not possessing or using nuclear weapons is a violation of international law. In 1994, the UN General Assembly (over American objections) asked the ICJ, "Is the threat or use of nuclear weapons in any circumstance permitted under international law?" In answering this question, the court was asked to contemplate the relevance of the laws of war in an age of weapons of mass destruction—a kind of warfare that the framers of just-war theory and international humanitarian law could not have comprehended.

---

[30] McGirk, Tim (2006) "Collateral Damage or Civilian Massacre in Haditha?" *Time,* March 19.

[31] Hanker, Thom (2006) "Inquiry Implies Civilian Deaths In Iraq Topped Initial Report," *New York Times,* May 19.

[32] Oppel, Jr., Richard A. and Mahmoud, Mona (2006) "Iraqis' Accounts Link Marines To the Mass Killing of Civilians," *New York Times,* May 29.

[33] Von Zielbauer, Paul and Marshall, Carolyn (2006) "Marines Charge 4 with Murder of Iraq Civilians," *New York Times,* December 22.

The ICJ's response to the query was complex and subtle but pleased virtually nobody. In order to answer the question posed by the General Assembly, the court first discussed some of the unique features of nuclear weapons:

> [N]uclear weapons are explosive devices whose energy results from the fusion or fission of the atom. By its very nature, that process, in nuclear weapons, as they exist today, releases not only immense quantities of heat and energy, but also powerful and prolonged radiation. According to the material before the Court, the first two causes of damage are vastly more powerful than the damage caused by other weapons, while the phenomenon of radiation is said to be peculiar to nuclear weapons. These characteristics render the nuclear weapon potentially catastrophic. The destructive power of nuclear weapons cannot be contained in either space or time. They have the potential to destroy all civilization and the entire ecosystem of the planet.[34]

Then, they examined the relevant portions of the laws of war, including the Geneva Conventions and the Hague Conventions and customary international humanitarian law. After carefully considering all of the legal and scientific data, the court ruled as follows:

> Certainly, as the Court has already indicated, the principles and rules of law applicable in armed conflict—at the heart of which is the overriding consideration of humanity—make the conduct of armed hostilities subject to a number of strict requirements. Thus, methods and means of warfare, which would preclude any distinction between civilian and military targets, or which would result in unnecessary suffering to combatants, are prohibited. In view of the unique characteristics of nuclear weapons, to which the Court has referred above, the use of such weapons in fact seems scarcely reconcilable with respect for such requirements. Nevertheless, the Court considers that it does not have sufficient elements to enable it to conclude with certainty that the use of nuclear weapons would necessarily be at variance with the principles and rules of law applicable in armed conflict in any circumstance.
>
> . . .
>
> Accordingly . . . the Court is led to observe that it cannot reach a definitive conclusion as to the legality or illegality of the use of nuclear weapons by a State in an extreme circumstance of self-defence, in which its very survival would be at stake.

Thus, while the court strongly hinted that the use of nuclear weapons was illegal, they ultimately refused to reach a final decision on the issue, at least insofar as it relates to "an extreme circumstance of self defense." Moreover, it is important to note that the court was only considering whether or not nuclear weapons were illegal, not whether or not their use was a war crime, although, as we've discussed above, there is an important connection between the two.

CONCLUSION

In this chapter, we have examined the two major international crimes that revolve around international armed conflicts. Something to keep in mind, however, is that the concept of an armed conflict is often ambiguous and that there are comparatively few *international* armed conflicts. That is, most modern wars are either civil wars (wars between different forces within

---

[34] Advisory Opinion on the Threat or Use of Nuclear Weapons.

a single state for domination) or insurgencies (guerilla campaigns against an existing government). These conflicts do not easily fit into the paradigm of international humanitarian law or the laws of aggression, which were designed to regulate the conduct of interstate conflict. The relevance of the laws of war to the current war against terrorism is also problematic. Radical Islam and al-Qaeda are not governments and do not sign treaties like the Geneva Conventions, a fact that has created a lot of problems for the U.S. government in dealing with suspected terrorists. (We will discuss this further in later chapters when we discuss terrorism and the war on terror in greater depth.) While they are obviously still an important part of international criminal justice, they have limited applicability in many modern conflicts.

In the next chapter, we will look at another set of international criminal laws that are prosecuted in international courts—crimes against humanity and genocide. Unlike war crimes and aggression, however, they do not require some sort of international armed conflict. As we will see, in some ways this makes them more relevant to civil wars, insurgencies, and other sorts of modern conflict but it also makes these crimes in some ways more controversial and they find a great deal more resistance than the notions of war crimes from the governments of sovereign states.

QUESTIONS

1. Do you consider yourself a realist? A pacifist? Or do you subscribe to just war theory? Does this impact on your view of the concept of war crimes?
2. What makes a person commit a war crime? Is it moral evil? The stress of combat? The nature of military command?
3. How should the courts understand the "superior orders" defense or the laws of command responsibility? Do you agree with the Yamashita court or with the My Lai court?
4. Should the use of nuclear weapons be a war crime on your view? Why or why not?

READING AND RESOURCES

The Crimes of War Project is an independent organization of scholars, journalists, and others who seek to promote the understanding of international humanitarian law. They have published a slick book (entitled *Crimes of War*) and have a useful website (http://www.crimesofwar.org) that includes balanced discussions of many important contemporary cases.

The *International Committee for the Red Cross* has an excellent website that has a great deal of detailed information on international humanitarian law as well as unbiased analyses of current global conflicts. The address for the ICRC website is http://www.icrc.org.

Roberts and Guelff, *Documents on the Laws of War,* 3rd ed. Oxford: Oxford University Press, 2000 is an anthology of all of the major treaties and other sources for international humanitarian law.

7

Crimes against Humanity and Genocide

❖

In this chapter we will discuss the two major "peacetime" international crimes. Like war crimes and aggression, these are crimes that are prosecuted by international courts like the ICTY, ICTR, and the ICC. However, unlike the crimes discussed in the previous chapter, the ones that we will look at here do not necessarily take place within the context of an armed conflict. Rather, they are crimes perpetrated by governments against civilians—usually their own citizens—during peace or (sometimes) war. While the laws of war have been around in some form or another since antiquity, the laws regarding crimes against humanity and genocide are of much more recent vintage, stemming largely from the aftermath of World War II and the world's revulsion at the atrocities committed by Nazi Germany. This means that they are less detailed than war crimes, but also more controversial.

CRIMES AGAINST HUMANITY

The term *crime against humanity* refers to a number of different criminal acts when they are perpetrated as part of a "widespread and systematic attack on civilians." Unlike war crimes, however, crimes against humanity may be committed in peacetime as well as during the course of an armed conflict and this attack on civilians can be either directed by a government or carried out by another organization (such as a guerilla army or a terrorist organization).

The term *crimes against humanity* was originally used in a criminal sense to describe the Ottoman massacre against the Armenians that was carried out during World War I. However, it was not used in a courtroom setting until the Nuremberg Tribunal for the Nazi

leadership.[1] There it was used to describe a host of activities (murder, enslavement, deportation, etc.) committed against civilian populations, *"before or during the war. . . . Whether
or not in violation of the domestic law of the country where perpetrated."*[2] There are two
parts of the Nuremberg definition that point to significant features of crimes against humanity: First, that these crimes do not have to occur during war (which distinguishes them from
war crimes), and second, it doesn't matter whether the activities were legal in the country
where they were committed. This early definition was then incorporated into customary
international law as well as into the statutes for the ICTY, ICTR, and ICC, with a few variations between them.

These two features of crimes against humanity make them more controversial than
war crimes. Simply put, because they limit the authority of domestic law and a national
government over the nation's citizens, crimes against humanity so conceived are a threat to
state sovereignty. Traditionally, political leaders have been willing to accept that warfare
should be limited; if for no other reason than that they would expect other countries to give
their own nationals the same protections that they provide. Additionally, war is a relatively
rare occurrence and so it would not bother these leaders very much to submit aspects of
them to some legal scrutiny. But, because they apply in both war and peace, crimes against
humanity go further than war crimes. This means that officials of any state at any time could
commit a crime against humanity. At Nuremberg, there was a great deal of debate about
whether to prosecute acts that occurred before the conflict began or whether to leave those
actions alone, considering them to be the legitimate right of a sovereign state over its
citizens, regardless of how repellant these actions may be. The anti-sovereignty side won
out and the scope of the prosecution was extended to include prewar actions of the Nazi
government, thereby creating the modern notion of crimes against humanity.

The two main features of crimes against humanity are that they are part of widespread
and systematic attack and they are usually perpetrated as part of a government policy. As one
scholar described these crimes, "They are not isolated or sporadic events, but are either part
of a government policy or of a widespread or systematic practice of atrocities tolerated,
condoned or acquiesced in by a government or a de facto authority."[3] This means that an individual may be accused of a crime against humanity only if they are acting as an agent of the
government or with the government's tacit knowledge. Single, isolated acts, regardless of
how heinous they may be, are not enough for it to be considered a crime against humanity,
and neither are widespread attacks carried out by organizations operating independently of
the state unless they are functioning as the sole authority in an area (what Cassese calls the
"de facto authority").

Specific Crimes against Humanity

The list of actions that are usually considered to be crimes against humanity is somewhat
long. It is important to notice, however, that a single act from the list below in isolation

---

[1] Cassese, Antonio, *International Criminal Law,* p. 67. Originally, these crimes were described by
some as "crimes against Christianity and civilization," but these terms were abandoned out of fear of
offending non-Christians. See also Bass, Gary, *Stay: The Head of Vengeance.*
[2] Nuremberg Charter, Article 6(c).
[3] Cassese, *International Criminal Law,* p. 64.

would *not* be considered a crime against humanity, unless it was part of a larger, organized campaign carried out with governmental authority or acquiescence.[4]

The following are among the various crimes that are considered to be crimes against humanity:

Murder—Committing unlawful homicide as part of a widespread attack against a civilian population.

Extermination—Extermination differs from murder in two ways. First, extermination is murder on a large scale. More importantly, however, extermination may involve not only direct forms of murder, but also killing by indirect means—by creating the conditions where large numbers of people die. Such extermination tactics could include denial of food and water, forced migration to inhospitable territory, or forced labor until death. As one international criminal case described extermination, "For the crime of extermination to be established . . . there must be evidence that a particular population was targeted and that its members were killed or otherwise subjected to conditions of life calculated to bring about the destruction of a numerically significant part of the population."[5] The exterminators do not need to fire a gun or otherwise directly cause the death of their victims for their acts to be acts of extermination.

Enslavement—Buying and selling human begins and keeping them under conditions of forced labor is enslavement. Although slavery has been illegal in most of the world for centuries, it is still practiced in certain parts of Africa and the Middle East. According to the Slavery Convention of 1926, "Slavery is the status or condition of a person over whom any or all of the powers attaching to the right of ownership are exercised." Later amendments to the Slavery Convention include debt bondage, serfdom, and marrying women against their will "on payment of a consideration in money or in kind to her parents, guardian, family or any other person or group." (We will discuss slavery in more depth in the chapter on human trafficking.)

Torture—The crime of torture was barred by the Hague Conventions, the Geneva Conventions, and almost all of the human rights treaties, although they each have slightly different definitions of the crime. In the Rome Statute of the ICC, torture is defined as "The intentional infliction of severe pain or suffering, whether physical or mental, upon a person in the custody or under the control of the accused; except that torture shall not include pain or suffering arising only from, inherent in or incidental to, lawful sanctions." But there are other definitions in international and domestic law, including the 1984 "Convention against Torture and Other Cruel, Inhumane, or Degrading Treatment or Punishment,"[6] and § 2340 of the U.S. Federal Code.[7]

---

[4] For more on this, see Chesterman, Simon (2000). "Altogether Different Order: Defining the Elements of Crimes Against Humanity," *Duke Journal of Comparative and International Law,* Vol. 10, 307.

[5] *Prosecutor* v. *Radislav Krstic,* Judgment, § 502.

[6] There torture is defined as "Any act by which severe pain or suffering, whether physical or mental, is intentionally inflicted on a person for such purposes as obtaining from him or a third person information or a confession, punishing him for an act he or a third person has committed or is suspected of having committed, or intimidating or coercing him or a third person, or for any reason based on discrimination of any kind . . ."

[7] There, torture is defined as "An act committed by a person acting under the color of law specifically intended to inflict severe physical or mental pain or suffering (other than pain or suffering incidental to lawful sanctions) upon another person within his custody or physical control." It is punishable by up to 20 years in prison.

All definitions of torture rely on a number of ambiguous terms: For example, how severe the pain must be is sometimes unclear under the law. Moreover, it is sometimes difficult to pinpoint where standard interrogation tactics, particularly aggressive interrogation tactics, end and genuine torture begins. What about cases where the lives of innocent people are at stake and torture may be the only way to gain crucial information in order to save them? In such cases, the exact line between harsh interrogations and "torture" is blurry. Governments, most notably the United States, have defended their right to aggressively interrogate suspected terrorists. We will return to the question of torture in a later chapter, when we discuss the suggestion that terrorists might be tortured for the purpose of gaining intelligence.

Rape, Sexual Slavery, and Forced Pregnancy—Historically, women were considered prizes of war and were often given very few legal protections in international law. Rapes and sexual slavery have likewise been used frequently to terrorize women into silence or to humiliate and silence the enemies of a government. However, a number of laws have developed over the last century in order to protect them from the worst sorts of abuses. Still, many feminist activists complain that rapes are insufficiently protected in international law, as we will see when we discuss rape in the context of genocide.

Apartheid—*Apartheid* originally referred to the racist practices of the former South African government. Between 1948 and 1994, the white South African government had strict laws that excluded black South Africans (who constitute the vast majority of South Africa's population) from political power and left them segregated and impoverished. While the apartheid system fell in South Africa in the early 1990s, the crime of apartheid was labeled a crime against humanity in the 1973 International Convention on the Suppression and Punishment of the Crime of Apartheid. Specifically, this convention says that a number of different acts "Committed for the purpose of establishing and maintaining domination by one racial group of persons over any other racial groups of persons and systematically oppressing them" are considered acts of apartheid. These acts include "Denial to a member or members of a racial group or groups of the right to life and liberty of person," "Deliberate imposition on a racial group or groups of living conditions calculated to cause its or their physical destruction," and, "submitting them to forced labor."

Persecution—Somewhat more ambiguous than other crimes, persecution refers to the general efforts to deprive fundamental rights to a person based on his or her gender, ethnic, racial, national, cultural, or religious identity. In some ways, persecution as a crime against humanity overlaps with the crime of apartheid, but may include cases that are not necessarily aimed at maintaining racial domination.

Imprisonment—Imprisoning people or depriving them of their basic liberties in violation of their human rights (such as the right to a fair trial) is a crime against humanity.

Deportation—*Deportation* refers to the forcible removal of a group from one country to another. A population transfer, the forcible removal of people from one part of a country to another part within the same country, is also covered under the crime of deportation. Frequently, large groups of people are deported from a country in an effort to make it "ethnically pure" or devoid of minority groups in a process referred to as "ethnic cleansing." In 1923, for example, the Greek government agreed with the newly formed Turkish government to deport citizens that didn't belong to their respective national religions (thus, many of the Greek Orthodox Turks were forced to move to Greece and

Greek Muslims were forced to go to Turkey). Such activities usually cause mass suffering and death and can leave millions of lives shattered in their wake.

Disappearances—In Latin America in the 1970s and 1980s, it was a common practice of a number of right wing governments to make hundreds of citizens whom they believed were their political opponents "disappear." The victim would be abducted off of the street or taken from their home late at night by members of the secret police or a similar organization, never to be seen again. Often the government or organization that carried out the disappearances did not acknowledge that the individual was ever in their custody (or even confirm that the individual was dead). This can make the lives of those who care for the disappeared victim particularly painful, as they do not know the whereabouts of the individual or their ultimate fate. Thus, the arrest, detention, or abduction of an individual without disclosing their location or fate is a crime against humanity.

GENOCIDE

The word is used, and *misused,* so often that it is hard to believe that the term *genocide* was coined only during World War II and became well known only as a result of the passionate efforts of one bookish Polish-Jewish lawyer. As a young man, Raphael Lemkin was horrified when he read of the mass murder of the Armenians by the Turkish-Ottoman government during World War I and vowed to fight government-sponsored mass murder of their own people. It didn't take long for such crimes of genocide to personally impact on Lemkin: During World War II, he was forced to flee Europe to the United States, where he became a professor at Duke University and from there campaigned to raise awareness about the genocide of his fellow European Jews. A number of Lemkin's own family members were murdered by the Nazis. Lemkin lobbied the U.S. government to stop the genocide and published a lengthy treatise *Axis Rule in Occupied Europe,* which catalogued Nazi policies toward the Poles, Jews, and others. Despite his efforts during the war, he was unable to seriously affect U.S. policy against Germany and to stop the slaughter of the Jews.

However, despite his weaknesses as a political activist, Lemkin was very good with words and he knew that the right words could open the world's eyes to what was going on under the Nazi regime. In order to do this he wanted to give a name to the crime that had previously been nameless—the attempt to annihilate an entire group through various forms of mass murder. Once it could be named, he believed, it could be criminalized and ultimately stopped. He settled on the term *genocide* as its label. The term is a combination of two Greek words—*genos* (meaning tribe or race) and *cidere* (to kill, as in *suicide* or *homicide*)—and denotes the effort to destroy a racial, ethnic, or other type of human group. The point of genocide is that the offender is not simply *killing* an individual or a group of people, but rather is aiming to wipe them out, destroying their existence on earth. This usually involves mass killing, of course, but it also can mean a lot more than this. As Lemkin himself described it:

> Genocide has two phases: one, destruction of the national pattern of the oppressed group; the other, the imposition of the national pattern of the oppressor. The imposition, in turn,

may be made upon the oppressed population which is allowed to remain or upon the territory alone, after removal of the population and colonization of the area by the oppressor's own nationals.[8]

Genocide is mass murder, but it is mass murder with an agenda: the destruction of a way of life and its replacement with another. Hitler was not simply ordering the deaths of the Jews and the Poles, he was trying to erase their existence on earth and fill their place with German Aryans—his "final solution" to the "problem of the Jews."

Lemkin's campaign against genocide did not end with the invention of the term itself, of course. At the Nuremberg Tribunal, he was able to convince the prosecutors to include "deliberate and systematic genocide, viz., the extermination of racial and national groups, against the civilian populations of certain occupied territories in order to destroy particular races and classes of people and national, racial, or religious groups, particularly Jews, Poles, and Gypsies and others" in the indictment of the Nazi leadership (although there it was considered a Crime against Humanity and not a separate crime). He was also instrumental in expanding on Nuremberg precedent by getting the international community to draft the "Convention on the Prevention and Punishment of the Crime of Genocide," making genocide an international crime. After his death, the term was added to the list of crimes punished by the ad hoc tribunals for Yugoslavia and Rwanda, as well as by the International Criminal Court. All of these developments resulted from the work of Lemkin and the willingness of the international community to heed his advice.

Modern Genocide

It is a sad reality that genocides have occurred throughout history and have been carried out in virtually all parts of the world by all kinds of people. The Old Testament tells of the annihilation of Midianites by the Israelites in the Book of Numbers—however, there were surely many more genocides like it in the ancient world.[9] Some of the conquests of the Roman Empire, involving mass killing, enslavement, and the capture of property could likewise be described as genocidal attacks. (The city of Carthage was reportedly destroyed by the Romans, its people killed or enslaved, and the earth tilled with salt so that nothing could grow there again.) In the nineteenth century, U.S. policy toward the Native American peoples, the Australian attitude toward their Aboriginal people, and the Belgian policies in the Congo could be characterized as genocides. Western and eastern, democratic and authoritarian, ancient and modern civilizations have carried out genocides in some form or another throughout the history of human civilization.

It was in the twentieth century, however, that genocide became a common feature of political conflict and it first began to attract public notice (and condemnation). The first twentieth-century genocide occurred during World War I. The Ottoman Turks, allied with Germans and the Austro-Hungarian Empire, carried out a policy of mass murder against

---

[8] Lemkin, Raphael (2002) "Axis Rule in Occupied Europe," in Power, Samantha. *A Problem from Hell; America and the Age of Genocide*. New York: Basic Books.
[9] For a discussion of the genocide of the Midianites, see Singer, Peter (2002), *One World*, New Haven: Yale University Press.

their Armenian citizens. Over a million Armenians were killed during the conflict—the many of them women and children. As Christians, the Armenians were sympathetic to France and England (the Ottoman's foes) and opposed the Ottomans, causing the government to carry out a policy of systematic mass murder against them. To this day the Armenian genocide is controversial in Turkey, where it is considered a myth that is blown out of proportion by anti-Turkey forces. Asserting that Armenians were victims of genocide can get a person arrested by the Turkish government on charges of "Insulting Turkish identity."[10] It was the killing of the Armenians that initially inspired Lemkin to develop the term *genocide,* and Hitler was said to have referred to the Armenian genocide when planning the annihilation of the Jews, asserting, "Who remembers the Armenians?"

Of course, the most infamous attempted genocide was committed against the Jews during World War II. Over 6 million Jews, along with various other groups labeled inferior by the Nazi government (Poles, communists, the disabled), were shot or gassed by the German SS or other military groups over the course of the war. Much of this was carried out in the infamous extermination camps like Auschwitz and Treblinka. Others died from starvation or exhaustion in "concentration camps" like Dachau and Buchenwald. Still others were herded into ghettos in cities like Warsaw and Prague, where they either died in squalor or were shot outright. Many Jews fled occupied Europe for England and the United States, while others fled to the British territory of Palestine to found the Jewish state of Israel. By the end of the war, only a small fraction of Europe's Jewish population remained on the continent and the Jewish people were forever changed.

The images of the skeletal, dying victims of the Nazi concentration camps are familiar enough now that they have lost much of their impact. However, there are a few things to keep in mind when thinking about the genocide of the Jews. At the time that the atrocities were taking place, few believed that such killings were possible, especially from a European country that was ostensibly more "civilized" than the rest of the world. Many even denied the hard evidence when it was presented to them in the form of witness testimonies. Moreover, much of the genocidal killing during the war did not take place in these camps, but rather were carried out by military units like the *Einsatzgruppen* ("Special Action Groups") that would gather together undesirable civilians in the countryside and shoot them by the hundreds. While the death camps were responsible for a great number of the Nazi murders, these death squads were responsible for killing about 1.3 million Jews in Eastern Europe.[11]

The Holocaust, as the genocide of the Jews has become known since, was not the only genocide of the war, however. Japanese policies in China could also be described as genocide. Rape, murder, and enslavement were carried out on a mass scale in Japanese-occupied Manchuria, where the Chinese *Han* people were butchered and starved to make room for Japanese colonization. Some were used for biological experiments in the Japanese military's efforts to develop its capacity to wage biological and chemical warfare. In the city of Nanking alone, approximately 300,000 Chinese men, women, and children were killed by the Japanese

---

[10] For a history of the Armenian genocide see Akcam, Taner (2006) *A Shameful Act: The Armenian Genocide and the Question of Turkish Responsibility.* New York: Metropolitan Books. Akcam was forced to flee Turkey as a result of his work.

[11] Rhodes, Richard (2002) *Masters of Death: The SS-Einsatzgruppen and the Invention of the Holocaust.* New York: Alfred A. Knopf.

military in 6 weeks. Homosexuals, the handicapped, and the Romani (Gypsies) were similarly targeted for extermination by the Nazis. World War II was unprecedented in the way that civilian groups were targeted for genocidal murder, and the Jews were not the only victims.

At the end of World War II, the world learned of the details of these killings and vowed "never again." After the war, the Genocide Convention was written and genocide was given a new international prominence. Not only did the Convention define genocide and label it "a crime under international law," it also required states pass laws to punish genocide and allow for the extradition of those accused of conducting it. While it is commonly believed that the Convention created a legal obligation to prevent genocide rather than just punish those who commit it, the text of the Convention itself is not as clear. Rather, Article 1 of the Convention says that genocide is a crime that states will "undertake to prevent and punish"[12] but does not *require* that they do so. Nonetheless, the Genocide Convention helped fulfill Lemkin's dream of making genocidal mass murder a thing of the past or at least to prevent it from being a prerogative of sovereign governments.

However, despite the high-minded rhetoric of Lemkim, the Convention, and the postwar years, genocide did not disappear from the planet after the Nazi regime was crushed. At the end of the Cold War, three horrifying genocides broke out: two in Africa and the other in Eastern Europe. While we have already discussed the conflicts in Rwanda and the former Yugoslavia when we analyzed the ICTY and ICTR, it should be pointed out that each of the conflicts had elements of genocide to them. In Rwanda, the Tutsi minority were described as "cockroaches" by the Hutu Power government and they were butchered by the thousands. In the former Yugoslavia, ethnic Serbians systematically targeted Croats, Bosnian Muslims, and Kosovar Albanians to make an "ethnically pure" Serbian state. In Darfur, Sudan (discussed below), the members of the "fur" minority were attacked by the government-backed janjaweed militia. In all of these cases, the response from the international community was very weak—they either denied that what was occurring was genocide or failed to make any serious response to the killings. (The UN Security Council similarly failed to do much about the atrocities.) In 1999, the United States, along with other NATO powers, began a bombing campaign to prevent the Yugoslav government from killing civilians in its Kosovo province but they did nothing to stop the killing of civilians in Bosnia or Rwanda.

Genocide in Darfur

Currently, a genocide is being carried out in Sudan, a troubled but oil-rich nation in Northern Africa. In that country's Darfur region (on its western side), a group, the fur, that is identified as "African" by the Sudanese government has been in a protracted struggle against the Sudanese government, which is usually described as "Arab" (both are Muslim).[13] In an effort

---

[12] However, governments have sometimes avoided calling genocides by their proper name in order to avoid having to do anything to stop the mass killings.

[13] While this conflict is often described in the press as a conflict between Arabs and Africans, in many ways this is misleading. Characterizing the people of Darfur as African and the Khartoum government as Arab is as much a product of Sudanese perception of their ethnic differences as it is any real difference between the different peoples. See Prunier, Gerard (2005) *Darfur: The Ambiguous Genocide*. Ithaca: Cornell University Press.

to stifle rebellion in Darfur, the government, based in the capital city of Khartoum, has enlisted the help of an Arab militia known as the janjaweed. According to public reports, the janjaweed have brutally attacked civilians in the Darfur region since 2003, raping and murdering hundreds of thousands of people. Many human rights activists and political leaders have denounced the Sudanese government and sought to bring the conflict to the world's notice.

Through the efforts of celebrities, activists and journalists, the Darfur crisis has been placed at the center of the world's attention. However, as with previous genocides, governments have been slow to respond to events in Darfur despite the loud public outcry. Sudan is a major oil exporter and some countries did not want to lose access to its resources. Other countries fear becoming involved in a protracted, messy conflict in the third world. However, in September 2004, the U.S. Secretary of State, Colin Powell, described the Darfur situation as a genocide, a characterization that the United States had previously resisted,[14] and it has tried to respond to the crisis in ways short of military intervention. Finally, in March 2005, the UN Security Council referred the situation in Darfur to the ICC to investigate genocide and other international crimes, and in February 2007, the ICC prosecutor accused two Sudanese ministers with crimes in Darfur. Alongside the efforts of the prosecutor, the international community is negotiating with the Sudanese government to stop the genocide (although these two tracks to stopping the genocide may conflict). However, because of its oil wealth, many countries are hesitant to be too confrontational with Sudan, fearing losing access to its resources or further aggravating the situation.

Legal Features of Genocide

The word genocide has been used so often in political debates that it has lost a lot of its rhetorical power. Along with the Holocaust, Rwanda, and Bosnia, it has been used to describe abortion, unfavorable economic policies, and language discrimination. Because the word is relatively new, it is sometimes hard to distinguish what cases constitute genocide and what acts are war crimes or crimes against humanity.[15] However, like any other crime, "genocide" has a very specific definition under the law. According to the Genocide Convention, genocide is "any of the following acts committed with intent to destroy, in whole or in part, a national, ethnical, racial or religious group, as such:

  a. Killing members of the group;
  b. Causing serious bodily or mental harm to members of the group;
  c. Deliberately inflicting on the group conditions of life calculated to bring about its physical destruction in whole or in part;
  d. Imposing measures intended to prevent births within the group;
  e. Forcibly transferring children of the group to another group."

Many antigenocide activists have complained about aspects of this definition. In particular, they complain that it limits the groups that can be victims of genocide to "national,

---

[14] BBC News, "Powell declares genocide in Sudan," Thursday, September 9, 2004, available at http://news.bbc.co.uk/2/hi/africa/3641820.stm.
[15] For different definitions of genocide, see Andreopoulos, George J. (ed.) (1994) *Genocide: Conceptual and Historical Dimensions*. Philadelphia: University of Pennsylvania Press.

ethnical, racial, or religious groups," but leaves out political groups. In the Soviet Union under the brutal dictator Josef Stalin, millions of people were killed on the basis of their politics—mass murder, but under the Convention at least, this is not genocide.

Along with the crime of genocide itself, the Genocide Convention also forbids crimes that are connected with genocide. For example, it outlaws conspiracy to commit genocide ("conspiracy" means agreeing to commit a crime, even if the crime itself is never committed[16]), inciting genocide (seeking to convince others to commit acts of genocide), and attempted genocide. In 1946, Julius Streicher a leading Nazi propagandist was executed in part on the basis of his anti-Semitic writings calling for the elimination of the Jews. In 2003, three leaders of the Rwandan media under the previous Hutu government were found guilty of conspiracy to commit genocide and incitement to commit genocide based on their public declarations such as a "Ten Commandments" which included instructions like, "Hutus must cease having any pity for the Tutsi," and, "Every Hutu male must know that all Tutsis are dishonest in their business dealings. They are only seeking ethnic supremacy." (Two of the defendants in this case were sentenced to life in prison, the other for 27 years.) These aspects of genocide are unique, as most international crimes do not explicitly include such inchoate (or "incomplete") crimes.

U.S. Federal Criminal Code's § 1091 also lists genocide as a crime punishable by either 20 years or by execution if the perpetrator commits homicide as part of the crime. There, genocide is defined by listing acts committed "with the specific intent to destroy, in whole or in substantial part, a national, ethnic, racial, or religious group as such—

1. kills members of that group;
2. causes serious bodily injury to members of that group;
3. causes the permanent impairment of the mental faculties of members of the group through drugs, torture, or similar techniques;
4. subjects the group to conditions of life that are intended to cause the physical destruction of the group in whole or in part;
5. imposes measures intended to prevent births within the group; or
6. transfers by force children of the group to another group"

However, under U.S. law, the crime is limited to acts that either are committed by American citizens or take place on U.S. soil. Other countries have similar laws against genocide with different restrictions on jurisdiction.[17]

There are several important issues in the legal definition of genocide that merit discussion: First, both international and the federal law require the criminal to have "special intent" to commit genocide. This means that in order to be convicted of genocide, the defendant must seek to destroy a group "in whole or in part." Murder, even mass murder, is not genocide unless it is part of such a larger agenda. This is significant because many atrocities that are aimed at an ethnic group may not be aimed at their destruction even if they ultimately cause such destruction. When the government of

---

[16] For more on the crime of conspiracy in international criminal law, see Fichtelberg, Aaron (2006) "Conspiracy and International Criminal Justice," *Criminal Law Forum,* Vol. 17, No. 2, 149–176.
[17] For a database of different national laws criminalizing genocide, see http://www.preventgenocide.org/law/.

Brazil was accused of perpetrating genocide against an indigenous ethnic group, its permanent representative to the UN replied that "The crimes in question were committed for exclusively economic reasons, the perpetrators having acted solely to take possession of the lands of their victims,"[18] and thus they were not genocide. Since the killings happened as part of a land grab, and not in an effort to wipe out the indigenous population, there was no genocide.

Second, for a crime to be genocidal, it must be aimed "at a national, ethnical, racial or religious group." But of course, race and ethnicity are fluid concepts. These categories are creations of a society and mean very little beyond that context. "Hutu" and "Tutsi" were inventions of the Rwandan people and their former Belgian colonizers. Similarly, some groups were left out of the list: mass killings of groups based on their political identity such as in Stalin's Russia or in Pol Pot's Cambodia is not a form of genocide, nor is the destruction of *cultural* groups by forcing an alternative way of life on them. According to one international ruling, what distinguishes groups that are potential victims of genocide are "constituted in a permanent fashion and membership of which is determined by birth, with the exclusion of the more 'mobile' groups which one joins through individual voluntary commitment, such as political and economic groups. Therefore, a common criterion . . . is that membership in such groups would seem to be normally not challengeable by its members who belong to it automatically, by birth, in a continuous an often irremediable manner."[19] This means that in order to establish genocide, the courts must look at the mindset of both the offenders and their victims: Did the killers believe that they were attacking members of an ethnic, racial, or religious group and did the victims see themselves as a member of this group? If the answer to these questions is "yes" then the attackers are committing genocide.

Important Genocide Prosecutions

As was mentioned above, there have been a number of significant international and domestic prosecutions for genocide since the end of World War II. Adolph Eichmann, a Nazi high official, was kidnapped from Argentina by Israeli security forces and smuggled into Israel for trial in 1961 (this case was discussed in detail in Chapters 5 and 6) was not charged with genocide, but rather with "Crimes against the Jewish people," which was described in a manner similar to genocide, but was a crime under Israeli, not international law. The media trials in the ICTR are another important example, but there are also a lot of others.

The most significant of the genocide trials since the end of World War II was the case of Jean-Paul Akayesu at the ICTR. Akayesu was the mayor of the Rwandan commune of Taba during the 1994 genocide. As Taba's mayor, he personally oversaw the murder of approximately 2000 Tutsi, many of whom had fled to Taba to escape the Hutu militias. Akayesu initially resisted participating in the genocide, but soon became an enthusiastic participant in the killings. In one mass killing, a number of Tutsi refugees begged to be shot to avoid a painful death. Akayesu is reported to have said to them, "There are no more bullets. Even if there were, we would not waste them on you," and ordered the Interhamwe

---

[18] Kuper, Leo (1981) *Genocide.* New Haven: Yale University Press. See also Cassese, *International Criminal Law,* pp. 103–105.

[19] *Akayesu,* § 511, cited in Cassese, *International Criminal Law,* p. 101.

militiamen to club them to death.[20] After the genocide was halted, Akayesu fled to Zambia, where he was arrested and sent to Tanzania for trial.

Akayesu was the first international trial for genocide. Because it was the first, the Tribunal had a lot of issues to settle about the nature of genocide as an international crime: What is a "group" that might be targeted for genocide? What does it mean to destroy a group "in part or in full?" and so on. This meant that the judges in *Akayesu* went a long way toward providing specificity and detail to the Genocide Convention's definition. This makes *Akayesu* arguably the most important genocide trial in history.

In 2001, four Rwandans were put on trial in Belgium for acts of genocide. One owned a factory, one was a professor, but of particular note were two Catholic nuns: Sister Gertrude (born Consolata Mukangango) and Sister Maria Kisito (born Julienne Mukabutera). They were each charged with complicity in Rwanda's genocide under Belgium's universal jurisdiction laws. When a group of Tutsi refugees sought shelter in their convent during the genocide, the nuns drove the Tutsis out of the church and proceeded to help the Hutu militia murder them, even helping obtain gasoline so that they could burn the Tutsis alive. It is estimated that 5,000–7,000 people were killed at the convent during the genocide.[21] (Many Belgians believe that particularly their country bears responsibility for the Rwandan genocide because of their historical links to that country.) The nuns were eventually transferred by the church to Belgium, where their actions were discovered and they were arrested. They were found guilty by a Belgian jury and sentenced to 12- and 15-year terms. (The factory owner was given 20 years and the professor 12.[22]) Many other religious figures were found guilty of participating in Rwanda's genocide, including three Catholic priests, a Seventh-Day Adventist minister and an Anglican bishop.[23]

Before he died in March 2006, Slobodan Milosevic was charged with genocide and complicity with genocide in Bosnia. It was alleged by the prosecutor that he ordered the killing of thousands of men and boys in detention facilities in territories under his control, causing serious bodily and mental harm to thousands of Muslim, including torture and beatings, and starvation, all of which the prosecution argued were "calculated to bring about the partial physical destruction" of the Muslim population. He died before his trial was completed, but in February 2007, the ICJ found that genocide had occurred in Bosnia and that the Serbian government bore some responsibility for it, but it left the criminal liability of Milosevic and others unclear.[24]

Saddam Hussein was put on trial for genocide before the Iraqi Special Tribunal—the court set up by the American-led coalition forces after toppling the Hussein government.

---

[20] This account is told in Neuffer, Elizabeth (1988) *The Key to My Neighbor's House: Seeking Justice in Bosnia and Rwanda.* New York: Picador. See also: McKinley, James C., Jr. (1996) "Ex-Mayor on Trial, a Rwanda Town Remembers," *New York Times,* September 27.

[21] Simons, Marlise (2001) "An Awful Task: Assessing 4 Roles in Death of Thousands," *New York Times,* April 30. See also, the Trial Watch report of the case: http://www.trial-ch.org/en/trial-watch/profile/db/facts/julienne_mukabutera_186.html.

[22] Simons, Marlise (2001) "Mother Superior Guilty in Rwanda Killings," *New York Times,* June 9.

[23] Simons, Marlise (2002) "Trials Test the Faith of Rwandans," *New York Times,* May 12.

[24] See "Case Concerning the Application of the Convention on the Prevention and Punishment of the Crime of Genocide (*Bosnia and Herzegovina* v. *Serbia and Montenegro*)." 2C February, 2007.

While Hussein was charged with many different crimes and was ultimately executed for crimes against humanity in the town of Dujail, he was also charged with genocide (although he was executed before the trial ended) against Iraq's Kurdish minority. These genocide charges resulted from the Anfal Campaign against rebel Kurds in northern Iraq. The Kurdish ethnic community has long fought against the Arab government (as well as the neighboring governments of Turkey and Iran), seeking to create an independent state of Kurdistan. In 1988, after a lengthy conflict between Kurdish forces and the government, Hussein ordered a full-scale war against the Kurdish people, including the use of poisonous gas against civilians. In total, approximately 182,000 people were killed by the Iraqi military in the campaign.[25] Hussein and six others were charged with the genocide, each pleading not guilty. However, Hussein himself was executed in December 2006 for the killings in Dujail before the completion of the genocide case. The remaing Anfal defendants were convicted in June, 2007 and sentenced to death.

Rape as Genocide

Rape has been an enduring feature of armed conflict throughout human civilization. Even modern, "civilized" militaries have been accused of committing widespread and systematic rape when they go to war. While rape has been clearly understood to be both a war crime and a crime against humanity in international criminal law, it is *not* listed in the Genocide Convention as one of the means to carry out genocide. Many feminist critics were outraged over this absence. Because the authors of the Genocide Convention were almost exclusively men, they ignored the unique ways that women suffer in genocidal conflicts.[26] Critics felt that international law overlooked the crucial importance of genocidal rape—arguing that rape has always been a tool of genocide that was ignored by governments and international bodies that were almost entirely run by men. Critics pointed out that rape is never mentioned in the Nuremberg proceedings, despite the fact that it was common practice during the war (as with all armed conflicts women were abused by soldiers serving on all sides). Thus the concerns of women were ignored in the male-dominated world of international criminal justice.

The feminist critics were correct. The rape of women has been a part of genocide from the beginning. (In the Book of Numbers, God commanded the Israelites to "Kill every [Midianite] woman that hath known men by lying with them. But all the women children, that hath not known a man by lying with them, keep alive for yourselves."[27]) In part this is because ethnic identity is closely linked to biology for many people—we believe that who we are is decided often by who our biological parents were. Other times rape is used to intimidate and insult an enemy or as a prelude to murder—one last humiliation before death. In modern Yugoslavia, Serbian forces created rape camps that were part

---

[25] Human Rights Watch, *Genocide in Iraq: The Anfal Campaign against the Kurds,* Middle East Watch Report, 1993.

[26] See for example, Mackinnon, Catherine (2006) *Are Women Human? And Other International Dialogues.* Cambridge: Belknap Press. Mackinnon has been one of the strongest proponents of prosecuting rapists under international criminal law.

[27] Numbers 31:17–18.

of their program to eliminate non-Serb populations. Rwanda saw the mass rape of the Tutsis. In virtually all genocides women were sexually abused as part of the killing—a fact that is often overlooked by (male) prosecutors.

Rape can be a weapon of genocide in a number of different ways. Because many societies are organized *patrilineally* (that is, the race or identity of the offspring is determined by the father[28]) the forced impregnation that results from some rapes can be a way to destroy the identity of a group.[29] Women who are forced to bear the children of men from other ethnic groups are seen to be destroying a community by severing the ethnic link between mother and child. Thus if a man of one ethnic group impregnates a woman from another, the child is removed from the mother's group and its people are a little closer to destruction. (Keep in mind what was previously said, however, that "ethnicity" is a construction and has no real scientific basis, so these opinions about ethnic identity are reflective of culture not biology.) Obviously, if rape and forced impregnation are carried on in a widespread fashion, this can prove to be very destructive for the future of an entire group in such schemas.

Rape can also be a weapon of genocide in some more concrete ways. The terror experienced by rape survivors can prevent them from living a normal life, forcing them into isolation, deep depression, or even suicide. Many rape survivors are scorned by their own people, who have labeled them "impure" and thereby unsuitable for marriage or for having children.[30] ("Blaming the victim" has often been a feature of humanitys' response to rape.) This means that rape survivors either are forced out to the margins of their society or they must flee somewhere else in order to escape persecution at home. Both of these tragic consequences have the effect of destroying a people and a way of life, even if they don't involve simple murder.

To remedy the absence of rape in the Convention, a number of important domestic and international rulings expanded the definition of genocide to include rape as a form of genocide:

In U.S. Federal Court, with the assistance of feminist legal scholar Catherine Mackinnon, a group of Bosnian women sued Bosnian Serb leader Radovan Karadzic under the Alien Tort Statute for rape and other crimes, asserting that they were part of the anti-Muslim, anti-Croat genocidal campaign conducted by Serb forces. The case, *Kadic* v. *Karadzic*[31] was the first to recognize rape as an element of genocide under international law. After proving unable to stop the prosecution by claiming immunity, Karadzic refused to participate in the trial and the defendants were awarded $740 million in damages by default. Although this was a civil, non-criminal case and despite the fact that the plaintiffs have not collected their money, the case had some political results. Conducted in the middle of the Bosnian war, *Kadic* v. *Karadzic* brought Serbian rape policies and their genocidal consequences to the attention of the general public.

---

[28] Rwanda is such a society. See Prunier, Gerard (1995) *The Rwanda Crisis: History of a Genocide.* New York: Columbia University Press, p. 15.

[29] See Fisher, Siobhan K. (1996) "Occupation of the Womb: Forced Impregnation as Genocide," *Duke Law Journal,* Vol. 46, No. 1, 91–133.

[30] For an example of this, see Bumiller, Elisabeth (1999) "Deny Rape or Be Hated: Kosovo Victims' Choice," *New York Times,* June 22.

[31] 70 F.3d 232, 240.

The other significant development toward the inclusion of rape as a tool of genocide was the aforementioned *Akayesu* case. As part of the killings in Taba, Akayesu oversaw the rapes of many Tutsi women and he was convicted of genocide in part because of these rapes. Despite the fact that he was not initially charged with rape as part of his participation in the genocide, the ICTR prosecutor was convinced by antirape activists to include the charge. In its judgment, the court concluded that Akayesu's acts constituted genocide by causing serious bodily and mental harm to members of a group in order to destroy them. As the tribunal ruled:

> Numerous Tutsi women were forced to endure acts of sexual violence, mutilations and rape, often repeatedly, often publicly and often by more than one assailant. Tutsi women were systematically raped, as one female victim testified to by saying that "each time that you met assailants, they raped you". . . . Furthermore, it is proven that on several occasions, by his presence, his attitude and his utterances, Akayesu encouraged such acts. . . . In the opinion of the Chamber, the above-mentioned acts . . . render him individually criminally responsible for having abetted in the preparation or execution of the killings of members of the Tutsi group and the infliction of serious bodily and mental harm on members of said group.[32]

In reaching its conclusions about rape, in *Akayesu* the ICTR firmly established that rape, a crime that was completely ignored at Nuremberg, was now officially a potential tool of genocide and could be prosecuted as such.

In still another case before the ICTR, a woman, Pauline Nyiramasuhuko, was charged with genocide for ordering the rapes of Tutsi women as part of a massacre carried out in the city of Butare, where she was a high political official. (She was indicted along with her son, a leader of the Interahamwe militia, and she was the first woman to be charged with genocide in an international court.) During the genocide, she had helped Hutu forces lure the Tutsis into the local stadium with promises of Red Cross assistance. When they arrived, they were surrounded by Interahamwe forces and murdered, but not before Nyiramasuhuko ordered that the Tutsi women be pulled aside to be raped by Hutu men.[33] Victims of the attacks produced horrifying tales of gang rapes, penetration with all manner of objects, and sexual slavery. One witness reported that a woman's baby was murdered prior to her rape.[34] As of this writing, Nyiramasuhuk's case is still in trial.

Cases like *Kadic* v. *Karadzic, Akayesu,* and *Nyiramasuhuko* show several things. First, that international criminal law has grown and changed in response to the new challenges that it must face. Second, they show that a carefully thought-out campaign by a group of activists can affect the machinery of international justice in profound ways, causing prosecutors and judges to consider new issues and prosecute crimes

---

[32] *Akayesu Judgment,* paragraphs 706–707.

[33] For an account of Nyiramasuko and the Butare massacre, see Landesman, Peter (2002) "A Woman's Work," *New York Times,* September 5. See also BBC News, "Rwandan denies genocide charges," January 31, 2005, available at http://news.bbc.co.uk/2/hi/africa/4223035.stm.

[34] de Brouwer, Anne-Marie (2005) *Supranational Criminal Prosecution of Sexual Violence: The ICC and the Practice of the ICTY and the ICTR.* Antwerp: Intersentia.

differently. Finally, they show that without the work of antirape, feminist legal scholars, the widespread use of rape in genocide would still be ignored by international courts and perhaps, by the general public. Thus, the inclusion of the crime of genocide in international criminal law shows the influence of feminist activists in the international criminal justice system, but also the somewhat disappointing reality that the international courts would probably not have discovered that rape can be genocidal on their own.

Genocide and "Ethnic Cleansing"

In the bloody wars in Yugoslavia during the 1990s, a new term was used, alongside *genocide, war crimes,* and *crimes against humanity* in order to describe the policy of the Bosnian Serbs towards their rival ethnic groups in the region: *ethnic cleansing.* While ethnic cleansing is not a *legal* term at this moment, it does match onto certain features of genocide and crimes against humanity and there has been a growing movement to understand ethnic cleansing as an independent international crime. The term refers to efforts to drive out members of an undesirable group either by force or by making conditions intolerable for them so that they have no choice but to leave an area. The goal of ethnic cleansing may or may not include destroying a group (which would be closer to genocide), but usually aims at removing them from an area so that members of another, preferred ethnic group may take their place. The point is to use whatever tactics are necessary in order to make a region "ethnically pure."

Although the term developed in the former Yugoslavia (it is a literal translation of the Serbo-Croatian expression *etnicko cisenje* and was reportedly first used in 1981[35]) history reveals numerous cases of ethnic cleansing before the term was invented. Native Americans were expelled from regions of the United States when they stood in the way of economic interests. In 1923, as a result of the Treaty of Lausanne, Greece and Turkey each expelled each other's ethnic groups from their territories, forcing Greeks who had lived in Turkey for millennia to move to Greece and vice versa.[36] In the aftermath of World War II, German-speaking peoples in the Sudentland (a part of what was then the central European country of Czechoslovakia) were forcibly removed from their homes and sent to Germany, with the consent of the Allied powers.[37] The list goes on and on. As long as national identity is linked with racial or ethnic identity, minority groups will be threatened with some form of ethnic cleansing as groups seek to make their land "ethnically pure."

---

[35] Petrovic, Drazen (1994) "Ethnic Cleaning—An Attempt at Methodology," *European Journal of International Law,* Vol. 5, 1–19.

[36] See Preece, Jennifer Jackson (1998) "Ethnic Cleansing as an Instrument of Nation-State Creation: Changing State Practices and Evolving Legal Norms," *Human Rights Quarterly,* Vol. 20, No. 4, 817–842.

[37] Waters, Timothy William (2006) "Remembering Sudetenland: On the Legal Construction of Ethnic Cleansing," *Virginia Journal of International Law.* For a longer historical view of ethnic cleansing, see Bell-Fialkoff, Andrew (1993) "A Brief History of Ethnic Cleansing," *Foreign Affairs,* Summer.

CONCLUSION

In this chapter, and in the previous one, we have discussed crimes that are punished internationally through the ICC or other international tribunals (although they are sometimes prosecuted domestically too). They are often considered more "political" than other sorts of international or transnational crimes, primarily because they are often committed by people with political power or by individuals who claim to be acting in the name of their national governments during a time of political or military conflict. Political leaders are usually the ones who are responsible for committing genocide, war crimes, and so on, not social outcasts like gang members or terrorists. Usually, political leaders operate beyond the reach of their domestic criminal justice systems, making international prosecutions necessary. On the other hand, accusations of war crimes and genocide are often used as political propaganda by rival governments—leaders often accuse other states of committing these crimes while ignoring the crimes committed by their own government or by their allies. This means charges of war crimes of genocide are sometimes viewed skeptically by the public, despite the horrors that they create.

In the following chapters, we will shift gears to look at another category of international crime. These crimes are not usually prosecuted in international courts, but rather are punished by individual states in their own domestic criminal justice systems. However, because of their global nature, they are often the subject of international treaties which set out their elements and allow states to cooperate to fight them. These crimes, including terrorism, drug and human trafficking, and cybercrime, are much more conventional crimes and often do not carry the political baggage of aggression, war crimes, or the subjects of this chapter. However, as we will see, they are in no sense less political or less controversial than genocide and war crimes, they only *seem* less so.

QUESTIONS

1. Why is genocide worse than other forms of mass murder? Is there something different about trying to destroy a group? If so, why?
2. Are there other acts that should be considered crimes against humanity? If so, what are they and why?

READING AND RESOURCES

Bassiouni, Cherif, *Crimes against Humanity in International Criminal Law,* a very in-depth study of the history and the law of crimes against humanity.

Power, Samantha (2002) *A Problem from Hell: America and the Age of Genocide,* New York: Basic Books. A Pulitzer Prize–winning history of genocide in the twentieth and twenty-first centuries.

Prevent Genocide is an NGO that helps raise awareness of genocide issues. Their website has some excellent resources on genocide law and genocide cases around the world. Their website is http://www.preventgenocide.org/.

The 2004 film *Hotel Rwanda* is an excellent account of the genocide in Rwanda as told by a survivor, as is the book by Philip Gourevitch (1998) *We Wish to Inform You That Tomorrow We Will Be Killed with Our Families: Stories from Rwanda,* New York: Picador.

An excellent website for monitoring international cases, in particular genocide trials, is http://www.trial-ch.org/.

8

International Terrorism

❖

Odds are that one of the main reasons why you are looking at this text is an interest in international terrorism. No member of this generation can forget where they were and what they were doing on the morning of September 11, 2001, when they first heard that terrorists had crashed two hijacked airplanes into the World Trade Center, killing thousands of innocent people. Likewise, few can forget the fear, anxiety, and uncertainty that quickly followed the attacks as everyone anxiously waited for the "other shoe to drop," that is, for the next terrorist strike. In response to the attacks, the country mobilized and was united in a way it had not been for over half a century. Politicians responded to people's fears and newfound patriotic sentiment in many different ways—some useful, and some not. One thing was clear on that morning, however: America and the rest of the world were no longer the same as they had previously been. Likewise, the criminal justice system, both in the United States and in the developing international system, would have to reckon with a new and pressing series of threats. Dangers that had sat comfortably on the back burner on September 10 could no longer be ignored.

Undoubtedly, American thinking about international crime and international criminal justice has been dramatically transformed by the September 11 attacks. But despite the new threats that Osama bin Laden and al-Qaeda presented, terrorism is a widespread phenomenon stretching far back in world history. Terrorism in one form or another has been a nearly universal element of political conflict since antiquity. Similarly, America has been forced to deal with terrorists of different stripes since its founding. Anarchists, radicals, and other underground organizations have carried out bombings, assassinations, and other violent acts since well before the republic was founded. The antebellum South saw pro- and antislavery activists engaged in acts that we would now describe as terrorism and after that war, bands of white Southerners such as the Ku Klux Klan (KKK) used terror tactics to suppress African Americans in the South for nearly a century. Similarly, when it has suited American political goals, the U.S. government has been willing to work with or even support groups that were considered terrorist organizations. American responses to terrorism did not begin with al-Qaeda or the rise of Islamic fundamentalism, much less on September 11, 2001, and America has not always been an implacable enemy of terrorism in all of its forms. Thus, the relationship between the American government (and the American criminal justice system) and terrorism has not always been so unambiguous as it is now. Of course, as we will see, even deciding who gets labeled a "terrorist" is not always a simple matter and present its own political challenges.

In order to combat terrorism, it is essential to understand the nature of this complex threat. In this chapter we will study the nature of terrorism along with its evolving character. This will be include analysis of the concept of "terrorism," discussing its common features and, methods, as well as providing some details about its history. Further, we will discuss some of the major terrorist organizations in the world, explaining the roles that they have played in both local and international conflicts. Then, in the next chapter, we will turn to an analysis of the various ways that American and international criminal justice systems have responded to terrorism, and what legal, political, and policing tools have been developed to help counter the terrorist threat. Like many other parts of international criminal justice, the concept of terrorism and the idea of a "war against terrorism" are politically charged topics. Everyone has their own views about who is or who is not really a terrorist and which terrorists are worse than others. This text has tried to be politically neutral but in a discussion of a subject as controversial and emotionally charged as terrorism, disagreement (even disagreement with this text) is not only inevitable but it is probably a useful exercise as well.

TERRORISM: WAR OR CRIME?

Since September 11, American politicians have frequently spoken of a "war on terrorism," or a "global war on terror." Many politicians and experts who have suggested that terrorism is better seen as a form of violent criminal activity analogous to the mafia have often been answered with criticism and scorn by critics. To call terrorism a mere "crime," so the argument goes, is to equate it with jaywalking, car theft, or other minor public nuisances. But to call the fight against terrorism a "war" is to suggest that the opponents are not simple lawbreakers but are rather bitter enemies of the United States, set on our absolute destruction. Crime is a pervasive problem, but one that is usually manageable by the government and by a well-functioning criminal justice system. War on the other hand, is usually a life-or-death struggle between two or more civilizations. The fight against terrorism, critics charge, is better seen as a mobilization of all parts of society into a war machine and resulting in a domestic security state where many peacetime comforts (and many of our cherished civil liberties) are considered luxuries to be put aside. In war, entire societies participate in the conflict in one manner or another. To equate terrorism with crime, to compare terrorists with drug traffickers or the Mafia, is to belittle the conflict and to underestimate the gravity of the terrorist threat, such critics argue.

Nowadays we are used to using the word "war" metaphorically. Politicians have spoken of a "war against drugs" or a "war on poverty" without calling for the massive sacrifices and curbing of individual liberties that World War I or the war of 1812 may have required. But regardless of whether the fight against terrorism is best characterized as war or as a law enforcement operation, many of the traditional tools of criminal justice will be essential to fight global terrorism. There is, strictly speaking, no battlefield where governments will fight against terrorists. Rather, the battlefield is in cities and towns across the globe, in bank accounts in Sweden and the Cayman Islands, warehouses in Jordan, Toronto, and New York, and restaurants in Paris and Baghdad. This means that military troops are not the only soldiers in the war against terrorism. Rather, the nation will also rely upon law enforcement agencies like the FBI, immigration services, and the municipal police to defeat terrorists. Police and investigators will pursue terrorists using skills like finger printing and profiling that they also use to investigate more conventional crimes. As with white-collar criminals and money launderers, government investigators will comb through banking records, seeking out important information about the financing of terrorist enterprises in order to shut them down. Most terrorists (though certainly not all) will be tried in a court of law for their activities and be sentenced to some form of criminal sanction, whether incarceration or the death penalty. Criminal justice professionals, not soldiers or intelligence experts, will frequently be on the "front lines" of the war against terrorism and to a great degree they will be responsible for safeguarding American safety. Thus, whether or not this is a "war" in any meaningful sense of the term, the conflict will in many cases be indistinguishable from the fight against more mundane foes.

There is a lot about the fight against terrorism that will be obscured if we rely too heavily upon the war metaphor in order to describe it. On one hand, wars usually have clear beginnings and clear endings. At the beginning, one country declares war against another. At the end, one side surrenders or their forces are utterly destroyed. This is unlikely to be the case in the fight against terrorism. When one terrorist force is destroyed or crippled, another is likely to take its place—perhaps without any training or without any formal acknowledgment of the event. Thus, when compared with traditional wars, it is unlikely that the United States will ever "win" the conflict against terrorism in any definitive sense of the term. Even if one terrorist organization were completely annihilated, as long as the political conflict which initially inspired the terrorists continues, there will likely be more volunteers willing to take their place.

Likewise, terrorists are not soldiers in any conventional sense of the word. Describing terrorist organizations as military forces overlooks a good deal of the complexity of their organization structures, their tactics, and their overall goals. As we will see, terrorists come from a variety of different backgrounds and use very different means to achieve their desired ends. The goals will differ depending on the ideology of the terrorist organization as well as the political and historical context in which the terrorists operate. Some may seek political autonomy for an ethnic minority, others may strive for a global political revolution, and others will even seek world destruction as part of a fanatical religious doctrine. There is no one identifiable terrorist army that can be engaged with and defeated. Al-Qaeda, for example, is not a single group with bin Laden as a "commander in chief," but rather it consists in a loose confederation of groups connected to each other in various ways, some operating with a great deal of independence. While terrorists are not criminals in the traditional sense of the term, it is equally implausible to say that they are soldiers in the conventional sense of the term, or that our fight against terrorism is a "war."

DEFINING TERRORISM

Despite the fact that everybody agrees that America is involved in a bitter struggle against terrorism, few people are quite sure what this means. There is no doubt that groups like al-Qaeda and Islamic Jihad are terrorist organizations and that the attacks on the World Trade Center and the Pentagon were acts of terrorism, but beyond these obvious facts, it gets fuzzy. Historically, the American government supported organizations such as the Contras in Nicaragua and the Mujahideen in Afghanistan that many considered to be terrorist organizations, deploying tactics that were designed to produce fear in their opponents. Additionally, some terrorist organizations also have elements that conduct legitimate political or social work along with those that use violence. The Irish Republican Army in Northern Ireland has always had its political wing, Sinn Fein, which has never been directly involved in terrorist activities and holds seats in the Irish parliament. Similarly, the Palestinian organization Hamas, the Islamic Resistance Movement, and Lebanese Hezbollah have both been involved in charity work and participated in democratic politics along with the armed attacks against Israelis. Finally, different terrorist organizations seem to be involved in very different kinds of activities (kidnappings, suicide bombings, robbery, etc.) with very different motives behind their acts. Some organizations such as the leftist Shining Path in Peru are motivated by a radical political ideology and seek social and political change, while others, like al-Qaeda, are driven by a sense of religious mission and see themselves as pious believers. All of this points to the fact that terrorism is a complex phenomenon that defies any easy definition.

These ambiguities have led some to reject the label "terrorist" as a way to make sense out of this new global threat. Rather, they argue that the term is a political concept only suited for attacking one's political opponents. Beyond its rhetorical value as a tool to demonize one's enemies, it isn't a very helpful concept. As one common saying puts it: "One man's terrorist is another man's freedom fighter." When an organization that is allied with the United States is involved in allegedly terrorist acts, it is either a necessary act of war or a regrettable accident according to American apologists, but when an enemy of the United States commits some atrocity, it is terrorism. A politician can quickly dismiss a group that he disagrees with by labeling them "terrorists." (In February 2004, the U.S. Secretary of Education referred to the National Education Association, the national teachers' union, as a "terrorist organization" for opposing his government's policies.[1]) Such critics argue that it would be much more productive to focus on the acts that are committed and the nature of the organizations themselves, rather than getting caught up with semantic questions about who is a terrorist and who is not.

Some critics likewise argue that terrorism scholars should distinguish between the violence committed by terrorist organizations and acts committed as a part of a genuine liberation struggle. While under the repressive and racist apartheid regime in South Africa, groups like the African National Congress (ANC) used violence against the white minority government and its supporters. Nonetheless, many consider the ANC's campaign necessary for bringing down apartheid and do not consider the ANC members to be terrorists. Similarly, over the previous century many groups fought against colonialist governments (such as the Algerian and Vietnamese struggles against France) often directing their

---

[1] Goldstein, Amy (2004) "Paige Calls NEA a 'Terrorist' Group," *Washington Post,* February 24, A19.

violence against civilians. Critics argue that we should distinguish between these groups, legitimate freedom fighters, and terrorist organizations like al-Qaeda. Unfortunately, for many, when one looks at their tactics free of a prejudice in favor of one cause or another, the difference between them is thin at best. They both kill innocents, and they both use fear to achieve their political goals. And while terrorism is clearly a difficult concept to define, it is probably less likely that scholars could reach a consensus about the definition of an authentic "liberation struggle."

Other critics have argued that most definitions of terrorism unfairly ignore terrorist acts committed by governments. That is, by focusing attention on organizations like al-Qaeda and the Shining Path, which are not a part of any existing government, as meriting special condemnation, scholars ignore the violence perpetrated by existing governments against innocent civilians. Ignoring the violence used by governments against their own people when defining terrorism overlooks the fact that governments kill many more people than any terrorist organization does. Acts like the U.S. bombings of Hiroshima and Nagasaki are much more bloody than all of the attacks carried out by al-Qaeda combined. Such critics argue that the threat of terrorism is a "red herring"—distracting people from the real harm done by currently existing political powers.

However, there is a difference between government-sponsored violence, even unjustified violence perpetrated against civilians, and the violence carried out by terrorist organizations. First of all, terrorists operate in secret and are not accountable for their acts before the UN and the rest of the international community. Although they are sometimes violated, international laws exist to help control the behavior of governments. Human rights law and international criminal law (discussed in Chapter 2) set out some basic rules that states must follow in treating their citizens—as well as those of foreign countries. States may be considered totalitarian regimes, oppressive states, or rogue regimes and be singled out for condemnation by other governments, the United Nations, or human rights NGOs. Because they invariably operate in secret, away from public scrutiny, terrorists are not similarly accountable. While oppressive states can be (and often are) more violent and more destructive than terrorist organizations, this is beside the point. The point of defining terrorism is not to figure out who is the worst sort of evildoer, but to understand a particular kind of violence—terrorist violence—and to set out the best responses to it. If we use the term *terrorist* to describe every group that does something wrong, we will water down the term and rob it of any of this power. (Here I am excluding the notion of *state-sponsored terrorism,* a concept that we will discuss later.)

Undoubtedly everyone's list of terrorist organizations will differ. Some will include a particular group that others would not. One definition would consider some feature of terrorism to be crucial while to another it might be secondary or even trivial. However, despite these differences, it is possible to distinguish certain activities as terrorism and certain groups as terrorist organizations. We can break down the concept of terrorism into four main components: *use of violent means, choice of targets, aims,* and *government affiliation.* All terrorist organizations will show some, if not all of these features as part of their criminal agenda. Some nonterrorist organizations will likewise manifest some of these features and most terrorist organizations will engage in other types of activities, so we should not treat these as absolutes. A warning: These categories are at best a rough guide for distinguishing terrorism and probably will not fit every case that is conventionally considered an act of terrorism. The distinction between terrorists and other violent groups (such as guerillas or insurgents) is never a black-and-white one. In the next chapter, we will expand upon this analysis by looking at federal and international criminal laws relating to terrorist activities and study the various legal definitions of terrorism that have been offered by these sources.

Use of Violent Means. Terrorists are invariably violent in character, or at minimum terrorists use an explicit threat of violence in order to intimidate others. Usually the violence is not tactical, that is, the violence is not a means to attain some material goal (such as an armed invasion of a country). Rather, terrorist violence is aimed at producing the maximum amount of fear in the public mind. This is why terrorists often carry out spectacular and shocking attacks such as large explosions, suicide bombings, or hostage taking. Of course, this violence does not have to be exclusively aimed at *killing* innocent people. Terrorists can hijack aircraft, destroy property, or forcibly steal money in order to achieve their ultimate political goals. A hijacking can be just as dramatic as a suicide bombing.

Some, however, have tried to portray political protests, particularly aggressive political protests as a form of terrorism, but unless these protests have an explicit or implicit threat that violence will ensue, they are most likely not terrorism.

Choice of Targets. Terrorists use violence but so do a lot of other groups. Militaries, police officers, and petty criminals use violence in one form or another in order to achieve their aims. One thing that distinguishes the violence used by terrorist organizations from other forms of violence is the willingness of these organizations to deliberately harm civilians instead of attacking traditional military targets. Palestinian terrorist organizations frequently attack Israeli restaurants, clubs, or cafes that are frequented by all types of Israelis (and non-Israelis) along with the attacks on Israeli military targets. Al-Qaeda attacked the World Trade Center, killing thousands of innocent civilians. In 1995, Timothy McVeigh deliberately killed hundreds of civilians in the Federal Building in Oklahoma City in order to declare war against the U.S. federal government. In each case, the terrorists sought to capture the world's attention by attacking non-military targets and killing individuals who had little if anything to do with the causes for which the terrorists fought.

In combat, conventional military forces also kill civilians of course, and civilian casualties are an inevitable part of every war. However, conventional military forces rarely do so as an explicit goal of their military activities. Usually, civilians are killed either accidentally or as a result of what is usually termed *double effect* or *collateral damage*. A military strike (say, against an enemy munitions factory) will almost inevitably kill civilian workers in the factory. However, despite the fact that the attacking force knew that these civilian deaths would be a result of their acts, they do not intend them. That is, if it were possible, legitimate military forces would avoid killing civilians and stick exclusively to military targets. Put more technically, the killing of civilians in wartime is usually considered legitimate if it is *foreseen* but not *intended.* Provided that the military target is in fact one that must be destroyed as part of the war effort and that the civilian deaths are proportionate to the strategic gain, then the killing is usually considered unfortunate but legitimate. Given certain restrictions, the principle of double effect allows for forces to knowingly kill noncombatants without being considered criminals or murderers. If soldiers deliberately kill civilians, they have committed a grave breach of the Geneva Conventions and hence they may be punished as war criminals.

The principle of double effect helps to distinguish terrorist killings from more conventional sorts of killings. Terrorists usually attack civilian targets deliberately, seeking to kill as many innocent people and cause as much destruction as possible. This allows them to have the maximum impact on the public consciousness and better publicize their agenda. Timothy McVeigh referred to the principle of double effect when he called the victims of the Oklahoma City Bombing as "collateral damage," but he was mistaken. His target was a government site, but he was well aware that it was full of civilians (including innocent children) and McVeigh took none of the precautions that legitimate combatants would use to minimize these casualties. He *wanted* those people to die. It is not enough to say that you have no desire to harm innocents; you must make an active effort to avoid doing so. To put the matter bluntly, legitimate combatants are forced to kill civilians at times. Terrorists try to kill civilians.

This aspect of terrorism may be controversial in some cases. First, it eliminates acts that are commonly recognized as terrorist acts, such as bombings of military targets. In 2000 members of al-Qaeda bombed a U.S. Navy ship, the *USS Cole* while docked at Aden, Yemen. Similarly, Lebanese terrorists killed over 200 Marines stationed in Lebanon in October 1983. These were military targets and would not be considered terrorist attacks under the part of the definition, despite their obvious brutality. Similarly, in 1945, the United States, on the order of President Harry Truman dropped atomic bombs on the Japanese cities of Hiroshima and Nagasaki, killing hundreds of thousands of people, almost entirely civilians. Many critics of American behavior in the world have suggested that these attacks are as much terrorism as the attacks on September 11. Whether or not this is true (the morality and legality of the Hiroshima and Nagasaki bombings have been a subject of endless debate by military scholars) is not that important for the criminal justice professional. As we will see, the conception of terrorism in this chapter will be different from the *legal* definition of terrorism developed by Congress (that will be discussed in detail in the following chapter).

Finally, "innocence" is in many ways as controversial a concept as terrorism itself. Many terrorist organizations rationalize their actions by refusing to recognize any distinction between enemy soldiers and innocent civilians. Such groups assert that *anybody* who supports a government they oppose, whether politician, soldier, or civilian, is a legitimate target. Others see any member of an enemy group, such as a religious, ethnic, or racial group as "the enemy" and thus believe that they can be freely targeted. However, under the Geneva Conventions (see Chapter 2), innocents are defined as "Persons taking no active part in the hostilities, including members of the armed forces who have laid down their arms and those [no longer in combat] by sickness, wounds, detention, or any other cause."[2] Thus even if an individual actively supports a government, they may not be targeted under law unless they are actively participating in a conflict. This means that an enemy combatant who surrenders is not a legitimate target, much less children eating in a pizzeria.

Clandestine Organizations. Terrorist organizations do not act openly and do not operate as official representatives of a government in the manner of traditional military forces. Conventional soldiers wear uniforms and carry weapons in the open; terrorists seek to "blend into" their surroundings and do not announce their presence. They usually try to appear as normal people until they strike. The Geneva Conventions require that combatants wear "A fixed, distinctive sign recognizable at a distance" and they must be "carrying arms

---

[2] Geneva Convention IV (1949), Article III.

openly."[3] In this sense, terrorists are much closer to spies or assassins, both of whom have no legal standing and are akin to common criminals under the international laws of armed conflict.

Aims. Terrorist organizations do not hold onto territory and they do not run governments. Their methods are purely destructive. They use violence in order to create a climate of fear among the general population that they hope will ultimately produce instability and chaos. Only when this fear is substantial enough can the terrorists and their allies achieve their real goals. When terrorists do gain political power, they usually abandon their previous method of fighting to become part of an established order and then oppose terrorism. The members of the Israeli terrorist organizations known as the *Irgun* denounced terrorist tactics after Israel became a Jewish state in 1948, and Irgun members became part of its government. The creation and cultivation of fear remains the predominant goal of terrorist organizations; traditional tactical goals such as capturing territory or destroying an enemy force, or broader strategic political goals (such as the construction of a government) are usually left to others.

Beyond this simple creation of fear, terrorists can have a vast number of different agendas. Some seek the establishment of a religious government, a *theocracy*. Others seek political independence for a particular ethnic group or the suppression of a different group. Other terrorist groups such as *ecoterrorists* (environmentalists who use violence against polluters and others who they believe harm the environment) simply seek to attract public attention to a cause, leaving others to deal with the larger political consequences. What makes a terrorist unique is not their goals, nor the fact that they use force to achieve these goals; rather it is the means that they use. Traditional governments use armed forces to fight other armed forces and avoid hurting civilians whenever possible. Terrorists use clandestine attacks that target innocents in order to create a climate of fear.

Government affiliation. Terrorists are usually not a part of any existing government, but rather work underground. Although they may receive material or financial support from a particular government, they themselves are not government representatives. This means that they do not have to answer to a group of citizens for their behavior. Many terrorists who claim to fight for the liberation of a group don't care whether or not they actually have the support of the people whom they claim to be representing. This means that terrorists are an example of the nonstate actors that we have discussed in earlier chapters. Like pirates before them, terrorists use violence against others without having to be accountable to any government or to any voters and, also like pirates, they usually do not have to answer to anybody for their deeds.

Because they are not part of a government, terrorists are not bound by the same rules as those who wage wars "out in the open." Nonstate actors do not sign treaties like the Geneva Conventions that govern the conduct of war (see Chapter 2) and thus terrorist organizations are not required to follow the laws of war. They are not required under international law to respect prisoners or civilians. However, as we will see in the next chapter, many have asserted that the status of terrorists as nonstate actors means that they don't receive many of the protections that the Geneva Conventions provide for conventional prisoners of war. Most terrorist

---

[3] Third Geneva Convention (1949), Article 3.

organizations gain a significant advantage from not being part of an actual government. They often can use it to avoid any of the responsibilities incumbent upon states. However, many terrorists crave the legal and political legitimacy that a normal representative of a state has and they often seek to become normal politicians as part of their ultimate plan.

Nonetheless, many terrorist organizations receive some form of covert support from recognized governments. Although no government officially acknowledges that they provide support for any recognized terrorist organization; many nonetheless secretly provide political, financial, military, and diplomatic support to them. Either these governments agree with the ultimate goals of the particular organization but cannot openly support them, or they simply want to use the terrorists as a tool to harass their enemies or for similar strategic purposes. The State Department lists six states as sponsors of terrorism: Cuba, Libya, Iran, North Korea, Sudan, and Syria, but this list is somewhat political.[4] A number of nations friendly to the United States but whose governments support terrorism are ignored. Pakistan and Saudi Arabia, for example, have pronounced elements in their governments that support various terrorist organizations (including al-Qaeda), but they are not considered state sponsors of terrorism as long as their governments remain friendly to the United States. The terrorists, themselves, however, are often distinct from the governments that support them and are usually not mere extensions of their sponsors. They often possess their own ideas and often work independently of their government sponsors. Sometimes, the terrorists will break with their sponsor government and conduct independent operations.

Exceptions. This is nobody's official list and it is important to realize that, despite the claims of some politicians, the concept of terrorism is not a clear one. Some organizations and acts that are labeled "terrorist" are not necessarily so and some organizations and actions that are not called terrorist may fit the description set out here. Further, the methods of fighting that are labeled "terrorist" are not always obviously wrong in every case (such as, arguably, the case of the African National Congress) and groups that are not commonly considered to be terrorist organizations commit many despicable acts of terrorism. Many military forces kill innocents as part of campaigns of intimidation or ethnic cleansing, but rarely does this get labeled "terrorism" by politicians or in the popular press. The targeting of innocent civilians has been a part of war through history and the belief that innocents should be protected is a recent phenomenon in law and politics. A student should critically evaluate any claim that somebody is a terrorist or that a group is a terrorist organization and reach a final conclusion only after careful, independent research.

A BRIEF HISTORY OF TERRORISM

Depending on how one chooses to define terrorism, its roots can be traced back to ancient India and Asia, or in a more modern context, to the French Revolution. Some of the earliest political murderers killed as a part of their religious rituals. In India, for example, the *thugee,* a group of religiously inspired killers, would strangle their victims while in drug-induced stupor as part of their religious practices. Likewise, the ancient world saw many organizations

---

[4] Iraq and Afghanistan were on the list in 2001, but were removed when the U.S. military and its allies changed their governments through military invasions.

that used clandestine methods and murder in order to achieve political change. When Rome occupied modern-day Israel during the first century, a group of killers known as the Zealots would sneak into towns and murder Roman soldiers and Israeli collaborators in an effort to force the Romans out of their lands.[5] From the eleventh to the thirteenth centuries, Islamic killers known as *Hashassins* (from hashish they smoked) murdered those they accused of defiling Islam in what is now Saudi Arabia.

It was in Europe, however, that terror became a conscious tool of political power. Maximilien Robespierre, the French dictator who held power during part of that nation's revolutionary period at the end of the eighteenth century, was the first person known to consciously and systematically use fear as a political tactic. During his rule, which became known as "the terror," he deployed arbitrary arrest and execution as tools for consolidating his power and stifling opposition. As Robespierre himself argued, terror is a necessary part of any government that must confront internal enemies:

> Without, all the tyrants encircle you; within, all tyranny's friends conspire; they will conspire until hope is wrestled from crime. We must smother the internal and external enemies of the Republic or perish with it; now in this situation, the first maxim of your policy ought to be to lead the people by reason and the people's enemies by terror. If the spring of popular government in time of peace is virtue, the springs of popular government in revolution are at once virtue and terror: virtue, without which terror is fatal; terror, without which virtue is powerless. Terror is nothing other than justice, prompt, severe, inflexible; it is therefore an emanation of virtue; it is not so much a special principle as it is a consequence of the general principle of democracy applied to our country's most urgent needs.[6]

Like later terrorists, Robespierre believed his own political goals to be more important than democratic government or principles of justice and he used any means necessary to achieve them. Most importantly, Robespierre (like the Italian political theorist Niccolo Machiavelli before him) thought that a carefully cultivated and controlled fear could be a tool of political power. During the terror, Robespierre used the guillotine to execute over 200 "enemies of the state" until a change of political fortunes in 1794 led to his own execution.

Since Robespierre, other political leaders have used terror to enforce obedience. Hitler, Stalin, and countless others relied upon widespread surveillance in order to destroy the trust among citizens, preventing them from openly discussing political issues. Random arrests and brutal executions were used systematically to spread fear and keep their citizens submissive. Fear has served as an effective political tool to hold on to power and keep unhappy citizens from rebelling against authority. Robespierre's tools and tactics have been taken up by dictators around the world and used as *state terrorism*. While we will shortly distinguish between state terrorism and most forms of modern terrorism, the systematic use of fear to achieve goals was primarily a modern, European invention.

---

[5] Kronenwetter, Michael (2004) *Terrorism: A Guide to Events and Documents.* Westport: Greenwood Press, pp. 24–25.

[6] Robespierre, M. (1794) Report upon the principles of political morality which are to form the basis of the administration of the interior concerns of the Republic. *Modern History Sourcebook: Maximilien Robespierre: Justification of the Use of Terror.* Cited in: Garrison, Arthur H. (2004) "Defining Terrorism: Philosophy of the Bomb, Propaganda by Deed and Change Through Fear and Violence," *Criminal Justice Studies,* Vol. 17, No. 3, September, 259–279, at 260–261.

It was not until the twentieth century that "terrorism" as we now know it became a recognizable problem and terrorist attacks became a common feature on the political landscape. It is here that individuals who were not officials of any recognized government used organized violence (frequently against civilians) in order to achieve their political aims. Radical political ideologies that bubbled up from the nineteenth century, such as Marxism and fascism, along with the rise of ethnic nationalism captured the popular imagination, leading many to reject the legitimacy of existing governments and work outside of them in order to create social change. A Croatian nationalist who sought independence for his own people committed one of the seminal events of that century, the assassination of Archduke Franz Ferdinand in the city of Sarajevo during the summer of 1914. This act of terrorism touched off World War I (a conflict that killed millions), which in turn planted the seeds of both World War II and the resulting Cold War between the Soviet Union and the United States. Terrorism not only started these conflicts, but terrorism also became a part of them, a weapon that all sides used against each other.

There are a number of important changes that led to the rise of terrorism in the twentieth century. On one hand, this period saw the rise of *ethnic nationalism.* Ethnic groups began demanding the right to self-rule (sometimes called *self-determination*) and saw the use of terrorist violence as a legitimate means to achieve this goal. These groups rarely had a government or a military of their own and instead had to rely on irregular forces to achieve their goals. Second, the twentieth century saw the rise of violent political philosophies such as Marxism and fundamentalist Islam that refused to recognize a line between innocent civilians and legitimate military targets, considering all citizens of a particular society to be "fair game" and vowing to achieve their goals regardless of the cost.

Finally, and perhaps most significantly, modern newspapers and other forms of mass media began to flourish in the twentieth century. Terrorists have always sought to affect public consciousness through acts of violence. Newspapers, radio, television, and, later, the Internet gave them a powerful new tool to do this. Violence and bloodshed always attract public attention and through its graphic coverage of terrorist attacks, the media allows terrorists to reach beyond those who are directly harmed by their violence and affect a much wider audience. An attack in Berlin can reach readers in London, Los Angeles, and Sydney in a matter of minutes and people thousands of miles away can feel the psychological impact of an event that has little actual impact on their lives. Violent acts can also serve either as a "recruitment poster" to attract others to their terrorist movement or as a way to garner public attention for their cherished cause. Whether or not one approves of their methods, it's clear that terrorist acts can help put a cause "on the map" and inform the public about a set of grievances, some of which might be legitimate. Prior to the twentieth century and the rise of the mass media, it was virtually impossible for small groups of determined outlaws to have such a profound impact on world consciousness, no matter how extreme their acts.

After the end of World War II, terrorism became a weapon used by the two remaining great powers. Since open war between the Soviet Union and the United States was not possible (both had nuclear weapons) the great powers would often use terrorist organizations as proxies. Both sides would take advantage of conflicts in smaller countries around the world, aiding and supporting terrorists and other irregular forces that would then seek their own goals. When the Soviet Union invaded Afghanistan in 1979, the United States gave economic, humanitarian, and military assistance to the rebel Afghan forces, called the *mujahideen,* that fought a guerilla war against the Soviets. After the Soviets withdrew from Afghanistan, the mujahideen helped to found the Taliban movement there, which ultimately succeeded in taking over Afghanistan in 1996. The Taliban then became the primary source of support for al-Qaeda and Osama bin Laden until they were toppled by the American invasion in 2002. Similarly, in the 1980s, the United States supported the contras, a rightist rebel paramilitary organization that sought to undermine the existing leftist government in Nicaragua by terrorizing its citizens. Thus, despite their current distaste for terrorism, the United States has supported organizations that were linked with terrorism, particularly when such groups assisted them in their fight against communism.

The Soviets, too, sponsored many terrorist organizations while fighting against the United States. Along with their support of radical leftist organizations in America, the Soviet Union gave aid to communist movements in South America and elsewhere, many of which committed attacks on innocent people. The USSR likewise supported organizations in Africa, Latin America, the Middle East, and Asia that committed atrocities against civilians in their quest for "peoples' liberation" and fought against American-sponsored guerillas. When it comes to supporting terrorism and terrorist tactics during the Cold War, both sides had their hands dirty (and to some extent, both are responsible for laying the seeds of modern terrorism).

TERRORISM, ISLAM, AND THE MIDDLE EAST

Terrorism has become central to events in the Middle East as well as in the larger Islamic world. Terrorists have played and continue to play a tremendously influential and tremendously destructive role in the course of political events throughout this part of the world. Many respected political leaders in the Middle East were once terrorists themselves and many other political leaders have supported terrorists, either openly or in secret. Similarly, many who oppose the current governments in the Middle East (both the Islamic governments and the non-Islamic governments) are members of terrorist organizations. To many in America, the Middle East and terrorism have become synonymous.

The reality of terrorism in the Middle East and in the broader Islamic world is much more complicated and subtle than it may initially seem. Middle Eastern terrorism is not merely a product of a simple-minded religious fanaticism. There is no single form of Middle Eastern terrorism. Rather, Middle Eastern terrorist organizations represent a complex mix of ethnic nationalism, socialist politics, fundamentalist religion, and legitimate political dissatisfaction. Similarly, there is no single objective for all Islamic terrorists, and many terrorists who operate in this part of the world do not share the goals of Osama bin Laden and al-Qaeda. While a comprehensive history of Middle Eastern and Islamic terrorism would require volumes, we can touch on a few of the central issues and events that have shaped Middle Eastern and Islamic terrorism over the last six decades.

Much Middle Eastern terrorism revolves around Israel, the Jewish state. While Jews trace their history in the region back tens of thousands of years, the modern state of Israel was only created in 1949, and consisted largely of Jewish refugees from Europe who had fled the Holocaust. However, it was founded on land that had previously been known as Palestine, was under British control, and was largely occupied by Muslim Arabs. In order to achieve their goals of expelling the British and establishing a Jewish state, Jewish settlers formed underground terrorist organizations like the Irgun and the Stern Gang that used bombs and political assassinations as a significant part of their method. Some of this violence was directed against the Palestinian people, seeking to drive them off of the disputed lands, but much of it was used against the British military. In July 1946, the Irgun used a bomb to destroy the King David Hotel in Jerusalem, killing 91 people, and in 1948, the Stern Gang assassinated Count Folke Bernadotte, a Swedish peace negotiator working for the United Nations to negotiate a peace agreement between the Jews and Palestinians in the area. When Israel achieved its independence in 1948, many of the leaders of these organizations renounced terrorism and some of these former terrorists became respected members of the Israeli political establishment. Menachem Begin, for example, a leading member of the Irgun who helped carry out the King David Hotel attack, became the Prime Minister of Israel in 1977. The fact that the Israeli state would not have existed without terrorism has continually made Israeli criticisms of Palestinian terrorism problematic.

However, the damage and loss of life caused by Israeli terrorism after the war was minor when compared with the half-century of Palestinian terrorism that followed Israeli independence. Many Middle Eastern states, particularly those surrounding Israel, believed the Jewish state to be illegitimate and refused to recognize its existence. Several states declared war on the new country (and many still refuse to call it a country, instead referring to it as "the Zionist Entity") and have since continually vowed to wipe Israel off of the map. Particularly after the 1967 war, which left the Israeli government in control of the West Bank, and the Gaza Strip (usually referred to as "the occupied territories"[7]) each of which was filled with Palestine refugees who had been forced to flee their home. These occupied territories became the home of an impoverished, angry, and increasingly desperate Palestinian population that turned to terrorism as a means to achieve their independence and reclaim their dignity. Many of these Palestinian refugees would become suicide bombers and other terrorists as Israeli settlers moved into these territories and began to claim them in the name of the Jewish people. Similarly, media coverage of the conflict, particularly in the Islamic countries, has angered many Muslims and led to popular sympathy for the refugees and funding for terrorist organizations like Hamas.

One of the most significant acts committed by Palestinian terrorists was the murder of 11 Israeli athletes during the 1972 Olympic Games in Munich, West Germany. A group of eight radical Palestinians, working under the title "Black September," held members of the Israeli Olympic team hostage until a bungled rescue attempt by the German police left five terrorists and all of the hostages dead. The terrorists had two goals, and succeeded at one: Their stated goal was to ensure the release of 234 hostages (all but two of them Palestinians held by the Israelis—the other two were members of the infamous German Baader-Meinhof gang), which failed utterly. The other aim of their efforts was to call world attention to the plight of the Palestinian people. No hostages were released, but the Palestinian cause was catapulted to the front pages of all the world's newspapers, where it remains today. As one Palestinian refugee put it, "From Munich onwards nobody could ignore the Palestinians or their cause."[8] The terrorists used the shock of violence and the reach of the mass media to promote their agenda in a way that sheer force of arms alone never could. The "Munich Massacre" as it has become known, signaled the beginning of the age of modern Middle Eastern terrorism.

---

[7] In August 2005, Israel abandoned the Gaza Strip.
[8] Cited in Dershowitz, Alan (2002) *Why Terrorism Works*. New Haven: Yale University Press, p. 46.

While many believe that al-Qaeda is linked to terrorism in Israel and the occupied territories, this group is in many ways different from Hamas, the PLO, and other traditional Palestinian terrorist organizations. Al-Qaeda was born out of Islamic fundamentalism, while Palestinian groups such as Black Friday were nationalist movements, more aligned with secular leftist movements than the religious ones. Al-Qaeda is as much opposed to Middle Eastern governments who do not meet their standards of a legitimate Islamic government as they are to the Jewish state. The connection between Islam and terrorism in the Middle East, and elsewhere in the world, is much deeper, broader, and more complex than events in Israel and the occupied territories. The roots of al-Qaeda are not in Palestine, but rather in Afghanistan and Saudi Arabia.

In 1979, the Soviet Union invaded the sovereign nation of Afghanistan, seeking to make it a communist satellite state. With the support of the U.S. government, the Afghan mujahideen fought a 10-year war against the Soviets and ultimately drove them out of the country. (Sometimes, this conflict is referred to as "Russia's Vietnam.") While Afghan independence was successfully defended, the end of the war left the country unstable and unable to effectively rule itself. Warlords and drug traffickers flourished in its lawless society, and different groups vied for political control of the backward nation. Ultimately, the Taliban, an ultra-fundamentalist group of Muslim religious scholars, succeeded in taking over the vast majority of the country. Under Taliban rule, human rights and intellectual freedom were suppressed in Afghanistan and a strict form of *Shariah* or Islamic law was imposed on its population. As part of its loyalty to other Islamic radicals, Taliban also gave both shelter and support to Osama bin Laden and his al-Qaeda organization, refusing to surrender him to the United States after he was determined to be the mastermind of the September 11, 2001, attacks. While the Taliban was removed from power as a result of the 2001 U.S. invasion of Afghanistan, the Taliban and Afghanistan remain an important part of the American war on terrorism. The United States has a sizeable military force working in that country searching for al-Qaeda operatives and the remnants of the Taliban government who still carry out strikes against U.S. and Afghan forces.

The second major influence on the development of al-Qaeda was their dissatisfaction with Middle Eastern governments in general and Saudi Arabia in particular. While nominally Muslim, many of the governments in these countries are in fact dictatorships of one form of another, many of which are both corrupt and oppressive. The government of Saudi Arabia, a hereditary monarchy, has been criticized by many fundamentalists for being too closely aligned with the United States and for the moral corruption of its wealthy royal family. Other, more secular countries such as Egypt, the former Iraqi government of Saddam Hussein, and Algeria, for example, have been bitterly attacked by Islamic fundamentalists. These countries responded to Islamic fundamentalist movements with harsh repression, which has in turn only emboldened the fundamentalists. As the birth place of the Prophet Muhammad, the Saudi government has been the primary enemy of al-Qaeda and its fundamentalist compatriots. In 1979, a group of Islamic radicals took over the Grand Mosque in Mecca, the birthplace of Muhammad, and held it for several weeks in protest against the behavior of the royal family and the presence of Westerners in the country (they were eventually defeated by Saudi troops, and the surviving militants were publicly beheaded). The development of Islamic fundamentalism and Islamic terrorism is as much a product of corrupt or autocratic Islamic governments as any acts perpetrated by Western governments or the existence of Israel, and al-Qaeda and its allies have attacked many Middle Eastern governments along with Western powers.

Bin Laden himself is a product of both Islamic fundamentalism and anger at the current Middle Eastern governments. A Saudi national, bin Laden is an heir to a construction fortune who abandoned the comforts of wealth and privilege in 1979 in order to assist the mujahideen in Afghanistan (where he helped found al-Qaeda to recruit more mujahideen). After the Soviet withdrawal from Afghanistan, bin Laden found his next mission when Iraq, under Saddam Hussein, invaded its small neighbor Kuwait in 1990. Bin Laden himself offered his own forces to help the Saudi government to liberate that country and protect Saudi Arabia but was refused in favor of allowing U.S. forces to repel Hussein's troops. Bin Laden was outraged by the presence of non-Islamic troops in the land of the Prophet and wound up supporting anti-government Saudi radicals. He was forced to leave Saudi Arabia in 1991 after criticizing the Saudi monarchy and has since traveled around Africa and the Middle East before settling in Afghanistan at the invitation of the Taliban government. After the U.S. invasion, his where-abouts have been unknown but he is currently being hunted in the southern mountain regions of Afghanistan along its border with Pakistan. Whether or not bin Laden is anything more than a figurehead or symbolic leader of the modern al-Qaeda organization, he has become the central figure in America's fight against terrorism: He is on the FBI's 10 most-wanted list and the United States still makes a concerted effort to find him.

Al-Qaeda and the Islamic terrorist movement have had an influence on many Muslims beyond those living in the Middle East. They have inspired Islamic radicals in many places with Muslim populations and political grievances to adopt many of their tactics, including forces in Chechnya, Indonesia, and the Philippines. Chechnya, a small region of southern Russia that has had a strong independence movement that has been radicalized and waged violent terrorist attacks in Russia including the 2004 attack on an elementary school in Beslan, Russia, which left over 300 dead. Jamaah Islamiah, a radical Muslim organization in Indonesia has helped carry out attacks against Western and Australian tourists in the resort town of Bali. Similarly, they have inspired "home-grown" Islamic terrorists in Europe, such as the July 7, 2005, London Underground subway bombers, with no known connection to al-Qaeda, who killed 52 people. To many alienated Muslims around the world, al-Qaeda has become a symbol of Islamic resistance to Western powers and western culture with an influence that has stretched far beyond its core membership in Afghanistan and Iraq.

There are several important modern non-Islamic terrorist movements outside the Middle East that have made infamous, but important contributions to modern terrorism. In the small island country of Sri Lanka off the southern coast of India, a group known as the Liberation Tigers of Tamil Eelam (LTTE) or "Tamil Tigers" is credited, alongside Hezbollah, with some of the first suicide bombings and have the record for carrying out the most suicide bombings.[9] The Tamil Tigers have fought (and continue to fight) for a separate homeland in the northern part of Sri Lanka for the Tamil ethnic minority and are notorious for using particularly brutal tactics in seeking to achieve their goals. Likewise in Europe, the Irish Republican Army (IRA) and ETA, the Basque separatist organization, have fought for political independence from England and Spain respectively, frequently using targeted assassinations or indiscriminate bombing in order to achieve their goals.

---

[9] Schweitzer, Yoram, "Suicide Terrorism: Development & Characteristics," http://www.dushkin.com/text-data/articles/30833/body.pdf and Sprinzak, Ehud (2000) "Rational Fanatics?" *Foreign Policy,* September/October, 66–84.

There have also been a number of prominent leftist terrorist organizations in Europe that have used bombings, assassinations, and kidnappings (among other tactics) to achieve their goals. Many, particularly in the 1960s and 1970s, saw a revolution coming in Western, capitalist societies that could only be induced through a systematic campaign of fear and violence. Bombings and targeted assassinations were used to help bring on a global socialist revolution. In the 1970s, the Baader-Meinhof gang (also known as the Red Army Faction, RAF) was a potent force in West German politics and frequently used violence. Baader-Meinhof sought to bring about a socialist state in West Germany and allied itself with the international communist movement (it took its name from the Japanese militant communist organization, the Red Army). The Baader-Meinhof gang had largely been destroyed by German law enforcement in the late 1970s, and much of the force behind these movements dissipated when the Soviet Union collapsed in 1989 and the Cold War ended. However, as we will see, a number of terrorist organizations with roots in radical communism are still active in South America and Asia.

AMERICAN TERRORISM

So far we have focused our discussion largely on international terrorism, but there are some important terrorist groups operating within the United States, many of which have links to organizations beyond our borders. During the 1960s and 70s, many radical leftist organizations carried out terrorist activities to undermine the American government and to express opposition to the war in Vietnam. These groups were largely Marxist or anarchist in orientation and sought to foment a socialist revolution in America analogous to the 1918 Russian Revolution that led to the creation of the Soviet Union. In one famous case in 1974, the Symbionese Liberation Army or SLA kidnapped Patty Hearst, the granddaughter of the powerful publishing magnate William Randolph Hearst. Two months later, police were shocked to see that Ms. Hearst had joined the SLA and participated in a bank robbery in San Francisco. She, along with the other SLA members, was captured shortly thereafter and sentenced to seven years imprisonment. (Heart's sentence was commuted by President Jimmy Carter after she served less than three years.) Another group, known as the Weather Underground, conducted bombings during the 1960s and 70s. Other organizations linked with the American Communist Party carried out attacks and robberies in the United States. The end of the Vietnam War and the student movement (along with vigorous investigations by the FBI) led to a sharp decline in American leftist terrorism.

In the 1990s, however, new forms of American terrorism developed, this time coming from the far right of the political spectrum. A number of groups who had grievances against the government and American society began a series of attacks against targets in the United States. Some opposed the power of the federal government over the states, others, the legalization of abortion, and some wanted to advance violent racist agendas. During the 1996 Olympics in Atlanta, Eric Rudolph planted a bomb at Centennial Park that exploded during a rock concert, killing one person (he had previously planted bombs at a bar in Atlanta frequented by homosexuals and at two different abortion clinics around the southeastern part of the country). More dramatically, in 1995 Timothy McVeigh a right-wing army veteran parked a truck loaded with fertilizer that he had converted into a powerful bomb in front of the Alfred Murrah federal building in Oklahoma City. The ensuing blast destroyed much of the building and killed 168 people. (McVeigh was quickly caught and was executed in June 2001.) Finally, in the aftermath of the September 11 attacks, a series of letters laced with deadly anthrax were sent out to prominent congressmen and media figures, which many suspected was the work of domestic right wing terrorists.

Finally, the less violent, but nonetheless dangerous ecoterrorism movement has recently made its presence felt. Groups such as the Animal Liberation Front (ALF) and the Earth Liberation Front (ELF) have defaced and destroyed property that they believed harm the environment or the welfare of animals. These groups believe that the only means by which to stop the destruction of the earth's natural environment is through violent and destructive action against those who harm it. In order to achieve their goals, they've destroyed lab equipment, releasing numerous lab animals, committed acts of vandalism against loggers and land developers, and carried out "tree spikings" (placing large metal nails into trees which can seriously injure loggers who use chain saws to chop down the trees). While it is certainly true that these organizations do not come close to matching groups such as al-Qaeda or right-wing terrorists like Timothy McVeigh (most ecoterrorists do not harm humans), they nonetheless constitute a growing threat in American society. The FBI estimates that over the past 20 years, ecoterrorists have caused over $100 million in damage, and John F. Lewis, the Deputy Assistant Director of the Counterterrorism Division of the FBI, asserted that "In recent years, the Animal Liberation Front and the Earth Liberation Front have become the most active criminal extremist elements in the United States."[10]

THE MODERN IRA

Since signing the "Good Friday Accords" in 1998, the IRA and Sinn Fein have been gradually disarming and abandoning violence as a tool for political change. But these political changes in Northern Ireland have also shown how resilient terrorist organizations can be and how they can quickly transform themselves and branch out into other criminal activities when the political situation changes. In December 2004, a group robbed a bank in Belfast and took away approximate £26.5 million (about $45 million). The robbery was professionally done (the robbers had kidnapped family members of some of the bank employees and forced them to serve as accomplices) and many immediately suspected that it was the work of the IRA. While investigating this crime, other IRA-run criminal operations such as money laundering schemes were discovered by detectives. It was clear to many that the IRA was transitioning from a political operation to a conventional criminal organization as a result of political changes in the UK.

Shortly after the Belfast robbery, IRA members took part in a brutal murder that shocked the British Isles and undermined the credibility of both Sinn Fein and the IRA. In a little bar in a corner of Belfast, two friends, Robert McCartney and Brendan Devine went to have a few pints of beer. The two were having a conversation when another approached them; he was a known member of the IRA with whom McCartney had some troubles in the past. The IRA member insisted that the two had made a rude comment about a female companion of his and demanded an apology. They refused and a fight quickly broke out. On the signal of the IRA member, a bottle was smashed over McCartney's head,

---

[10] Testimony before the Senate Judiciary Committee, May 18, 2004.

a hand reached out from behind his head, pulling his neck back, and a knife was slashed across his throat. McCartney died shortly thereafter.

The fight was not inspired by politics, but rather by a personal disagreement between the patrons, like a million other bar fights that take place throughout the world. What makes this unique is that after the attack, the killers informed the bar patrons that they were on "IRA business" and that nobody should interfere with them. Traditionally, a code of silence among the Irish Catholic community has protected the IRA from police investigations. (The Northern Irish Police Service has often been associated with the British "occupiers".) The McCartney family, however, refused to be cowed and have since sought to raise public awareness of the crime, insisting that their brother's killers be brought to justice. This, in turn, has harmed the IRA's reputation as a legitimate alternative to British rule. (Perversely, Sinn Fein leaders offered to have the killers executed by the IRA itself rather than surrendering them to the police.) The McCartney sisters even met with President George W. Bush, who supported their efforts to bring their brother's killers to justice.

These types of events show that the line between terrorism and other sorts of crimes can be a thin one. Like any other organization, a terrorist organization must adapt to new circumstances or face extinction. This has led some of them to change from an idealistic, if violent force for political change into a group of thugs aiming only for wealth and power. Other organizations, such as the Sendero Lumenso in Peru (discussed below), have likewise crossed the line from political radicals to paramilitary drug lords by working with cocaine producers to obtain money to fund their activities. Further, as the McCartney case shows, terrorists are frequently disposed to use violence in other contexts, especially after their organization has outlived its usefulness as a part of a political struggle. Some scholars argue that, given the Good Friday Agreement, this is the current situation of the IRA: Either its members will reconcile themselves to a peaceful future as part of a democratic Northern Ireland or they will slip into pure, apolitical organized criminality.

MOTIVATIONS OF TERRORISTS

Defining terrorism is clearly a difficult task. No less difficult (or controversial) is explaining their motivations. Theories about what makes an individual or group resort to terrorism serve as a Rorschach, "ink blot," test of sorts. What one sees depends to a large degree upon what one looks at and what one wants to see. A psychologist, for example, might focus on the personal experiences of the terrorist, and on his or her individual emotional problems or other personal issues that lead them to embrace such an extreme cause. A sociologist will examine a terrorist's behavior in relation to their larger demographic population, examining their race, education, and so on and searching for broad commonalities among terrorists. Political scientists may see the motives of terrorists as political issues, and view terrorism as a response to real or perceived oppression and as a tactic in the struggle for political power. Finally a moralist may resort to language of good or evil: a terrorist does what he does because he is evil. Different disciplines are trained to look at the world through different lenses and it makes perfect sense that they would each find different things interesting in searching for the motives and causes of terrorism.

It's certainly tempting to search for a single answer to the question of what causes a person to resort to terrorism, particularly one that puts the terrorist in a bad light. It's convenient to portray terrorists as crazy or evil, but it's probably not very helpful. Terrorists may use morally repugnant methods to achieve their ends, but their motives are in many ways rational as are the means that they use to achieve them. Terrorists may be wrong, but they are not necessarily insane. Further, different terrorists and different terrorist causes are likely to possess different mind-sets, attracting different types of people with different beliefs and values. A religiously motivated terrorist is likely to be a very different kind of person than a nationalist fighting for an independent homeland or a communist seeking to change the global economy. As one prominent psychologist of terrorism has put it, "Even the briefest review of the history of terrorism reveals how varied and complex a phenomenon it is, and how futile it is to attribute simple, global, and general psychological characteristics to all terrorists and all terrorism."[11]

The different ideologies behind terrorists preclude any simple explanation of terrorist motivations; likewise, the different experiences of different terrorists makes it difficult to explain. Some terrorists are extremely wealthy (such as bin Laden), others, such as many Palestinian terrorists, are quite poor. Most of the September 11 attackers were college educated, while many IRA members are not. Men and women are both capable of becoming terrorists, and members of every culture and ethnic group can be terrorists. Thus, just as there is no single form of terrorist organization, there is no single archetypal terrorist that can be used to explain or understand terrorist motivations from a criminological perspective.

SUICIDE BOMBINGS

The belief that sacrificing one's life in the name of an important cause is noble and praiseworthy is a nearly universal one. "Martyrdom" or death in defense of a religious cause is found in all major religions. Christianity celebrates its early martyrs who were brutally killed by the Roman Empire for refusing to renounce their religion and early Islam tells many tales of sacrifice including the martyrdom of early Shiite's (and their leader Husayn) in the city of Karbala. Those who carry out dangerous operations fully expecting to die as a result of their actions are often lauded as patriots and heroes of their home country. Three-hundred Greek warriors held off almost a million Persian soldiers for three days at the battle of Thermopylae (480 BC) and were slaughtered to the last man, but they became heroes of the ancient world (and even have been glorified in contemporary cinema). The poet Alfred, Lord Tennyson immortalized the suicidal "Charge of the Light Brigade" (where over two-hundred British Cavalrymen were killed in the Crimean War against Russia), asserting "Their's not to reason why, / Their's but to do or die." The Japanese military used Kamikaze pilots to sink Allied ships during World War II, deliberately flying their explosives-packed planes into the side of the enemy ships. Suicidal tactics have always been an important part of warfare and, in many contexts have been highly praised by Western and Non-Western peoples alike.

However, the notion of a "suicide bomber," an individual who straps a large explosive onto his body, seeks out appropriate targets, and detonates the bomb in their proximity is a relatively new phenomenon. The difference, of course, is that suicide bombers *must* die in order to achieve their desired goals. In most suicide attacks, the Kamikaze pilots being a notable exception, those who carry out the mission have some hope (however thin)

---

[11] Reich, Walter (1998) "Understanding Terrorist Behavior: The Limits and Opportunities of Psychological Inquiry," in Reich, Walter (ed.), *Origins of Terrorism: Psychologies, Ideologies, Theologies, States of Mind.* Washington: Woodrow Wilson Center Press, pp. 262–263.

of surviving their mission—their deaths are a likely consequence of their acts, usually not a necessary or desired one. Records show that the Liberation Tigers of Tamil Eelam in Sri Lanka first used suicide bombers but it has been widely adopted by Islamic terrorists in the Middle East and turned into a religious act of the highest order.

Strategically, of course, suicide bombers can be very effective weapons. A single person with explosives strapped to his body can seek out his target. He can move when his target does, and if the opportunity to strike fails to present itself, the bomber can wait for a better chance to detonate his explosives. This makes the bomber a kind of cheap and effective "smart bomb," capable of causing great carnage at relatively little financial expense. Traditional military forces must spend millions for the intelligence data and satellite technology necessary to locate their desired target and then millions more for the guidance systems that will produce the same effect as one individual with a hand-made belt composed of crude explosives.

More powerful than the physical damage caused by suicide bombers is their psychological impact. Suicide bombers show a willingness to die for a cause, either out of a sense of desperation or due to religious fanaticism. This self-destructiveness heightens the sense of fear that terrorists often seek to create, a fear that the terrorist enemy is somehow inhuman or superhuman in nature. Most people do not consider committing suicide for one's cause "normal." Thus suicide attacks can serve as powerful propaganda tools for the terrorists, amplifying their emotional impact for allies and enemies alike. However, suicide tactics undermine a bedrock premise of Western society and Western criminal justice: that people generally want some kind of material gain for their political or criminal activities. As we will see in the next chapter, such suicidal terrorism also poses unique problems for any criminal justice system that relies on the self-interest of individuals in order to deter crime.

MAJOR TERRORIST ORGANIZATIONS: A BRIEF LIST

Here is brief list of some of the major terrorist organizations working in the world today. As there is very little reliable intelligence, we will refrain from making any estimates regarding the size of each of these organizations.

Major Islamic Terrorist Organizations

Abu Sayyaf   Largely operating in the southern Philippines, the Abu Sayyaf group is aiming for an independent Muslim state in that region. It has allied itself with other pacific Islamic terrorist groups (such as Jamaah Islamiah), with al-Qaeda, and with Philippine mobsters. They have carried out a protracted war with the Philippine government, frequently bombing civilian and military targets, and have kidnapped (and sometimes killed) foreign civilians.

Al Qaeda   The most well known Islamic terrorist organization, al-Qaeda was founded in 1989 by Osama bin Laden and a few of his allies in the Mujahideen in Afghanistan. Al-Qaeda sees itself as a "defensive group" that is geared toward protecting Muslims from countries who they perceive as enemies of Islam, and toward expelling Western forces from the Middle East. As an extension of this, they target "apostate regimes," that is, regimes that they believe are insufficiently Muslim, such as Saudi Arabia, Syria, and Iraq.

Along with the September 11 attacks and the attack on the *USS Cole,* al-Qaeda has carried out numerous other attacks against U.S. citizens and foreign nationals. Among their largest attacks are an earlier, failed attempt to destroy the World Trade Center in 1993, and the successful bombings of the U.S. embassies in Nairobi, Kenya, and Dar es Salaam, Tanzania, in 1998. Similarly, al-Qaeda, alongside remnants of the former Taliban government, has been involved in attacks against American troops and other forces currently in Afghanistan. Al-Qaeda runs training camps throughout the world that train jihadists to attack the United States and allied governments.

While al-Qaeda has been seriously wounded by operations carried out by the U.S. government and its allies since the September 11 attacks, it has in many ways transformed itself into a more complex, less centralized institution. "Splinter" organizations have taken up the title of al-Qaeda, sometimes without any official relation to Osama bin Laden. For example, the Jordanian terrorist Abu Musab al Zarqawi founded an organization known as "al-Qaeda in Iraq" in order to aid the anti-American and anti-government insurgency in that country and claims allegiance to al-Qaeda and bin Laden. (Al Zarqawi was killed by U.S. forces in Iraq.) Al-Qaeda in Iraq has also been active outside of Iraq, recently attacking sites in neighboring Jordan.

Hamas   Hamas is an Islamic Palestinian organization working in Israel and the Palestinian territories. Its name is an acronym for the organization's title "Islamic Resistance Movement" in Arabic. Hamas is one of the largest and most influential and active Palestine terrorist organizations. It was founded as an outgrowth of the "Muslim Brotherhood," an Egyptian Islamic fundamentalist movement, and has since become the largest party opposing the mainstream Palestinian government. Its ultimate aim is the destruction of Israel and the creation of an Islamic state in all of Palestine. Toward this end it has carried out dozens of suicide attacks against Israelis in Palestine and in Israel. Along with Hamas, Palestinian Islamic Jihad (PIJ) functions as a splinter group that carries out independent attacks against Israelis. Also, Hamas has a political wing that has run candidates in various Palestinian elections and is popular among many Palestinians who consider it to be an honest alternative to the corruption of the Palestinian Authority and the mainstream Fatah party. In 2006, Hamas won a majority of the seats in the Palestinian parliament, and in the Summer of 2007, it forcibly took control of the Gaza Strip, leaving the West Bank to its rivals.

Hezbollah (or Hizbollah)   A Lebanese Shiite organization, Hezbollah (or "the Party of God") operates in Lebanon and is closely linked with the Shiite government of Iran and the Sunni regime in Syria. It was founded in 1982 when Israel invaded Lebanon and has since worked to found a Shiite Muslim state in Lebanon and to harm Israeli citizens. Like Hamas, Hezbollah has a political and social wing that is involved in peaceful political activities in Lebanon. In July–August 2006, Israel invaded southern Lebanon to root out Hezbollah forces there. Israeli forces were partially successful, but Hezbollah remains a powerful force in Lebanese politics.

Jamaah Islamiah   This Muslim organization (its name means "Muslim Community") operates primarily in Indonesia and is dedicated to the creation of an Islamic state throughout the South Pacific. It has carried out several attacks in Indonesia, including two bombings in the resort city of Bali (one in October 2002 and the other in

October 2005) that have killed over 200 people. The organization has recently been weakened by the arrest of some of its leaders, but remains an active threat in the South Pacific and has links with al-Qaeda.

Nationalist Terrorist Organizations

Irish Republican Army (and Splinter Group: "The Real IRA")   The IRA in some form or other has been fighting for Irish independence and later the reunification of the northern Irish counties since the mid-nineteenth century. Henry VIII conquered Ireland in the sixteenth century, but movements for independence developed shortly afterwards. After over two centuries of fighting, the southern, predominantly Catholic, counties separated from the protestant UK and became an independent state in 1921. But as part of their agreement, England kept the northern region of the Irish island on account of its large Protestant population. Since that agreement, the IRA carried out bombings, assassinations, and other attacks throughout the twentieth century in an attempt to force the English out of Northern Ireland.

Since the 1998 "Good Friday Accords," the IRA has largely ceased its military activities, its weapons have been decommissioned and its military units deactivated. However, some radicals rejected the agreement and have broken off from the IRA to continue a violent struggle for Irish independence. They left the organization to form "the Real IRA," which has continued conducting terrorist attacks throughout Northern Ireland and the UK. The Real IRA is blamed for the 1998 Omagh bombing, which killed 29 people, including a pregnant woman and two babies.

Along with the IRA and its splinter organizations, there are a number of Protestant terrorist organizations that have fought against the Irish Catholics and sought to keep Northern Ireland unified with the UK. These "Ulster" or "loyalist" organizations ("Ulster" is another name for the Northern Irish provinces) such as the "Ulster Defense Association" and the "Ulster Volunteer Force" have carried out bombings and shootings in an effort to keep the Irish provinces British. Like the IRA, the loyalist factions have a political wing known as the Ulster Unionist Party that currently has one seat in Britain's Parliament.

Al Aksa Martyrs Brigade (or "al-Aqsa Martyrs Brigade")   A radical offshoot of the Fatah party, it is one of the major political factions in Palestine. While it does carry out suicide attacks like Islamic terrorist organizations, the Martyrs Brigade is not a purely Islamic terrorist organization. Unlike Hamas and Islamic Jihad, the Martyrs Brigade is closer to a Palestinian nationalist organization than a religious one.

ETA   While Spain is now a single, unified nation for the most part, historically this was not always so. It was formed out of a number of different ethnic and cultural groups, only some of whom use Spanish as their native language. The Basque ethnic group of northern Spain and southern France was bitterly suppressed under the Spanish fascist dictator Francisco Franco. ETA grew out of resistance to Franco, and from his death in 1975 until 2006, it fought for Basque independence using bombings, train derailments, and assassinations. Reports of its membership ranged from 20 to several hundred. Like the IRA, ETA also has a "legitimate" political wing that was banned by the Spanish government, which also waged an all-out war against ETA, and dramatically reduced the organization's numbers. Its name is an abbreviation of Euskadi Ta Azkatasuna, which in the Basque language means

"Basque Homeland and Freedom." In 2006, ETA officially abandoned the use of violence as a means to achieve Basque independence.

Liberation Tigers of Tamil Eelam ("Tamil Tigers")   In the northern part of Sri Lanka and the southern region of India is an ethnic group known as the Tamil. The largely Hindu Tamils have had an uneasy relationship with other Sri Lankans and have fought various struggles either for autonomy or for independence. The Tigers have been waging a civil war against the Sri Lankan government and its Buddhist majority since the 1970s, using military strikes and political assassinations, including the 1991 assassination of Indian prime minister Rajiv Gandhi. Currently, as a result of a 2001 ceasefire, the Tigers have been granted a large measure of autonomy in the northern region of Sri Lanka (where they helped coordinate efforts to respond to the December 2004 Tsunami). This situation, however, is quite fragile and could change at any time.

These terrorist organizations are not the only nationalist terrorist organizations presently functioning. They are only the biggest and most active. Many states have their own, fringe groups that seek independence for a minority group, some of which perpetrate violence against innocent civilians.

American Terrorist Organizations

The 1995 attack on the Alfred Murrah federal building in Oklahoma City crystallized the fact that a number of violent right wing organizations are active in the United States. Religious fundamentalists such as Erich Rudolph believe that the liberalization of modern society has corrupted America and must be stopped through violence if necessary. Terrorist organizations exist on both ends of the political spectrum, however, and there are many leftist organizations that seek political change through violence. Although the relations between these organizations (and their connections with international radical organizations) are complex, here is a short list of some of the major movements and organizations that dot the landscape of American terrorism.

Militia Organizations   Extreme rightist groups have formed their own paramilitary or militias that they see as part of a defense against an illegitimate federal government that threatens individual rights. While most militias are "weekend warriors," some have taken the struggle against the government seriously, engaging in criminal activity and terrorism to seek radical changes in the U.S. government. Timothy McVeigh was a part of one of these organizations.

Racist Organizations (Neo-Nazis and the Ku Klux Klan)   Affiliated with the militias are a number of different neo-Nazi organizations that have engaged in acts of violence and terror in the United States. While some of these organizations are peaceful (if obnoxious) political organizations that work through the democratic system, others are not. These groups see the development of a multicultural society in America as a threat to the "white race" and some seek to instigate a "race war" that will lead to the extinction of non-white Americans. Their ideology is spelled out in one of the seminal texts of American racist terrorism, the *Turner Diaries* by William Pierce, a quasi–science fiction account of a civil war wherein African-Americans and Jews attempt to destroy "white America." Many terrorists (including McVeigh) used this text as the blueprint for their enterprises, a manual for igniting a race war in America.

The roots of the Ku Klux Klan go back to the end of the Civil War, when confederate veterans organized to prevent the newly freed slaves from gaining any kind of political power. Membership has ebbed and flowed over the years, but over the last two decades, KKK rolls have suffered a steep decline. Devastated by police investigations, lawsuits, and internal splits, the KKK has been seriously weakened in America. In response, the Klan has tried to recast itself as a mainstream organization, using figures like David Duke (ostensibly a politician) to reform its public image and to distance itself from its terrorist roots.

Close to the KKK are so-called neo-Nazi organizations that take inspiration from Hitler's Germany. Organizations like the American Nazi Party and the White Aryan Resistance have sought to spread racial hatred and anti-immigrant sentiments and sometimes lash out violently at their perceived enemies. Neo-Nazis were implicated in the 1984 murder of Alan Berg, a Jewish radio host in Denver, Colorado. American Neo-Nazis have worked to forge connections with their European counterparts, seeing themselves as part of a grand, transnational Aryan nation. Some recent reports have even claimed that neo-Nazi organizations have joined with Islamic terrorists, bonding over a shared anti-Semitism.[12] However, despite the fact that the American Nazi Party often attracts a great deal of public attention, their numbers are likely small and their relation to real Nazi and fascist ideology is tenuous at best.

Another significant piece of the puzzle of American right wing terrorism is the so-called Christian Identity movement. This movement, a radical interpretation of traditional Christian doctrine, sees whites as God's chosen people and other races, along with the federal government, as in league with Satan. As former FBI director Louis Freeh described the movement's tenets: "Adherents believe that Jews have increasingly gained control of the United States Federal Government and are attempting to enslave the white population by enacting laws subjugating the white people, such as affirmative action, pro-choice, and anti-gun statutes." Thus for the Christian Identity movement, race war, antigovernment actions, and religious war are all part of the same struggle. A number of killings and robberies across the country have been attributed to this movement and its believers have joined with other rightist organizations such as the KKK and the militias. Thus the Christian Identity movement involves a blend of right wing politics, fundamentalist Christianity, racism, and anti-Semitism.

It should be noted that there are many on the American right including racial supremacists and militia members who are not terrorists and do not support the actions of McVeigh and his ilk—

At the other end of the political spectrum are a number of radical leftist organizations that use violence to achieve their political ends. While there were several Marxist and anarchist organizations working in the United States during the 1960s and 1970s such as the Weather Underground and the SLA, they have largely disappeared and have been replaced by ecoterrorists and similar groups. These tend to be loosely organized groups of activists who carry out acts of vandalism such as graffiti along with more serious acts of

---

[12] Gartenstein-Ross, Daveed (2005) "The Peculiar Alliance: Islamists and Neo-Nazis Find Common Ground by Hating the Jews," *The Weekly Standard,* August 31.

destruction (including arson). As a matter or policy, ecoterrorist organizations do not harm people, however. Here are the two best-known ecoterrorist organizations:

Earth Liberation Front (ELF)   As mentioned above, the ELF commits acts of vandalism and arson throughout the globe in an effort to stop what they believe is the destruction of the environment by corporations and private industry. Among the acts perpetrated by ELF are setting fire to housing developments and "tree spiking," placing large nails in trees to damage logging equipment and sometimes injure the loggers themselves.

Animal Liberation Front (ALF)   Like ELF, ALF commits acts of vandalism and destruction throughout the country in order to protect animals from abuse and cruelty. Its roots are in the antihunting movement in England in the 1970s, but it currently focuses on a number of different animal cruelty issues, including meat, fur, and the use of animals in scientific research.

Other Terrorist Organizations

Aum Shinrikyo   A Japanese cult that borrows many of its beliefs from Hinduism and Buddhism, Aum Shinrikyo (translated as "Supreme Truth") is a form of millennial cult—a religious movement that centers its belief around the imminent end of the world. Aum Shinrikyo seeks to promote this end through various destructive acts. In 1995, cult members released sarin gas (a powerful nerve agent) in a Tokyo subway, killing 12 and injuring 6,000 Japanese commuters. The members of Aum Shinrikyo who committed the act (including the cult's leader Shoko Asahara) were arrested and sentenced to various punishments (including death for Asahara). In 2000, the Aum Shinrikyo renounced terrorist tactics and changed its name to Aleph, but is still considered an active terrorist organization by the U.S. State Department and some suspect that members of the organization are still trying to realize Shoko Asahara's doomsday vision.

Shining Path and Tupac Amaru   The Sendero Lumenoso (or "Shining Path") was founded by a Peruvian philosophy professor named Abimael Guzman to carry out a Maoist revolution in the impoverished South American country. Maoism is a radical form of communist theory that advocates a peasant revolution and the use of violence in order to form a socialist society built around economic equality for all. The Shining Path carried out numerous bombings throughout Peru in the 1980s and 1990s and was known for carrying out brutal attacks against those who did not support their movement. The organization was dealt a severe blow, however, when Guzman was arrested in 1992, but nonetheless it still remains active in rural Peru.

The Tupac Amaru (or MRTA, short for Movimiento Revolucionario Tupac Amaru) is another leftist terrorist organization that has been active in Peru. Taking its name from an Incan king who was killed by the Spanish conquistadors, the MRTA has sought to remove foreign influence in the country and to turn Peru into a Marxist state. It has carried out assassinations and taken hostages in Peru since the mid-1980s. The Tupac Amaru briefly received attention in the United States when an American citizen, Lori Berenson, was accused of being an MRTA member by Peruvian forces and was sentenced to life in prison in 1996. Later that year, a group of 14 Tupac Amaru radicals took over the home of the Japanese ambassador in Lima and held the ambassador and a number of Japanese and Peruvian citizens hostage for five months. (They were, in part objecting to the close economic links between Japan and Peru and also protesting the policies of the Peruvian president, Alberto Fujimori, who was of Japanese descent.) Peruvian government commandos raided the embassy and killed all 14 Tupac Amaru operatives, including their leader. Since that raid, there has been significantly less activity from the group but they have still conducted a few minor strikes against radio stations and government officials.

QUESTIONS

1. What do you think makes a person a terrorist?
2. Is there a difference between a terrorist act and a terrorist organization? That is, can groups like Hamas that have both a terrorist and a humanitarian component be "partially" terrorist?
3. Do you think that suicide bombers are uniquely dangerous? What does the phenomenon of suicide bombers say about the terrorist groups that use them? What does it say about the bombers themselves?
4. Of the American terrorist organizations currently active, which do you think is most dangerous and why?

READING AND RESOURCES

Many websites purport to be the "official" website for terrorist organization, and some of these sites may be run by individuals with connections to the actual terrorists. However, these sites are often inaccurate and biased and should be avoided by anybody conducting serious research into terrorism; likewise with books on terrorism. Many books that purport to analyze terrorism often approach the issue from a politically biased viewpoint. Avoid books that seek to point fingers at American politicians (such as "How the liberal elite supports terrorism" or "How the right wing allows terrorists to threaten our freedoms").

One particularly useful text on Islamic terrorism and al-Qaeda is Benjamin, Daniel, and Simon, Steven, *The Age of Sacred Terror,* Random House, 2002.

Another good text is Hoffman, Bruce, *Inside Terrorism,* Potomac Books, 2005.

Here is a sight providing some useful information about ELF and ALF: http://www.animalliberation.net/.

The Council on Foreign Relations is a bipartisan "think tank" (that is, a collection of scholars who often advise politicians and other government officials) that has an excellent and balanced discussion of terrorism: http://www.terrorismanswers.org/.

The National Memorial Institute to Prevent Terrorism has a website that combines a lot of useful information about terrorism. It has a great deal of statistical data about terrorism. Its address is http://www.tkb.org/.

The Southern Poverty Law Center runs a website that keeps track of U.S. hate groups, including right wing terrorist organizations: http://www.tolerance.org/.

The U.S. State Department puts out an annual report entitled "Patterns of Global Terrorism." It can be accessed at http://www.state.gov/s/ct/rls/pgtrpt/.

9

Terrorism and the Criminal Justice System

❖

In the previous chapter we set out to understand the nature of terrorism as well as the threat that it poses for America. In this chapter we will explore some of the different ways that the U.S. government, either unilaterally or in coordination with foreign governments, has responded to the unique threats posed by international terrorism. We will emphasize the aspects of the fight against terrorism that are of particular interest to criminal justice professionals and largely skip over military, economic, and political responses to terrorism (although these are clearly relevant to the overall fight). Thus, we won't discuss the invasion of foreign countries that support terrorism, diplomatic efforts to discourage the support of terrorists, or the isolation of terrorist-friendly nations, regardless of their obvious relevance for the overall struggle. These are clearly important parts of the fight against terrorism, but since they don't involve criminal justice professionals, it is best to put them aside here.

Terrorists are an exceptional type of criminal. The character of terrorists, the beliefs that motivate them, and the types of the crimes that they commit create a distinctive threat and pose unique challenges for governments and for criminal justice professionals. Some terrorists are suicidal fanatics who cannot be deterred by conventional criminal sanctions. Others reject the legitimacy of the entire political order, including the existing criminal justice system. Nonetheless, criminal justice professionals have a unique and important role to play in the fight against terrorism. In this chapter we will explore some of the actual responses that the American government has developed to counter terrorist threats, particularly after September 11, 2001. Thus, we will look at post-September 11 legislation (like the USA Patriot Act) as well as new criminal justice institutions that were developed by the federal government (such as the Department of Homeland Security) to coordinate the government's response to terrorism. In addition, we will examine some other possible responses that have been suggested by politicians and scholars—including the use of torture to gather information about imminent terrorist attacks. Many of the criminal justice system's responses to terrorism are premised on a theory of what makes a terrorist "tick" and so our analysis here will make some references to the material in the previous chapter.

At present, many aspects of the fight against terrorism are in a state of flux. A number of difficult political, legal, and constitutional questions about how to handle suspected terrorists, and legal determinations about what rights suspected terrorists deserve, are still under dispute in American courts, as well as in courts overseas. This means that the analysis offered here will be both tentative and sketchy. In a few years, the criminal justice system's various approaches to fighting terrorism may look radically different from what they are today, depending on the outcome of certain Supreme Court rulings, the results of future presidential elections and, of course, the new tactics used by the terrorists themselves.

Nonetheless, there are a number of crucial issues that the criminal justice professionals and policymakers must confront and a number of different strategies have been settled on by federal and local governments for fighting terrorism and these are the subject of this chapter. First, we will examine the legal questions surrounding the war on terror and some of the laws that are designed to combat terrorism. Then, we will examine some of the criminal justice tactics that have been specifically formed in order to confront terrorism, including the attempt to develop special military tribunals to try suspected terrorists. Finally, at the end of the chapter, we will examine some crucial and controversial law enforcement issues involving the unique threats that terrorists pose, specifically the use of torture and other extreme tactics to gather intelligence about terrorist plans.

Similarly, some of the aspects of the war on terrorism are only partially related to the field of criminal justice. As we will see, in the fight against terrorism, the line between criminal justice activities and other antiterrorism efforts is often blurred. Agencies like the National Security Agency (NSA) are not formally part of the criminal justice system, but to the extent that they are using the tools of criminal justice (such as wiretapping) to bring down terrorist cells in the United States or abroad, we will consider them to be involved in criminal justice activities. To stick to a narrow definition of criminal justice in this chapter would be to overlook many important features of this struggle. As the fight against terrorism is a multifaceted effort, relying on the efforts of law enforcement alongside other agencies that are not formally a part of American criminal justice, we will have to think broadly about the government's role in antiterrorism efforts.

CRIMINAL JUSTICE, INTELLIGENCE, AND COUNTERTERRORISM

The war against terrorism presents a number of different challenges for the American criminal justice system. At the most fundamental level, however, it poses a question about the proper role that law enforcement organizations play in a democratic society. Law enforcement traditionally carries out a number of different tasks, ranging from controlling deviant behavior (by investigating crimes and arresting lawbreakers) and maintaining social order (preventing large-scale unrest; for example, by quelling riots) to more mundane law enforcement tasks. Less often, however, it plays an intelligence gathering role: actively searching out information regarding threats to the American government and to the American people. During World War II, the FBI sought out enemy spies in the United States and likewise during the Cold War, it diligently pursed communist agents operating here. In this intelligence role, the criminal justice system is not reacting to crimes that have taken place, or crimes that are in preparation, as much as diligently pursuing would-be enemies before they have done anything overt to harm the state or society. The police are monitoring threats presented by innocent people rather than responding to extant criminal activity.

There are some other important differences between intelligence gathering activities and traditional law enforcement activities. Intelligence gathering refers to the pursuit of information by government organizations regarding the behavior of foreign agents. Intelligence gathering efforts are largely ongoing affairs and may include spying on people who are not suspected of any overt criminal activity. Criminal investigations, on the other hand, are much more limited and are usually constrained by constitutional principles regarding unreasonable searches and seizures. For example, criminal investigations require probable cause in order to get a warrant from a judge. Intelligence gathering has significantly lower standards for conducing investigations and fewer limitations. As one criminal justice scholar has argued,

> The police collect evidence within court-recognized standards for investigations . . . Intelligence agencies are not held to investigative standards for evidence. Their job is to gather as much information as possible, evaluate its reliability, and utilize it in national defense. The real difference between intelligence gathering and law enforcement is not based on bureaucratic rivalries about differing missions, but differences based on the constitutional use of power.[1]

One of the most significant transformations in American criminal justice following the September 11 attacks is the blurring of the line between these two uses of government power and its implications for the role of government and the bill of rights. If terrorism is not viewed as a crime, but rather as analogous to the behavior of foreign spies, then much of American criminal justice may be undergoing a "paradigm shift"—a dramatic transformation toward a very different role and dramatically expanded powers.

WAR, TERRORISM, AND THE CONSTITUTION

In the last chapter, we talked about whether the fight against terrorism is a "war" or should be described in a different way. There, the discussion was only theoretical. In this chapter, this question has important political and legal consequences, some of which go to the heart of the nature of the American government as set out in the Constitution. According to Article II, Section 2 the Constitution, the president is Commander in Chief of the armed forces and has very wide powers when acting in this way (unlike his civilian powers as Chief Executive which are more limited). Congress, on the other hand, is not as powerful in this area, having the ability to declare war and "the power of the purse," that is, the power to withhold funds from the military when Congress disagrees with the president's policies. Nonetheless, the president is not a dictator, he cannot do whatever he wants by claiming to be acting as a military leader; rather his power as Commander in Chief has been reigned in by the courts and by Congress over the 200 plus years since the Constitution was written.

---

[1] White, Nathan R. (2004) *Defending the Homeland.* Belmont: Thompson Wadsworth, p. 19.

When the president acts as Commander in Chief in a war authorized by Congress, he is much more powerful than he is in his normal civilian role. He can hold prisoners of war without a trial, he can requisition materials for the war effort without paying for them, etc. Essentially, he can do whatever he deems necessary to win the war. However, Congress has not officially declared a war since World War II despite being engaged in numerous military operations since then. Thus, there is a substantial "gray area" between full-scale war and peacetime and the president's powers in these situations are not clearly set out by the Constitution. When Congress has given him specific authority to act as Commander in Chief, even if they have not officially declared war, he may obviously do anything that Congress allows. When Congress has not authorized him to use his war powers, but he feels compelled to act as Commander in Chief, then he is significantly weaker, although he is not powerless. Thus there is a continuum of powers that the president might have in his military role: acting under a declaration of war, acting without congressional authority (but not necessarily against congress), or acting against the will of Congress. In each of these situations, the president has different levels of power, and Congress has a good deal of say in this power. As one Supreme Court Justice put it, "When the President takes measures incompatible with the expressed or implied will of Congress, his power is at its lowest ebb."[2]

This issue has been an important one in the fight against terrorism. In September 2001, shortly after the attacks on the World Trade Center and the Pentagon, Congress passed the "Authorization for the Use of Military Force"[3] (or AUMF) which gave the president power to use force against terrorists and their supporters. Here is the relevant portion of the text:

> the President is authorized to use all necessary and appropriate force against those nations, organizations, or persons he determines planned, authorized, committed, or aided the terrorist attacks that occurred on September 11, 2001, or harbored such organizations or persons, in order to prevent any future acts of international terrorism against the United States by such nations, organizations or persons.

The language Congress used in the AUMF is both broad and ambiguous—it's not quite clear what limits are given to the president, that is, what is "appropriate force"? While the AUMF is not a "declaration of war" per se, it does authorize the president to use force against terrorists and their supporters and has served as the basis for many of the controversial actions taken by the president since the attacks; however, some judges and Constitutional scholars believe that he has overstepped his proper Constitutional bounds.

TERRORISM AND THE LAW

As we observed in the last chapter, there are different forms of terrorism and there is no consensus on what it means to be a terrorist. The law likewise provides many different (and not completely compatible) definitions of terrorism. One scholar has found nearly 150 different definitions of terrorism in the American legal system![4] Each of these different legal definitions pick out different things. Some focus on the activities that constitute terrorism (hijacking,

---

[2] *Youngstown Co.* v. *Sawyer,* 343 U.S. 579 (1952), Justice Jackson, Concurring.
[3] S.J.Res.23.
[4] Nicholas J. Perry, "The Numerous Federal Legal Definitions of Terrorism: The Problem of Too Many Grails," 30 J. Legis. 249.

bombings, etc.), while others emphasize the terrorist's motives (attempts to force political change through intimidation and fear), or where the actions take place (usually, they emphasize crimes that occur overseas). Further, some statutes criminalize activities that aren't really terrorist acts in and of themselves but rather are actions that aid or support terrorists. Finally, some legal approaches to terrorism focus on defining a terrorist *group,* while others aim at prosecuting *individuals* who have already committed terrorist acts. Here, we will hit only the "highlights" of the federal laws against terrorism.

State Department

The U.S. State Department keeps an official list of terrorist organizations and posts it on their website[5] but their analysis is limited to foreign organizations that "Threaten the security of U.S. nationals *or* the national security (national defense, foreign relations, *or* the economic interests) of the United States." Thus domestic terrorist organizations are excluded from the list, as are organizations that are sometimes considered to be terrorist by other countries, but are on good terms with the U.S. government. This means that their list, however helpful, cannot be considered exhaustive or completely accurate. Moreover, their list is not a legal document (the State Department does not make law), but it nonetheless serves as a good guide for understanding some aspects of the government's views about what terrorism consists in.

On their site, the State Department also lists a number of *activities* that they consider to be acts of terrorism. These include:

1. The highjacking or sabotage of any conveyance (including an aircraft, vessel, or vehicle).
2. The seizing or detaining, and threatening to kill, injure, or continue to detain, another individual in order to compel a third person (including a governmental organization) to do or abstain from doing any act as an explicit or implicit condition for the release of the individual seized or detained.
3. A violent attack upon an internationally protected person (as defined in section 1116(b)(4) of title 18, United States Code) or upon the liberty of such a person.
4. An assassination.
5. The use of any—
   a. biological agent, chemical agent, or nuclear weapon or device, or
   b. explosive, firearm, or other weapon or dangerous device (other than for mere personal monetary gain), with intent to endanger, directly or indirectly, the safety of one or more individuals or to cause substantial damage to property.

Federal Criminal Code

There are a number of crimes related to terrorism and terrorist organizations set out under Federal criminal statutes. Chapter 113B (§§ 2331–2339(C)) of the U.S. Federal Code outlines terrorism as a unique category of criminal activity and follows the 1978 "Foreign

---

[5] http://www.state.gov/documents/organization/45323.pdf.

Intelligence Surveillance Act" (FISA) and the 1996 "Antiterrorism and Effective Death Penalty Act." Under the current version of the U.S. Code, the term *international terrorism* refers to activities that:

a. involve violent acts or acts dangerous to human life that are a violation of the criminal laws of the United States or of any State, or that would be a criminal violation if committed within the jurisdiction of the United States or of any State;
b. appear to be intended—
    i. to intimidate or coerce a civilian population;
    ii. to influence the policy of a government by intimidation or coercion; or
    iii. to affect the conduct of a government by mass destruction, assassination, or kidnapping; and
c. occur primarily outside the territorial jurisdiction of the United States, or transcend national boundaries in terms of the means by which they are accomplished, the persons they appear intended to intimidate or coerce, or the locale in which their perpetrators operate or seek asylum;[6]

(Terrorism also works as an aggravating factor in a crime, allowing for additional punishment. To commit a murder is one offense, to commit a murder as a terrorist implies additional punishments.)

Along with individual acts of terrorism, the Federal Criminal Code lists a series of related activities as criminal offenses. For example, it is illegal to provide "material support" to a terrorist organization, a crime that is punished up to 15 years. If the terrorist attack causes a death, this material support can lead to a life sentence. The term *material support* has a very broad definition. It can be providing "Currency or monetary instruments or financial securities, financial services, lodging, training, expert advice or assistance, safehouses, false documentation or identification, communications equipment, facilities, weapons, lethal substances, explosives, personnel, transportation, and other physical assets, except medicine or religious materials." (18 U.S.C. § 2339B) Similarly, the Federal Code outlaws unapproved financial transactions with states that support terrorism (§ 2332(D)), and harboring or concealing terrorists. Thus, the Federal Code sets out a comprehensive legal approach to terrorism, not only criminalizing the act itself, but also forbidding a number of different terrorism-related activities.

Like other sorts of organized crime, terrorist organizations are also considered to be a *criminal conspiracy* under the law. A conspiracy is an agreement by a group of people to engage together in criminal activities—and the agreement itself is a criminal act. Law enforcement can use conspiracy as a tool to arrest somebody before they have carried out their plan. Jose Padilla, the "dirty bomber," was charged with being a part of a widespread conspiracy, "To murder, kidnap, and maim persons in a foreign country." In June 2006, a group of would-be terrorists were arrested in Miami under federal conspiracy statutes for being in an operation that was "more aspirational than operational."[7] Presumably then, all individuals who are part of al-Qaeda may be prosecuted for being part of a criminal

---

[6] 18 U.S.C. § 2331.

[7] Shane, Scott and Zarate, Andrea (2006) "F.B.I. Killed Plot in Talking State, A Top Aide Says," *New York Times,* June 24.

conspiracy, regardless of what over criminal acts they themselves have committed. Obviously, this can be useful because it allows law enforcement to move in and arrest a terrorist before they actually do strike, or even before they *attempt* to strike—all they have to do is agree to carry out terrorist attacks in order to be arrested.

The Moussaoui Trial

Zacarias Moussaoui, a French citizen of Moroccan ancestry, was arrested for immigration violations by FBI in Minneapolis, Minnesota, on August 17, 2001. He had trained in Afghanistan, studied radical Islam in England, and had attended flight school in the United States. Shortly after the September 11 attacks he was suspected of involvement with the crime and was quickly labeled as the "20th hijacker" by the press. While he was most likely not a part of the actual September 11 plot, he clearly was connected to al-Qaeda and may have been intended for a later operation. Nonetheless, prosecutors charged him with being part of al-Qaeda and bearing responsibility for the deaths in the World Trade Center and the Pentagon. Prosecutors put him on trial in federal court in Alexandria, Virginia, and asked that Moussaoui be given the death penalty. As of this writing, he is the only person to be tried in American courts for involvement in the September 11 attacks.

Moussaoui was charged by federal prosecutors with criminal conspiracy and, unlike other suspected al-Qaeda members, he was put on trial before a conventional, civilian criminal court with a jury and public proceedings. After a tumultuous, nearly four-year trial, which included numerous delays, struggles with defense counsel, and multiple outbursts from Moussaoui (including shouting "I am al-Qaeda" to the courtroom), he was convicted. While the prosecutor sought Moussaoui's execution, the jury ultimately settled on six life terms in prison. While they conceded that he was responsible for the September 11 deaths, jurors believed that he was only a minor player in the conspiracy and that his status as an immigrant in France, as well as questions about his mental competence mitigated his crime. After the sentence, Moussaoui tried to retract his guilty plea, asserting that he now believed that he could get a fair trial "even in America." However, it was too late and he was transferred to the supermax prison in Colorado.

The Moussaoui trial showed both the possibilities and the challenges of prosecuting suspected terrorists in civilian, criminal courts. On one hand, Moussaoui was a confrontational and uncooperative defendant, refusing to work either with his attorneys or with the judge. Often such defendants seek to turn the courtroom into a propaganda tool to expose the injustice of their system and to inspire others to follow their lead. (This was a concern at Nuremberg too. Public trials that gather attention can often be used as a platform for political radicals.) On the other hand, there is every reason to believe that Moussaoui himself persuaded nobody in the Islamic world or elsewhere. He did not seem like an inspired or holy man to many, but rather struck observers as delusional and inept. Even Osama bin Laden denied any close connection to Moussaoui.[8] Moreover, no crucial intelligence was revealed in the proceedings, a fear which many have about public trials for terrorists. Whether or not a savvier defendant could do better, the Moussaoui case shows the possibilities for prosecuting suspected terrorists in civilian courts.

---

[8] Shane, Scott (2006) "Bin Laden Is Said to Talk Of Moussaoui," *New York Times,* May 24.

Lynne Stewart: Terrorist or Attorney?

The laws that are used against terrorist crimes are complex and what it means to "support terrorists" is no simple matter. Often, the line separating legal, but ethically questionable behavior and the criminal support of terrorism is not completely clear, even for legal experts. The term *material support* set out in the Federal Code is so broad that there is a real danger that one could inadvertently provide such support. This fact explains the 2002 case of Lynne Stewart. Stewart was the attorney for Sheikh Omar Abdel Rahman, the "Blind Sheik." Among his alleged crimes, Rahman planned the assassination of Egyptian prime minister Anwar Sadat in 1981 and helped organize the 1993 (failed) attempt to destroy the World Trade Center, a crime for which he was sentenced to life in prison. A lifelong radical attorney, Stewart has represented many unpopular clients and even endorsed certain forms of violence to create social change.

The judge in Rahman's trial forbade Stewart from passing on any messages from her client to the general public while representing him. When Stewart made a public statement that Rahman no longer supported a ceasefire in Egypt between Islamic radicals and the Egyptian government, she was promptly arrested and charged with providing material support to terrorists. As part of the trial, secretly recorded conversations between Stewart and Rahmen were presented as evidence against Stewart (usually, these conversations fall under attorney–client privilege, the principle that interactions between criminal defendants and their lawyers are private). Stewart claimed that she was simply trying to keep her client's case in the public eye in order to assure that Rahman's trial would be subjected to public scrutiny and to convince the government to return Rahman to Egypt. Her lapses, she argued, were only a minor offense. Further, Stewart never provided financial or military assistance to terrorists and thus there was nothing "material" about her support. Nevertheless, in February 2005, Stewart was found guilty for supporting terrorists and in October 2006, she was sentenced to 28 months in federal prison.[9]

Stewart's case raises important questions about the relations between terrorism, lawyers, and the criminal justice system. Criminal defendants have the right to a zealous defender, and usually defendants have a right to expect that their interactions with their lawyers will be confidential. Some have accused Stewart of using attorney–client privilege as a shield to pass on information to terrorists, asserting that when she passed on Rahman's message to the press, she stopped being Rahaen's lawyer and became an active part of a terrorist network. Others, including many defense attorneys, have charged the government with using the case to intimidate attorneys who wish to defend terrorists in American courts, causing them to think twice before they take on accused terrorists.

Given the facts of this case, do you think that there was a message being sent by the government to those who defend terrorists? Did Stewart cross the line? What could she have done to protect her client without violating the law?

---

[9] Preston, Julia (2006) "Lawyer, Facing 30 Years, Gets 28 Months, to Dismay of U.S.," *New York Times,* October 17.

The USA Patriot Act

Along with the expanded definition of terrorism set out in the Federal Code, the U.S. government has also developed a number of important and controversial legal tools since September 11 to investigate and prosecute suspected terrorists. Traditionally, law enforcement has treated terrorist groups like any other form of organized crime, and used similar legal tactics in order to investigate and prosecute them. Concerns about protecting the privacy of innocent civilians restricted the ability of law enforcement to conduct surveillance operations of suspected terrorists and rules of habeas corpus and limitations on gathering evidence restricted their ability to detain and interrogate them. However, after September 11, many politicians and criminal justice officials argued that the new threat of terrorism requires novel legal weapons. Because terrorists plan their operations abroad or work with foreign nationals to develop their schemes, law enforcement should treat them differently from traditional criminal operations and different rules ought to apply.

More controversially, many politicians and legal scholars believed that the new dangers presented by al-Qaeda required a reevaluation of the traditional balance between the liberty of American citizens and the security of the nation. Traditionally, criminal law has placed great value on the rights of the accused. Following English jurist William Blackstone, many believed that it is "Better that ten guilty persons escape [punishment] than that one innocent suffer." The fear of a totalitarian government that trampled the rights of its citizens and the horror of punishing an innocent person outweighed the damage caused by the individual criminal who might escape prosecution. Thus, the criminal justice system has always been oriented toward protecting the rights of accused criminals rather than capturing and punishing the guilty (at least in theory; in practice, the system has often been tilted against poor or minority defendants). But when the actions of one of these guilty individuals can lead to the deaths of hundreds, if not thousands of people in a terrorist attack, many argued that Blackstone's formula required reexamination. After September 11, many questioned the balance between liberty and security that had been developed in American law and argued for a new set of laws that could allow law enforcement officers to effectively counter terrorists, even at the expense of civil liberties.

After September 11, the federal government reexamined its capacity to combat terrorism, and Congress gave federal law enforcement authorities some dramatic new powers. In October 2001, after almost no debate in either the House of Representatives or the Senate, Congress passed the "Uniting and Strengthening America by Providing Appropriate Tools Required to Intercept and Obstruct Terrorism Act" (or USA PATRIOT Act) giving federal authorities radical new powers to combat terrorism and other forms of organized crime. Advocates for this legislation argued that a number of legal, civil rights regulations preventing the effective investigation and prosecution of terrorist organizations had hamstrung law enforcement and that the emphasis on civil rights endangered the country. Further, they argued that many of the laws that governed criminal investigations (such as laws regulating wiretapping) were outdated because they were not designed for modern electronic technologies such as email and the World Wide Web. Had law enforcement had the proper investigation and surveillance powers, the al-Qaeda plot could have been discovered and the cells broken up before the September 11 attacks. (The FBI had argued for many of the legislation's provisions prior to September 2001.) Supporters argued that these new laws were necessary and overdue, while critics have argued that these new powers represent a dire threat to civil liberties and open the door to the abuse of government power.

Most generally, the USA Patriot Act blurs the lines, mentioned above, separating law enforcement and intelligence operations. It does this in several ways: First, it significantly expands the power of investigators to monitor various sorts of electronic communications in cases involving national security. Previously, under the 1978 FISA statutes, law enforcement officials were authorized to monitor incoming and outgoing telephone calls in relation to an intelligence matter without being required to show "probable cause" to a judge. They merely had to show that the surveillance was "part of an ongoing investigation" into a foreign power in order to get the warrant. While investigators could not listen to the content of the message without an actual warrant, they could monitor what numbers were dialed out of a particular phone (called "pen registers") and what phone numbers called a particular phone number (referred to as "trap and trace"). The USA Patriot Act expanded this power to a wide array of other electronic communications including email and websites. This means that, without showing probable cause to a judge, the FBI may monitor an individual's email activity and Web activity to a fairly high degree. Proponents of this part of the Act argued that technology had developed to the point where old surveillance methods were outdated and ineffective because a large number of terrorist communications were now electronic.

The USA Patriot Act likewise expanded the ability for law enforcement to request what are known as "sneak and peak" warrants. Under traditional search warrant regulations, law enforcement officials are required to notify the owner of the property that they have searched the premises and specify what they have taken. Sneak and peak warrants do not require that police offers notify the owner in this fashion. These warrants allow law enforcement officials to clandestinely enter a house or other residence, investigate and remove whatever material they desire and leave without letting the owners know that they were ever there. The USA Patriot Act was the first explicit law that authorized these warrants (traditionally, judges have allowed them, but they have occupied a legal "grey area"—they were legally controversial but were sometimes allowed by judges). Critics have charged that this changes a warrant from an open, official act of a government to a secretive tactic of breaking and entering, creating an unacceptable intrusion into the private life of citizens who have not been accused of any particular crime. Defenders charge that this is the only way to investigate what suspected terrorists are up to without alerting them to the fact that they are being observed and thereby changing their behavior, causing them to cease to be useful sources of intelligence.

Unlike conventional criminal investigations, warrants for national security investigations need not go through traditional judicial channels. There is a special federal court, known as the Foreign Intelligence Security Court (FISC) that works in secret and reviews requests from the Department of Justice and the Attorney General regarding warrants in foreign intelligence matters. In theory, the FISC is meant to make sure that the DOJ is not abusing the power to conduct counterintelligence operations. In practice, the court tends to be a "rubber stamp" for federal investigations. In 2002, the FISC authorized all but one wiretap request.[10]

[10] Crank, John P. and Gregor, Patricia (2004) *Counter-Terrorism after 9/11*, Newark: Lexis-Nexis Publishers.

It is clear that there is a balance to be struck by criminal justice professionals and law-makers between the requirements for combating terrorism and the need to protect the very freedoms that terrorists wish to destroy. Historically, citizens of democracies have been willing to give up some of their rights in order to protect liberties. When England suffered a plague of bombings by the IRA in the 1970s, the government assumed powers to arrest and detain individuals for great lengths of time without a trial. Concerns about losing civil liber-ties and undermining democracy are very abstract when compared to the concrete acts of destruction that terrorists are capable of inflicting on innocent people and the fear that their threats provoke. However, dictators have sometimes used a "fight against terrorism" as an excuse to destroy democratic governments. As former Attorney General John Ashcroft argued before Congress in late 2001: "To those who pit Americans against immigrants, cit-izens against non-citizens, to those who scare peace-loving people with phantoms of lost liberty, my message is this: Your tactics only aid terrorists for they erode our national unity and diminish our resolve. They give ammunition to America's enemies and pause to America's friends. They encourage people of good will to remain silent in the face of evil." As some scholars have observed, whenever "freedom" is opposed to "security" in the mod-ern world, freedom almost inevitably loses.

The Warrantless Wiretapping Controversy

In December 2005, the *New York Times* revealed that President George W. Bush had authorized the National Security Agency (NSA) to monitor phone conversations of suspected terrorists without applying for a warrant from the FISA courts.[11] The revela-tion led to anger on both sides. Supporters of the administration wanted the editors of the newspaper to be prosecuted for revealing state secrets and thought that the article had damaged America's ability to fight terrorists by alerting them to the fact that they could be monitored. Opponents of the administration felt that the act, in direct defiance of the FISA law, amounted to an impeachable offense and argued that the president should be thrown out of office. Perhaps most controversially, the president never went to the FISC to get permission to wiretap the lines even after the wiretapping had been carried out.

The White House argued that the president was constitutionally authorized to act as Commander in Chief to conduct the surveillance operations. The lawyers further argued that the AUMF gave the president the legal authority to conduct wiretaps without the permission of the FISA courts. As the lawyers argued, "History conclusively demon-strates that warrantless communications intelligence targeted at the enemy in time of armed conflict is a traditional and fundamental incident of the use of military force authorized by the AUMF."[12] These arguments are controversial, and in August 2006 a Federal Judge in Detroit ruled the wiretaps unconstitutional (the Department of Justice is appealing the ruling).[13]

---

[11] Risen, James and Lichtblau, Eric (2005) "Bush Lets U.S. Spy on Callers Without Courts," *New York Times,* December 16.
[12] US Department of Justice Memorandum (2006) "Legal authorities supporting the activities of the National Security Agency described by the president." January 19, p. 2.
[13] *ACLU* v. *NSA,* Case No: 06-CV-10204.

The Department of Homeland Security

Along with the adoption of the USA Patriot Act, the federal government underwent another major shakeup after September 11, 2001. Many believed that better coordination between the different branches of the federal government could have stopped al-Qaeda before they struck. In the wake of the attacks, there were a number of efforts to reform the federal law enforcement, security, and intelligence bodies so that they would be better able to anticipate future attacks and respond to those that should occur (along with other disasters). The most dramatic of these reforms was the creation of the Department of Homeland Security (DHS), a new federal agency with a cabinet-level position, the Secretary of Homeland Security, who reports directly to the president. The theory behind this is that a high-profile, politically powerful branch of government would be better suited to protecting the nation and simultaneously coordinating an effective response to terrorist attacks and other disasters.

The DHS consolidates 22 different agencies with over 180,000 personnel and has taken on a dizzying array of tasks. The department is divided up into four major sections or "Directorates," each of which is headed by a commissioner or undersecretary who answers to the Secretary of Homeland Security. It should be noted that the DHS is not solely involved in fighting terrorism, but must also deal with other threats to the security of the nation, including natural disasters and illegal immigration. This means that for many of parts of the DHS, terrorism is not the sole or even the primary part of their job. Here is a list of some of the major organizations that are now a part of the DHS:

Border and Transportation Security (BTS)   One of the ways that the DHS protects the nation from terrorist attacks is by keeping track of those who enter the country and likewise preventing undocumented and potentially dangerous aliens from getting in. Several of the September 11 hijackers were not supposed to be in the United States at the time of the attacks but as immigration was not adequately policed, they were able to operate undiscovered. Thus the organization previously known as the Immigration and Naturalization Service (INS) became the Immigration and Customs Enforcement bureau (ICE) and Customs and Border Protection (CBP) under the DHS. Further, the BTS also handles the security of U.S. airports under the Transportation Security Administration (or TSA—these are the people who inspect your luggage at the airport before you board your flight).

Emergency Preparedness and Response (EP&R)   The purpose of the EP&R division is to coordinate responses to disasters (both man-made and natural) as well as to be prepared for future disasters. This means that, along with radiological, biological, or other forms of terrorist attack, the EP&R is responsible for preparing for, and coordinating response to, natural disasters like floods, hurricanes, and fires. Obviously, this is a tremendous task and in order to carry it out, the EP&R merged with the Federal Emergency Management Agency (FEMA—formally an autonomous government agency) and builds upon their work in coordinating disaster relief efforts.

Science and Technology Service (S&T)   The S&T is the research wing of the DHS. It is in charge of developing technology and equipment that will help other parts of the DHS and the law enforcement community at large anticipate and prepare for future terrorist attacks.

Information Analysis and Infrastructure Protection   The term *infrastructure* refers to those institutions that provide basic needs to Americans, including water and energy supplies. For example, power plants (and particularly nuclear plants) are thought to be potential targets for terrorist strikes and a serious attack on these could kill thousands and cripple the basic functioning of society. This means that the security of these structures requires constant study.

The Secret Service and Coast Guard   The Secret Service, previously part of the Treasury Department, has historically protected the president and other important government officials on one hand, and protected the economic security of the nation by apprehending counterfeiters on the other. Insofar as the economic security of the country could be undermined by counterfeiting of American currency or by assassinating prominent public officials, these agents have played an important role in protecting the homeland. Likewise, the Coast Guard, whose job is to patrol and protect the American coastlines, searching for unlawful smuggling and rescuing troubled ships, has become a part of the DHS in times of peace, at least. (In times of war it becomes a part of the Department of Defense, however.)

The DHS has had critics from the beginning. Some of these skeptics have argued that the DHS just adds one more layer of bureaucracy to the federal government. The jobs assigned to the Secretary of Homeland Security have been so nebulous and the bureaucracy under his command is so huge, that some feared creating another sprawling, ineffective bureaucratic beast that would not make Americans any safer. This perception was exacerbated by the use of "color codes" to establish threat levels and the recurring dire warnings of threats (which were often suspiciously timed), which were mocked by critics and late-night talk-show hosts. Similarly, the FEMA division of the DHS was publicly attacked for failing to adequately respond to the devastation caused by Hurricane Katrina in August 2005. Others critics fear the power wielded by the head of such a centralized government agency, believing that such a great amount of concentrated power could easily be abused, creating a "big brother" organization that would control the lives of ordinary citizens in unacceptable ways.

It is difficult to determine whether or not the critics of the DHS have been correct. As with the USA Patriot Act, many of the DHS antiterrorism operations are carried out in secret and so experts cannot publicly evaluate them. The DHS is new and it may take many years for their ultimate role to be clearly defined. Further, it is difficult to measure its effectiveness. One cannot arrive at any definitive conclusions based upon what has *not yet* happened or compare it to what would have happened had there been no DHS. While it is true that (as of this writing) there have been no major terrorist attacks in the United States since September 2001, it is fallacious to conclude that this is a consequence of the efforts of the DHS or the USA Patriot Act and not a result of other factors. Determining the cause of events is difficult enough, determining the causes of nonevents is nearly impossible.

Unlawful Combatants and Military Tribunals

Since the September 11 attacks, the U.S. government has struggled with finding the appropriate way to classify and handle the suspected terrorists that they have arrested or captured on the battlefield. On one hand, they are prisoners of a war that Congress has authorized the president to conduct. On the other hand, this is a war with indefinite boundaries against an enemy that has no recognizable government. Further, it is a struggle that may never have a final conclusion. Giving a president too much power in such circumstances could easily lead to abuse, but at the same time the president needs a free hand to fight a dangerous and secretive enemy. Nowhere is the tension between conceiving the fight against terrorism as "war" and as "law enforcement" as acute as it has been in the detention and treatment of suspected al-Qaeda and Taliban members.

Shortly after the 2001 attacks, President Bush made a number of controversial declarations regarding the treatment of suspected terrorists. He declared that the prisoners at Guantanamo Bay were "unlawful combatants" (or "enemy combatants"), meaning that, at the president's determination, they could be held indefinitely without a trial. Moreover, according to the White House, they were not prisoners of war and therefore they did not get the POW protections that are spelled out in the Geneva Conventions (as was discussed in Chapter 6, the Geneva Conventions set out the basic laws of war including the treatment of prisoners of war). Further, the president ruled that these prisoners could be put on trial in special military tribunals that gave the defendants fewer rights than they would receive in civilian courts. For example, the tribunals as envisaged by the White House did not allow the defendant to see all of the evidence presented against him and allowed hearsay (second-hand) evidence that would not be allowed in a U.S. court. The president claimed the unilateral authority to make these determinations without the input of Congress and without the scrutiny of the Supreme Court.

The approach set out by the White House was largely rejected by a number of subsequent Supreme Court rulings. Most recently, the Supreme Court rejected the White House's approach to handling the terrorists held at Guantanamo Bay. In a ruling entitled *Hamdan* v. *Rumsfeld,* the court held that the prisoners at Guantanamo Bay were entitled to protection under the Geneva Conventions and that the president alone could not create tribunals to prosecute the suspected terrorists. Any courts that put detainees on trial would have to be set up by Congress, and "Common Article 3" of the Geneva Conventions (that prevents "cruel, inhuman, and degrading treatment," discussed in Chapter 6) must be applied to these prisoners.

Since the *Hamdan* ruling, Congress has developed legislation to give suspected terrorists a trial with more protections than those provided by the White House, but which allowed military officials to tightly control the procedures. On October 17, 2006, President Bush signed the Military Commission Act of 2006, which gave him the authority to set up military tribunals for enemy combatants. (An individual is determined to be an enemy combatant by a "Combat Status Review Tribunal" or CSRT, another quasi-judicial body that examines the evidence against a suspect.) Enemy combatants are put on trial and may be convicted and sentenced by the commission, which may apply the death penalty. While these commissions give defendants some of the rights that one would find in a civilian court or in a military court martial, they are denied other basic rights. The act also limited the ability of prosecutors to punish Americans for war crimes such as violations of Common Article 3, making it easier for government agents to engage in torture and other violent acts against prisoners with impunity.[14] The military commission act specifically

---

[14] Scheffer, David (2006) "How the Compromise Detainee Legislation Guts Common Article 3," *Jurist,* September 25 (available at http://jurist.law.pitt.edu/forumy/2006/09/how-compromise-detainee-legislation.php).

prevents those determined to be enemy combatants from appealing to a civilian court, denying them the right of *habeas corpus.*

As of this writing, nobody has been put on trial before the military commissions although a number of important suspected al-Qaeda members have gone before CSRTs and some individuals have been charged with war crimes. In March 2007, David Hicks, an Australian national, was charged by the Commission's prosecutor with providing material support to terrorists[15] and suspected al-Qaeda member Khalid Shaikh Mohammed acknowledged responsibility for planning the September 11 attacks during CSRT proceedings.[16]

Racial Profiling?

One of the most contentious issues in modern American law enforcement has been the use of "racial profiling," that is, using the racial makeup of citizens as a guide to their potential criminality. Traditionally, law enforcement has used racial profiling as a means for targeting African Americans and other minorities for searches and questioning (giving rise to the "Driving While Black" phenomenon), a tactic that has been bitterly attacked by civil rights advocates as a form of racism. However, given the fact that an overwhelming number of terrorists were of Arab, Middle Eastern, or South Asian descent and given the dangers of letting terrorists slip past airline security many have reevaluated the role that racial and ethnic distinctions should play in terrorism. Millions of people travel on planes and trains each day and racial and ethnic markers may be one useful way to determine who might be a terrorist threat and who might not. Without using visible clues such as dress and race to determine who to stop and search before boarding an airplane, security officials will no doubt waste a large amount of their time inspecting individuals who have no relation to terrorism.

Racial profiling is a complex political, legal and ethical problem and can refer to a lot of different things. Between the extremes of stopping an individual solely because they are a member of a minority group and using racial characteristics to find a specific individual wanted for a specific crime lie a whole host of activities, some legal, some not. The courts have ruled that police officers may use an APB that uses racial characteristics (such as an APB for an "Asian male") as grounds for stopping an individual.

Whether or not racial profiling certain groups is legal, it is nonetheless unofficially practiced throughout the transportation industry. Many individuals of Arab or Middle Eastern descent report being stopped by airport security services much more often than other ethnic groups. Anecdotal evidence likewise points to the fact that individuals who "look Muslim," having beards and dressing in a Middle-Eastern fashion, are stopped and searched by airport security officials. Alongside Driving While Black, some have complained about FWA, "Flying While Arab."

However, as we saw in the last chapter, terrorists, including Islamic terrorists, come from all racial and ethnic backgrounds. The Abu Sayyaf group consists largely of ethnic Filipinos. Jamaah Islamiah's members are Indonesian. Many Muslim radicals have come out of Bosnia and Kosovo in Eastern Europe and appear to be white by most

---

[15] "Australian Is Charged In Terror Case," *New York Times,* March 2, 2007.

[16] Liptak, Adam (2007) "Suspected Leader of 9/11 Attacks Is Said to Confess," *New York Times,* March 15.

American standards. John Walker Lindh, a white American from Southern California, was arrested in Afghanistan and pled guilty to aiding the Taliban. Likewise, a number of terrorists hail from parts of Africa where people possess ethnic traits similar to African Americans, such as Zacharias Moussaoui, who comes from Morocco. In his fictional account of future terrorist attacks, a former Bush administration counterterrorism expert surmised that the next generation of terrorists to attack targets in the United States will most likely not be Arabs. (As one of his fictional terrorists writes, "We do not look like you think we do. And we will kill you until you leave our holy lands."[17]) Thus even if the court system concedes that law enforcement may use some form of racial profiling in airport security and other places where terrorist attacks are likely, it is not likely that racial profiling will stop all Islamic terrorists.

Terrorism and Torture

There are many who wish to expand the powers of the president to fight terrorism even further. After September 11, 2001, a number of legal scholars began to assert that, under limited circumstances, law enforcement authorities should be authorized to torture suspected criminals, especially suspected terrorists who might possess valuable intelligence about impending attacks on Americans. The classic case (often called "the ticking-bomb terrorist") involves a terrorist who knows the location of a bomb that could soon kill hundreds or thousands of people, but refuses to disclose where it is hidden. In such cases, it is difficult to argue that torture is obviously wrong and that it is preferable that many innocents die than one guilty individual undergo short-term, if serious pain. As a part of the fight against terrorism, a number of ethicists and legal scholars have suggested that torture is morally justified in cases such as these and they have begun to articulate some principles that might provide a rationale for terrorism and express its limits. Others, however, have been equally strident against the use of torture in any circumstance, even against terrorists.

Historically, the vast majority of governments have used torture against their internal and foreign enemies, and in recent times many states, some of them democratic, have resorted to torture in one form or another. Israel, for example, used numerous "stress techniques" (such as sleep deprivation and forcing a prisoner to crouch in uncomfortable positions for great lengths of time, along with other forms of physical force) on Palestinian prisoners in order to extract information from them about terrorist operations. (Israeli courts outlawed many of these techniques, however.) The British government used torture against suspected Northern Irish terrorists and the French government used systematic torture against Algerian separatists who sought independence from France. In less democratic states throughout the world, leftist, rightist, religious, and secular governments have used torture against terrorist (or perceived terrorist) threats with little hesitation. When faced with violent extremist movements, the use of torture is the rule, not the exception among governments throughout the world.

Traditionally, the American government has opposed torture as a form of intimidation or interrogation against suspected terrorists or other forms of criminals. Evidence gained through torture, like any other form of unlawfully obtained evidence, falls under the

---

[17] Clarke, Richard (2005) "Ten Years Later," *The Atlantic Monthly,* January/February.

exclusionary rule and cannot be used at trial. As we saw in Chapter 5, evidence gained through interrogation methods used by foreign law enforcement officials that "shock the conscience" can be excluded from an American criminal trial. Likewise the Eighth Amendment to the U.S. Constitution outlaws the use of "cruel and unusual punishment," which is taken to outlaw the use of torture. The United States ratified the international Convention against Torture in 1988 and has frequently criticized foreign governments that practice torture. As we saw in the Pinochet case (discussed in Chapter 4), torture is considered to be a crime against humanity for which there is no immunity for heads of state. Generally speaking, torture is considered anathema to American criminal procedure, American criminal law, and to American political and moral values.

Since September 11, however, the American government has reevaluated its stance toward certain forms of torture in public and (many believe) secretly used torture techniques or exploited legal loopholes in order to torture suspected terrorists in order to obtain information about their activities. Usually the information gained through interrogation is not used to prosecute the suspected terrorists (the present administration has not focused on prosecuting suspected terrorists), but rather to prevent future attacks and to learn the location of active terrorists who might be neutralized by American agents. Traditionally, torture has been labeled a violation of the Geneva Conventions, but government officials have begun to reevaluate what constitutes "torture," accepting interrogation methods that had previously been considered torture, thereby giving interrogators a measure of freedom to use physical force during interrogations. Alberto Gonzalez, while White House Counsel, the president's attorney, argued that the unique nature of the fight against terrorism made a number of the traditional legal protections against torture (to use his term) "quaint." Many observers have argued that these views led to a lax environment that tacitly if not explicitly allowed torture to happen under American command and created an environment that dehumanized Arab prisoners, culminating in the scandal at Abu Ghraib, where American soldiers brutally tortured captive Iraqi prisoners.

The American government has also used a tactic known as "rendition" in order to evade laws against torturing prisoners. Rendition refers to the case where prisoners are handed over to foreign governments with more lenient torture policies than those in the United States. ("Extraordinary rendition" refers to cases where the president and not the courts authorize the transfer.) The United States essentially uses these foreign and frequently totalitarian governments as proxies, gaining the intelligence that the foreign government extracts from the victim without having any legal accountability for their acts and without violating domestic American law. Suspected terrorists are flown by private jets owned by dummy corporations that serve as "fronts" for the CIA to countries such as Syria, Egypt, or Pakistan where they are beaten and tortured for information.[18] At present, American officials acknowledge that they carry out renditions but assert that they gain reassurances from the states that receive the suspected terrorists that they will not torture their prisoners. A number of former detainees who were eventually released have gone public with their allegations, and at present, some are suing the U.S. Government over their renditions. Whether or not the U.S. government is aware of or secretly condones the use of torture, handing over suspected terrorists to brutal regimes raises a number of thorny political, legal, and moral problems.

---

[18] Mayer, Jane (2005) "Outsourcing Torture," *The New Yorker,* February 14.

When the pictures of torture and humiliation of Iraqi prisoners from Abu Ghraib prison in Iraq appeared in the Western press in the spring of 2004, the ugly realities surrounding torture came to light. Many Americans were shocked by the images of American troops torturing Iraqi prisoners in brutal and humiliating ways especially given the cheery expressions that many of the torturers had in the photographs and the sexual nature of a great deal of the events portrayed. The military rushed to prosecute those who committed the acts and the president publicly apologized for them, asserting on Arab television that "What took place in that prison does not represent the America that I know."[19] Further, groups and individuals began to report about torture tactics that were used on the prisoners at Camp X-Ray and Camp Delta in Guantanomo Bay. Nonetheless, since Abu Ghraib, a number of incidents of torture carried out by U.S. forces have been reported in Iraq and Afghanistan.

Terrorism raises many morally complex and troubling issues regarding the limits on interrogations and the application of torture. Many terrorists are fanatical about their causes and are frequently willing to accept most traditional forms of punishment as part of their "martyrdom" and thus are not as likely to be intimidated by traditional interrogation tactics. Likewise, the destruction of human life, property, and security that terrorism can cause are much worse than more traditional crime. Finally, the threat of abuse of the power of torture is ever-present as law enforcement and intelligence officials misuse the power to torture to force confessions from innocent civilians or to quiet the sort of dissent that is normally an acceptable part of democratic society. This means that, in order to successfully fight terrorists, new and aggressive forms of interrogation and intelligence gathering may be needed.

These issues have been widely debated in government and in the media. Vice President Dick Cheney has argued for giving intelligence officials the right to use certain forms of torture against suspected terrorists. In October 2005, the Senate voted on a proposal to ban the use of "cruel and degrading treatment" by U.S. officials.[20] The bill's main sponsor was John McCain, a Vietnam veteran who was tortured while in captivity. However, critics pointed out that the law left numerous loopholes that allowed for government officials to conduct torture. Leaving aside these political battles, the appropriateness of the use of torture and the acceptable limits for the interrogation of violent, fanatical terrorists will undoubtedly be an issue for ongoing debate.

There is a very practical question about the use of torture as an interrogation technique. Many intelligence experts reject torture as a technique of interrogation but not on humanitarian grounds. Rather, they argue that torture is useless as a tool to gather intelligence. Under excruciating physical pain, people are inclined to say anything that they believe their tormentors wish to hear in order to cease their pain. Thus, torture victims report confessing to crimes that they did not commit and identifying innocent individuals as fellow terrorists in order to please their captors and end the suffering. Gerry Conlon, a suspected IRA terrorist, was tortured into confessing for a bombing that he did not commit, and under pressure, pointed to several of his friends, who were equally innocent,

---

[19] Statement of President Bush, G. W. (2004). On the Al-Hurra station. MSNBC, May 5.

[20] "Cheney pushes senators for exemption to CIA torture ban," *USA Today,* November 4, 2005.

as fellow terrorists. It was only after the "Guilford Four" had served 15 years in prison that the misbehavior of the British Police was exposed and the falsely accused terrorists set free.[21] Cases like this underscore the point that, even if moral issues are put aside, torture may not be a particularly desirable tool for law enforcement to use against terrorists.

Deterring Terrorists?

In the previous chapter, we discussed the unique nature of terrorist tactics and the fanatical nature of modern terrorism. These aspects of terrorism place particular challenges before the modern criminal justice system. While there is a widespread belief that most *traditional* criminals may be deterred from their antisocial behavior by threats of some form of punishment, terrorists pose unique challenges. As far as motives for criminal behavior go, religious beliefs are different from the selfish pursuit of wealth or power. For believers, religious motives are more powerful than any possible worldly harm that could be placed upon them by the criminal justice system, such as incarceration. Many terrorists are willing, even happy, to sacrifice their lives for their cause, believing that they will be rewarded in the afterlife for their actions, referring to their acts as "martyrdom operations" and eagerly anticipating the benefits of heaven. Further, those who die in the service of their cause are frequently considered heroes to be emulated by others. Even Timothy McVeigh is viewed by many domestic terrorists as a hero to be emulated in the cause of white supremacy. It is highly unlikely that such individuals could be easily deterred by threats of incarceration or even execution in the way that street criminals are.

The political issues that the large-scale use of suicide bombers by terrorist forces raise are profound ones for any criminal justice system. A great amount of the modern criminal justice system relies upon an individual's fear of punishment or death as a form of deterrence, that is, as a way to ensure that most rational individuals obey the law out of a kind of "enlightened self-interest." The threat of imprisonment or execution is meant to keep in line individuals who would otherwise violate the rules of society. But if the criminals themselves are willing, even eager, to die for their particular cause, then there is little that these traditional threats can do to deter them. This means that the sanctions that support the entire criminal justice system won't be enough to stop them from their intended goals in many cases. The nihilistic attitude of suicidal terrorists and their eagerness to sacrifice lives (their own and others) present a serious challenge to the institutions of criminal justice.

Further, many terrorists feel that there is no possible means to promote their causes other than by resorting to terrorist violence. Frequently, terrorism is the last resort turned to once all peaceful means available to promote their cause have failed. Encouraging those who seek political change to work through legitimate political organizations or to vote misses the fact that most terrorist organizations only develop when such nonviolent methods have proven fruitless.

At a minimum, many terrorists feel that they must continue to press their cause through violence so that other, less extreme, efforts to resolve a political dispute may be

---

[21] The story of Gerry Conlon and the Guilford Four was told in the book and movie *In the Name of the Father.*

effective. In Northern Ireland, Sinn Fein relied on pressure from their violent compatriots in the IRA to force the British government to negotiate for home rule. In such cases, moderate and extremist political forces deliberately or indirectly work in collusion to press for political or social change. This means that terrorists frequently feel that they have no option but to continue harming innocents. Even if there are other tools to achieve change, terrorism has the ability to keep public attention on issues that would otherwise be forgotten.

These facts make formulating criminal justice policies for handling terrorists a particularly difficult task for modern criminal justice professionals. If the threat of long-term incarceration or even the threat of execution will not discourage terrorists from carrying out their plans, then both general and special deterrence seem to fail as reasons for punishing terrorists. Execution may ultimately only encourage future terrorists by creating a group of martyrs who inspire a new generation of terrorists. Further, open, public criminal trials for accused terrorists may only provide them with a forum from which they might expound their doctrines, risking the possibility that the accused terror-ist might persuade converts to his or her cause or gain a great deal of sympathy from the general public. A charismatic terrorist can sway public opinion in his or her favor or inspire others to join them in waging violent war against innocent civilians. Hence, the appeal of military tribunals, despite the concern that they might not provide a fair trial for accused terrorists, is that they may be carried out in secret thereby robbing the terrorist of such a lucrative propaganda tool.

In the previous chapter we pointed out that many terrorist organizations lack a firm organizational structure, preventing governments and criminal justice systems from easily destroying them. Even if the US caught the al-Qaeda masterminds such as Osama bin Laden and punished them, others would probably rise from the "grass roots" to continue their fight. To this extent, terrorist organizations resemble the mythical hydra, the many-headed creature that, when one head is lopped off, grows two more. This, coupled with the fanaticism of many modern terrorists makes the prospect of a complete solution to the terrorist threat through the use of the tools of the criminal justice system highly dubious. Of course, this does not mean that the criminal justice system as it presently functions is irrelevant to the fight against terrorism; it simply means that its powers to stop and deter terrorism are limited.

Refusing to punish terrorists at all is, of course, not a realistic option and something must be done with them. At least incarceration will prevent a terrorist from participating in further attacks. It may not be able to deter future terrorist attacks, but it can incapacitate terrorists by keeping them away from the innocent public. To this extent, punishment has a role to play in the fight against terrorism. Likewise, incarcerated terrorists might be reformed—being taught the difference between acceptable and unacceptable outlets for the political and spiritual isolation. Such reformed terrorists could be very useful for public relations efforts to delegitimize terrorism as a tactic of political struggle. Whether or not the modern prison system is appropriately equipped for such tasks is another matter, how-ever. As there is very little evidence criminal incarceration reforms conventional criminals, so there is likewise little reason to believe that current prison conditions could change hardened terrorists.

All of this suggests that the criminal justice system cannot formulate a complete response to terrorism. While it is certainly true that terrorists may be investigated like conventional criminals, they cannot be treated like conventional criminals for purposes of punishment. In order to counter terrorists thoroughly, criminal justice responses must be supplemented with political, economic, and military efforts. These additional efforts can address the root political causes of terrorism as well as the governments that support them. As we will see shortly, when we discuss international drug smuggling, the criminal justice system is only part of the puzzle of international crime—other approaches, whether economic or political, can make a significant contribution in the fight against international crime.

Noncriminal Approaches to Defeating Terrorism

One novel approach that has been developed for fighting terrorist organizations does not rely on criminal sanctions at all, but rather seeks to cripple terrorists by using civil suits to rob them of their sources of funding. Private lawsuits by the families of terrorist victims have focused on the wrongful deaths they have caused and target the publicly known organizations that fund them as well as the states that sponsor terrorist acts. The Antiterrorism Act of 1996 strips governments that sponsor terrorism of their traditional legal immunity in U.S. Federal Courts. Such suits have been used effectively against right wing groups like the Ku Klux Klan in the United States by organizations like the Southern Poverty Law Center, shutting down their operations by robbing them of funding.[22] By hitting terrorist supporters "in the wallet," civil suits can help drain terrorist organizations of political and financial support without having to resort to the traditional tools of law enforcement.

Like incarceration or execution, the promise of suing terrorists out of existence is somewhat limited, however. While the terrorists themselves may be hurt by a lack of support and funding, this will not necessarily prevent them from carrying out attacks or recruiting new members. The funds that are required for conducting most terrorist operations are not significant, particularly when compared to conventional militaries. Frequently states fund terrorist organizations clandestinely and deny there is any connection between themselves and terrorists—making effective lawsuits a difficult proposition. Likewise, a great deal of funding for terrorists comes from the secret donations of private individuals through informal transactions with no detectable paper trail. Finally, many terrorist organizations raise their own funds, through illegal activity such as the manufacture and distribution of illegal drugs. As we will see in the next chapter, terrorist organizations in Latin America have made a great deal of their money by participating in cocaine trafficking operations, usually by running protection rackets for the traffickers. While tools such as civil suits can be helpful for fighting terrorism and allow the victims of terrorism to find some kind of compensation for their suffering, it is unlikely that these strategies alone will significantly harm terrorists or interrupt their activities.

The criminal justice system's response to terrorist threats must be seen against a broader political backdrop. The FBI and the Department of Homeland Security seek to fight terrorism using its own tools, but so do politicians and diplomats. Many terrorist organizations rely upon the goodwill and support of sympathetic governments and cannot

---

[22] The Associated Press, "Klan Loses Suit over Fire: Jury Awards $37.8 Million," July 25, 1998.

function effectively without them. This means pressure from a powerful and wealthy country like the United States can force these governments to crack down on terrorists and their supporters or cut off the financial or logistical support for terrorist organizations. Political solutions to terrorism are not a complete solution (after all, many terrorist groups are not supported by governments or would continue to function were their patron governments to cut them off), but they are an important part of the fight against terrorism.

There is no single "silver bullet" that will work effectively against every type of terrorist organization. As we saw in the previous chapter, each terrorist group has its own unique structure, belief systems, and goals and each must be approached differently. The strategies that worked effectively against the IRA in Northern Ireland would probably not work against an Islamic radical group in the Middle East. Similarly, an absolute prohibition on any negotiations with *any* terrorists or acceding to any of their demands may run the risk of overlooking aspects of the terrorist's causes that are legitimate and may likewise be the interest of many peaceful people. To refuse to discuss the situation in Palestine because of the behavior of Hamas would lead to ignoring serious problems that affect people who do not support Hamas operations. Simply because terrorists have taken up a cause does not mean that this cause is inherently wrong. Terrorist organizations must be confronted with a variety of techniques, and a combination of political, military, and law enforcement approaches is most likely to be effective. Terrorism is a complex phenomenon and while the military, local, federal, and international law enforcement communities have an essential role to play in the fight against it, these are not the only tools that can be used.

QUESTIONS

1. Given the unique problem that terrorism raises for a criminal justice system, what are the ways that criminal justice professionals may effectively deal with terrorism? Are there any good options to deal with terrorists?

2. What is the proper balance between the additional security that acts like the USA Patriot Act provide and the privacy and liberty that all Americans cherish? Does the act go too far in allowing the government to observe Americans? How might the act be improved?

3. What are some ways that the American criminal justice system might work toward defeating terrorism? Is there a way that the corrections/penal system may be changed so that it might be better suited to handling terrorists?

READING AND RESOURCES

The website of the Department of Homeland Security is http://www.dhs.gov/.

Two organizations that monitor civil rights in the United States are the Electronic Privacy Information Center (EPIC), http://www.epic.org/, and the American Civil Liberties Union (ACLU), http://www.aclu.org. Both are critical of the U.S. government and the USA Patriot Act.

The Rand Corporation is an independent "think tank" that has a special program to study homeland security. Its website is http://www.rand.org/ise/security/.

Senator Patrick Leahy (D-VT) has a useful website that provides an overview of the provisions of the USA Patriot Act: http://leahy.senate.gov/press/200110/102401a.html.

Berkowitz, Peter, *Terrorism, the Laws of War, and the Constitution,* Hoover Press, Stanford, 2005. A nice anthology of legal experts addressing the three recent enemy combatant cases.

Cole, David, and Dempsey, James, *Terrorism and the Constitution,* New Press, New York, 2002.

Crank, John P., and Gregor, Patricia, *Counter-Terrorism After 9/11,* Newark: Lexis-Nexis Publishers, 2004.

Yoo, John, *The Powers of War and Peace: The Constitution and Foreign Affairs after 9/11,* University of Chicago Press, 2005. A conservative attorney's arguments for expanding presidential powers in wartime.

10

International Drug Trafficking

❖

There is no doubt that illegal drugs are ubiquitous in American society today.[1] There is probably nobody in your class or in your social circle who has not been exposed to illegal drugs in some form or another, and many, if not most, have tried them. For many young people, drugs, particularly marijuana, is the recreational activity of choice—an innocuous way to spend a Friday evening with friends. On the other hand, cocaine is the choice for the wealthy, while ecstasy, methamphetamine, and crack cocaine serve other sections of society. Virtually every day some new drug or a variant on an old drug is introduced into American popular culture and television, movies, and music constantly refer to drug use as being a normal part of American life. Despite four decades of effort from the U.S. government, drugs have become a widespread and widely accepted part of American society.

Of course, behind all of these drugs is money—big money. And pursuing this money are dangerous people who are willing to kill to get it. Many of these drugs cannot be produced in the United States—they require a great deal of space and equipment to grow and process and such operations would quickly attract the attention of local law enforcement officials. Other ingredients, such as the opium poppy require certain climatic conditions to grow properly, meaning that they cannot be grown within U.S. borders. This means that they must be produced elsewhere and secretly trafficked into the United States or Europe where they may be passed on to other dealers and ultimately sold on to consumers.

Like everything else in the global economy, the global market for illegal drugs is ruled by the basic economic principles of supply and demand. Drugs are demanded by the

---

[1] *Drugs* is a somewhat misleading term. Not all of the substances that we call "drugs" have a legitimate medical use as the term seems to imply. Many people prefer terms like *narcotics* to describe these substances, but this term ignores the fact that many illegal substances have stimulant, not narcotic effects. In this chapter we will use the term to refer to any illegal substance that has substantial effect on the brain's functions.

citizens of wealthier countries, and they must be provided by somebody, either at home or abroad. Many of the drugs that are consumed in the United States must come from abroad for three major reasons: First, the criminal justice institutions in the United States, particularly law enforcement, are much stronger, more effective, and more honest than elsewhere in the world. A huge amount of U.S. government resources are aimed at tracking down and arresting drug producers and the penalties for drug crimes are stiff under American law. This means that it is safer to produce and process a drug abroad and import it into the United States than it is to make it here. Second, equipment and labor are cheaper elsewhere. Just as it is often cheaper to produce a shirt in China and have it shipped to the United States than to manufacture it here, it is often cheaper to produce drugs abroad and then have them shipped in to consumers. Finally, the key ingredients of some drugs require a specific climate that is not found in the United States. For example, coca plants, the primary ingredient of cocaine, only grows in a very select environment particularly prevalent in the Andean region of South America. These limitations on drug production and the great distances between drug producers and drug consumers have helped turn international drug trafficking and drug smuggling into billion-dollar industries.

At the level of the consumer, the drug user in the United States, much of the violence and suffering that the international drug trade causes remains invisible. Consumers only see the drug itself (and their dealer) they don't see the harm that is generated by its overseas production and domestic distribution. Further back along the supply chain, the forests of northern California, the jungles of Peru and Bolivia, or the poppy fields of Afghanistan, the manufacturing and trafficking of illegal drugs are often an integral part of war, violence, and official corruption. Describing drug use in the modern world as a "victimless crime" overlooks the victims that are scattered along the pathways that drugs take from producer to consumer—not to mention the lives that are ruined by addiction at home. Taken as a whole, the international trade in drugs is part of a dangerous, violent world, regardless of whether or not one thinks that they should be legalized or that their consumption is ultimately harmless.

In this chapter, we will examine aspects of the international drug trade and the international criminal justice system's response to it. We have already discussed some aspects of this issue in Chapter 5 when we discussed the role of the DEA in international law enforcement, but here we will return to that issue with a little more focus and in a little more depth. Nonetheless, we have already seen that, alongside terrorism, the international drug trade has been one of the primary engines of international criminal justice. Before September 11, stopping the international illegal drug trade was the primary motive for the United States to turn its criminal justice system outward and take an interest in illegal activity that takes place overseas. Countries that have been ambivalent about international courts and international law, like the United States, have been strong supporters of international institutions that help them to fight drug smuggling. Because the United States (alongside Europe) is one of the largest importers of illegal drugs, and their consumption has torn apart many of its cities, and cost the nation billions of dollars in law enforcement, prison, medical care, and other expenses, the United States has a vested interest in keeping down international drug smuggling. Prior to the war on terrorism, politicians often talked about a "war on drugs" as the great struggle of our times, a war that was fought on the streets of American cities as well as in the jungles of Latin America and the poppy fields of Pakistan and Afghanistan.

On the far end of the supply—demand chain, many poor nations in South America and Asia gain a great deal from the illegal drug trade. In states like Bolivia, coca has become an economic staple for poor rural farmers, providing income when few other salable products can be grown. The Bolivian government, under its socialist president Evo Morales, has supported the cultivation of coca leaves, ostensibly for uses other than refining into cocaine[2] and Morales himself is a former coca farmer.[3] Growing opium poppies in Afghanistan is one of the few ways that the farmers of this impoverished and war-torn country can make enough money to survive—and it is often approved, at least tacitly, by many local authorities. Drug traffickers in many of these countries are not seen as vicious criminals, but rather as folk heroes or Robin Hoods, helping the poor and foiling corrupt government officials—an image that many of these traffickers actively cultivate among their people. While America is a committed fighter in the war on drugs, not everybody in the world shares our enthusiasm.

It is undoubtedly true that, economically speaking, narcotics cultivated and processed for trafficking contribute a great deal to the economies of many countries around the world, but they have also been disastrous for many of them. While poor farmers are able to feed their families because they grow crops like opium or coca, drug sales often help finance their oppression. They fund both sides of bloody civil wars in Colombia and Peru, and despite aggressive efforts by their governments, in cooperation with the U.S. government, drug production remains entrenched in the local economies and in the lives of many people. Kidnappings, assassinations, and corruption are an ever-present part of international drug trafficking, not to mention the devastation that the finished product causes.

There are two major schools of thought in the drug war: Those who believe in cutting off the supply of drugs and those that wish to reduce the demand for them. In the United States, the vast majority of funding is focused on choking off the drug supply at its source or in transit rather than reducing public demand for illegal drugs. These approaches emphasize criminalizing drug production and drug trafficking, catching and punishing those who wish to make and sell drugs. We can call this a criminal justice approach to drugs. Others, those seeking to reduce demand, aim to educate the public about the dangers of drug abuse and help drug abusers come clean. These people take a "harm reduction" approach, seeking to reduce the harm done by drugs rather than preventing people from buying them. Some argue that drug production and drug smuggling cannot be stopped unless demand goes down—that there is a close relationship between the demand for drugs and their supply. They maintain that stopping the flow of drugs into the country would only raise their prices, thereby making trafficking a more lucrative enterprise, and more tempting for those who wish to make a quick buck. Both approaches have shaped international drug policy but here we will emphasize criminal justice approaches.

---

[2] Forero, Juan (2006) "Bolivia's Knot: No to Cocaine, But Yes to Coca," *New York Times,* February 12, p. 4.

[3] BBC Profile: Evo Morales (http://news.bbc.co.uk/1/hi/world/americas/3203752.stm).

THE HISTORY OF THE INTERNATIONAL DRUG TRADE

Drug trafficking was not always a criminal matter. In fact, it is really only in the last century that international drug trafficking has been considered a crime, or that drugs themselves have been the subject of serious government regulation. Prior to this, narcotic drugs were a normal, ordinary part of international trade and were left largely unregulated. Many respectable companies made profits by importing opium from Turkey and the Middle East and then selling it in Asia; many drugs that we now consider to be among the most dangerous, such as heroin and cocaine, were used medicinally and were widely praised for their beneficial properties.

One of the central turning points in the pre-twentieth-century history of drugs were the two "Opium Wars" fought in China during the mid-nineteenth century. The Chinese Imperial government, fearing that the opium trade was destroying its people, sought to ban opium and stop its importation. The sale of opium in China was a major source of revenue for the British East India Company, and in two wars (one from 1834 to1843 and the other from 1856 to1860) the British government used its massive military to force the Chinese government to allow the importation of opium. (England also won temporary ownership over the city of Hong Kong through these wars, relinquishing it only in 1999.) It was not until the beginning of the twentieth century that the international community began to seriously address the problem of opium abuse, which then served as the impetus for the regulation of other drugs.[4]

Since the Opium Wars, Western views about drugs have changed significantly. In the early twentieth century, concern about the destructive effects of the abuse of narcotics led the U.S. government to begin regulating their use and to control their importation and exportation. Over the course of the century, a number of international treaties were created to help control the flow of drugs and international organizations developed to help monitor and control the production of illegal narcotics (more on these later). The Shanghai Opium Commission was led by the United States to study the impact of opium use and led to the Hague Opium Treaty in 1912. This treaty set some of the basic principles of the international regulation of narcotics, many of which still guide international antidrug trafficking treaties today. These include regulations for lawfully producing, processing, and transporting in narcotics along with collective efforts to outlaw narcotics and fight drug trafficking.[5] Opium was banned in the United States in accordance with this treaty by the Harrison Narcotics Act of 1914. Other narcotic substances, such as marijuana and cocaine, followed a similar trajectory: Their use was often widespread and commonplace, only to be banned when their negative effects were better understood and publicized. Marijuana was set on the path of criminalization in the United States by the passing of the1937 Marijuana Tax Act. (Now, marijuana is considered as dangerous as heroin and more harmful than cocaine under U.S. law.) Even alcohol was banned from 1918 until 1929 under the Eighteenth Amendment of the U.S. Constitution. Of course, these substances represent only a

---

[4] For a history of early international efforts to combat heroin, see Willoughby, W. W. (1925) *Opium as an International Problem.* Baltimore: The Johns Hopkins Press.
[5] Paust, et al., *International Criminal Law,* p. 1052.

small number of the drugs that were eventually to become available to users around the world, and new treaties were negotiated as new drug problems emerged.

By all accounts, recreational drug use soared in the Western world in the 1960s. Changing social morals and the glorification of drugs in popular culture led younger generations in the United States and Europe to experiment with illegal narcotics, causing their use to become widespread and "normalized" (that is, it was no longer considered shocking or unusual to be using drugs). Marijuana was the drug of choice in America during the 1960s and soon after, American soldiers returned home from Vietnam with heroin addiction in shocking numbers. Studies of urban crime in America discovered a strong connection between heroin addiction and street crime. New drugs like LSD were also first popularized in this period.

At the time antidrug policies in America were not focused primarily on law enforcement, but rather balanced criminal justice with harm reduction. Much of the U.S. government's efforts to fight heroin abuse, for example, relied on methadone, a heroin substitute that was given to addicts to help them cope with withdrawal. In 1971, President Nixon changed the face of U.S. antidrug efforts by declaring a "war on drugs" and making illegal narcotics "public enemy number one." To confront the problem, he proposed a massive government campaign to eradicate drug use in the United States—focusing primarily on criminal justice responses. As part of this development, Nixon signed the Controlled Substances Act of 1970 (usually referred to as the CSA of 1970) which, among other things, created the DEA to help consolidate federal law enforcement's antidrug efforts. While we have already discussed the role of the DEA as a force in international law enforcement in Chapter 5, its influence on both American and international drug policy cannot be overstated. Along with working with overseas law enforcement through American embassies, the DEA functions as the central federal police body in the war against drugs. The CSA of 1970 also replaced previous antidrug laws with new ones and included a set of "schedules" that determined the dangers posed by different drugs and established the punishments for possessing or trafficking them. Drug producers, traffickers, and dealers were arrested in large numbers and the United States was locked into a "law enforcement first" approach to illegal drugs, a strategy that has gone largely unquestioned ever since.

Drug smuggling into the United States has likewise gone through various stages. Like any other business, the international drug business has sought to respond to the demands of the market, and with each new stage of drug use in the United States and elsewhere there has been a shift in patterns of international drug trafficking and the organized criminals who run them.[6] As demand for one drug increases, those regions that supply them become more involved in drug trafficking. During the 1960s and early 1970s, small planes smuggled marijuana across the U.S.–Mexican border. However, during the 1970s and 1980s, cocaine became extremely popular in America and the drug production and trafficking system shifted south to Colombia, Bolivia, and Peru. Heroin has been popular in the United States (but much more popular in Europe) and

---

[6] See: Williams, Phil (1993) "The International Drug Trade: An Industry Analysis," *Low Intensity Conflict & Law Enforcement,* Winter, Vol. 2, No. 3, 397–420.

synthetics like ecstasy and methamphetamines have come to the United States from Europe. Some groups are organized like legitimate businesses with chief executives and lower-level personnel who are delegated authority over specific matters. Others are loose and less formal, relying on ethnic, familial, or cultural ties to run an effective trafficking operation. Nigerian traffickers, for example, rely on ethnic ties to ferry heroin from Asia to America, but ultimately use carriers who are unlikely to arouse suspicion (usually white women) to bring drugs into the United States.[7] There is not a single type of drug trafficking organization, but rather they take on a variety of forms based upon what drug is being smuggled, where it is being smuggled from, and who is organizing and profiting from the drug sales.

While cocaine and heroin are still important parts of the international drug trafficking industry, other drugs such as LSD ("acid"), methamphetamine, and ecstasy (MDMA) have become increasingly popular and have also changed the dynamics of the international drug trade. Unlike their predecessors, these drugs are synthetic and thus do not require the organic base products that are available in only small parts of the world. This means that they can be manufactured cheaply in labs virtually anywhere, relying on commercially available materials, making them much easier to manufacture domestically. At a minimum, their synthetic basis frees such drugs from the region-based production of opium and cocaine, shifting some drug production to Europe and the United States (although it remains strong in Mexico). Similarly, with developments in hydroponics technology, marijuana can now be grown indoors, virtually anywhere and with enough secrecy to elude law enforcement searches. While cocaine and opium remain region-specific drugs, the modern era has seen a decentralization and globalization of drug production such that many popular drugs can now be manufactured virtually anywhere in the world.

Virtually all major organized criminal gangs are involved in international drug trafficking in some form or other. Along with the Colombian cocaine cartels and the mafia, Nigerian gangs, Israeli gangs, and Chinese triads engage in producing, processing, and transporting drugs around the world. Because the drug trafficking process is a complex one, stretching from across borders and cultures and requiring elaborate setups, organized criminals play a crucial role in the international drug trafficking network. They can connect the various actors together and handle the logistical complexities of the trafficking process, buying planes, paying mules, and dividing the drugs for distribution to local dealers and consumers. Other organized criminals are parasites on the drug trafficking process, controlling crucial trafficking corridors (such as Tijuana) and demanding tribute from the traffickers. However, these gangs are only part of the picture, usually engaged in the processing and transportation of the drugs. At the production level, many drugs are grown by poor farmers who sell them to middlemen. Also, along the way, corrupt politicians and law enforcement officers take their cut. At the distribution level, trafficking is often much more dispersed and drugs often change hands numerous times before they are consumed. Thus, while organized crime is essential to the international drug trafficking network, they are only part of a much larger world.

---

[7] See: *Ilicit*, p. 73 and Briggs, Michael and Lehman, Daniel J. (1995) "Nigerian Smugglers Make Chicago a Heroin Hub," Chicago Sun-Times, April 3, Section: NEWS, p. 1.

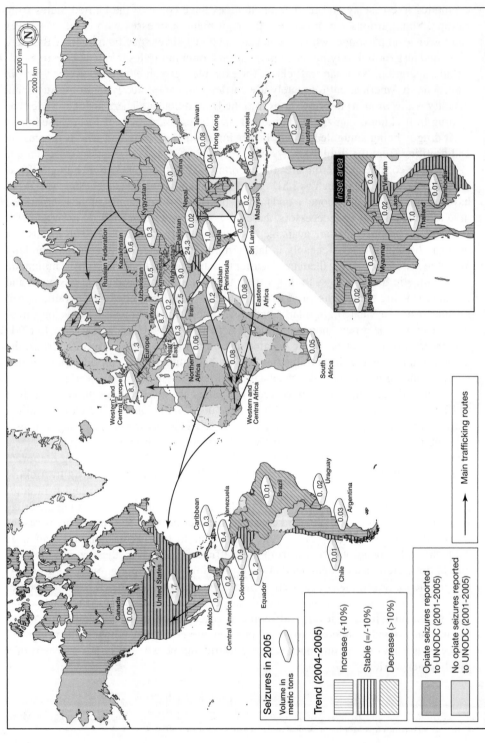

FIGURE 10.1 The International Heroin Trade
Source: UNODC World Drug Report

DRUG TRAFFICKING INTO THE UNITED STATES

The U.S. government has labeled sites that "exhibit serious drug trafficking problems and harmfully impact other areas of the country" as "High Intensity Drug Trafficking Areas" (HIDTAs).[8] Many of these areas are located along American borders or in cities with major international airports. According to the UNODC and the U.S. government, the vast majority of drugs enter the United States through Mexico. Cocaine and heroin in particular travel overland from Latin America to the border where they are brought into the United States by mules (either by foot or hidden inside vehicles). Some of these drugs enter through the Caribbean using small planes that secretly fly into Florida or other secluded sites around the gulf of Mexico. Some *pollos* (individuals who are smuggled into the United States to find work—see Chapter 11 for details) carry drugs with them as they enter the United States to look for work.

Other drugs, however, enter the United States from Canada and overseas, from Europe and Asia. They can arrive hidden in shipping containers, secretly stored inside legitimate cargo, or hidden on or inside the bodies of drug mules. Marijuana grown in Canada (so-called "B.C. Bud") has been smuggled into the United States over waterways using canoes or thrown off of planes into remote woodlands attached to signal beacons that alert their recipients of their location.[9] Many of the synthetic drugs manufactured in Europe are brought into the United States stored inside luggage on flights from Brussels or Amsterdam flying into Chicago or New York.[10] (However, increases in airport security after September 11, 2001, have forced smugglers to find new routes into the United States.)

Almost every federal law enforcement organization deals with drug trafficking in some form or another. Antitrafficking operations are carried out first and foremost by the DEA, which runs federal antidrug operations in the United States as well as overseas. However, the CBP (Center for Border Protection, see Chapter 5 for details) maintains security along the U.S. border, meaning that they carry out a large number of antidrug operations in that region. The Coast Guard (also part of the Homeland Security Department) is responsible for interdicting maritime trafficking.[11] The U.S. State Department's Bureau for International Narcotics and Law Enforcement Affairs advises the government on international antitrafficking issues. State and local law enforcement likewise play an essential role in stopping drug trafficking although they have limited jurisdiction at U.S. borders and other points of entry.

---

[8] The National High Intensity Drug Trafficking Area Program: Annual Report 2004. Available at http://www.whitehousedrugpolicy.gov/publications/policy/hidta04/.

[9] Kershaw, Sarah (2005) "Violent New Front in Drug War Opens on the Canadian Border," *New York Times,* March 5, Section A, p. 1.

[10] Wren Christopher (1999) "Seizure of Ecstasy at Airport Shows Club Drug's Increase," *New York Times,* October 29 and Rashbaum, William (2000) "Drug Experts Report a Boom in Ecstasy Use," *New York Times,* February 26.

[11] Although the *Posse Comitatus* Act prevents the military from performing law enforcement duties, federal law makes a special exception for the Coast Guard. See 18 U.S.C. § 1385. See also Podgor, Ellen S., *Understanding International Criminal Law,* p. 49.

Mules

The 2004 film *Maria Full of Grace* (*Maria, llena eres de gracia*) tells the story of a Colombian "drug mule"—a person paid by smugglers to ferry contraband across international borders. Maria, who is paid (and later threatened) by Colombian traffickers to transport cocaine from Colombia to the United States, swallows the drug in a pure form, tightly wrapped in latex balloons, before boarding a plane to New York. Upon landing she and her fellow mules are taken by the American branch of the Colombian smuggling unit to a hotel, where they are kept hostage until the drugs pass through their system, are cleaned, and then sent on for distribution and sale. However, not all of the mules make it. One is caught by customs officials at the New York Airport. Another's balloons burst in her stomach before she can pass them and, in a particularly gruesome scene, the drug smugglers cut her body open in a bathtub to extract her "cargo." After further trauma, Maria herself eventually gets the money she is owed by the dealers and decides to stay in the United States to raise her unborn child.

Swallowing and then passing drugs (sometimes called or "body packing") is only one way that drug mules transport their cargo across international borders—they may also carry it packed in stashed aerosol cans, strapped onto their bodies, formed into jewelry, or sewn into the lining of their clothing. Swallowing is really only suitable for the most valuable cargo as the human body cannot safely contain a great quantity of material. Also, its risks make it a particularly expensive mode of transportation. Other traffickers have found even more creative ways to get drugs to their foreign markets. The U.S. government recently reported that purebred animals were being used to smuggle heroin from Colombia into the United States by surgically implanting bags of liquid heroin into their stomachs.[12] Other customs officials have found horses, snakes, and fish used as mules (for the snakes, the drugs were hidden beneath false bottoms of tanks that held poisonous cobras).[13] Some of the human mules are eager to earn the cash that the smugglers offer, but others are blackmailed or threatened into making the trek.

One of the most famous recent groups of drug mules are known as "The Bali Nine." The nine young Australians ranging in age from 19 to 29 were arrested in Bali (a small Indonesian island, popular as a vacation spot for Australians) while attempting to smuggle approximately 18 pounds of heroin out of Bali and into Australia. Some were arrested at Ngurah Rai airport with heroin strapped to their torso and legs, while others were found in hotels scattered throughout the island. Most of the mules had made previous trips to Bali, and when they were questioned, some claimed that they were forced or threatened by the alleged ringleader (Andrew Chan) and his "muscle" (Myuran Sukumaran) into carrying the drugs back home.[14] Of the nine, the two ringleaders were sentenced to death, over the objections of the Australian government, while the other seven were sentenced to life imprisonment (reduced to 20 years for two). The case has harmed relations between the two countries, as Australians object to what they believe is an unjustly harsh Indonesian criminal justice system. Cases like this show how tempting muling can be as well as how risky a job it is.

---

[12] Baker, Al and Rashbaum, William K. (2006) "Heroin Implants Turned Puppies Into Drug Mules, U.S. Says," February 2. Powell, Sian, Jakarta (2006) "I was forced to smuggle: Bali drug mule," *The Australian*, February 8, p. 6.

[13] Speart, Jessica (1995) "The New Drug Mules," *New York Times Magazine,* June 11, p. 44.

[14] AAP (2006) "Bali duo sentenced to death," *Sydney Morning Herald,* February 14.

Opium from Asia: The Golden Triangle, the Golden Crescent

The world's two primary sources of opium, the main ingredient of heroin, are the so-called "golden triangle," stretching across Burma, Thailand, and Laos, and the "golden crescent," consisting of Pakistan, Afghanistan and Iraq (although there is some production in Latin America). While all of these states are significant producers, the *center* of opium trafficking is clearly Afghanistan. According to the UNODC, 89% of the world's opium is produced in the undeveloped Muslim nation. In contrast, only 8% comes from the golden triangle (primarily from Myanmar), while the rest is from other nations in the region or from Mexico and Colombia.[15]

For at least the next decade, Afghanistan "Will determine the size and development of the world's main opiate markets."[16] This is the case for several reasons. First, the country is very poor and one of the few sources of significant revenue has been growing opium poppies for processing into heroin. Second, Afghanistan has been plagued with civil wars and foreign invasions in recent decades. These conflicts have prevented an effective central government from establishing itself, hindering law enforcement, and leaving the functions of government to local clans and warlords that do not have an interest in stopping the lucrative drug trade. For years heroin traffickers have relied on this instability and lawlessness to grow and process the drugs, and export opium and heroin with near impunity. Finally, the country's rough, mountainous terrain provides many remote and difficult-to-access locations where farmers can grow opium poppies without fear of interference from whatever limited government actually exists in the country at any given time. All of these features together make Afghanistan a "perfect storm" of opium production.

While continually the largest source of opium production, Afghanistan's production has changed over the years in response to political changes in the region. Prior to the American invasion of Afghanistan in 2001, Afghanistan was run by the Islamic fundamentalist group known as the "Taliban." Under the Taliban government, heroin was banned as un-Islamic, but the militant Islamic leadership was either unable or unwilling to do anything serious about opium production during their rule.[17] According to the UNODC, Afghan opium cultivation and production actually increased under Taliban. Whether or not they were genuine, Taliban antiopium efforts were largely moot, as much of the production took place in the north of the country in areas beyond Taliban control.[18]

After the 2001 invasion of Iraq, the U.S.-backed government that replaced the Taliban has had an even more difficult time preventing opium cultivation, as it has been unable to effectively control the remote regions where the cultivation takes place. Despite a sharp decrease in 2001, opium cultivation and production has dramatically increased since the U.S. invasion to such extremes that the UNODC warned that "Afghanistan has already become a narco-economy in the sense that drugs are now Afghanistan's largest employer, income generator, source of capital, export and foreign investment."[19]

---

[15] UNODC World Drug Report, 2006, p. 61.

[16] UNODC World Drug Report, 2005, p. 9.

[17] Wren, Christopher (2000) "U.N. Forsakes Effort to Curb Poppy Growth by Afghans," *New York Times,* September 18.

[18] Naim, Moses, *Illicit,* p. 69.

[19] UNODC press release, June 28, 2006, available at,
http://www.unodc.org/unodc/press_release_2006_06_28.html.

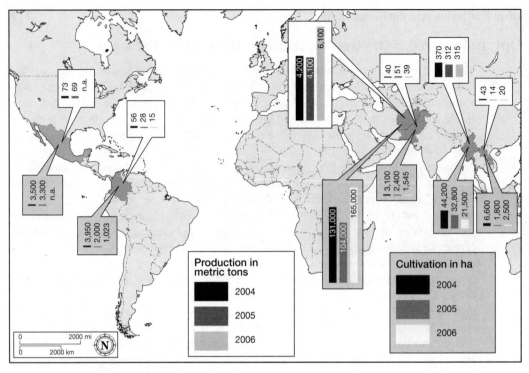

FIGURE 10.2   Opium-Producing Regions of the World
Source: CIA website. http://www.cia.gov/cia/publications/heroin/flowers_to_heroin.htm

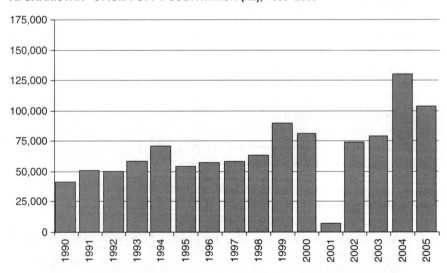

FIGURE 10.3   Afghan Opium Production (in Hectares)
Source: UNODC World Drug Report, 2006

The second largest producer of opium in the world is Myanmar, formerly known as Burma, which makes up the backbone of the golden triangle. Here, opium is shipped primarily into China and Australia, and either consumed there or passed on to Europe. As in Colombia and Afghanistan, large-scale drug trafficking operations in Myanmar are a part of violent political movements and separatist warfare: Much of the trafficking in Myanmar is done by the "United Wa State Army"—a rebel group operating in the northeast region of the country. While Wa Army officials claim to be cracking down on drug trafficking, they are nonetheless accused of being deeply involved in heroin and opium trafficking and have also been involved in manufacturing and selling the amphetamine known locally as "Yaa Baa" (or "crazy drug"), which is used in the region as a work aid or as a recreational drug.

Unlike the golden crescent, the golden triangle has seen a marked decrease in heroin production over the last several years, balancing out the postwar increase in Afghanistan. This decrease has occurred primarily as a result of tough government policies against drug traffickers, along with weather conditions that have made poppy cultivation more difficult. Antitrafficking efforts have produced similar results in Thailand and Laos. (Drug trafficking is a capital offense in most of these countries.) Myanmar's government, which is a military dictatorship that gives its people few civil rights, has set a goal of being opium-free by 2014. The UNODC in its *2005 World Drug Report* asserted that these governments may prove successful in their effort to completely eradicate illegal narcotic cultivation and manufacturing in the region. This is one of the few regions where law enforcement alone seems to have resulted in a significant decrease in drug production operations.

South America—"Narcoterrorism" and Cocaine Cartels

South America, in particular the region surrounding the Andean mountains, is the source of virtually all of the world's cocaine. Coca, the plant that provides the base ingredient for cocaine, has been grown in the Andes for centuries and its leaves are chewed by the rural population as a mild stimulant.[20] Archaeologists found evidence of coca use in precolonial Incan civilization, and up to the 1920s, cocaine was an ingredient in Coca-Cola. It was banned as an illegal drug only in 1914 under the Harrison Act and is currently listed as Schedule II drug by the U.S. government. According to the UNODC, approximately 50% of all of the world's cocaine comes from Colombia, 32% from Peru, and 15% from Bolivia. Each of these countries is plagued by corruption, violence, and in the cases of Peru and Colombia, civil war, all of which are intimately tied to illegal drug production.

Prior to the 1970s, cocaine was smuggled into North America and Europe in small quantities by mules. However, skyrocketing demand and the development of new smuggling tactics by the Medellin Cartel turned small-scale cocaine operations into billion-dollar enterprises, tying together farmers, cocaine processors, smugglers, and dealers into a single, smooth operation. The image of cocaine as a chic drug of wealthy sophisticates and club dwellers fueled demand in the United States and the invention of crack cocaine in

---

[20] US Department of Justice website: "A History of Cocaine," http://www.usdoj.gov/oig/special/9712/appc.htm#N_1_.

the 1980s—a variant of cocaine that is cheap and thus more easily available to poor drug users (not to mention much more addictive)—only increased its value. To fill the demand, cartels developed a sophisticated network of planes, cars, and ships to funnel the drug into the United States. In Tijuana, the dangerous Arellano Félix gang is known for running a complex network of tunnels underneath the U.S.–Mexico border that are used to bring drugs in, taking a cut in the profits.

The cocaine industry in South America is intimately bound up with political instability and civil war in both Peru and Colombia. In both of these countries, right wing and left wing rebel groups are involved in drug trafficking, using their profits to buy weapons and supplies to continue waging war against their governments. Radical organizations like the Sendero Luminoso in Peru and the FARC (Columbian communists—see Chapter 8), as well as reactionary organizations like United Self-Defense Forces of Colombia, have all been involved in cocaine trafficking in some form or another—usually extracting protection money from the traffickers. The cocaine dealers themselves have also become part of this war, often supporting one side against the others or engaging in their own violent actions against a government bent on bringing them to justice. The Cali Cartel (see below) carried out armed attacks against the Colombian government and used car bombs against civilians in order to intimidate the government. The term *narcoterrorism* was coined to refer to the use of bombings and other terrorist tactics by drug traffickers and has now become a general category to describe both these tactics and the use of cocaine to fund insurgencies throughout the globe.[21]

The Colombian Cocaine Cartels

The history of drug trafficking has gone through different stages, with different organizational structures, different regions, and different drugs having temporary dominance over the others. The cocaine cartels that ran drug trafficking from Colombia from the 1980s until they were crushed by U.S. and Colombian forces in the 1990s are prime examples of this trend. Flamboyant, powerful, and ruthless, to many the cartels' leaders were romantic figures. They made millions of dollars (perhaps billions), while becoming folk heroes to many of the Colombian people who saw them as champions of the poor. To others, they represented only terror, crime, and violence—killing or kidnapping anybody who stood between them and their profits.

The two most famous of these were the Cali and the Medellin Cartels, business rivals in the 1980s and 1990s. They are credited with revolutionizing the drug trafficking industry and sending large-scale shipments of the drug into Europe and the United States through a network of traffickers. The Medellin Cartel was run by several drug traffickers, including the infamous drug lord Pablo Escobar. Escobar was a ruthless businessman who reportedly offered a $2,000 bounty for the death of each Colombian police officer. He is alleged to have destroyed a civilian airliner, killing over one hundred people, taken numerous hostages, and killed dozens of public officials in order to prevent his extradition to the

---

[21] Smith, G. Davidson, (1991) "Commentary No. 13: Terrorism and the Rule of Law: Dangerous Compromise in Colombia," Canadian Security Intelligence Service, October (available at http://www.csis-scrs.gc.ca/en/publications/commentary/com13.asp).

United States. The Medellin Cartel basked in the spotlight, funding numerous public works projects around their native city, giving Escobar the nickname "Robin Hood of Medellin." In 1982 he even served in the Colombian legislature, insuring that he was immune to criminal prosecution under Colombian law during his term. He ran the Cartel until his death in a shootout with Colombian police officers in December 1993 (his fellow cartel leaders have all either been killed or arrested).

The leaders of the Cali Cartel, named after the Colombian city that served as its headquarters, were less flamboyant and less violent than Escobar and his colleagues, but were nonetheless wildly successful at manufacturing and distributing Colombian cocaine, ultimately outstripping their Medellin rival. Sometimes known as the "gentlemen's cartel," the Cali cartel was founded and run by Gilberto Rodríguez-Orejuela and his brother Migel, who preferred bribery and other, less violent tactics for developing and expanding the drug trade. However, this did not stop them from assassinating rivals and government officials who stood in their way. Gilberto Rodriquez-Orejuela was arrested in 1995 but continued to run the organization from prison until released for good behavior in 2002. He was rearrested in 2005 and extradited to the United States, where he and Miguel were sentenced to 30 years in prison.[22]

Extraditing the cartel members to the United States for trial was a difficult process, but one that was necessary given the weakness and corruption of the Colombian criminal justice system. Many judges were unwilling or unable to prosecute leaders in Colombian courts, either because they feared for their safety or because they were on the payroll of the cartels. Judges and prosecutors who handled drug trafficking cases were often assassinated. Other cases simply "disappeared" from the criminal justice system entirely, the paperwork vanishing and the traffickers allowed to go free. The kingpins who were caught and sentenced by the government were often allowed to continue conducting their business inside lavish cells fitted with hot tubs and supplied with a steady stream of drugs, alcohol, and prostitutes. When the Colombian government initially proposed extraditing drug traffickers to the United States, the cartels responded with a wave of bombings, assassinations, and kidnappings that ultimately forced the government to relent and cease all extraditions. It was only in the late 1990s, with an influx of new antidrug funds and political changes in the Colombian government, that they allowed for leaders to be extradited.

Both cartels were run in a top-down, corporate fashion, with all major decisions being made at the top and carried out by subordinates. They used elaborate financial and insurance schemes to underwrite their operations and they kept close tabs on their subordinates. Many who did business with the Cali Cartel had family close to the cartel who could be quickly and harshly punished if they tried to cheat them. They often invested their profits in legitimate enterprises such as hotel chains and agriculture. (One estimate claims that 30–40% of all construction in the Cali region of Colombia was funded by cartel money.) Drugs were only a part of the vast financial empires run by the cartels.

While quite successful for some time, the structure of the cartels made it difficult to maintain their business without their leadership in place. The downfall of the cartel leadership in the 1990s led to structural changes in cocaine trafficking in the Andean region. Whereas the cartels represented large-scale organizations that controlled all facets of the cocaine business, from production to processing to transportation, and used

---

[22] Aguayo, Terry (2006). "Cali Cocaine Brothers Plead Guilty," *New York Times,* September 27.

elaborate accounting schemes to conduct their business, the trafficking business has since become more fragmented. Now different groups control different aspects of the cocaine business, each contributing its own share and making its own "cut" of the profits. This approach makes trafficking enterprises less vulnerable to targeted law enforcement operations. When one link of the trafficking chain is arrested, the others may continue to function as they had before, simply seeking out new, already existing enterprises to replace the old ones. With the large cartels, the arrest or death of the leadership undermined the entire structure. This approach, referred to as the "kingpin strategy," destroyed the cartels, but clearly did not destroy cocaine production in South America.[23] It only changed it.

DRUG TRAFFICKING INTO EUROPE

Alongside the United States, Europe is the biggest market for illegal drugs. While, as in the United States, cannabis is the most popular drug in Europe, heroin is also much more popular there than in the United States, and cocaine use among Europeans is on the rise. Expanding demand, coupled with Europe's wealth and high standard of living, makes it an attractive market for international drug traffickers.

Heroin

Much of the heroin trafficked into Europe comes from the golden crescent in central Asia. It makes its way there through a variety of different routes. The most common path is via the "Balkan route," which flows from Afghanistan to Iran through Turkey and then through the states that comprise the former Yugoslavia. The other route is the so-called "silk route" or the "northern route," which mirrors the road taken by ancient silk traders, bypassing Iran and entering Europe through the central Asian republics. Turkish and Kurdish organized criminals are major heroin traffickers into Europe, backed by Albanians and other Eastern European gangs, although the UN reports that "Much of the retail trade in Western Europe . . . is now in the hands of criminal groups of West African origin."[24]

Cocaine

Because of its origins in South America, cocaine makes it to Europe through very different channels than heroin does. The two primary entry points are Spain and the Netherlands, but other countries, particularly those that do not closely monitor international flights, are also suitable entry points. From there, the drug is either used locally or moved on to other regions with a high demand for the drug. While cocaine abuse is high throughout Western Europe, it is particularly strong in Spain, England, and the "Benelux" countries (Belgium, the Netherlands, and Luxembourg).[25] As Dutch and Spanish law enforcement have

---

[23] Treaster, Joseph B. (1993) "U.S. Altering Tactics in Drug War," *New York Times,* September 17.
[24] 2005 World Drug Report, p. 49.
[25] Ibid., p. 78.

cracked down on cocaine smuggling, new routes have developed into Europe through western Africa.[26] While cocaine use has decreased in North America, it has risen in Europe in recent years.

Synthetics

Europe is not only a consumer of illegal drugs; it is also a significant supplier of drugs—particularly synthetics. It is the source of 80% of the world's ecstasy, the majority produced in Belgium and the Netherlands.[27] Much of it is smuggled abroad by Russian and Israeli criminal groups who bring it to the United States, where its euphoric and stimulant properties have made it an important part of "rave culture."[28]

OTHER SOURCES OF DRUG TRAFFICKING

While Europe and the United States are the largest importers of illegal drugs, and South America and Asia are the biggest producers of them, many other countries in many other parts of the world contribute to the global drug problem. In 1980, shortly after obtaining power, Iran's Islamic government executed 200 known drug traffickers, but every day, new groups of smugglers ship heroin from Afghanistan or Pakistan into Iran for its eager customers.[29] Despite such antidrug measures, there are approximately 1.2 million drug addicts in Iran (out of a population of approximately 68 million), with the majority hooked on heroin originating from Afghanistan.[30] With approximately 1.5 million addicts, Russia, too, is one of the largest consumers of Afghan heroin. Marijuana use has been on the rise around the globe and amphetamines have been increasingly popular in Asia. While Western, democratic societies have struggled to contain drug abuse and the influx of illegal substances that drive it, drug abuse and drug trafficking are both worldwide problems.

Likewise drug production goes far beyond the Andean cocaine industry and the two Asian heroin-producing regions. Small amounts of opium are produced in Latin America and smuggled north or to Europe. While synthetic drugs often originate in Europe, they can be produced anywhere in the world. According to the UNODC, marijuana is grown in 176 different countries and is the most commonly abused illicit substance.[31] The largest amounts are grown in Mexico and the United States, and these crops are almost exclusively for American consumers, but it is also grown in the Ukraine for Russians and Europeans and is legally grown in the Netherlands. The stimulant *khat* is grown in Africa

[26] International Narcotics Control Board 2005 Report. Available at http://www.incb.org/incb/annual_report_2005.html.

[27] White House Office of National Drug Control Policy, Fact Sheet http://www.whitehousedrugpolicy.gov/publications/pdf/ncj201387.pdf.

[28] US Department of Justice National Drug Threat Assessment: http://www.usdoj.gov/ndic/pubs11/13846/mdma.htm.

[29] Gouverneur, Cedric (2002) "Iran loses its drugs war," *Le Monde Diplomatique,* March.

[30] Hiro, Dilip (2005) *The Iranian Labyrinth.* Nation Books, p. 324.

[31] World Drug Report, 2006, p. 103.

and the Middle East, but has made its way into Europe and the United States.[32] While the more "traditional" illegal narcotic industry is still rooted in Latin America and Asia, drug production has moved all over the world.

"NARCOSTATES": GOVERNMENTS AND DRUG TRAFFICKING

In most of the states where drug trafficking is a major problem, it usually takes place against the will of the government or because the domestic criminal justice system is unable to stop it. In most of these cases, either political instability or massive corruption prevents the government from acting against the traffickers and allows them to flourish. However, there are some governments that have trafficked in drugs as a way to raise money for themselves. In particular, the Panamanian government in the 1980s under Manuel Noriega and present North Korea have been accused of trafficking in drugs, although the problem may be more widespread than this.

North Korea, led by the dictator Kim Jong II, is one of the least open, most autocratic nations in the world. The vast majority of North Koreans (unlike their Southern counterparts) are kept in abject poverty and have even reportedly resorted to cannibalism in order to get enough nourishment to survive.[33] However, the leadership lives in splendor and commands one of the largest militaries in the world. One of the ways that they have managed to maintain this elaborate lifestyle and destructive economic model is by manufacturing and selling illegal drugs abroad. In 1999, Egyptian authorities caught North Korean diplomats with 506,000 tablets of rohypnol (a common "date rape drug"), the largest cache of the drug discovered up to that time.[34] In 2003, the Congressional Research service reported at least 50 documented cases linking North Korean diplomats to international drug trafficking.[35] Along with synthetic drugs such as rohypnol, North Korea has also been linked to opium and heroin production and money counterfeiting. These problems, coupled with North Korea's pursuit of nuclear weapons, make it one of the most dangerous states on earth.

In 1989, the United States invaded the small Central American nation of Panama, after disclosing that its leader, the dictator Manuel Noriega, was involved in cocaine trafficking. Referred to as "Operation Just Cause," the United States used over 20,000 soldiers to seize the country and arrest Noriega. He was put on trial in U.S. criminal court and sentenced to 40 years in prison, where he remains today.

Such cases of states acting like criminal enterprises pose big problems for the international community. As we saw in Chapter 5, the powers that international law grants sovereign states includes giving diplomats and heads of state immunity from criminal liability.

---

[32] Gardiner, Sean (2006) "That Darned Khat: In search of New York's most elusive drug," *The Village Voice,* November 21.

[33] Faison, Seth (1997) "Grim Tales of Want From the North Korean Border," *New York Times,* April 27.

[34] Kaplan, David E. (1999) "The Wiseguy Regime," *U.S. News and World Report,* February 15, p. 37.

[35] Perl, Raphael F. (2003) "Drug Trafficking and North Korea: Issues for U.S. Policy," CRS Report for Congress, Congressional Research Service, December 5. Available at: http://fpc.state.gov/documents/organization/27529.pdf.

Similarly, embassies and certain diplomatic materiel are considered inviolable—they cannot be searched by law enforcement even if they have strong reason to believe that they may contain illegal materials like drugs or weapons. These powers give unscrupulous nations like North Korea and Panama the ability to engage in criminal behavior without fear of getting caught or being punished. On the other hand, government officials are often hesitant to do anything about the illegal behavior of diplomats or foreign officials. Immunity and inviolability are important principles of international law, and if one state is willing to breach international law in order to catch foreign drug traffickers (or other types of criminals for that matter), they run the risk of undermining an international order that they themselves benefit from. Their own diplomats and officials could be arrested in retaliation. This means that governments may not be able stop "gangster states" like North Korea from breaking laws by selling drugs or participating in other kinds of criminal behavior.

INTERNATIONAL LAWS AGAINST DRUGS

Prior to the 1960s, the international laws dealing with drug issues were scattered, complex, and uncoordinated. Numerous treaties dealt with different drugs in different ways. In 1961, under the guidance of the UN's Narcotic Commission, a number of states gathered together to fill in the gaps created by the prewar treaties and conventions, streamlining the process of international drug regulation. Out of this came the Single Convention on Narcotic Drugs (SCND), which simplified and expanded the international community's regulation in the manufacturing, sale, and distribution of illegal drugs.[36] Along with the SCND, the Convention on Psychotropic Substances, completed in 1971, and the UN Convention against Illicit Traffic in Narcotic Drugs and Psychotropic Substances of 1988 fill out the backbone of the international drug control regime.

Paust, et al. summarizes these principles of the international narcotic control system that developed out of the SCND:

1. The production (harvesting), manufacture, import, export, trade, distribution, consumption and possession of certain drugs must be limited to medical and scientific purposes.
2. The narcotic supplies of country obtained by manufacture and/or import must be limited to quantities needed for medical and scientific purposes.
3. The national administration of narcotic regimes is subject to control by international organs.[37]

Like the CSA of 1970, the modern international control systems breaks down drugs into four "Schedules" ("I" being most serious "IV" being least.) They also require that states

---

[36] Bayer, I., Ghodse, H. (1999) "Evolution of international drug control, 1945–1995," *Bulletin on Narcotics,* Vol. LI, Nos 1 and 2.
[37] Paust, et al., *International Criminal Law: Cases and Materials,* p. 1054.

pass laws to control the flow of drugs across their borders (however, it does not require that states outlaw all drugs). Also, the SCND created a body known as the International Narcotics Control Board (INCB) that helps monitor world narcotics patterns and evaluates national drug policies to ensure that they are complying with their international obligations. These treaties work together create an international legal system meant to allow the effective and profitable sale of safe drugs for medical purposes while preventing their sale for abusive purposes.

A number of international institutions play roles in the international drug trafficking regime set out by the SCND. The Commission on Narcotic Drugs is a UN body consisting of 50 members that sets global drug control policy. (Its members are appointed by the UN's Economic and Social Council.) The World Health Organization monitors substances, making recommendations to the commission about how they should be scheduled. As mentioned above, the INCB monitors the efforts of governments to fight drug trafficking and makes recommendations on reform. They also publish an annual report on the international drug control system.[38] Alongside these, the UNODC operates as the umbrella organization for the UN's antidrug regime, producing its own annual *World Drug Report* as well a number of studies on special topics in the global drug trafficking industry.

U.S. LAWS AGAINST INTERNATIONAL DRUG TRAFFICKING

As we discussed in Chapter 3, many U.S. laws involving drug trafficking have extraterritorial jurisdiction. That is, they authorize the American government to punish activities that take place overseas and do not require that the criminal acts occur on U.S. soil or involve U.S. citizens to be criminal offenses under U.S. law. Beyond this, we will not discuss the individual drug statutes that criminalize drug trafficking, but rather mention a few of the specific laws that are used to combat international traffickers. We have already mentioned one of the most significant of these laws: The Anti-Drug Abuse Act of 1986 requires that the president certify that a state is cooperating in the fight against drug trafficking and can result in economic sanctions against states that fail to meet American expectations.

The Maritime Drug Law Enforcement Act (MDLEA) makes it, "Unlawful for any person . . . on board a vessel subject to the jurisdiction of the United States . . . to possess with intent to manufacture or distribute, a controlled substance."[39] The MDLEA also authorizes the Coast Guard to board any "Vessel registered in a foreign nation where the flag nation has consented or waived objection to the enforcement of United States law by the United States" as well as ships that do not carry the flag of any state, so-called "stateless vessels."[40] U.S. courts have ruled that the Coast Guard does not need to provide grounds for suspicion to stop and search a U.S. flagged or stateless vessel, leaving one commentator to assert that the MDLEA is "one of the most sweeping grants of police authority ever written into U.S. law."

---

[38] It is available at their website http://www.incb.org/.

[39] 46 U.S.C. App. § 1903(a).

[40] Merriam, Michael J. (1996) "NOTE: United States Maritime Drug Trafficking Search and Seizure Policy: An Erosion of United States Constitutional and International Law Principles 19," *Suffolk Transnational Law Review,* 441.

According to Coast Guard statistics, in 2006 Guard ships intercepted over 230,000 pounds of cocaine and more than 9,000 pounds of marijuana (with over 200 arrests).[41]

The Foreign Narcotics Kingpin Designation Act was signed into law in 1999, to give the government power to hurt international drug traffickers without bringing them before American judges. The FNKDA, "provide[s] authority for the identification of, and application of sanctions on a worldwide basis to, significant foreign narcotics traffickers, their organizations, and the foreign persons who provide support to those significant foreign narcotics traffickers and their organizations, whose activities threaten the national security, foreign policy, and economy of the United States."[42] Each year the president designates a number of individuals as "significant international narcotics traffickers" and directs the Treasury Department to impose economic sanctions against them. Likewise, the act punishes those who aid individuals designated as drug traffickers by up to 10 years in prison or a $10 million fine.[43] As of this writing there are 187 entities or individuals listed as significant traffickers and the U.S. government has worked to isolate these individuals politically as well as financially.[44] While the FNKDA is not the same as criminal prosecution, the financial isolation it provides can be a very effective force against international traffickers.

LAW ENFORCEMENT TACTICS

As we saw in Chapter 5, preventing the trafficking of illegal drugs has been a central motive of many of the developments in international law enforcement—most of which have been spearheaded by the United States. The UNODC and the WCO both are intimately involved in efforts to stop international drug trafficking by studying patterns of international drug trafficking, advising national governments about how to improve their policies, helping states cooperate on trafficking issues, and assisting states to streamline their customs procedures so that illegal drugs will be discovered more easily. The DEA has expanded its operations through American embassies abroad, helping American and local law enforcement agencies develop new tactics for fighting against trafficking operations and providing valuable intelligence about international drug traffickers. Since we have already covered most of these subjects already, we will only briefly discuss some specific antidrug actions undertaken by the U.S. government overseas.

In 1999, the Colombian government, with the aid and support of the United States, developed "Plan Colombia," a multi-year, $7.5 billion effort to fight Colombian cocaine with American financial support. The goal of this program was to boost Columbia's own ability to fight the drug cartels and tip the scales in favor of the Columbian government. Among the projects funded by Plan Colombia are the spraying of Colombia cocaine fields with powerful herbicides and outfitting the Colombian military with high-tech U.S. military equipment, such as Black Hawk Helicopters, to fund the operations. Additionally, the

---

[41] http://www.uscg.mil/hq/g%2Dcp/comrel/factfile/.

[42] For a fact sheet on the Act, see http://www.whitehouse.gov/news/releases/2005/06/20050602–2.html.

[43] White House Fact Sheet (available at http://www.whitehouse.gov/news/releases/2001/06/20010601–3.html).

[44] US Treasury Department Fact sheet, "What You Need to Know About U.S. Sanctions Against Drug Traffickers" (available at http://www.treasury.gov/offices/enforcement/ofac/programs/narco/drugs.pdf).

United States has placed several hundred American military personnel in Colombia to serve as intelligence analysts, trainers, and armed, military advisors in large-scale counter-narcotics operations.[45] Critics of the plan point out that the Colombian military has been accused of human rights abuses and that the United States has spent some $3 billion in support of Colombian antidrug forces with little sign of success in reducing the availability of cocaine on American streets.[46] Nonetheless, the U.S. government still officially supports Plan Colombia and Congress reauthorized the program when its mandate expired in 2005.[47]

Among the controversial tactics used in Plan Colombia is the spraying of herbicides (chemicals that kill plant life) over coca and opium plots. Additionally, experts have encouraged Colombian farmers to grow alternative crops to replace their coca and opium plants. These spraying efforts have been moderately successful, but it is a risky tactic: several planes have been shot down while spraying the plants and in many cases, the coca growers merely replanted their coca and opium after the planes left. Other farmers have simply moved their operations elsewhere.[48] Additionally, environmental activists have raised concerns about the negative environmental and health effects of spraying herbicidal chemicals over populated land.[49] In 2005, the Colombian government sprayed 138,775 hectares of coca fields and 1,624 hectares of opium poppies (the largest amount to date), while according to UN statistics overall coca cultivation in the Andean region increased slightly after a sharp downward trend in the late 1990s (see Figure 10.4).[50] Efforts to promote replacement crops such as palm oil and pineapple have been similarly disappointing as the income generated by growing coca is often significantly better than other, legal crops.[51]

Similar herbicide-spraying operations haven taken place in Afghanistan to destroy the region's opium crop. While the Afghan government has not authorized spraying, citing health concerns, farmers in rural villages have reported mysterious planes spraying local opium fields. (Both the U.S. and UK governments deny authorizing the spraying, despite the fact that the U.S. government controls Afghan air traffic.[52])

---

[45] Forero, Juan (2004) "Congress Approves Doubling U.S. Troops in Colombia to 800," *New York Times,* October 11.

[46] Brinkley, Joel (2005) "Anti-Drug Gains in Colombia Don't Reduce Flow to U.S.," *New York Times,* April 28.

[47] Shields Elinor (2005) "US weighs costs of Plan Colombia," BBC News, July 5 (available at http://news.bbc.co.uk/2/hi/americas/4627185.stm).

[48] Veillette, Connie (2005) "Plan Colombia: A Progress Report," CRS Report for Congress, June 22 (available at http://www.fas.org/sgp/crs/row/RL32774.pdf).

[49] "Anti-Drug Gains in Colombia Don't Reduce Flow to U.S.," *op cit.*

[50] US State Department (2006) *International Narcotics Strategy Report* (available at http://www.state.gov/p/inl/rls/nrcrpt/2006/vol1/html/62106.htm).

[51] Jones, James C. (2004) "Alternative Development in the South American Andes: Report of Findings," December (Under contract with United Nations Office of Drugs and Crime) (available at http://ciponline.org/colombia/0509jone02.pdf).

[52] BBC News, "Afghan concern at opium spraying," Tuesday, 30 November 2004 (available at http://news.bbc.co.uk/2/hi/south_asia/4054657.stm) and Gall, Carlotta "Afghan Poppy Farmers Say Mystery Spraying Killed Crops," *New York Times,* December 5, 2004. See also: Various Authors, "Impact Assessment of Crop Eradication in Afghanistan and Lessons Learned from Latin American and Southeast Asia," *Senlis Council,* January 2006 (available at http://www.senliscouncil.net/modules/publications/009_publication).

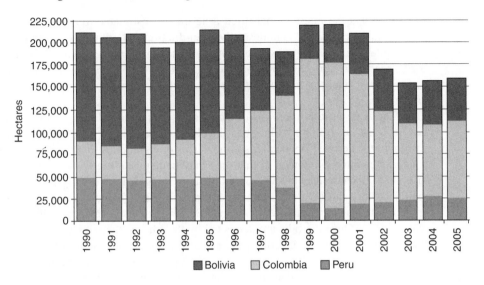

FIGURE 10.4 Global Coca Bush Cultivation (in Hectares)
Source: UNODC World Drug Report, 2006

MONEY LAUNDERING AND INTERNATIONAL DRUG TRAFFICKERS

The massive profits generated by the international drug trade have created new problems for the traffickers. The billions of dollars they make cannot be spent in large quantities if they can be traced back to their illegal sources. To spend this "dirty money" would invite investigation and a quick arrest. Additionally, the large amounts of cash that drug traffickers handle are just too heavy, bulky, and insecure to be an effective way to do business. This means that the money must be "laundered," that is, cleansed of any connection between the money and its origins, before traffickers can openly deposit it in banks, spend it in large quantities, or invest it in legitimate businesses.[53] Money laundering requires the help of otherwise legitimate financial institutions to conceal the sources of the dirty cash and to transfer it abroad where the traffickers can access it for their personal use. This means that money laundering is the point where the dark and violent world of international drug trafficking intersects with the apparently respectable and legitimate world of international high finance. All too often, the "straight" world of bankers, lawyers, and accountants succumbs to the lure of international narcodollars.

Nobody knows quite how much money is laundered each year and money laundering was criminalized in the United States only in 1986 with the Money Laundering Control Act.

---

[53] The U.S. Customs Service defines money laundering thuly: "Money laundering is the process whereby proceeds, reasonably believed to have been derived from criminal activity, are transferred, transformed, converted, or intermingled with legitimate funds, for the purpose of concealing or disguising the true nature, source, disposition, movement, or ownership of the proceeds. The goal of money-laundering is to make funds derived from, or associated with, illicit activity, appear legitimate." Cited in Richards, James R. (1998) *Transnational Criminal Organizations, Cybercrime, and Money Laundering,* Boca Raton: CRC, p. 44.

But, given that the international illicit drug trade is estimated to be somewhere around $400 billion per year and countless other non-drug-related criminal enterprises, including white-collar criminals and terrorists, rely on money laundering services, it is undoubtedly big businesses. (Estimates run as high at $1.5 trillion dollars per year.) It is even reported that dishonest financial institutions often bid competitively for an opportunity to launder drug trafficking profits.

There are usually three major steps in the money laundering process: *placement, layering,* and *integration.*[54] Placement involves the investment of illegal monies (usually cash) into the crooked financial institution. This often requires that the bills be smuggled from one country to another so that they may be deposited in the appropriate financial institution. Because the amounts of cash that are smuggled are usually small (usually less than $10,000—the U.S. government requires reporting financial transactions over that amount), the cash carriers are nicknamed Smurfs, and cash smuggling is referred to as "Smurfing."[55] Once the bills are deposited by the smurfs, the money is laundered by the financial institutions in a layering process. Layering involves a series of complex international financial transactions, where money is rapidly shifted from one financial entity to another in order to avoid detection by law enforcement personnel. Often, the launderers will use loopholes in a country's banking regulations or exploit financial privacy laws that prevent the money from being observed by financial regulators. They may also use correspondent accounts that allow for financial transactions between domestic and foreign banks to hide the money or set up dummy overseas corporations where the banks invest it to conceal its source. Finally, at the integration stage, the money is returned to the original investor, cleaned of any trace of its illicit source, while the financial institution has taken its own cut from it.

Drug traffickers frequently use offshore banks in small countries like Macao, the Cayman Island, Aruba, and Nauru to launder their money. These banks operate under regulations that are much looser than in other parts of the world and rely on their bank secrecy laws to obscure the nature of their business. Some of these countries, like Nauru, have few other sources of income and can only survive by operating as a haven for questionable financial institutions or dummy corporations. However, it is not only these countries that launder drug money: American banks such as Citibank and Riggs bank have been found to have engaged in laundering activities. States like Delaware and Nevada have strict corporate secrecy laws that make them ideal cites for establishing dummy businesses to launder money and stash the laundered profits.[56]

Governments have cooperated to develop a number of financial, legal, and law enforcement institutions to track down laundered funds. In addition to antidrug trafficking operations, antilaundering efforts have been boosted by a concern that laundered funds are supporting terrorist organizations around the world the fight against international drug trafficking with the fight against terrorism. (It doesn't hurt that most governments keep the confiscated funds to fill their own coffers.) Prior to the treaties, different states treated financial crimes related to illegal activities very differently and had very different banking and corporate secrecy laws. The 1988 United Nations Convention against Illicit Traffic in

---

[54] See the UNODC report on money laundering: http://www.unodc.un.or.th/money_laundering/.

[55] *United States* v. *Stephen A. Saccoccia,* Nos. 93–1618, 93–2208, 94–1506 58 F.3d 754; 1995 U.S. App. LEXIS 15956; 42 Fed. R. Evid. Serv. (Callaghan) 355 (June 28, 1995).

[56] Bonner, Raymond (2000) "Laundering of Money Seen as 'Easy', " *New York Times,* November 29.

The Ten Fundamental Laws of Money Laundering [57]

1. The more successful a money laundering apparatus is in imitating the patterns and behavior of legitimate transactions, the less the likelihood of it being exposed.

2. The more deeply embedded illegal activities are within the legal economy and the less their institutional and functional separation, the more difficult it is to detect money laundering.

3. The lower the ratio of illegal to legal financial flows through any given business institution, the more difficult it is to detect money laundering.

4. The higher the ratio of illegal "services" to physical goods production in any economy, the more easily money laundering can be conducted in that economy.

5. The more the business structure of production and distribution of non-financial goods and services is dominated by small and independent firms or self-employed individuals, the more difficult the job of separating legal from illegal transactions.

6. The greater the facility of using checks, credit cards and other non-cash instruments for effecting illegal financial transactions, the more difficult it is to detect money laundering.

7. The greater the degree of financial deregulation for legitimate transactions, the more difficult it is to trace and neutralize criminal money.

8. The lower the ratio of illegally to legally earned income entering any given economy from outside, the harder the job of separating criminal from legal money.

9. The greater the progress towards the financial services supermarket and the greater the degree to which all manner of financial services can be met within one integrated multi-divisional institution, the more difficult it is to detect money laundering.

10. The greater the contradiction between global operation and national regulation of financial markets, the more difficult the detection of money laundering.

Narcotic Drugs and Psychotropic Substances has a provision that requires signatories to track money laundering and confiscate any funds associated with drug trafficking:

Article 5

Confiscation

1. Each Party shall adopt such measures as may be necessary to enable confiscation of:
   a. Proceeds derived from offences established in accordance with article 3, paragraph 1, or property the value of which corresponds to that of such proceeds;
   ...

---

[57] From UNODC website http://www.unodc.org/unodc/en/money_laundering_10_laws.html. See also Wren, Christopher S. (1996) "Business Schemes Change Dynamics of the Drug War Bottom of Form," *New York Times,* May 5.

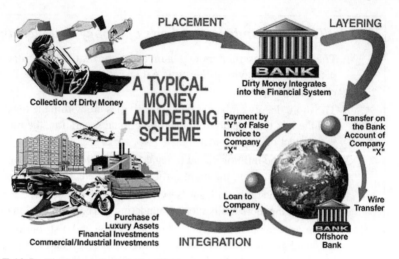

FIGURE 10.5   The Money Laundering Cycle
Source: UNODC website. http://www.unodc.org/unodc/en/money_laundering_cycle.html

2. Each Party shall also adopt such measures as may be necessary to enable its competent authorities to identify, trace, and freeze or seize proceeds, property, instrumentalities or any other things referred to in paragraph 1 of this article, for the purpose of eventual confiscation.

3. In order to carry out the measures referred to in this article, each Party shall empower its courts or other competent authorities to order that bank, financial or commercial records be made available or be seized. A Party shall not decline to act under the provisions of this paragraph on the ground of bank secrecy.

Agreements like these allow states to standardize their responses to global money laundering and work together to ensure that more dirty money is discovered and seized by national governments.

Along with international treaties, the "Group of Seven" (or G-7), the major economic powers of the world, created the Financial Action Task Force on Money Laundering (FATF) that monitors international money laundering and global terrorist financing.[58] Formed in 1989, the FATF produces an annual list of states that are not adequately policing their financial institutions, recommends changes to improve their standing, and can even institute countermeasures for states that do not make the necessary reforms. As part of this effort, each country has developed a Financial Intelligence Unit (FIU) that monitors the transactions of its financial institutions and reports suspicious activity to the appropriate government agencies. These national FIUs (there are over 100) coordinate their information through an intergovernmental organization known as the "Egmont Group" (after the castle in Brussels where the organization was formed in 1995) that allows them to share information and encourage the further development of FIUs around the world.[59]

---

[58] Their website is http://www.fatf-gafi.org/.
[59] Their website is http://www.egmontgroup.org/.

The American Justice and Treasury Departments actively search for money laundering from drug traffickers and often work through the DEA, the IRS, the FBI, and customs officials to conduct sting operations and catch money launderers—even setting up phony financial institutions to entice drug traffickers.[60] The Bank Secrecy Act of 1970 requires transactions of more than $10,000 to be reported to the Treasury Department. The Treasury Department's Financial Crimes Enforcement Center (finCEN), which is the American FIU, monitors financial transactions under the Bank Secrecy Act, works with law enforcement, and advises foreign governments about money laundering.[61] The Foreign Narcotics Kingpin Designation Act makes it a crime (punishable up to 30 years in prison) to provide financial support to individuals designated by the president to be significant narcotics traffickers and the Bank Secrecy Act requires U.S. financial institutions to report any suspicious financial transactions.[62] In January 2006, the Treasury Department released its first Money Laundering Threat Assessment[63] resulting from an interdepartmental working group that studied money laundering crimes throughout the United States.

ALTERNATIVE APPROACHES TO DRUG TRAFFICKING

A great deal has been written about the war on drugs. Many have called for novel strategies to fight drug trafficking, including aggressive new tactics and harsh new punishments for drug traffickers. Some have even suggested that the ICC be given jurisdiction over international drug traffickers.[64] However, critics maintain that in 35 years, the war on drugs has had little effect on drug use in the United States—pointing out that over the long term, despite billions of dollars and countless lives, drug use has consistently risen since the war on drugs was declared in 1971. They argue that harsh punishments for drug dealing unfairly discriminate against the poor and minorities and that the only solution to the war on drugs is to end it and search for new ways to confront the worlds' drug problem. Some have suggested that drugs be decriminalized or legalized, so that law enforcement can be channeled elsewhere. Others have suggested that drugs be treated akin to a public health problem, not a criminal justice problem—seeking to educate potential drug abusers and treat those who currently use them rather than arresting and punishing those who supply the abusers.

The United States has one of the strongest antidrug policies in the world, focusing almost exclusively on interdicting smuggled drugs and doling out criminal punishment for those who produce, traffic, and sell illegal narcotics. Other countries have decriminalized

---

[60] For a short list of these operations, with code names like "Operation Dinero" and "Operation Polar Cap," see Chepesiuk, Ron (1999) *Hard Target: The United States War Against International Drug Trafficking: 1982–1997.* Jefferson: McFarland Press, pp. 211–222.

[61] http://www.fincen.gov/.

[62] This, in turn, has led to the practice of "structuring." That is, manipulating transactions to avoid BSA reporting requirements.

[63] Available at http://www.treasury.gov/offices/enforcement/pdf/mlta.pdf.

[64] Yacoubian, George S. (2003) "Should the Subject Matter Jurisdiction of the International Criminal Court Include Drug Trafficking?" *International Journal of Comparative Criminology,* Vol 3, No. 2, December, 175–190(16).

certain drugs and have a less stringent penal policy for those who sell or traffic in drugs. States like the Netherlands, where marijuana and other "soft drugs" are legal or decriminalized and drug abusers are dealt with less harshly than in the United States, still have drug abuse problems and have additionally become magnets for those who wish to smuggle drugs into states and other places where they remain illegal. The drug culture in the Netherlands has allowed the country to become a production center for synthetic drugs and an important link in the international drug smuggling chain. (On the border between Germany and the Netherlands are numerous drive-through marijuana "coffee shops" where Germans may quickly buy the product and then return home.) Other states have experimented with legalizing or decriminalizing drugs with important results.[65] One state's drug policies—even a country as small as the Netherlands—can have dramatic effects beyond its borders.

To get into this debate would go far beyond the subject of this text. Nonetheless, we can point out a few of the costs of the drug war internationally, as well as the successes that the drug war has had abroad. As we have already seen, the war against drugs has been destructive to many poor farmers in the Andean region as well as in the opium producing regions without providing significant results, but on the other hand the antiopium efforts in the golden triangle have been significantly more effective at stopping the flow of heroin from the region. As with terrorism, the American focus on drugs has caused some resentment among governments around the world, particularly in Latin America where many poor farmers survive on their coca crops. American drug policies have cost taxpayers a great deal of money done significant damage to other countries (Colombia in particular), but whether they have prevented an even greater harm is difficult to determine.

CONCLUSION

In this chapter, we have examined the nature of the *international* drug trafficking threat as well as the efforts by both the American and international criminal justice systems to deal with the problem. Like terrorism, drug trafficking is a "hot button" issue of international criminal justice, gathering a great deal of international attention and resources and it will most likely continue to do so for the near future. It is also a continuing subject of media fascination—primetime crime dramas and popular movies glorify the fast lives of Latin American drug lords. While many of these images are myths, the reality is that international drug trafficking will be lucrative as long as there is a market of eager would-be consumers, and the drug trafficking world will always attract a mix of the poor and desperate along with the greedy and violent.

In the next chapter, we will look at a group of international crimes that, while largely ignored for decades, have recently also become the focus of a great deal of American and international attention: human smuggling and human trafficking. Like drugs, international human trafficking relies on a market eager for illicit goods from overseas. Unlike drugs, however, the product being smuggled abroad is a living, breathing human being with a mind and a will of its own. On account of this, human smuggling is a

---

[65] See Serge, Sandro (2003) *Controlling Illegal Drugs* Somerset: Aldine Transaction.

significantly more complicated criminal activity and although the global human trade is much smaller than the trade in illegal drugs, it nonetheless results in a despair that rivals the ravages of drug abuse.

QUESTIONS

1. Do you think that efforts to fight drug abuse that seek to cut off the supply of drugs to the United States and other countries are effective? Why or why not? Would a demand-based approach work better?
2. What do you think should be done with "narcostates"? Should military force be used against them? Do you think diplomatic approaches would be better? Is there another approach that you think would work better?

READING AND RESOURCES

The majority of online resources on drug trafficking are pushing a political agenda. Many of them are seeking to "unmask" what they believe are the falsehoods that surround the war on drugs and call for the legalization or decriminalization of drugs. Thus, if you are doing research online about drug trafficking, you should be very careful about the sources that you look at, and be very critical about the information that they provide. Even government sources may be biased on this very controversial issue.

The UN Office of Drugs and Crime puts out an annual report on drug use and drug trafficking around the world. You can find it at http://www.unodc.org/unodc/en/world_drug_report.html.

The website for the INCB is http://www.incb.org/. There, they publish an annual report on drug use and drug control efforts around the globe.

The U.S. Department of Justice's National Drug Intelligence Center publishes and annual Drug Threat Assessment which includes a host of valuable information about drug use in the United States as well as information about international drug trafficking into the United States. Its website is http://www.usdoj.gov/ndic/.

PBS' *Frontline* series produced an excellent four-hour documentary on the fight against drugs, including interviews with a number of significant drug traffickers and antidrug government officials. It is widely available at university libraries. It is entitled *Drug Wars* and you can access information about it (including transcripts and videos) at http://www.frontline.org/.

11

Slavery, Human Smuggling, and Human Trafficking

❖

Every year millions of people cross international borders illegally. Many do it eagerly; others are coerced into making the trip or are lured abroad under false pretenses. Many of those who cross borders by choice seek to escape social and economic misery at home. Others are seeking respite from war, oppression, and famine. This new migration, largely from Eastern Europe, South and Central American, Africa and Asia is a part of the new global economy, and new sorts of crime that have accompanied it. Alongside illegal drugs, pirated DVDs, and other illicit goods, the shipment of human beings across borders for work has become a central part of modern, globalized crime.

Of course, many of these travelers who seek financial gain abroad never make it to their final destination. They are stopped by local police forces or immigration services at the border, arrested and promptly sent home. Some die by accident or are murdered while making the sometimes treacherous crossings across scorching deserts or vast oceans. Many who do manage to arrive at their destinations only find new kinds of despair—abandoned to gritty ghettos on the suburbs of Berlin, Paris, or New York. Others fall into even worse situations than the ones they experienced at home. They are sold into a life of slavery where they are kept prisoner and forced to have sex with strangers in dark, filthy brothels or toiling in sweatshops for little or no money. However, some are able to make a decent living in their new homes, working menial jobs and sending their excess money back to their families at home—inspiring many others to make the dangerous trek. Although unlawful emigration is a risky proposition, as long as national borders separate poverty from opportunity and freedom from oppression, there will be individuals who are willing to break the law to improve their situation.

Nowhere is this gap between rich and poor states more apparent than on the border between the United States and Mexico. Nowhere in history has there been a wider income disparity across adjacent national boundaries and such a tempting goal for would-be illegal immigrants. Along the 2,000-mile border, mostly consisting of desert and the Rio Grande River, thousands of agents of the U.S. Customs and Border Protection (CBP, part of the Department of Homeland Security) seek to hold back the tide of illegal border crossings. By most accounts, they are largely unsuccessful. Each year, thousands of men, women, and children seek to enter the United States to find a better life. Some are caught and sent back, where they simply turn around and try again the next day. Many make it through, working in low-wage agricultural and service jobs for menial pay, sending home much of their paycheck, and frustrating many American citizens and government officials. Likewise in Europe, governments carefully monitor their borders to prevent African and Asian immigrants from getting into their countries and right wing politicians rant about the "invasion of Europe" to an increasingly receptive European public.

In Istanbul, Turkey, immigration has a very different face. Here, women from Eastern Europe (mostly from poor Eastern European countries like Ukraine and Moldova) are lured to Turkey to find relatively well paying service work to support their families at home only to become sex workers in that country's brutal underground prostitution market. Some knowingly enter into a life of prostitution there, catering to the desires of locals as well as to sex tourists, ultimately returning home with money for food and medicine for their families. However, many believe that they are going abroad to become waitresses, nannies, or maids, but are in fact forcibly sold into sexual slavery when they arrive. Some of these women work in Turkey until they are no longer useful or are arrested by authorities and returned to their poverty. Others are transported to the Middle East or elsewhere and kept enslaved by vicious pimps—often never to be seen again. Few of these women ever make it home and many die at the hands of their captors.

HUMAN TRAFFICKING AND HUMAN SMUGGLING

This chapter deals with the international market for people and the illegal transportation of people across borders. However, one should be careful to distinguish between the forcible and the free movement of people across borders without authorization—both are illegal but are very different activities and are handled differently by the criminal justice system. *Human trafficking* is the illegal transportation of individuals against their will for profit— the buying and selling of individuals as property. Such trafficking is often, though not always, accompanied by the transportation of these individuals across international borders. Slaves transported against their will from one country to another in order to work have been trafficked, but one can stay within one's own country (or even within one building) and still be a trafficking victim. On the other hand *human smuggling* is the illegal transportation of people across borders for money. People who enter countries unlawfully or people who are willingly transported across borders by someone else, have been smuggled and are considered to be lawbreakers and illegal immigrants. Both acts violate domestic and international laws, but in different ways.

Differences between Human Trafficking and Smuggling

Trafficking	Smuggling
Must Contain an Element of Force, Fraud, or Coercion (actual, perceived or implied), unless under 18 years of age involved in commercial sex acts.	The person being smuggled is generally cooperating.
Forced Labor and/or Exploitation.	There is no actual or implied coercion.
Persons trafficked are victims.	Persons smuggled are violating the law. They are not victims.
Enslaved, subjected to limited movement or isolation, or had documents confiscated.	Persons are free to leave, change jobs, etc.
Need not involve the actual movement of the victim.	Facilitates the illegal entry of person(s) from one country into another.
No requirement to cross an international border.	Smuggling always crosses an international border.
Person must be involved in labor/services or commercial sex acts, i.e., must be "working."	Person must only be in country or attempting entry illegally.

Source: The U.S. State Department website (http://www.state.gov/p/inl/rls/fs/49768.htm)

However, despite these neat categorizations, the lines between smuggling and trafficking are not always clear and there are many cases where these two categories overlap. As we will discuss further below, often people are tricked into willingly crossing borders illegally for work. They are led by guides who instruct them in lying to customs and border officials or sneaking past border patrols and they willingly do so. However, when they arrive at their destination, their passports are confiscated by their guides and they are then kept as slaves or sold on to a pimp or to other criminals who exploit them for profit. Sometimes, they are then transported across further borders against their will to be held as slaves elsewhere. In other cases, smuggled immigrants are held prisoner and either forced to work to pay off the debts they incurred for their travel or they are held prisoner until their relatives pay off this debt. Thus in practice, there is a good deal of ambiguity. Likewise, both categories are frequently dealt with by the same law enforcement organizations and thus should be discussed together.

All countries allow foreigners to enter their borders under certain conditions. In most cases, a would-be traveler needs to get a visa from their destination country's government (usually through their embassy) and possess a passport from one's home country (the State Department issues passports to American citizens) in order to reside lawfully in a country. However, some borders, such as the U.S.–Canadian border and many separating European nations, do not require a visa to cross. In some cases, travelers need only show their IDs, in others (such as in Europe), one can cross national borders on trains, airplanes, or freeways without ever being stopped by border guards or inspections by customs officials. In most countries, however, individuals may be arrested, prosecuted, or deported without such documentation. For example, under § 1325 U.S. Federal Code, "Any alien who

1. enters or attempts to enter the United States at any time or place other than as designated by immigration officers, or
2. eludes examination or inspection by immigration officers, or
3. attempts to enter or obtains entry to the United States by a willfully false or misleading representation or the willful concealment of a material fact, shall, for the first commission of any such offense, be fined under title 18 or imprisoned not more than 6 months, or both, and, for a subsequent commission of any such offense, be fined under title 18, or imprisoned not more than 2 years, or both."

However, while illegal immigration is a crime, in most cases aliens are simply sent back to their home country or country of origin without prosecution.

SLAVERY AND HUMAN TRAFFICKING

Slavery has been outlawed throughout the globe for over a century and the ban on slavery is considered one of the bedrock principles of international human rights law. The Universal Declaration of Human Rights asserts that "No one shall be held in slavery or servitude; slavery and the slave trade shall be prohibited in all their forms." Likewise, the ICC Statute defines, "Rape, sexual slavery, enforced prostitution, forced pregnancy, enforced sterilization, or any other form of sexual violence of comparable gravity" as a crime against humanity and alternatively, as a war crime.[1] The American Civil War was fought in part to end the practice in the United States and the Thirteenth Amendment of the Constitution asserts that "Neither slavery nor involuntary servitude, except as a punishment for crime whereof the party shall have been duly convicted, shall exist within the United States, or any place subject to their jurisdiction." Nonetheless, the reality is that slavery has been practiced and is still practiced throughout the world in different forms, and it remains a part of the underground economy of this country, where immigrants are forced to labor as slaves in back-alley sweatshops and women are kept imprisoned as prostitutes in New York, San Francisco, and Los Angeles.

While slavery and human trafficking are closely linked in that most people who are trafficked are forced into a life of slavery, there is a subtle difference between the two. Trafficking involves the buying and selling of people, while slavery involves holding these people against their will and forcing them into labor. Many traffickers are only middlemen

---

[1] However, as we discussed in Chapter 2, such acts must be "committed as part of a widespread or systematic attack directed against any civilian population" (Article 7(1)) to be considered a crime against humanity. It is also described as war crime when part of an armed conflict.

or transporters who do not actually keep slaves themselves. A legal definition of human trafficking was spelled out in the "Protocol to Prevent, Suppress and Punish Trafficking in Persons Especially Women and Children" (a supplement to the United Nations Convention against Transnational Organized Crime) in 2000. There, trafficking is defined as,

> the recruitment, transportation, transfer, harbouring or receipt of persons, by means of the threat or use of force or other forms of coercion, of abduction, of fraud, of deception, of the abuse of power or of a position of vulnerability or of the giving or receiving of payments or benefits to achieve the consent of a person having control over another person, for the purpose of exploitation. Exploitation shall include, at a minimum, the exploitation of the prostitution of others or other forms of sexual exploitation, forced labour or services, slavery or practices similar to slavery, servitude or the removal of organs.[2]

Notice that there are a number of different ways that a person may be enslaved and there are a number of ways that the slave's labor can be exploited by his or her "owner" (including, horribly enough, the use of slaves as resources for organs). All of these different categories are meant respond to the numerous ways that individuals have been enslaved in the modern world and the ever-innovative modern slave trade.

The Slavery Convention (which entered into force in 1927) defines slavery as "the status or condition of a person over whom any or all of the powers attaching to the right of ownership are exercised," and there are many different ways that an individual can be enslaved. Most of us are familiar with the plantation slavery practiced in the antebellum South, but this form of slavery (sometimes called "chattel slavery" because the slave is considered to be the absolute property of the slave owner and has no rights whatsoever) is only one of many ways that humans can be enslaved. For example, *debt bondage,* or *indentured servitude,* means that an individual is held prisoner and forced to work in order to pay off an outstanding debt. *Sexual slavery* entails holding a person, usually a woman or a child, prisoner and forcing them to perform sex acts for somebody else's profit. There are also lesser known forms of slavery such as *marital bondage,* where an individual, again usually a woman, is "given" to another family to be married against her will, usually in exchange for money or other kinds of compensation. There is no single kind of slavery and each of these is practiced in different forms in different places around the world.

Slavery is illegal everywhere and it is a crime under both international and domestic law throughout the world. Legally speaking, it does not matter, in most cases, whether or not the victim is transported across borders—slavery is a crime. Like the crimes mentioned in Chapter 2 (genocide, war crimes, etc.), slavery need not affect other countries for it to be considered an crime under international law. The difference between war crimes/genocide and slavery is that in most cases slavery does not fall under the jurisdiction of the ICC— unless it is also a war crime or a crime against humanity. Nonetheless, there are several treaties that ban slavery and it is considered a violation of *jus cogens* principles of international law (as was discussed in Chapter 2, these are laws that no government can exempt itself from). This means that in the vast majority of cases slavery crimes must be prosecuted in domestic courts under domestic laws—there is no other legal option.

---

[2] Article 3(a). It is also important to note that the treaty states that "The consent of a victim of trafficking in persons to the intended exploitation . . . shall be irrelevant" (Article 3(b)).

In lawless countries or those with a great deal of corruption, this can create big problems for those seeking to end slavery and human trafficking through the tools of criminal justice. Without the intervention of an international court (or the UN Security Council), there may be little legal recourse in lawless states where slavery is practiced.

It is impossible to know with a great degree of certainty how many people are enslaved around the world or how many people are trafficked.[3] Like other illicit industries, slavers and human traffickers do not willingly divulge information about their activities. Likewise, governments do not necessarily want to make their countries' slave practices known to the larger world. This is especially true in countries with governments that tacitly allow slavery or with law enforcement bodies that are too corrupt or incompetent to stop slavery practices within their borders. Some countries such as Sudan (see below) use slavery as tool of civil war: internal enemies are enslaved by allies of the government in order to crush rebellion. To compound the problem, well-meaning antitrafficking organizations often exaggerate the numbers of people trafficked in order to attract public attention. To make matters even more difficult, despite the fact that there are a number of international agreements dealing with slavery and some with human trafficking, not everybody agrees on what circumstances constitute slavery and what human trafficking is, exactly. For example, forced marriage may be considered slavery in one culture but may be an accepted practice in another, and importantly, it may not be counted as slavery when government officials tally up their national slavery statistics. These factors make definite figures for slavery and human trafficking very difficult to uncover.

Nonetheless, some scholars and government officials have made responsible estimates regarding global slavery and human trafficking. According to the U.S. State Department, approximately 600,000–800,000 people are trafficked across international borders each year—the vast majority women, and about half of them children.[4] Kevin Bales, from the NGO "Free the Slaves," estimates that there are 27 million slaves in the world. As he analyzes these numbers, "The biggest part of the 27 million, perhaps 15 to 20 million, is represented by *bonded labor* in India, Pakistan, Bangladesh, and Nepal . . . Otherwise slavery tends to be concentrated in Southeast Asia, northern and western Africa, and parts of South America . . . There are more slaves alive today than all the people stolen from Africa in the time of the transatlantic slave trade."[5] While other experts have placed the number as high as 200 million (the population of many large countries), these are probably too high.[6] Regardless of the exact numbers, it is clear that slavery is a world-wide problem that destroys millions of lives.

In seeking to understand how slavery and human trafficking work in the modern global marketplace, scholars point to "push" and "pull" factors that influence these criminal enterprises. "Push" factors are those aspects of a society that make it a likely target for human traffickers by creating a ready pool of potential victims. The primary factors pointed out by scholars are (1) government corruption, (2) high infant mortality, (3) a very young population, (4) low food production, and (5) conflict and social unrest. On the other

---

[3] Tyldum, Guri and Brunovskis, Anette (2005) "Describing the Unobserved: Methodological Challenges in Empirical Studies on Human Trafficking," *International Migration,* Vol. 43 Issue 1–2.

[4] U.S. State Department, *Trafficking in Persons Report,* June, 2005, p. 6.

[5] Bales, Kevin (1999) *Disposable People: New Slavery in the Global Economy* Berkeley: University of California Press, p. 8.

[6] *Op cit.* For national population data, see United Nations Population Network http://www.un.org/popin/.

hand, "pull" factors are those that lead traffickers to bring trafficked people to that country, things that are appealing to traffickers. While conceding that such factors are less helpful in predicting where people will be trafficked to, push factors are the age demographics of the destination country (they usually have a large number of men over the age of 60), the amount of official corruption, the quantity of food, and a low level of infant mortality.[7]

While the most common form of human trafficking is the forcible transportation of women as prostitutes and sex slaves, others are trafficked as domestic laborers, factory workers, or mine laborers. Anywhere that goods can be produced more cheaply with forced labor, labor regulations are not enforced, and police powers are corrupt or inept, human beings will be bought, sold, and enslaved.

Operations of Human Trafficking

Bales has isolated eight major stages that comprise the trafficking process from beginning to end. While these stages may differ from place to place, they serve as a good rough guide for how traffickers prey on desperate and naïve victims.

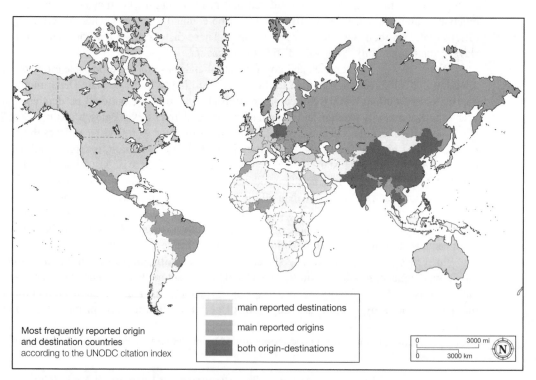

Most frequently reported origin
and destination countries
according to the UNODC citation index

main reported destinations

main reported origins

both origin-destinations

0   3000 mi
0   3000 km   N

FIGURE 11.1   Reported Human Trafficking: Main Origin, Transportation, and Destination Countries
Source: UNODC Report, "Trafficking in Persons: Global Patterns, 2006"

---

[7] Bales, Kevin (2005) "Human Trafficking: A Worldwide Concern," in Bales, Kevin, *Understanding Global Slavery: A Reader.* Berkeley: University of California Press, p. 140.

1. *The Context of Vulnerability*—Traffickers often locate victims based on their surroundings (poverty, lack of opportunity, etc.). Thus, they search out places with the aforementioned push factors.

2. *Recruitment*—Victims are often approached by members of their own community, ethnic group, or tribe, usually appearing affluent, who promise them lucrative opportunities away from home. Rarely are trafficking victims forcibly abducted. Rather, they are lured away from the safety of their homes, leaving willingly.

3. *Removal*—This is the most delicate part of the trafficking process, where the trafficker begins to assert control over his or her victim. Usually the victim consents to leaving home, believing that they are on their way to a better life elsewhere. At this point, the victim is still consenting to his or her situation. (However, as was noted above, the laws governing trafficking do not consider the victim's consent to leave home as relevant to the crime of trafficking.)

4. *Transportation*—As was already mentioned, trafficking doesn't necessarily mean transporting victims across international borders. Nonetheless, at this point, the victim has been completely removed from his or her home and the traffickers have begun to solidify their control over their victims by remaining their only familiar face. At this point, some victims may still not be aware of the fact that they are being trafficked. They may still believe that they are simply being smuggled and may help conceal their status by lying to local law enforcement or customs officials.

5. *Establishment of Control*—Usually when the victim arrives at his or her destination, the traffickers begin the process of "breaking down" their victims. In international trafficking, the victim is usually deprived of their travel documentation (passports, visa, etc.) to prevent them from returning home. For sex slaves, this usually involves beatings, rapes, and humiliation that are meant to reconcile the victim to her new circumstances. In other cases it might mean extended periods of isolation or forcing the victim to ingest powerful drugs that distort her thinking processes.

6. *Arrival*—Usually, when the victim arrives at her final destination (which may be the first of many locations) the traffickers, from their first handlers to those who deliver the "cargo," have made extensive efforts to make their victims malleable and submissive to the will of their new "owners." If they have done their job correctly, the trafficking victim no longer has the will to escape and will do all that is demanded of them.

7. *Exploitation*—As we've already discussed, slaves are exploited in numerous forms. Some are put to work as prostitutes, others in factories or in plantations, others in the homes of the wealthy.

8. *Resolution*—The end of the exploitation of slaves may mean many different things. Some are simply released to their own devices. Others are killed. Some are fortunate enough to escape from their captors and find their way to freedom. Nonetheless, the victims may not be completely free from their enslavement once the exploitation has fully run its course. Some may be threatened or blackmailed into silence or shunned by their community. Some even become traffickers themselves. Many suffer lingering trauma after their release. Like survivors of military conflicts, the scars of human trafficking victims often run very deep and do not easily go away.

Who Traffics?

Human trafficking is not a simple process. Unlike drugs, which can be carried in your pocket, or stashed in a suitcase, holding and transporting a human being against their will is immensely difficult and complex. Each of the stages that were mentioned above requires the coordinated activity of a number of people—particularly when the trafficked individual is brought across national borders. Documents must be acquired or forged, boats and cars must be manned, and authorities must be eluded or bribed. Finally, the will of the victim herself must be broken and she must be kept secluded and guarded, sometimes constantly, to prevent discovery or escape for the trafficker to make his profits. All of this takes time, energy, and resources far more than one individual can muster. This means that, almost without exception, human trafficking is carried out by organized criminal gangs of some sort.

Andrea Di Nicola, a researcher with the Joint Research Centre for Transnational Crime breaks down the types of trafficking groups into four main categories[8]: *Individual entrepreneurs* (or amateur smugglers) who work independently to obtain, transport, or exploit trafficked individuals. These may include individuals who taxi trafficked individuals or individuals who lure others into positions of vulnerability and then sell them to traffickers. *Homemade businesses/small enterprises* that operate as "subcontractors" for larger trafficking networks. *Medium and large enterprises,* such as the Turkish Mafia, Albanian gangs, and Nigerian organized gangs, are usually region-specific and operate in more than one country. *Multinational enterprises* organize vast international trafficking networks that may stretch across many different countries. Since trafficking is a process and not a single action, it can be the case that any or all of these groups may be involved in a single case of human trafficking.

Many different criminal organizations around the world are involved in the human trafficking business and it is a truly global enterprises, with coordination between various groups across national boundaries. The Russian, Turkish, and Chinese mobs, and the Mafia are all involved in some level with human trafficking as are smaller organizations operating throughout the Balkan region of Eastern Europe. The Yakuza, the infamous Japanese organized criminals, have been known to be involved in the trafficking of women from China into Japan for sex work.[9] There are even reports that UN Peacekeepers in the Balkans have been both using trafficked women and assisting in the trafficking process.[10] However, the trafficking business seems to be "decentered," that is, there is not one organization that runs the trafficking operations around the world. Rather the different groups that Di Nicola cites operate at various stages of the trafficking process and interact with each other at various times, each making money for its part in exploiting the trafficking victim.

---

[8] Di Nicola, Adrea, "Trafficking in Human Beings and the Smuggling of Migrants," in Reichel, Philip (ed.), *Handbook of Transnational Crime and Justice,* pp. 181–203.

[9] http://www.icmpd.org/uploadimg/OCandTR.pdf.

[10] Amnesty International, " 'So does it mean that we have the rights?' Protecting the human rights of women and girls trafficked for forced prostitution in Kosovo," (http://www.amnestyusa.org/news/document.do?id=1391B6E5EE9C8A9780256E7E0041EE72).

Sexual Slavery

Sexual slavery is practiced in some form throughout the world. While some willingly sell their bodies for money, many argue that prostitution is by nature a forced, exploitative form of labor—even where it is conducted legally or with the consent of the victim. Nonetheless, internationally, prostitution and the trafficking of women are intertwined. It is common practice in parts of Asia for poor women to be abducted or sold to individuals by friends and kept prisoner in brothels for money. Many children who are trafficked are sold to pimps who use them to make money from eager pedophiles. According to the State Department, 80% of the people who are trafficked across international borders are women (and 50% are minors), the vast majority of which are put to work in brothels or independent prostitution rings. Sometimes these women are initially sold by their family, who often don't consider a daughter to be an asset, in order to provide income to help the rest of the family survive. Usually, after they are purchased, they are "broken" by their new "owners"—including repeated rapes, beatings, and degradation designed to prevent the woman from seeking to escape to freedom. They are usually forced to have sex with dozens of men each day, given a small portion of their proceeds (if any), and cruelly beaten.

In its cross-border form, traffickers often rely upon desperate, sometimes naïve women who are misled by businessmen, friends, and neighbors about their overseas employment prospects. Frequently, these women are lured to foreign countries with promises that they will be given relatively high paying jobs as domestic servants or waitresses in respectable homes or restaurants. Once they are overseas, however, their passports are confiscated by their "guides" and they are held prisoner in filthy brothels by vicious pimps. Other times, they are seduced by an apparently loving partner who convinces her to go abroad for a new life. When she arrives at her new "home," he then betrays her, sometimes after a bogus "marriage," selling her to traffickers and abandoning her to her fate. "Marriage services" operating in Eastern Europe purport to introduce women to Western men who are interested in marrying them. However, when they arrive, they are deprived of their freedom and put to work in strip clubs or brothels. Deceptions like these are crucial tools for traffickers—allowing them to quickly replenish their supply of women, which, given the nature of the sex trade, often has a high turnover rate as regular clientele tire of the available women.

To make matters more difficult for these sex slaves, prostitution is a crime in most countries and in many cases the trafficked women are treated as criminals themselves if they are caught, rather than being protected as victims. Many criminal justice systems prefer to view trafficked women as criminal prostitutes and as illegal aliens rather than as victims of slavery. Most are forced to return to their country of origin, which they had been desperately trying to escape. Others are prosecuted and imprisoned by local authorities. If they are returned home to a society that stigmatizes sex work and sexually active women, they will be shunned by their community if they are exposed. Thus, they are often left poor, rejected by their community, and emotionally or physically maimed by their experiences. There are even some reports that HIV-positive women who return to the nation of Myanmar

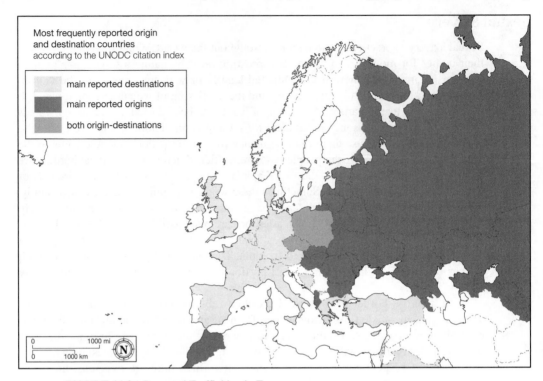

FIGURE 11.2   Reported Trafficking in Europe
Source: UNODC Report, "Trafficking in Persons: Global Patterns, 2006"

(a repressive dictatorship in South Asia) are executed by the government.[11] In the global trafficking of sex slaves, there has been a strong tendency for governments to blame, and often punish, the victims.

Europe   Since the fall of the Soviet Union, extreme poverty, corruption, and lack of opportunity in the former Soviet Republics have forced many women in Ukraine, Moldova, and Russia to travel abroad to find work, leaving them vulnerable to trafficking, slavery, and other sorts of exploitation. This vulnerability, coupled with the lawless nature of much of the Balkan region of Eastern Europe, which was devastated by a series of wars in the 1990s, and the power of local organized criminal gangs, has created an environment ripe for sex slavery and human trafficking. Europol has reported that approximately 90% of the women trafficked in Europe were from former Soviet states and the Ukrainian

---

[11] Murray, Alison, "Debt-bondage and trafficking: Don't believe the hype," in K. Kempadoo and J. Doezema (eds), *Global Sex Workers: Rights, Resistance, and Redefinition,* New York, Routledge, 1998, pp. 51–64. Cited in Miller, Jody, "Global Prostitution, Sex Tourism, and Trafficking," in Renzettie, Claire M., Goodstein, Lynne, and Miller, Susan, *Rethinking Gender Crime, and Justice,* Roxbury Publishing, 2006, pp. 139–154.

government estimates that 100,000 Ukrainian women were trafficked during the 1990s. Nicknamed "Natashas," the "Natasha trade" generates billions of dollars each year for Russian and Eastern European organized gangs.[12] Organized criminals run brothels throughout the Balkans and Western Europe (including Belgium, German, and the Netherlands) where women are used by local men as well as UN peacekeepers stationed in the former Yugoslavia.[13] Others are sold on to work in Asia and the Middle East. Because they are viewed as ethnically white and are often blond-haired, they have a unique appeal in a world where certain physical characteristics are considered desirable by many men.

However, Russian and East European women are not the only women who are trafficked into European brothels. Women are often brought in from Africa and Asia to cater to the sex tourists who haunt the notorious red light districts of Amsterdam, Brussels, and Frankfurt. One Italian diplomat suggested that 60% of the prostitutes working in Italian brothels are from Africa and many of these are, presumably, victims of trafficking in one form or another.[14] The largest group of trafficking victims that were discovered in Belgium during actions in 1999 were originally from Nigeria, one-fifth of which were men (the second largest group were Chinese), and in the Netherlands, about one-third of all trafficking victims were from outside of Europe.[15]

Other Forms of Slavery

Much of the data shows that the majority of people trafficked into slavery are held as sex slaves; however, they are not the only slaves in the world. These other forms of slavery and human trafficking have developed primarily for purposes of forced labor, including agriculture, industrial labor, or begging for change from tourists. Most of these cases are tragic, but some are bizarre: Hundreds of children have been kidnapped and transported to the United Arab Emirates from Bangladesh, Pakistan, and Eastern Africa to serve as jockeys in the camel races that are very popular there. (These races are quite dangerous and children have been killed when they fall off their mounts or have suffered abuse from their handlers.[16]) Others have been kidnapped to serve as soldiers or to work in factories,

---

[12] Malarek, Victor, *The Natashas: Inside the New Global Sex Trade*, Arcade Publishing, New York, 2004. Hughes, Donna, "The 'Natasha' Trade: Transnational Sex Trafficking" *National Institute of Justice Journal*, January, 8–15. Mameli, Peter. "Stopping the illegal trafficking of human beings: How transnational police work can stem the flow of forced prostitution." *Crime, Law & Social Change* 38: 67–80, 2002.

[13] Mendelson, Sarah E., "Barracks and Brothels: Peacekeepers and Human Trafficking in the Balkans," Center for Strategic and International Studies Report, February. (available at http://www.csis.org/ruseura/humanrights/trafficking/#pubs).

[14] Wallace, Melanie R., "Note: Voiceless Victims: Sex Slavery and Trafficking of African Women in Western Europe" 30 Ga. J. Int'l & Comp. L. 569.

[15] International Organization for Migration, "New IOM Figures on the Global Scale of Trafficking," *Trafficking in Migrants, Quarterly Bulletin,* April 2001 (available at http://www.iom.int//DOCUMENTS/PUBLICATION/EN/tm_23.pdf).

[16] U.S. State Department Trafficking in Persons Report (June 2005), p. 12. See also, BBC News, "Help for Gulf child camel jockeys," December 2, 2004 (http://news.bbc.co.uk/1/hi/world/middle_east/4063391.stm).

mines, or in plantations around the world. Chocolate production in the Ivory Coast has been linked to slavery, and slaves in India have been used to pound rocks into sand.[17] Anywhere that there is a desperate need for cheap, tedious or dangerous labor, there is a risk that people will be trafficked and enslaved.

Sudan and Slavery   When modern slavery is discussed by activists and diplomats, one nation is commonly cited as the most egregious offender: the troubled African nation of Sudan. One of the poorest and most brutal countries in the world (as was discussed in Chapter 7, the Sudanese government has also been accused of genocide in its western province, Darfur), Sudan has been embroiled in a brutal civil war between its Muslim northern people, who are of Arab descent, and its Christian and Animist (worshiping traditional, local deities) south for most of the last six decades. This war, which has begun to ebb, has resulted in the enslavement of thousands of members of the Dinka tribe in southern Sudan as part of a bloody civil war. Government forces, working with rival tribes, have captured women and children in the south and then used them as forced agricultural labor.

In an effort to free enslaved Sudanese Christians, some activists in the United States have begun "buying back" slaves from their "owners." While the intentions behind this are noble, the practice has generated many criticisms from antislavery NGOs. Some have argued that buying slaves their freedom only encourages further enslavement, making slaves a ready source for cash. Rather than treating the crime, they maintain, it is more important to address the deeper causes of slavery: war, poverty, and an ethic that allows one human being to claim another as property.[18] As the NGO Human Rights Watch writes, "When the crises in Sudan are brought to an end, slavery will also come to an end."[19] Antislavery activists who engage in the practice argue that they cannot wait for the end of a long war to stop global slavery. "The international community has failed for nearly two decades to end slavery in Sudan through peace talks. In the absence of viable alternatives, we cannot, and we will not, fail to rescue the slaves now."[20] Whether a noble project to obtain freedom for oppressed Africans, or a naïve, misguided effort that ultimately makes the Dinka people worse off—the ultimate solution to the problem of slavery in Sudan cannot be obtained by merely addressing the immediate issues and avoiding the deep political, religious, and economic conflicts that fuel the slave trade in Africa. Like so many other aspects of criminal justice, slavery, in Sudan, or elsewhere, is a product of many different social forces, making a single solution to the problem very difficult, if not impossible, to provide.

---

[17] Raghavan, Sudarsan, and Chatterjee, Sumana "Slaves to chocolate: Children suffer to harvest a treat they rarely get to taste," *The Gazette* (Montreal, Quebec) June 23, 2001, p. B1. Melwani, Lavina "Bitter Chocolate," *India Today,* August 8.

[18] Lewis, Paul, "UN Criticism Angers Charities Buying Sudan Slaves' Release," *New York Times,* March 12, 1999.

[19] Human Rights Watch Report, "Slavery and Slave Redemption in Sudan," March 2002, http://www.hrw.org/backgrounder/africa/sudanupdate.htm.

[20] Jacobs, Charles (President, American Anti-Slavery Group), Letter, *New York Times,* May 2, 2001.

Trafficking in the United States

While slavery has been illegal in the United States since the Civil War, illegal slavery and human trafficking are still practiced throughout the country. Just as in the rest of the world, some of those who are trafficked into the United States are made to work in sweatshops and domestic labor, and others are put to work in brothels. Most of those trafficked in the United States are brought from elsewhere (there is little trafficking of native American citizens).[21]

Many of the sex slaves in the United States are brought into the country from Latin America, Asia, and to a lesser extent from the former Soviet countries. They are often victimized by members of their own ethnic groups, who exploit their overseas connections and facility with the foreign cultures in order to lure them. Thus, Asian criminal organizations traffic Asian men, women, and children, while Russian and Latin American organizations usually traffic people from their own respective countries. According to an FBI report, among the Asian gangs that are involved in human trafficking and human smuggling, 45% are Chinese, 29% are Vietnamese, 7.3%, Korean, and the remaining consist of Lations, Cambodians, Filipinos, and other Asian groups.[22] Each organization has its own dynamics. According to Amy O'Neill Richard (a CIA researcher), Asian gangs tend to work in "a loose confederation of organized entrepreneurs or enterprises" while Russian traffickers working in Florida are probably run by individual Russians and "not necessarily organized crime."[23] Much of the profits from trafficking enterprises are then turned into other criminal enterprises either in the United States or abroad.

Recently, under President Bush, the government has made a concerted effort to deal with human trafficking. Congress passed the *Victims of Trafficking and Violence Protection Act of 2000* (VTVPA), designed to help combat trafficking and to protect its victims who, as undocumented aliens, often find themselves in a difficult situation. The VTVPA did several things that are meant to assist the United States and other governments fight trafficking: Most concretely, it toughened the punishments for trafficking under federal law from 10 years (maximum) to 20 years. Likewise, it made it a crime (punishable by up to 20 years) to knowingly provide or obtain labor, "by threats of serious harm to, or physical restraint against, that person or another person."[24] It also required that the State Department prepare reports for all countries receiving U.S. financial assistance, evaluating their efforts to combat human trafficking, collated in the annual Victims of Trafficking Report. It authorizes the president to help other countries fight trafficking, including developing laws against trafficking, investigating and prosecuting traffickers, and educating the public about the dangers of trafficking.

Because some trafficked individuals are scared into silence out of a fear that they would be imprisoned as illegal immigrants or returned to their home country, the VTVPA

---

[21] Landesman, Peter, "The Girls Next Door," *New York Times,* January 25, 2004.

[22] FBI, Asian Criminal Enterprise Unit, Trafficking in Asian Aliens, July 1998. Cited in Richard, Amy O'Neill, *International Trafficking in Women to the United States: A Contemporary Manifestation of Slavery and Organized Crime,* Center for the Study of Intelligence Monograph, November 1998.

[23] Ibid., p. 13 and p. 15 respectively.

[24] H.R. 3244, 106th Cong. § 112(a) (2000).

offers protection to the victims. The Act will often allow them to stay in the United States "if after an assessment, it is determined that such individual is a victim of a severe form of trafficking and a potential witness to such trafficking (Sect. 107(c)(3))." This gives trafficking victims an incentive to flee their traffickers and to testify against them rather than scaring them into silence out of a fear that they will be returned to their home where they could be subject to retaliation. Special visas (a "T Visa" and a "U Visa") have been created to assist victims of trafficking in order to allow them to remain in the country under certain circumstances.[25] However, the VTVPA does *not* give trafficking victims American citizenship.

At the federal level, trafficking is handled primarily by the Trafficking in Persons and Worker Exploitation Task Force under the Department of Justice's Civil Rights Division, created by the VTVPA to handle federal human trafficking cases. Its primary duties are the investigation and prosecution of human trafficking cases as well as an outreach program that works with trafficking victims, antitrafficking NGOs, and local law enforcement personnel.[26] Many states and large cities (such as New York) have similar task forces that help with preventing slavery and human trafficking.[27]

Strategies to Combat Human Trafficking and Slavery

Experts, activists, and criminal justice professionals have struggled to develop strategies to confront human trafficking and slavery to function alongside traditional criminal prosecution. Some have focused on cutting off the supply of slaves, others the demand, and still others have sought to find novel tools to fight against trafficking. Here are a few of the most common strategies that have been discussed in the relevant literature:

Educating Potential Victims   Some groups have tried to make potential victims aware of the scams used by human traffickers so that they may be more on guard against them. Many human traffickers rely on the trust of community members and the appearance of financial success to lure new victims (some former slaves even return to help recruit a new generation of slaves). Some, particularly those who wish to become prostitutes, do not understand the violence, lack of control, and degradation that they will be subject to when they consent to be trafficked. Others, desperate to escape poverty may be willfully blind to the fact that, once they become slaves, their chances of getting out are remote. "A dose of reality" for those who are considering becoming prostitutes can help prevent some of the most flagrant abuses.

Curbing Demand   Some have sought to fight human trafficking by attacking the "demand" side of the supply–demand chain. This can be done in a number of ways. Making customers of prostitution aware of the exploitative relations that trafficked women are subject

---

[25] U.S. Department of Justice Press Release, January 24, 2002. Available at http://www.usdoj.gov/opa/pr/2002/January/02_crt_038.htm.

[26] Their website is http://www.usdoj.gov/crt/crim/tpwetf.htm.

[27] Spangenberg, Mia, "International Trafficking of Children to New York City for Sexual Purposes," http://www.ecpatusa.org/pdf/trafficking_report_ final.pdf.

to can reduce the number of customers for exploited labor (although it probably won't completely eliminate it). Also, citizen activism campaigns that boycott companies that rely on slave labor abroad can force foreign countries to change their labor practices. Under the antislavery banner, activists have organized boycotts of corporations like Nike, the Gap, and Nestle, shining a spotlight on slavery and forced labor practices in Africa and Asia.

Citizen Activism   Some citizens have acted through NGOs or Church organizations to free slaves. Some have helped indentured servants save money to buy their own freedom, others have put up their own money to buy slaves from their "owners." As we have discussed above with the case of Sudan, the issues regarding slavery buybacks are complex and may produce unintended results (such as, ironically enough, an increase in slavery).

Criminalization   Law enforcement around the world actively seeks to uncover and crush human trafficking operations. This may involve active sting operations or the reliance on former trafficking victims to provide the intelligence necessary to break up the operations. Both Interpol and Europol work to fight international human trafficking, and Interpol runs the Interpol Child Abuse Image Database (ICAID) to monitor the exploitation of children on the Internet. Similarly, the UNODC's Global Program against Trafficking in Human Beings helps train local law enforcement in confronting issues in human trafficking.

Legalized Prostitution and Sex Trafficking

In the face of an inability to completely stop "the oldest profession," some countries have either legalized or decriminalized prostitution in an effort to make it a safer and less exploitative industry. The Netherlands, famous for the Red Light District in its most famous city, Amsterdam, had long turned a blind eye to prostitution within its borders and finally legalized the practice in 2000. Many of the sex workers in the country argued that legalization would allow them to organize and gain protections that are usually denied to workers in illegal trades. Proponents of decriminalization argued that regulation, in lieu of criminalization, makes prostitution safe and humane, thereby eliminating the trafficking, slavery, and exploitation that are endemic to the global sex trade.

Critics, on the other hand, have argued that legalization only deepens the exploitation of women that is inherent in the practice of prostitution. The Coalition Against Trafficking in Women (CATW), an NGO, has argued that prostitution can never be fair to women and that they will always be abused as long as they sell sex for money—there is no such thing as "fair prostitution." Further, the excess regulation that has resulted from the legalization of prostitution in the Netherlands has forced the illegal immigrants who work as prostitutes to go underground out of fear that registering with government officials will lead to their expulsion from the country.[28]

It would go far beyond the subjects of slavery and human trafficking to address this issue here. However, it is not clear that the legalization of prostitution would affect the *international*

---

[28] Daley, Suzanne, "New Rights for Dutch Prostitutes, but No Gain," *New York Times,* August 12, 2001, p. A1.

trade of sex slaves into or out of Europe (or anywhere else). Other legal activities that are linked with slavery (such as agriculture, camel racing, etc.) use trafficked and coerced labor despite the fact that they are legal activities—the criminal aspect of these activities simply moves underground. Nonetheless, as we have repeatedly discussed, globalized crime is linked to the globalized economy, and so changes in how goods are bought, sold, and regulated by governments is sure to affect how women who provide sexual services are treated by the industry.

HUMAN SMUGGLING

While both human trafficking and human smuggling deal with the illegal transportation of human beings, human smuggling raises very different issues for criminal justice than does human trafficking. For one thing, unlike human trafficking, where individuals who are trafficked are innocent victims who are transported against their will or under false pretenses, in human smuggling both the smuggler and the one who is smuggled are engaged in illegal activity. Likewise, human smuggling does not involve the brutality and degradation that is frequently associated with trafficking where victims are frequently beaten and tortured as a part of their captivity. Finally, smuggling is usually a temporary relationship between an individual and his smugglers—once the migrant has been brought safely to his or her destination, he or she is let go to pursue work in their new location while the trafficking victim is held in captivity until they have exhausted their moneymaking potential or die. Of course, as was already mentioned, in many cases the boundaries separating people who are trafficked and those who are smuggled is a thin one and smuggling can easily turn into trafficking; nonetheless, they are clearly different sorts of phenomena and should, on the whole, be kept separate.

Of course, human smuggling cannot be completely disconnected from the issue of illegal immigration and the general public's dislike of it. (There's a slight difference between human smuggling and illegal immigration—illegal immigrants or undocumented aliens are those people who cross borders and work abroad without proper authorization, while smuggling is the act of bringing in people to work as illegal aliens. A person could be an illegal alien without being smuggled by somebody else—if he or she independently entered a country illegally.) At the most basic level, objections to illegal immigration is tied up with questions about labor in the modern economy. Workers who enter the United States and Europe come from places with far fewer opportunities for work and significantly lower standards of living. Even this is relative as North Korean workers seek opportunities in countries like China, some of whose workers in turn seek to get into the United States in search of even better opportunities there. Because of this, new immigrants, particularly illegal immigrants, are often willing to work for wages that are much lower than those for natives who work at similar jobs. Many argue that this drives down the price of labor, hurting those who seek to make a living in unskilled markets such as agriculture and food service. (Defenders respond that cheap labor is required for producing cheap goods, which meet the consumer demands, and were the goods brought to market without illegal labor, they would be too expensive for most shoppers.)

Many other critics maintain that human smuggling and illegal immigration have a number of deleterious effects on society beyond their simple economic consequences.

Human smugglers are frequently used to smuggle other sorts of contraband such as drugs and illegal arms and critics argue that one cannot separate these forms of smuggling. More deeply, for many countries, large-scale illegal immigration poses an existential threat for many countries. That is, in many countries, it is sometimes believed that illegal immigration not only creates economic and crime problems, but threatens the existence and the identity of countries that have existed for centuries. America has always been an immigrant nation and has a multiethnic and multiracial population. However, most European nations, and most countries around the world for that matter, tie their national identities to ethnic identities. That is, one must be ethnically French in order to be "truly French," whereas a person can be considered an American regardless of where he or she was born or the color of their skin. An Arab may have lived in Germany his or her entire life and not be considered "German," whereas, for many, one can be an American very quickly and comparatively easily. In these situations, many immigrants cannot, or will not, assimilate to mainstream European society and instead reside in culturally isolated ghettos. Thus, the influx of foreigners with different cultural traditions has created a great deal of tension in many European communities, even those such as the Netherlands with a long tradition of tolerance for different types of people. As we will see, these fears (not far below the surface of American culture) have had political consequences in Europe and the United States when thinking about immigration and human smuggling.

Since September 11, 2001, the issue of human smuggling and illegal immigration has also become involved with a completely novel set of issues—terrorism and national security. Three of the al-Qaeda hijackers were in the United States illegally and in a strange twist, as a result of a bureaucratic mix-up, two of the hijackers were granted visa extensions six months *after* they helped destroy the World Trade Center.[29] Many have argued that our relatively porous borders, through which thousands of people can get in or out of the country undetected, make us vulnerable to terrorists who would not be able to enter the country by other means. The U.S.–Canadian border is the longest undefended border in the world and most people do not need a passport to enter the country—making it vulnerable to abuse by terrorists. While some have cynically exploited the fear of terrorism to crack down on immigration, securing the borders and carefully controlling who is allowed into the country is clearly an important part of protecting Americans. Thus, the U.S. government put Customs and Border Protection under the Department of Homeland Security.

Europe and Immigration

As in the United States, there is a tremendous human smuggling and illegal immigration problem throughout Western Europe. Frequently, would-be immigrants from Africa and Asia (particularly poor countries such as like Pakistan, Afghanistan, and Morocco) seek entry into France, Italy, Germany, or England in order to find work. Some come to Europe through the Andalusian coast in southern Spain, some through the Canary Islands off the coast of Africa. Others cross the Adriatic Sea, seeking passage into Italy. Still others attempt to get into England through the "Chunnel," the underground tunnel that connects Calais, France, to England.

---

[29] Schmitt, Eric, "4 Top Officials On Immigration Are Replaced," *New York Times,* March 16, 2002.

As in the United States, most immigrants to Europe come in order to improve their financial situation, working in menial jobs of various sorts, although some come to Europe to escape political repression at home. Frequently, human rights and immigration experts distinguish between "asylum seekers," refugees, and illegal immigrations. Under the Refugee Convention of 1951 asylum seekers are individuals who have a "well founded fear of prosecution" in their home countries. Once they have shown this, they may apply for asylum in a country. If it is provided, they are considered refugees and may legally reside there. If they seek to stay in a country without being granted asylum, or attempt to sneak in without documentation and without an asylum application, they are considered illegal immigrants. Obviously, a majority of people who are smuggled into western European countries are not going through traditional legal processes and are probably not making formal requests for asylum. (If a person's asylum application is refused they are usually sent home.)

Immigrants enter or are smuggled into Europe through a variety of different routes. As most of the immigrants in Europe come from Africa, Eastern Europe, and the Middle East they must either cross overland through Greece or the states comprising the former Yugoslavia, fly by plane, or cross the Mediterranean ocean. Usually, the route from Asia takes migrants overland through Turkey, the Balkans, and then Germany or Austria. The most direct route from Africa to Spain is across the Strait of Gibraltar, the narrow, 21-mile strait that separates Spain from Morocco.[30] Because the more direct water routes into Europe are often watched, smugglers often travel to the Canary Islands, a small collection of islands under Spanish rule located west of Morocco.[31] Then, they either stay in Spain or move on through Europe, taking advantage of the loose border regulations in the European Union, to England, France, or Germany where they attempt to stay and find employment.

The smuggling of illegal immigrants is usually coordinated by organized criminals in Europe, many of whom have roots in the countries that the immigrants come from. In December 2005, the Italian, British, and French police forces teamed together to shut down a ring that was smuggling Iraqi Kurds into Europe, an organization that was led by a former Iraqi Kurd who was living in Rome.[32] Similarly, human smuggling operations that seek to get Russians and East Europeans into western Europe, the United States, or Israel are run by Russian mobsters. These organizations often help immigrants acquire fake documentation, such as passports, visas, and work permits which they either forge or obtain from legitimate sources using false supporting documents.[33]

In many parts of Europe, the existence of refugees, asylum seekers, and migrant laborers has generated a good deal of animosity among the native populations. This, in turn, has popularized right wing political parties and neo-fascist organizations that have made anti-immigration the centerpiece of their political programs. In the Netherlands, Austria, and France, anti-immigration parties have shown a surprising level of popularity

---

[30] Interpol, "Human Smuggling," (at: http://www.interpol.int/Public/THB/PeopleSmuggling/Default.asp).

[31] Dixon, Martha (2004) "Migrants flock to Canaries," BBC News 26 October (http://news.bbc.co.uk/2/hi/europe/3950701.stm).

[32] "53 Are Accused Of Smuggling Kurds to Europe," *New York Times* (Reuters), December 16, 2005.

[33] Europol, "Organized Illegal Immigration into the European Union." (available at http://www.europol.eu.int/publications/SeriousCrimeOverviews/2005/organised%20illegal%20immigration2005.pdf).

in elections. In France, Jean-Marie Le Pen, the leader of the Front National came in second in the 2002 national elections in an anti-immigrant platform that many found racist, and in Austria, Jörg Haider, a Nazi apologist used anti-immigrant sentiment as a tool for (fleeting) political power. Anti-immigrant sentiments have also inspired neo-Nazi movements throughout Europe, as young, white skinheads have taken out their frustration on immigrants from all over the world. In late 2005, the deaths of two young Arab French boys sparked rioting in the frustrated Arab and African communities that occupy the suburbs of Paris, prompting calls for a "get-tough" policy from the French government and a new enthusiasm for anti-immigrant policies among the French electorate. Mainstream political parties have sought to stop the flow of illegal immigrants without making recourse to the far right solutions of mass deportations. Whether or not they *can* be successful, it is clear that illegal immigration is a central problem for European societies and presents a serious challenge to their traditional ways of life.

Smuggling into the United States

The vast majority of illegal immigrants that come into the United States come from Mexico and to a lesser extent, the rest of Latin America. Most are economic migrants, coming here to find a better life through low paying agricultural, construction, or service industry work, growing fruit, cleaning hotel rooms, and building houses throughout the country. At one time, it centered around the border states (California, New Mexico, Arizona, Texas), but has since spread far beyond the southwestern states and now illegal immigrants work on farms and other businesses throughout the United States. Many of these workers toil in difficult, manual labor for low wages and often send a great deal of their salary back across the borders to their families at home. Their numbers are large: the U.S. Census Bureau estimates that there were approximately 7 million illegal immigrants in the United States in 2000—a number that has surely increased since.[34] How many of these people were smuggled by professionals and how many entered the United States independently (or entered legally and then overstayed their visa) is difficult to ascertain.

As in Europe, the presence of illegal immigration to the United States has produced a great deal of anger from many Americans who fear being overwhelmed by the Latino presence in the country and resent the fact that these immigrants violate the law to enter the country. Some have complained about the criminal activity (including vandalism, robbery, and drug smuggling) that accompanies the illegal crossings. Outrage has led to the formation of a number of independent citizen action groups such as the "Light Up the Border" campaign founded by Muriel Watson in 1990 which would shine hundreds of car headlights onto the border once a month to dramatize the lawlessness that they saw.[35] More recently, organizations like the Minutemen have "guarded" the border, and illegal vigilante organizations have shot and killed immigrants who attempt to enter the United States. Some have accused these organizations of racism against these immigrants, while others see them as dealing with a problem that the government has been unwilling to

---

[34] http://uscis.gov/graphics/shared/aboutus/statistics/2000ExecSumm.pdf.
[35] Mydans, Seth, "As Sun Sets, Tempers Rise at Border," *New York Times*, June 22, 1990, Section A, p. 12.

confront. While anti-immigrant sentiments have always been a part of American history (there was strong opposition to Irish and Italian immigrants in the nineteenth century, for example), the anger directed at illegal immigrants from Latin America has been striking in its strength, particularly given the crucial role that these immigrants play in the economy of American agriculture.

Not all immigrants are treated alike under U.S. law, however. Some immigrants are welcome, regardless of whether they have a visa or permission to enter. Political issues often affect how the government treats immigrants who come to the United States. Some, for example, are considered to be refugees fleeing poverty or oppressive governments. Cuban refugees are treated differently from others because of American opposition to the Cuban government—a communist dictatorship ruled by long-time American nemesis Fidel Castro. Rather than being returned when they are caught, Cuban refugees are subject to the so-called "wet foot/dry foot" test, which says that Cubans may claim asylum and be granted a green card if they reach dry land in the United States but if they are intercepted at sea, they are turned back. (In January 2006, 15 Cubans were sent home when they were intercepted on bridge pilings in the Florida Keys after a court ruled that the pilings did not constitute American soil.[36]) Haitian refugees have likewise been a difficult issue for law enforcement to deal with. The miserable conditions in Haiti, one of the poorest countries in the Western Hemisphere, saddled with political instability and violent military coups have caused many to flee by ship to the United States. In some cases, then, the politics of a particular region and its relations with the United States have a strong influence over who is considered a refugee and who is an illegal immigrant.

Snakeheads, Coyotes, and Pollos   The two most common origins of illegal immigrants to the United States are Latin America and Asia and each has developed its own human smuggling operations and smuggling routes. Chinese smugglers, known as "snakeheads," often charge up to $35,000 to bring an immigrant into the United States. Immigrants are often taken on long, arduous, and circuitous journeys stowed aboard freighters, flying in small aircraft or on commercial airlines while using false papers, and traveling by foot until they arrive in the United States. Often their travels are dangerous and they are subject to physical abuse, sexual abuse, and deprivation during their journey—including a lack of food and proper sanitation facilities. In June 1993, the "Golden Venture," a Panamanian-flagged ship carrying almost 300 Chinese immigrants ran aground off the coast of New York City. Under orders from the crew, the desperate, starving immigrants leapt from the bow of the ship into the freezing water, where 10 died.[37] In March 2006, the organizer and financier of the smuggling operation, Cheng Chui Ping (aka "Sister Ping"), received 35 years in federal prison for the operation.[38] While many scholars and criminal justice professionals believe that the snakeheads are linked with Chinese "triads," the title of

---

[36] "Cubans who landed on piling sent back," *Seattle Times* (The Associated Press) Tuesday, January 10, 2006.

[37] Smith, Paul J., "Chinese Migrant Trafficking: A Global Challenge," in Smith, Paul J. (ed.) *Human Smuggling: Chinese Migrant Trafficking and the Challenge to American's Immigration Tradition,* The Center for Strategic and International Studies, 1997.

[38] Preston, Julia, "Ringleader Gets 35-Year Term in Smuggling of Immigrants," *New York Times,* March 17, 2006, p. B5.

Chinese criminal organizations, or Chinese street gangs,[39] others maintain that the Chinese human smuggling organizations are amorphous, temporary operations that do not resemble the traditional organized crime units studied by criminologists.[40]

When they finally arrive in the United States, they are often treated very poorly by their handlers. Placed in "safe houses," they are frequently held prisoner by the snakeheads until their families pay off the large outstanding debts they owe for their journey (usually, they only provide a small down payment for the trip, paying the remaining balance upon arrival).[41] Once out, they often work menial jobs in the food service sector (cooking in Chinese restaurants) or in garment factories, living in shared quarters and sending much of their excess money home.[42] Many stay and ultimately work through the snakeheads to send for their family members that they left behind in China. Others marry local Chinese or others with American citizenship and ultimately become a part of mainstream American society.

The other major smuggling route into the United States is along the U.S.–Mexican border. Here, the price for entry into the United States is much lower (experts suggest that it usually costs somewhere between $800 and $2,000 for the trip), but the risks are equally high. While many immigrants travel independently into the United States, the expansion of border patrols and the creation of barriers has forced many would-be immigrants to turn to professional human smugglers.[43] Known as *coyotes* (or *pateros*), these smugglers help the immigrants, known as *pollos,* Spanish for "chickens," sneak across the border, using footpaths far removed from border patrols and from the notice of most American citizens. They usually travel in the dead of night arriving at safe houses set up by the *coyotes* for the immigrants at various points along their route. Sometimes these underground railroads end at the border, but they can stretch far into the United States, helping immigrants reach destinations as far as New York, Chicago or Seattle. Coyotes make millions of dollars each year from *pollos* who come to the United States for work, many of whom make the same trip several times a year.

Many *coyotes* honestly help the chickens sneak across the border and aid them in finding new homes—many are former *pollos* themselves.[44] However, some immigrants report being robbed by the coyotes or abandoned by them mid-journey and left to survive in the oppressive desert heat. Some *pollos* are robbed by other bandits who roam the deserts on the borders and take their money and belongings. Each year, hundreds of immigrants die

---

[39] Chin, Ko-Lin, *Smuggled Chinese: Clandestine Immigration to the United States,* Temple University Press, 1999, pp. 38–42.

[40] Zhang, Sheldon, and Chin, Ko-lin, "Enter the Dragon: Inside Chinese Human Smuggling Organizations," *Criminology* Vol. 40 Issue 4, p. 737 (November 2002).

[41] Chin, Ko-Lin, "Safe House or Hell House? Experiences of Newly Arrived Undocumented Chinese," in Smith, Paul J. (ed.) *Human Smuggling,* pp. 169–195.

[42] Chin, Ko-Lin, *Smuggled Chinese,* p. 181.

[43] Guerette, Rob T., and Clarke, Ronald V., "Border Enforcement, Organized Crime, and Deaths of Smuggled Migrants on the United States–Mexico Border," E*uropean Journal on Criminal Policy and Research* (2005) 11: 159–174.

[44] Spenser, David, "This Coyote's Life," *NACLA Report on the Americas,* Vol. 33, No. 3, November/December 1999.

along the border,[45] with many notably gruesome cases. In 1987, 18 immigrants were abandoned by their smugglers in a sealed boxcar in over 100-degree heat, killing all of them. In 2003, 19 immigrants suffocated in the back of a trailer while being transported across the border—resulting in the prosecution and imprisonment of nearly a dozen smugglers.[46] In yet another case, deaf immigrants were held prisoner by traffickers in New York City and forced to beg for money.[47] While there doesn't seem to be evidence that *coyotes* are linked to the trafficking in drugs and other contraband across the U.S.–Mexican border, experts suggest that stricter border enforcement has made the smuggling business more ruthless and the trips into America more dangerous.[48]

While both human smuggling and illegal immigration are activities that violate the law, they are not moral equivalents. There is a difference between those who come to the United States in search of a better life, albeit illegally, and those who profit off of their desperation. Nonetheless, in such cases who is the real "criminal" and who is the "victim" are unclear (the smuggled individual? The American people?). The smuggled individual has violated the law. The smuggler, however, is a criminal of an entirely different magnitude.

While we have focused on Europe and the United States in this brief survey, it is important to recognize that human smuggling is a problem virtually everywhere in the world. Australia has continually struggled to deal with immigrants who come in large ships from Afghanistan, Pakistan, and countries throughout Asia. In one notorious case, the Australian government raided a Norwegian ship, in August 2001, that had picked up a number of immigrants from Afghanistan, Sri Lanka, and Pakistan in order to keep them from coming onto Australian soil.[49] (They were eventually taken to the tiny island nation of Nauru, where they have since been held and denied contact with the rest of the world.) Likewise, the Japanese and Chinese governments must deal with North Koreans seeking to escape the poorest, most oppressive country in the world.[50] Any country with neighbors worse off than they are must deal with immigrants seeking a better life there just as there will almost always be those who are willing to profit off of their desperation by helping smuggle them across borders.

Like so many other problems in criminal justice, the solutions to human smuggling and human trafficking cannot be solely a matter of crafting and enforcing adequate criminal laws. No matter how strict the laws against smuggling and no matter how many officers

---

[45] Romero, Simon, "Patrolling the Border for Migrants From Mexico, With a Humanitarian Goal," *New York Times,* July 20, 2005.

[46] Blumenthal, Ralph (with Maureen Balleza and Wendy Grossman) "3 More Convicted in Deaths of Immigrants in a Trailer," *New York Times,* February 9, 2006.

[47] Sontag, Deborah, "Poor and Deaf from Mexico Betrayed in Their Dreams," *New York Times,* July 25, 1997.

[48] Spener, David, "Smuggling Migrants through South Texas: Challenges Posed by Operation Rio Grande," in Kyle David, and Koslowski, Rey, *Global Human Smuggling: Comparative Perspectives,* Johns Hopkins University Press, 2001, pp. 129–165.

[49] Magner, Tara, "A Less than 'Pacific' Solution for Asylum Seekers in Australia," *International Journal of Refugee Law* (2004) 16(1): 53–90.

[50] Human Rights Watch Report (2002) "The Invisible Exodus: North Koreans in the People's Republic of China," November http://www.hrw.org/reports/2002/northkorea/.

are placed along American borders, immigrants will continue to seek a way into the United States or into Europe as long as there are no more attractive offers in their home countries. Law enforcement may mitigate the effects of such acts and cut down on the number of illegal immigrants entering their countries, but they cannot completely stop them. North Korea, the most totalitarian, autocratic government on earth, cannot stop as many as 300,000 people from leaving its tightly guarded borders and seeking a better life in China. The roots of the human smuggling problem are not "criminal," that is, they are not the result of bad people straying from the straight and narrow path—rather, they are economic principles of supply and demand. People on the other side of U.S. borders have few prospects where they are and see collusion with smugglers as the only way to improve their situation. Likewise, the cheap labor that illegal aliens can provide for America is necessary to help provide cheap goods and services, such as inexpensive fruits and vegetables for American dinner tables. Were American farmers required to hire American citizens for such labor, the prices would probably be significantly higher, which would, ironically enough, make American consumers turn to produce grown in Mexico and Latin America. Criminal justice professionals such as police officers and border patrol officers must deal with the "sharp end of the stick" of human smuggling and illegal immigration. But this is only the symptom that arises from much larger issues. The *root cause* of such activities is not criminal deviance, but rather are economic principles of free markets, principles which have proven to be surprisingly powerful in human history.

While human trafficking is also rooted in economic disparities between rich and poor countries and the desire of many people to improve their situations, there is probably good reason to believe that this may be treated more directly as a criminal justice problem. Because human trafficking is on a smaller scale than human smuggling—significantly less people are trafficked than are smuggled—there is more reason to believe that many of its most despicable perpetrators can be stopped. Two hundred years ago, the chattel slavery industry was a global business with huge profits. After the Civil War, this organized slave trade was ultimately dismantled and there is little reason that modern slavery and modern human trafficking could not meet a comparable demise. On the other hand, prostitution has been around probably as long as societies have been functioning, and, in many parts of the world, the line between consensual and forced prostitution is difficult to draw. Global efforts, led primarily by the United States, but also organized by international human rights NGOs, have gone a long way toward understanding, fighting, and ultimately ending the practice of human trafficking.

QUESTIONS

1. To what extent can human trafficking, slavery, and human smuggling be treated as criminal problems and to what extent should they be treated as economic issues or issues of social inequality? What would be most effective in fighting these crimes: policing or changing government policies?

2. Do you think that illegal immigration and human smuggling are a threat to American security? Why or why not?

3. Is human smuggling a victimless crime? If not, then who are its victims?

READING AND RESOURCES

The two most informative sources regarding human trafficking are the UNODC's human trafficking website (http://www.unodc.org/unodc/en/trafficking_human_beings.html), which includes lengthy annual reports on the issue and the U.S. State Department's website regarding trafficking in persons (http://www.state.gov/g/tip/), which includes the State Department's reports regarding worldwide trafficking practices that are mandated by the VTVPA.

The Polaris Project is a nongovernmental organization that is dedicated to fighting human trafficking. Their website is http://www.polarisproject.org/. They also run a useful information website: http://www.humantrafficking.com/.

The International Organization for Migration studies many different aspects of migration, including human trafficking and human smuggling. They also help run counter-trafficking programs around the world. Their website is http://www.iom.net/.

The website for the Coalition Against Trafficking in Women is http://www.catwinternational.org/.

The website for U.S. Immigration and Customs Enforcement (part of the Department of Homeland Security) is http://www.ice.gov/.

The National Criminal Justice Reference Service's (NCJRS) "In the Spotlight" website links to a number of important government studies on human trafficking. Their website is http://www.ncjrs.gov/spotlight/trafficking/publications.html.

Dating back to 1839, Anti-Slavery International is the oldest currently existing antislavery organization in the world. Their website is http://www.antislavery.org/. They also have a useful affiliated site: http://www.freetheslaves.net/.

Kevin Bales is the President of Free the Slaves and has written two excellent books on slavery and human trafficking. The first is *Disposable People: New Slavery in the Global Economy,* University of California Press, Berkeley, 2000, and the second is entitled *Understanding Global Slavery: A Reader,* University of California Press, Berkeley, 2005.

Another recent text that takes a critical look at Western, academic approaches to studying the trafficking of women is Kempadoo, Kamala, *Trafficking and Prostitution Reconsidered,* Paradigm Publishers, Boulder, 2005.

The Center for Immigration Studies is a nonpartisan think tank devoted to studying immigration into the United States. Its scholars have written some interesting pieces about "criminalizing" illegal immigration. Their website is http://www.cis.org/.

12

Copyright Piracy and Cybercrime

❖

If the motor of globalization is the pursuit of illicit and licit profit, the wheels of globalization are made from computer technology. There has always been international trade and for as long as trade has been taxed and regulated by governments there has been smuggling. What makes the modern era different is that advances in technology have drastically increased the speed of international trade along for certain types of goods that can be traded easily, safely, and in great quantities. Of course, jets can traverse the globe in a matter of hours, but more significantly computer technology has allowed information to travel around the globe almost instantaneously. With the development of the Internet, any computer can be connected to virtually any other computer anywhere in the world. Users can access all kinds of information, download various forms of entertainment, and share ideas with others with similar tastes. Within the last two decades, this communications revolution that has changed the face of global society. It has similarly transformed global crime.

While counterfeiters and intellectual property thieves (also known as "pirates") have been a concern for states for a very long time, the inventions of the last few decades have changed how these criminals operate. The Internet has amplified their capacity to create "bootleg" copies of material and to quickly ship them abroad. The digitization of analog media, that is, taking sounds and pictures and converting them into the ones and zeroes that can be loaded on to computers or disks, makes copying films, movies, and software much easier than it previously had been. DVDs and CDs produced in Hollywood along with other copyrighted and trademarked products can be quickly copied by the thousands in factories in Bombay, Taipei, or New York, and sold on the streets for a fraction of what an official commercial product would cost. (A blank disk costs only a few pennies, as does the packaging—the vast majority of the cost for store-bought movies and CDs are the royalties that go to the companies that produce the materials.) Producing bootlegs of digital material is quick and inexpensive, making the sale of pirated music and movies a serious threat to many modern industries.

Customs officials can monitor border crossings and the Coast Guard can be on the lookout for ships or planes loaded with contraband goods entering into U.S. waters, but the transfer of data over the Internet creates a host of unique problems for the criminal justice system. Nobody can completely stop the transfer of data over the Internet without crippling their nation's economy, which needs rapid, global digital communication to be competitive. Billions of bits of data jet around the world constantly and only a small fraction of these involve illegal material. But this open communications network presents a host of problems. Tech-savvy thieves can find ways to secretly trade data in ways that government officials cannot observe and unsavory individuals can collect and share dangerous or harmful material. The Internet knows no borders and the criminals who use it to engage in illegal activities often need not concern themselves with them, either.

While media pirates and other counterfeiters are causing serious damage to the film and software industries, another important group of criminals are also taking advantage of the wired global economy: hackers. Using their computer skills and code-breaking skills, they hack into secure computer systems, stealing information or impairing the system's ability to function properly. They release computer viruses that can shut down millions of computers around the world and cause billions of dollars of losses from missing data or from lost work hours. Their motives are often ambiguous: Some do it for a sense of pride, others for money, and some are driven by a radical political agenda—spreading a particular vision of the world or working in the service of a foreign government. Regardless of their motives, a single, highly trained expert using a computer in Manila, Frankfurt, or San Francisco can cause great damage to the global economy and to global society simply by pushing a few buttons.

In some ways, cyberspace is the high-tech version of the "high seas"—vast, difficult to control and regulate, but essential to the modern global economy. Like the real high seas, cyberspace is full of unsavory characters anxiously searching the horizon for potential victims, and smugglers who use its size to conceal for their illegal activities. While the United States plays an important role in regulating the Internet, like the high seas, cyberspace is essentially stateless, owned by no single organization or country. While the Westphalian political order of sovereign states (discussed in Chapter 2) always struggled to regulate the high seas, the Internet has amplified these problems and forced politicians, criminal justice professionals, and legal experts to develop new and creative ways to handle this new frontier. Too much regulation can stifle new development in computer technology. Too little control could result in anarchy.

In this chapter we will discuss two major areas where criminals have used computers and other recent technological inventions to make illegal profits or cause mayhem around the globe: intellectual property theft and cybercrime. Intellectual property theft, "IP theft," or "IP piracy" is the unauthorized reproduction and distribution of copyrighted or patented material. These materials can be books, music, or movies, but they can also be patented drugs or other forms of copyright technologies such as microchip designs or brand logos. We will focus here on the piracy of films, software, and music, but also consider the production of other counterfeit goods such as designer clothes and accessories, electronics, and other name-brand consumer goods. "Cybercrime" refers to the use of computers for illegal purposes, either in order to steal secret information or money, or to cause wanton destruction, such as unleashing viruses or causing computer systems to crash. While cybercrime and intellectual property theft are different types of criminal behavior, they share one common trait: modern technology and globalization have greatly amplified their ability to wreak havoc on economies and societies. Without the development of computer technology and the Internet, IP theft and hacking would not be the destructive forces that they have become.

Of course, there is plenty of cybercrime and intellectual piracy occurring strictly within U.S. borders. You and many of your friends may be involved in the illegal downloading of music or movie files from the Internet and you might have purchased a "knock-off" purse or shoes. Counterfeit Prada handbags may be made in the United States and they can be easily bought in New York, Chicago, or San Francisco. Similarly, many hackers are based in the United States and exclusively target U.S. companies like Microsoft or Google. But for the most part, American law and the American criminal justice system are both well equipped to handle such cases. They can be investigated by American prosecutors and, when caught, the perpetrators can be tried under American law. It is when these crimes straddle international borders, when Chinese citizens are pirating American movies, Indian sellers are pirating German software, or Indonesian hackers break into Israeli government servers, that they become issues for international criminal justice. International copyright piracy and international cybercrime are both likely to be international or transnational sorts of crimes, given the nature of the Internet and these require that governments work together to stop them. It is these sorts of cases that we will discuss in this chapter.

International intellectual property theft and cybercrime prevent special challenges for international criminal justice. On one hand, cultural and political differences affect how intellectual property laws are viewed around the world, dictating how reliably they are enforced. Many societies do not see these forms of piracy as inherently wrong. Instead they view them as a normal part of commerce. This makes it very difficult for a government to mobilize its society against IP theft, regardless of how much damage it causes. Many developing countries see intellectual property laws as a tool of wealthy, advanced countries (who own the vast majority of copyrights, patents, and trademarks) to keep their societies poor and, particularly in relation to pharmaceuticals, sick. They believe that other values, like the well-being of a society or the free exchange of goods, should be more important than protecting copyrights owned by American businesses. The sidewalks of cities like Bombay, Madrid, and Shanghai are littered with vendors selling bootleg movies and software, offering the latest CDs from popular musicians alongside bootleg copies of Microsoft Windows or other valuable pieces of software, and they make no bones about their origins. Similarly, the criminal justice systems of many states are ill-equipped to handle the fast-paced, ever-changing world of cybercrime where the tools of the trade and the tactics used by advanced cybercrooks often change rapidly and criminal justice professionals and legislators must struggle to keep up.

INTELLECTUAL PROPERTY, COPYRIGHT, AND INTERNATIONAL LAW

"Intellectual property," "trademark," and "copyright" refer to the legal tools that allow people and businesses to own, buy, and sell their ideas and words. Unlike physical objects such as real estate, cars, or computers, words and ideas cannot be physically possessed or controlled by an individual. Ideas, once spoken, cannot be physically protected from anybody who wants to take them and copy them for their own use. Gates and guards cannot be put around songs or movies to protect them from being illegally copied. Rather, intellectual property law requires the existence of political and legal institutions along with a general willingness among citizens to respect these types of property. While in much of America the right of an individual to own his ideas is taken for granted and there is, generally speaking, a great deal of respect for the principle of IP, this is not always the case in other countries.

Of course, many people you know (and possibly you, yourself) illegally download music or movies from the Internet and, undoubtedly, many of the other users who you share files with are somewhere very far away. And if you have ever traveled overseas, whether to Europe, Asia, Latin America, or Africa, you have probably seen blankets spread out or booths set up on sidewalks filled with scores of counterfeit CDs, DVDs, or software for sale at a fraction of the price an official copy would go for at a retail store. Intellectual property issues are a particularly important problem in a globalized economy: In many societies, intellectual property is not considered an important legal principle and such cultures do not have a problem with widespread violations of copyright law—it's simply not considered wrong to pirate a movie. (To an extent, this is also true in the United States, where many users guiltlessly trade music or movies online.) Further, many developing countries feel that intellectual property rights do not benefit their societies as they prevent their businesses from utilizing patented ideas to their fullest potential. These factors make the protection of intellectual property uniquely challenging. Many otherwise law-abiding citizens don't believe that it is a crime to use somebody else's ideas or artistic creations without compensating them.

There are three major types of intellectual property violations: *Copyright infringement,* where intellectual property is reproduced and sold without authorization (such as trading music on line or selling pirated DVDs in a store), *trademark counterfeiting,* which involves the unauthorized use of a trade mark such as a brand name (such as selling a fake Gucci purse or fake Nike shoes), and *stealing trade secrets* (such as research data or secret food recipes). While all of these are important violations of intellectual property, we will focus primarily on the first two as these are the most common and widespread forms of IP theft. Theoretically at least, the protection of intellectual property and the prevention of these types of crimes foster creativity and innovation in the private sphere. Inventors will be more inclined to work on their ideas, writers and musicians will be more inclined to create compelling work if they know that they will profit from their ideas, and as a consequence society as a whole will benefit from the fruits of their labor. Whether or not this is true, it is the fundamental principle underlying modern intellectual property law.

Films are usually pirated in several different ways. To get the most recent films, pirates will sneak a video camera into a movie theater and secretly record the movie from the screen. Then, the pirates will copy it, manufacture a cover, and distribute it to retailers. Often these "cammers" work in teams with other members looking out for security and preventing the screen from being obscured. Obviously, the quality of such films is not great, but camming is a fast way to get first-run films onto the black market. Moreover, since many movies are shown in one part of the world before being distributed overseas, these bootleg videos can actually beat a first-run Hollywood movie to a particular market. Once a video has been released on DVD, however, it is much easier to copy it and sell it around the world. (To avoid DVDs from being sold abroad at an inappropriate time, most DVDs are "region encoded"—that is, they are designed to work only in DVD players sold in a particular part of the world and will not function elsewhere—although software exists that allows pirates to negate region encoding.)

DVDs can also be pirated like bootleg software, which is usually pirated in two major ways. First, software can be copied onto disks and sold commercially with any material such as installation codes, and so on, that is needed to install and use it. More advanced pirates working in what are known as "warez groups" will "crack" a software program, modifying its software to remove any copy protection. The resulting cracked software, called "warez," is then either sold or distributed freely online, usually on special servers. Many times the software or movies are posted online and then downloaded by pirates who burn the material onto CDs or DVDs and then sell them on the street.

Most of these warez groups do not pirate movies and software for money but rather do it for the thrill of the activity. The warez scene is very hierarchical and members of the different groups report a strong competitiveness, taking great pride in being the first group to get a new film or piece of software posted online. Often, they will accompany their releases with markers indicating the name of the group who posted the software giving them bragging rights in "the scene." In order to get their hands on the latest releases, warez groups will sometimes turn to people who work in the entertainment or DVD industry in order to obtain advanced copies of new movies. These warez groups usually coordinate their actions over a small, exclusive network of users (sometimes called "darknet"), which may include users from anywhere in the world, and are very careful with whom they interact.[1] It is likely that the members of a warez group have never met each other face-to-face and know each other exclusively through their online nicknames. While warez groups do not seek profits for themselves, they nonetheless facilitate those who make millions off of bootleg movies. Once warez have posted a movie or program online, they usually trickle down from exclusive warez scene servers to publicly accessible file-sharing servers such as Limewire where they can then be downloaded by anybody. Often bootleggers in Russia and Asia get their material from the warez groups, downloading the files, burning them onto DVDs and selling them on the street just days after their initial release.

INTELLECTUAL PROPERTY IN CHINA

Copyright piracy has been particularly bad in China—one of the largest and fastest growing economies in the world—and the threat that Chinese pirating outfits present for American industry has made it a centerpiece of international antipiracy operations. Hollywood films are popular and are often openly sold by the thousands for a fraction of their retail cost. Faux designer goods stock the shelves of respectable stores, and software is sold in stores whose owners freely admit that many of their goods are counterfeit. According to the U.S. Department of Commerce 85–95% of all copyrighted works are pirated and 69% of all counterfeit goods seized by U.S. Customs originate in China. Some experts estimate that upwards of 90% of the CDs and DVDs sold in China are illegal bootlegs.[2] Trade experts

---

[1] Department of Justice, Cybercrime Division, "Illegal 'warez' organizations and Internet piracy." (Available at http://www.usdoj.gov/criminal/cybercrime/ob/OBorg&pr.htm.)

[2] Flynn, Laurie, "U.S. Discloses Moves to Stop Piracy of Intellectual Property," *New York Times,* September 22, 2005, Section C; Column 1; Business/Financial Desk; p. 7.

believe that Chinese piracy has been extremely damaging for U.S. movie and software businesses and has resulted in a trade loss of $2.8 billion.[3] As the Chinese economy continues to grow, there is good reason to believe that Chinese intellectual property theft is one of the most serious threats to U.S. business in the world today.

There are numerous reasons for China's rampant piracy. The country's rapidly growing economy and large population (over 1.3 billion people—the largest in the world[4]) have led to a huge demand for high-tech goods. While legitimate versions of movies, software, and name brand merchandise are available, a number of piracy groups are willing and able to provide them to shops quickly and cheaply. Because IP laws have not been rigorously enforced in China, they can do so with very little risk. Further, because Chinese businesses own very few patents and copyrights on their own, the government does not have a strong economic incentive for protecting intellectual property. For the Chinese government, intellectual property is often viewed as a trade issue, a matter of concern for other governments that must be addressed in order to conduct business with them. It is not seen as a criminal issue that harms Chinese society or its economy. (Critics contend that the only copyrights that are rigorously enforced are those held by Chinese companies, such as the 2008 Olympics logo.[5]) Finally, some scholars maintain that the respect for intellectual property that is found in the U.S. and European cultures has no parallel in Chinese history, making intellectual property theft an acceptable and mainstream activity there.[6]

The U.S. government and private industry have worked together to stop piracy and protect intellectual property in China. While enforcement of intellectual property law is flawed in China and Chinese courts have only weakly responded to complaints from companies, the American government has used a number of different tools to attempt to force a change in Chinese policies. U.S. businesses have lodged complaints to the U.S. Trade Representative regarding piracy issues under U.S. trade law, leading to the threat of serious trade sanctions against China.[7] The U.S. government has also threatened to take the Chinese government to the World Trade Organization (WTO) (China joined the organization in 2001), arguing that China's refusal to adequately protect intellectual property amounts to unfair trading practices.

To some extent, the Chinese government has attempted to respond to American and European concerns and threats and cracked down on piracy.[8] Developments in Chinese law, including recent decisions from the high court of China, put pressure on intellectual

---

[3] Israel, Chris, U.S. Coordinator for International Intellectual Property Enforcement, "Piracy and Counterfeiting in China," Testimony before the US-China Economic and Security Review Commission, and Nowak, Pete, "Lawsuits against pirates urged to test ruling; Cases will strengthen the system after disappointing judicial interpretation of copyright law, US trade official says," *South China Morning Post,* January 24, 2005, *Business Post,* p. 4.

[4] CIA World Factbook (https://www.cia.gov/cia/publications/factbook/geos/ch.html).

[5] Fowler, Geofrey A., "China's Logo Crackdown," *Wall Street Journal,* November 4, 2005, Section B, p.1.

[6] Alford, William P., *To Steal a Book is an Elegant Offense: Intellectual Property Law in Chinese Civilization* (Studies in East Asian law), Stanford University Press, Stanford, 1995.

[7] Mertha, Andrew C., *The Politics of Piracy: Intellectual Property in Contemporary China,* Cornell University Press, 2005, pp. 41–52 and Sanger, David E., "President Imposes Trade Sanctions on Chinese Goods," *New York Times,* February 5, 1995.

[8] Lague, David, "China Begins Effort to Curb Piracy of Computer Software," *International Herald Tribune,* May 30, 2006.

property theives, and strengthened the enforcement of IP laws in China. China has also agreed to expand the criminal prosecution of Chinese pirates and to launch public antipiracy campaigns to try to get Chinese society to choose legitimate copies of films and software over bootlegs. The Chinese government reports that the number of pirates prosecuted has increased, but according to the U.S. trade representative, they do not effectively deter pirates. While the Chinese government has made reforms to its intellectual property practices, according to the U.S. government "[intellectual property rights] infringement in China remains rampant, and [intellectual property rights] infringement levels reported by U.S. industry have not improved."[9]

PIRATED FILMS, TERRORISM, AND INTERNATIONAL ORGANIZED CRIME

Warez groups are informal organizations of computer users who connect online, but many other more conventional organized criminal gangs are engaged in pirating intellectual property and selling counterfeit goods. Experts report that Russian gangs and Asian gangs eagerly engage in pirating movies and software for sale on the streets to those who lack the technical capacity to download free copies from warez groups. Similarly organized criminals sell counterfeit designer clothes and accessories, counterfeit electronics, and any other goods that rely on brand recognition to be sold.[10] According to justice department officials, criminal gangs control all aspects of the pirating process, particularly abroad—from manufacturing, distribution, retail sales, and even export (bootleg DVDs and counterfeit goods are frequently brought into the United States from abroad for sale on the black market).[11]

Recently, some experts have asserted that there is a link between film pirates and international terrorists, claiming that terrorist organizations are involved in the sale of counterfeit movies and their profits are used to kill Americans. Similar claims have been made with other conventional crimes, such as bootleg cigarettes that reportedly fund Hezbollah terrorists in Lebanon.[12] Other terrorist organizations in Pakistan and Afghanistan have been linked to counterfeiting designer clothes.[13] Interpol testimony before the U.S. Congress has claimed that while there may be no direct link between IP theft and terrorism, there are indirect connections. Groups engaged in IP theft often support terrorist causes and may provide funds for them. "Most terrorist groups do not take responsibility for the development and control of counterfeit production and distribution; rather they benefit indirectly from funds

---

[9] U.S. Trade Representative, "2005 Report to Congress on China's WTO Compliance" available at http://www.ustr.gov/assets/Document_Library/Reports_Publications/2005/asset_upload_file293_8580.pdf.

[10] Myers, Willard H., "The emerging threat of transnational organized crime from the East," *Crime, Law & Social Change,* 24: 181–222, 1996. 181.

[11] "International Copyright Piracy: A Growing Problem with Links to Organized Crime and Terrorism," Hearing before the Subcommittee on Courts, the Internet, and Intellectual Property of the Committee on the Judiciary, U.S. House of Representatives, March 13, 2003.

[12] US Fed News, "Two Men Plead Guilty to Cigarette Racketeering Enterprise the Funded Hezbollah," July 10, 2006.

[13] Mazer, Roslyn A., "From T-Shirts to Terrorism," *Washington Post,* September 30, 2001; p. B02.

remitted to them from sympathizers and militants involved in IPC."[14] While there is no definitive evidence that pirated films fund terrorism, many suspect that there are links—a point that has been frequently mentioned by antipiracy trade organizations to encourage people to shun counterfeit goods and pirated movies.

THE U.S. GOVERNMENT AND INTELLECTUAL PROPERTY

Intellectual property is a complex part of U.S. law and has both civil and criminal components. As a legal principle, it is enshrined in the U.S. Constitution, which gives Congress the power, "To promote the progress of science and useful arts, by securing for limited times to authors and inventors the exclusive right to their respective writings and discoveries."[15] Beyond this, there are numerous federal criminal laws that deal with different violations of intellectual property rights. The Digital Millennium Copyright Act makes it a crime to upload films. Likewise, the Family Entertainment and Copyright Act makes it a crime to video-record films (punishable by up to 3 years or 6 years for repeat offenders). None of these statutes require that the copyright violations be committed for profit, meaning that the warez groups who violate copyrights without receiving any monetary gain are nonetheless criminally liable for their actions.

The U.S. government has been actively engaged in fighting IP violations at home and abroad, using a number of different tools that combine law enforcement, education, diplomacy, and civil actions. The Department of Justice's Computer Crime and Intellectual Property Section handles most cases of IP theft, including those with international dimensions. In 2005, the Bush administration unveiled its "Strategy Targeting Organized Piracy" (STOP), monitoring foreign IP practices and teaching U.S. businesses and foreign officials how to protect their intellectual property from foreign piracy and counterfeiting.[16] STOP also involves stepping up efforts to seize counterfeit goods smuggled into the United States and targeting the funds of alleged counterfeit goods traffickers.

The U.S. Department of Justice, the Customs Department, and foreign law enforcement agencies have cooperated on a number of successful large-scale international antipiracy operations. "Operation Buccaneer" was a 2001 antipiracy operation coordinated between the United States, the United Kingdom, Australia, Finland, Sweden, and Norway, focusing on shutting down one of the oldest and best-known warez group entitled "DrinkorDie." Buccaneer concluded with the execution of 58 warrants worldwide and the arrest of dozens of warez providers for conspiracy and copyright infringement. "Operation Site Down" was a similar operation that took on global pirates that involved law enforcement in 10 different countries and multiple arrests.[17] Finally, in 2004 "Operation Fastlink"

---

[14] Noble, Ronald K., "The links between intellectual property crime and terrorist financing," Testimony before the United States House Committee on International Relations, July 16, 2003.

[15] United States Constitution, Article I, Section 8, Clause 8.

[16] Flynn, Laurie, "U.S. Discloses Moves to Stop Piracy of Intellectual Property," and Krim, Jonathan, "Anti-Counterfeiting Initiative Launched; Four U.S. Agencies Team Up for Effort," *The Washington Post,* October 5, 2004, Financial; E05.

[17] "Justice Department Announces International Internet Piracy Sweep," Department of Justice Press Release, June 30, 2005. (Available at http://www.usdoj.gov/opa/pr/2005/June/05_crm_353.htm.)

saw the coordination of the United States, Belgium, Denmark, France, Germany, Hungary, Israel, the Netherlands, Singapore, Sweden as well as Great Britain. Such operations require the coordination of U.S. and foreign law enforcement agencies and will likely be a continuing feature of international antipiracy efforts. Whether or not they actually can change the behavior of members of the warez scene, however, is not entirely clear.

The U.S. Patent and Trademark Office has appointed an Intellectual Property Attaché to serve in the Chinese and Indian embassies, lobbying these states to improve their IP laws and helping them crack down on piracy. In January 2006, Attorney General Alberto Gonzales appointed Christopher P. Sonderby, a former federal prosecutor, as the "Intellectual Property Law Enforcement Coordinator" for Asia. Along with serving as the Legal Attaché for Thailand, Sonderby will help coordinate investigations in the region, assisting U.S. and foreign law enforcement personnel with IP issues.[18]

INTERNATIONAL EFFORTS TO STOP COPYRIGHT PIRACY

In response to the problem of global IP theft, the international community, working alongside businesses that work in arts and other IP-heavy industries, have created several legal and political institutions to strengthen the worldwide protection of intellectual property. Many of the international bodies that exist to boost global trade have also been used to foster and protect intellectual property around the world.

The most important international organization, both for boosting international trade and protecting intellectual property, is the WTO. Although it is the subject of much misunderstanding and criticism by antiglobalization activists, it plays a crucial role in the global economy. The WTO was created at the end of World War II to facilitate free trade, on the belief that trade between states would help prevent another catastrophic war. The central job of this organization is to support international trade and prevent the erection of unfair trade barriers between states. Thus it seeks to prevent taxes, subsidies, and tariffs that a government might use to give their own industries an unfair advantage over their foreign competitors. The WTO has conducted several rounds of trade talks to facilitate trade, and out of the Uruguay Round of trade negotiations, the agreement on Trade-Related Aspects of Intellectual Property Rights (TRIPS) was formulated. TRIPS sets out minimum standards for intellectual property protections that WTO member countries must meet.

Along with the WTO at the TRIPS agreement, a number of other public and private international organizations help regulate intellectual property The World Intellectual Property Organization (WIPO) is the branch of the UN based in Geneva, Switzerland, that promotes the regulation of intellectual property around the world. The WIPO has over 180 member states and traces its roots back to the beginnings of international intellectual property law. Among its tasks is helping states develop and harmonize intellectual property law and to allow patent owners to streamline the process of globally registering patents. Among the issues that WIPO has been involved in is the banning of "cybersquatting"—the registering of Internet domain names and then selling them to the highest bidder and other

---

[18] U.S. Department of Justice, News Release, January 5, 2006. (Available at http://usinfo.state.gov/ei/Archive/2006/Jan/10-176639.html.)

misuses of the Internet domain names.[19] Similarly, the World Customs Organization plays an important role in protecting intellectual property globally.

On the law enforcement side, Interpol helps coordinate domestic police organizations in handling transnational copyright infringement and intellectual property theft. It has a special division, the Intellectual Property Crime Action Group that focuses exclusively on fighting these sorts of crimes. They have helped conduct a number of transnational anti-counterfeiting and antipiracy operations. "Operation Jupiter-South America," for example, involved a series of raids against counterfeiters carried out by Brazilian, Paraguayan, and Argentinean police forces along side a number of private intellectual property industries that seized millions of dollars in bootleg CDs and DVDs, and counterfeit cigarettes. They have also worked extensively in Europe to help the various national police organizations counter music piracy, including an attempt to sell stolen Beatles recordings in London.[20]

THE PRIVATE SPHERE

Unlike most crimes, violations of intellectual property law only indirectly harm the general population. That is, street crime and terrorism affect people's lives and their sense of well-being in very immediate ways, but most people who don't work in the IP world feel the immediate affects of IP theft. In fact, most people see great benefits from free access to software, movies, and music. They may hurt everyone in the long run, when musicians and software development are stunted because nobody can profitably produce these goods, but this is remote from the everyday experience of most people. Rather, the victims of copyright piracy are first and foremost the businesses and corporations that profit from their intellectual property, such as movie companies, music producers, artists, and software companies. Thus, much of the political "muscle" behind the movement against intellectual property theft has come from private businesses, not from politicians responding to public demand.

This means that private industry plays an essential role in fighting global IP theft. Usually working through trade associations (that is, groups comprised of and funded by companies that work in a particular field), they actively lobby governments to toughen their copyright protections and help them crack down on the online distribution of music, software, and movies. They often work with national and international law enforcement to help set up operations that crack down on pirates (the aforementioned Beatles case involved the cooperation of the International Federation of the Phonographic Industry). Further, they often sue websites and software companies like Napster that facilitate the online trade in pirated software or even target the online traders themselves.

While there are dozens of intellectual property-oriented trade organizations that work to combat IP theft, the biggest is probably the International Intellectual Property Alliance (IIPA).[21] The IIPA is an umbrella organization made up of several different

---

[19] Clausing, Jeri, "A Challenge to Domain-Name Speculators," *New York Times,* April 5, 1999, Monday Section C, p. 4.

[20] Varga, George, "Tapes of Beatles are recovered," *The San Diego Union-Tribune,* January 11, 2003, p. A-1; and Interpol, "Significant Cases," http://www.interpol.int/public/nancialCrime/IntellectualProperty/Cases/.

[21] Their website is http://www.iipa.com/.

American IP trade groups that monitors worldwide piracy problems, lobbies government agencies dealing with IP issues, and produces in-depth country reports on piracy problems around the world. Often the IIPA will request that the U.S. Trade Representative put states with bad IP polices on the so-called "Special 301" list, that is, states that are subject to economic retaliation (such as trade restrictions) under the 1988 Omnibus Trade and Competitiveness Act.

CYBERCRIME

While copyright pirates use technology to illegally mass-produce consumer products, "cybercrime" is the use of technology as a tool for committing crimes. That is, cybercriminals use computers and the Internet to steal money or wreak havoc as they see fit. Conventional criminals use guns to commit their crimes; cybercriminals use software, Internet connections, and lines of code for theirs. While the term denotes a complex array of different activities, cybercrime is defined by one scholar as, "computer-mediated activities which are either illegal or considered illicit by certain parties and which can be conducted through global electronic networks."[22] Like other criminal activities, the motives that drive cybercriminals range widely: Many (of course) are motivated by financial profit, but some have ideological agendas, and some, like traditional hackers, are driven simply by curiosity and the fun of going somewhere where one is not allowed.

Criminologists break cybercrime down into two major categories: conventional crimes that use computers as a tool and computer-specific crimes. The first category includes child pornography, fraud, extortion, and so on. These have always been crimes, of course, but the Internet magnifies the ability of criminals to operate and greatly increases their reach. As former Attorney General (current Secretary of Homeland Security) Michael Chertoff stated before Congress, "Criminals are migrating online because they can reach more victims quickly, can collaborate with other criminals, can disguise their identities, and can use the global nature of the Internet to remain anonymous."[23] The other category of crimes includes hacking into computer systems and releasing destructive viruses onto the Internet. These are crimes that never existed prior to the invention of computers and the Internet.

Hackers

Originally, at least, a hacker was a person who used his or her computer skills in order to break into otherwise secure computer systems or other forms of communications technology. The first hackers were also known as "phreakers"—technicians who used special whistles and other artificial sounds to hack into phone lines and make long-distance calls free of charge. Almost all of the original hackers who operated in the 1970s and 1980s were American and operated according to a "hacker ethic"—a value system that asserted that

---

[22] Loader, Brian, and Douglas, Thomas *Cybercrime: Security and Surveillance in the Information Age,* Routledge (2000) p. 3.

[23] Statement of Michael Chertoff, Assistant Attorney General Criminal Division, U.S. Department of Justice, before the Subcommittee on Crime Committee on the Judiciary. U.S. House of Representatives, June 12, 2001. (Available at http://www.cybercrime.gov/cybercrime61201_MChertoff.htm.)

information should be freely available to all. Many of these original hackers sought to break into secure computing systems solely for the challenge that it presented: breaking codes and entering secure areas was fun and was considered an end in itself, regardless of any potential monetary gain. Often, they would not do a great deal of damage to the systems that they hacked, using their activities to boast of their skills to their fellow hackers. Some, referred to as "white hat hackers," would contact a business after breaking into their system and point to the flaws in the computer's security system so that systems programmers could make the appropriate changes.

Since its somewhat innocent beginnings, however, the hacker world has expanded and found numerous ways of making money illegally. In many ways, cybercrime and hacking have become virtually synonymous: now most people who hack into secure computer systems are engaged in criminal activity of some sort or another. While computer crime is constantly changing as cybercriminals discover new ways of using their skills for illicit profits, here we will briefly focus on some of the more common types of computer crime currently in use.

Stealing Confidential Information

The original hackers sought to break into secure computer systems solely for the challenge that their security systems posed, the thrill of going somewhere that was forbidden to them. However, it was only a matter of time before hackers began to use their code-breaking skills for illegal profit. Breaking into systems can give a hacker access to all sorts of confidential information, even financial records, that they can then use for personal enrichment. Often this will be credit card numbers, social security numbers, or other confidential information that they can then turn into profit. Much of this information, especially social security numbers, can be used for identity theft, when the numbers to apply for credit cards are known and the loans must ultimately be paid by the victim. Approximately 10 million Americans each year are victimized by identity theft in one form or another and many of these thieves find their victims online.[24]

Cybercriminals have numerous means for gaining access to personal information over the Internet. Sometimes the information is fraudulently obtained from the owner himself, tricking the person into providing the information to what they believe is a reputable site. In 2003, federal prosecutors charged 3 members of the Gambino crime family with running a pornographic website that offered "free tours." When viewers gave their credit card information (allegedly for age verification), the criminals used the numbers for unauthorized purchases. Investigators believe that the credit card numbers were used to steal over $200 million from their owners.[25]

Another common means that cybercriminals use to obtain confidential information is called "phishing." Phishing involves the creation of bogus websites that are replicas of legitimate sites such as online banks or auction sites. Unsuspecting victims

---

[24] US Department of Justice, *National Strategy To Combat Identity Theft,* May 2006. NCJ 214621, pp. 49–50. (Available at http://www.cops.usdoj.gov/mime/open.pdf?Item=1732.)
[25] Glaberson, William, "3 Are Accused of Swindling Visitors to Internet Sex Sites," *New York Times,* March 19, 2003.

are contacted through email and told that they must enter private information such as credit card data, website passwords, and so on to these dummy sites for any number of seemingly legitimate reasons. Then this information is used by the cybercriminals to make unauthorized purchases or sold on to third parties who use them for various illegal activities. The dummy websites are then quickly shut down before law enforcement has any chance to discover the real identity of the thieves. Another tactic is "Trojan Horse" software (also known as "crimeware") that implants itself onto a person's computer and secretly records the user's keystrokes, electronically transferring them to the criminals without the user's knowledge.[26] As law enforcement and Internet security companies discover effective ways to ensure your computer's security, cybercriminals develop new ways to gain access to your private information online.

Electronic Blackmail

Using confidential information to steal money is only one way that hackers use their ability to access confidential information to make themselves money. It takes a great deal of trust on the part of consumers to give their credit card information to a website, and companies that process online financial transactions stake their reputations on their ability to keep the information they hold secure. This makes financial companies with a substantial online presence a tempting target for electronic blackmail. When hackers break into secure computer services containing the financial information of a company's customers, they often hold on to the information threatening to expose the company's weaknesses and release the confidential data unless they are paid substantial sums of money. In January 2000, a cybercriminal who operated under the handle "Maxim" and claiming to be from Russia posted the private financial information from 25,000 users of the website CD Universe when the company refused to pay the $100,000 that he demanded.[27]

Other times Internet companies can be blackmailed by being threatened with so-called "denial of service attacks." To carry out theses attacks, hackers use special programs that assault a company's website with bogus request for information, emails, or other forms of electronic "noise," either overwhelming a website, causing it to shut down, or slowing it down to the point where few legitimate users are willing to wait for access to it. Frequently, these hackers use "botnets" to carry out their attacks. Botnets are programs that secretly implant themselves in other computers (which are then referred to as "zombies"). Once turned into zombies, these computers can then be commandeered by the hacker to do their bidding—sending emails and other actions that comprise a denial-of-service attack. These collections of infected zombie computers are run by so-called "botherders" who often rent them out to individuals to conduct denial-of-service attacks. The criminals then threaten to continue the attacks and destroy the company's ability to

---

[26] Zeller Jr., Tom, "Cyberthieves Silently Copy Your Passwords as You Type," *New York Times,* February 27, 2006.

[27] Markoff, John, "Thief Reveals Credit Card Data When Web Extortion Plot Fails," *New York Times,* January 10, 2000. Also, see: MacIntyre, Ben, "From Russia with menace: hacker," *The Australian,* January 12, 2000 Section, p. 8.

conduct business online unless they are paid off.[28] Numerous companies have reported being blackmailed in such a way and Eastern European hackers in particular have used botnets to blackmail online businesses.

Cyberterrorism and Cyberwarfare (Information Warfare)

Many hackers who vandalize websites and shut down computer systems are driven by political ideology. Most of these so-called "hacktivists" or "cyberterrorists" are independent operators who use their skills in the service of a political cause that they passionately subscribe to.[29] Other times they work in small groups of like-minded individuals who coordinate their efforts online. During a recent flare-up of the Palestinian–Israeli conflict, Palestinian hackers briefly shut down over 700 Israeli websites, either disabling them or defacing them with messages like, "You are killing Palestinians, we will hijack your servers."[30] While cyberterrorists using their hacking skills to cause serious harm to a nation's infrastructure and causing physical harm to innocents is a serious threat, there are at present no known cases of such serious attacks.[31] Rather, terrorist sympathizers with computer skills generally use their talents to design websites for terrorist organizations, coordinating terrorist activities, recruiting new members, or raising funds for their operations. Denial-of-service attacks on public websites sympathetic to other points of view have been the worst damage caused by cyberterrorists, leading many scholars to argue that at present cyberterrorism is not a serious threat.

Other cybercriminals work as agents of foreign governments, using computer technology to gain advantages in military or political conflicts. ("Information warfare" refers to the use of information in the form of intelligence or propaganda to gain the upper hand in a conflict and is as old as war itself.) Information warriors hack into government computer systems to learn secrets about a rival's military capabilities or to disrupt their enemy's communications. Other government agents hack into enemy news sites or television transmissions in order to spread propaganda, creating confusion and uncertainty among enemies. Still others seek to hack into the computer systems that operate a state's infrastructure (its electrical grids, nuclear facilities, and computer servers) in order to

---

[28] See: Thomas, Daniel, "Websites face more attacks BLACKMAIL: The number of sites being held to ransom is on the increase," *Financial Times* (London, England) May 31, 2006, Wednesday, *Digital Business;* p. 4 and Pollitt, Michael, "The Online Mafia: Cyber Gangsters are Using Computer Networks to Blackmail Businesses," *The Independent* (London), December 15, 2004, Wednesday First Edition; Features, p. 11.

[29] Cybercrime scholars usually distinguish between hacktivists and cyberterrorists. The former want to disable computer systems and websites that they disagree with. Cyberterrorists seek to cause physical harm to others using computer systems. See: Weimann, Gabriel, "Cyberterrorism: How Real Is the Threat?" United States Institute of Peace, Special Report, Washington, D.C., December, 2004 and, Denning, Dorothy, "Activism, Hacktivism, and Cyberterrorism," in Ermann, David, M. Shauf, Michele S. (eds), *Computers, Ethics, and Society,* Oxford University Press, 3rd ed., 2002, pp. .

[30] Al Jazeera website, "Pro-Palestinian hackers hit Israeli sites," Thursday 29 June 2006. (Available at http://english.aljazeera.net/NR/exeres/84000EB1-908C-4A44-9B32-BFC0FE201B31.htm.)

[31] Conway, Maura, "Cyberterrorism: Media Myth or Clear and Present Danger?" in Jones, Irwin (ed.)*War and Virtual War: The Challenges to Communities,* Rodopi, Amsterdam, 2004, pp. 79–98, and Weimann, Gabriel, *Terror on the Internet, The New Arena, the New Challenges,* United States Institute of Peace Press, Washington DC, 2006.

disrupt them. Governments (including the United States) are constantly developing ways to use computers to spy on each other or harm each other's defense-related computer systems should war break out. While the United States has not been the victim of any open attack by an enemy government, many experts have suspected that the United States' infrastructure is presently being "cased" by hacker agents of an unknown foreign government.[32]

ANTICYBERCRIME LAWS

Since cybercrime is a relatively new phenomenon, with new features and methods constantly appearing, it has resisted the formulation of clear legal codes by governments. In 1986, Congress passed the "Computer Fraud and Abuse Act" designed to regulate the use of computers and prevent some of the most obvious forms of cybercrime.[33] Among other things, the act prevents the use of computers for theft, the breaking into secure computer systems to cause damage to it, and the intentional release of virus programs.[34] This law has been supplemented by later bills, including the 2001 USA Patriot Act (see Chapter 7 for more details).

One of the significant problems with prosecuting cybercrime is criminal jurisdiction over cyberspace. The Internet doesn't occupy a particular physical place like a bank or a house, but is rather a complex global network of computers and cable networks with users who may operate from anywhere on earth, accessing a computer anywhere else on earth. This makes it difficult to determine precisely where a computer crime has taken place: Is it at the place of origin (where the criminal logged onto the Internet)? Is it at the location where the "victimized" computer is (say, the bank server)? This matters a great deal because some countries have not outlawed many types of cybercrime and cannot prosecute them. Without an appropriate legal basis for prosecuting a cybercriminal and given the requirement of double criminality (the principle that a state can extradite suspected criminals only if the act is criminal in *both* the extraditing state and the receiving state—see Chapter 5), states often cannot assert jurisdiction over cybercriminals abroad.[35]

Because of the international character of the Internet, domestic laws alone are clearly not enough to thoroughly outlaw cybercrime. The author of the "I love you" virus that disabled millions of computers around the world in 2000 and cost over $6 billion in lost productivity[36] escaped prosecution because there were no cybercrime laws on the books in the Philippines (where he lives).[37] Effective policing of cybercrime requires the coordination of

---

[32] See the PBS Frontline Documentary "Cyberwar," 2003 (http://www.pbs.org/wgbh/pages/frontline/shows/cyberwar/).

[33] Greenhouse, Linda, "House Approves Measure to Make Computer Fraud Fraud a Federal Crime," *New York Times,* June 4, 1986.

[34] 19 U.S.C. 1030.

[35] For a detailed analysis of the jurisdictional issues in prosecuting cybercrime, see Brenner, Susan W., and Koops, Bert-Jaap, "Approaches to Cybercrime Jurisdiction," *Journal of High Technology Law,* Vil IV, No. 1, 2004, 1–46.

[36] See Festa, Paul and Wilcox, Joe, "Experts Estimate Damages in the Billions for Bug," CNET News.com (May 5, 2000). (Available at http://news.cnet.com/news/01003-200-1814907.html.)

[37] Weber, Amalie M., "Annual Review of Law and Technology: VIII. Foreign and International Law: A. Cyberlaw: Cybercrime: The Council of Europe's Convention on Cybercrime," *Berkeley Technology Law Journal,* Vol. 18, 425–446 at 426.

many, if not all, of the world's governments. While there has yet to be a comprehensive international treaty on the subject, there have been some efforts to develop an international legal code against cybercrime: The Council of Europe's Cybercrime Convention was the first multilateral treaty to deal with the issue of cybercrime. Written in 2001 (the United States attended the Council's meetings and has signed the treaty), the Convention lists and defines some of the most significant forms of cybercrime and requires that parties to the treaty criminalize these.

Along with the jurisdictional problems presented by cybercrime, there are a number of other important challenges presented by this field of criminal activity. Computer technology changes almost daily. New programs, new hardware, and new programming tools develop all of the time, and cybercriminals frequently share their new insights with each other on online chat rooms and bulletin boards. This makes cybercrime an ever-changing phenomenon, with one method quickly replacing another before law enforcement can develop effective tools to counter it. Law enforcement must work very hard to keep up with cybercriminals and the constant demand for new technology to keep up with the hackers can strain the budget of law enforcement organizations. To compound the problem, skilled computer professionals who work against hackers can usually earn a great deal of money working for Internet security companies in the private sector—making it extremely difficult for law enforcement to hold onto talented personnel.

Cybercrime According to the Convention

Here is a list of the major crimes set out by the Council of Europe's Cybercrime Convention. Each party to the treaty promises to criminalize these acts in their domestic legal systems while providing "adequate protection of human rights and liberties."

Illegal access   "The access to the whole or any part of a computer system without right . . . with the intent of obtaining computer data or other dishonest intent, or in relation to a computer system that is connected to another computer system."

Illegal interception   "The interception without right, made by technical means, of non-public transmissions of computer data to, from or within a computer system."

Data interference   "The damaging, deletion, deterioration, alteration or suppression of computer data without right."

System interference   "The serious hindering without right of the functioning of a computer system by inputting, transmitting, damaging, deleting, deteriorating, altering or suppressing computer data."

Misuse of devices   "The production, sale, procurement for use, import, distribution or otherwise making available of:

  i. a device, . . . designed or adapted primarily for the purpose of committing any of the [established] offences.
  ii. a computer password, access code, or similar data by which the whole or any part of a computer system is capable of being accessed."

Computer-related forgery   "The input, alteration, deletion, or suppression of computer data, resulting in inauthentic data with the intent that it be considered or acted upon for legal purposes as if it were authentic, regardless whether or not the data is directly readable and intelligible."

Computer-related fraud   "The causing of a loss of property to another person by:

a. any input, alteration, deletion or suppression of computer data,
b. any interference with the functioning of a computer system, with fraudulent or dishonest intent of procuring, without right, an economic benefit for oneself or for another person."

Offences related to child pornography   "producing [distributing, possessing, procuring] child pornography for the purpose of its distribution through a computer system."

Offences related to infringements of copyright and related rights   "The infringement of copyright [or] related rights, as defined under the law . . ."

Anticybercrime Efforts

Most of the world's national law enforcement agencies have mobilized both together and separately in order to fight against cybercrime. The American Department of Justice's Computer Crime and Intellectual Property Section[38] handles most national cybercrime issues, while its Office of International Affairs helps coordinate international investigations and cooperates with foreign police agencies investigating cybercrime. Most other countries have similar units in their law enforcement organizations that focus on computer crime. Interpol coordinates international conferences on cybercrime and has several regional working groups on the topic, facilitating conversations between different national cybercrime experts. The European Union's Falcone Program, a continent-wide anti-organized crime unit has trained a number of European law enforcement officers in ways to investigate and prosecute cybercriminals. Moreover, police organizations throughout the world often share cybercrime data through less formal means.

Each computer has its own unique "IP address"—short for "Internet Protocol address"—that law enforcement and Internet security companies can use to track down people who use the Internet for illicit purposes. Likewise, emails usually have a header that can be used to trace the email back to its original sender. While skilled hackers are capable of masking their IP Address and hiding the sources of their emails, less experienced users are often caught when they mistakenly believe that their Internet interactions are anonymous.[39] If government agents are incapable of locating the source of the criminal activity, they can use any number of other ways to lure the cybercriminals out of hiding by posing as legitimate business or as minors interested in a sexual encounter.

---

[38] Their website is http://www.cybercrime.gov/.

[39] For a more in-depth discussion of the investigation of cybercrime see: Orton, Ivan, "The Investigation and Prosecution of a Cybercrime," in Clifford, Ralph D. (ed.), *Cybercrime: The Investigation, Prosecution, and Defenseoof A Computer-Related Crime* (2nd ed.), Carolina Academic Press, Durham, 2006.

Federal authorities conduct semi-frequent exercises that involve mock cyberattacks carried out by special teams of government hackers. The results of these "No-Notice Interoperability Exercises" (NIEX) are usually kept secret, but most often involve a "red team" of government hackers seeking access to secret government computer systems or manipulating government or infrastructure computer systems.[40] ("Blue teams" defend the computer systems, seeking to stop the red team's incursions.) In "Eligible Receiver," a NIEX that was conducted in 1997, a team of 35 hackers using only software that was freely available online were able to find and exploit crucial weaknesses in the Pentagon's computer systems, including U.S. Pacific Command, and displayed an ability to take down critical aspects of the Pentagon's defense systems.[41] NIEXs have been used to hack into a number of different computer systems, providing a valuable tool for the U.S. government anticyberwar and cybercrime efforts.

As with IP theft, many anticybercrime efforts are conducted in cooperation with private Internet security companies. Companies like Microsoft, Symantec, and McCaffee are constantly searching for ways to defeat hackers and other cybercriminals. They regularly update their computer security software to deal with any new viruses that are created by hackers and inform their subscribers about new threats to their privacy. Unlike conventional law enforcement organizations, these companies have large budgets and armies of well-paid experts whose job is to track new developments in cybercrime. These experts search out new ways to encode Internet transmissions to prevent third parties from accessing them and build "firewalls" that prevent unauthorized programs from accessing a particular network. Additionally, most companies that do business on the Internet have computer security experts on staff to prevent security breaches and manage any that do occur. These experts then may choose to contact the FBI or other law enforcement officials if they believe that they have been the victims of cybercrime.

Constitutional Issues

Along with houses and cars, the Fourth Amendment's provisions regarding unreasonable search and seizure also apply to computer systems. In general, a search is considered reasonable if it does not violate an individual's "reasonable expectation of privacy."[42] In most cases, users have such an expectation when it comes to their own computers or other electronic storage devices (such as diskettes or flash drives), particularly when they are not attached to a network. Computers are usually treated like "closed containers" that cannot be opened without a warrant.[43] The USA Patriot act modified the laws governing electronic searches, giving the

---

[40] Gellman, Barton, "Cyber-Attacks by Al Qaeda Feared," *The Washington Post,* June 27, 2002, p. A01.

[41] Verton, Dan, *Black Ice: The Invisible Threat of Cyberterrorism,* McGraw-Hill, New York, 2003, pp. 31–35. See also Frontline, "Cyberwars" (Documentary, PBS).

[42] *Katz* v. *United States,* 389 U.S. 347, 362 (1967) (Harlan, J., concurring).

[43] In *US* v. *Runyan,* 275 F.3d 449, the 5th Circuit Court of Appeals ruled that once a disk has been opened by a private party, each separate file on that computer is not protected and may be searched by law enforcement without a warrant. Thus, while disks are closed containers, the files themselves are *not* each discrete containers. It should be noted that different Appeals Courts have ruled differently on this issues (see http://www.cybercrime.gov/s&smanual2002.htm#_I_).

federal government new powers to monitor electronic transmissions such as email and searches on the World Wide Web (see Chapter 7 for a more detailed discussion of the USA Patriot Act). However, there is little analysis of the Fourth Amendment issues involved in searches of computers that are located abroad by U.S. law enforcement officials (say an electronic search of a computer located in Bangkok from an FBI office in Washington DC).[44] These "remote searches" of computers overseas represent numerous challenges for modern constitutional law.

In the case of *United States* v. *Gorshkov,* the court ruled that in many cases, remote, cross-border computer searches are constitutional. Vasily Gorshkov was a Russian hacker who had illegally gained access to numerous Internet businesses, obtaining access codes and other confidential financial information from them. Gorshkov, with an accomplice, Alex Ivanov, then used this information to blackmail the various companies, seeking large amounts of money to re-secure the sites. The defendant was lured to the United States by federal law enforcement officials who used a job offer from a dummy Internet security company to get them into U.S. jurisdiction. As Gorshkov showed off his hacking skills to his "interviewers," the FBI recorded his keystrokes and, after his arrest, used this data to access his Russian servers, gaining evidence that led to his conviction.[45]

Although the search was conducted without a judicially authorized warrant, the Federal Appeals Court ruled that it was nonetheless constitutional. Specifically, the court ruled that although the material was searched by American officials without a warrant, the principle of *Verdugo-Urquidez* applied. That is, despite the fact that he entered the United States of his own free will (unlike the defendant in *Verdugo-Urquidez*), the defendant lacked the "substantial connection" that was required for Fourth Amendment protection. Moreover, the court ruled that copying the material from Gorshkov's computer did not constitute "seizure" as spelled out by the Fourth Amendment as nothing was taken from the accused.

Cleary, there are still a lot of constitutional questions that law enforcement will have to deal with while investigating international cybercrime. Computer technology develops at an extremely fast pace and judges and legal experts can only struggle to keep up. Nonetheless, there are a number of concerns that courts must balance along with law enforcement's need to effectively counter cybercrime: the right of citizens to privacy on their computers as well as diplomatic concerns regarding the sovereignty of foreign nations are important values that may conflict with the need to catch cybercriminals.

---

[44] For one analysis of the issue of searches, see Young, Stewart, "*Verdugo* in Cyberspace: Boundaries of Fourth Amendment Rights for Foreign Nations in Cybercrime Cases," Michigan Telecommunications and Technology Law Review, Vol. 10, No. 1, 2004, pp. 139–174. See also Moseley, Jeremy A., "Note: The Fourth Amendment and Remote Searches: Balancing the Protection of 'The People' with the Remote Investigation of Internet Crimes," 19 ND J. L. Ethics & Pub Pol'y 355.

[45] For more details on the case see http://www.usdoj.gov/criminal/cybercrime/ivanovIndict2.htm; Young, "Verdugo in Cyberspace," *op cit,* pp.151–15, and Seattle Times staff and news services, "Russian hacker gets three years." *The Seattle Times,* October 5, 2002, p. B3, and Cha, Ariana Eunjung, "A Tempting Offer for Russian Pair." *Washington Post,* May 19, 2003, at A1.

THE INTERNATIONAL TRADE IN CHILD PORNOGRAPHY ON THE INTERNET

The Internet has been a tool for people with all kinds of different interests to network and share ideas and information with like-minded individuals. Most of these are perfectly harmless, of course, but people with illegal desires also hunt for resources and material on the Internet. Along with terrorists, drug traffickers, and other criminals, pedophiles have made use of the Internet in a variety of ways: sharing pornographic material, comparing notes with each other, and luring children into situations where they can be raped, abused, or worse. In December 2005, the *New York Times* wrote a lengthy article about a boy named Justin Berry who ran an Internet website where he sold pornographic videos of himself to pedophiles around the world.[46] Almost weekly, a news story appears detailing a law enforcement strike against an Internet pedophile ring, and a great number of these rings span the globe, linking pedophiles from Asia, Europe, and the United States in the shared exploitation of children.

National and international law enforcement have worked together to try and prevent the exploitation of children over the Internet. The 1996 Child Pornography Prevention Act criminalized the production and distribution of electronic images of children (including images of adults that are doctored to resemble children). Another law, the Child Online Protection Act passed by Congress in 1998, regulates the distribution of material that is "harmful to minors" over the World Wide Web. (This law is currently undergoing a court challenge and remains in a "legal limbo.") The Children's Internet Protection Act requires that public libraries filter Internet access, preventing children from accessing inappropriate material.[47] The FBI's Innocent Images National Initiative is an interagency effort, under the Bureau's cybercrime division charged with investigating child pornography online as well as the use of the Internet to lure or exploit children.[48]

There have been numerous anti-child pornography operations conducted transnationally. In 2002, *Operation Artus* resulted in the arrested of 30 suspected pedophiles located across the globe, including nine in the United States. The operation began with the arrest, by German police, of a German national who had founded an Internet chat room that facilitated the distribution of pornographic images of children.[49] *Operation Candyman* stemmed from an e-group on the popular site Yahoo! that shared pornographic images of children, resulting in numerous arrests in the United States and abroad.[50] *Operations Ore* and *Avalanche* began when a Texas computer entrepreneur was arrested for distributing child pornography and resulted in the arrest of thousands of people in the United States

---

[46] Eichenwald, Kurt, "Through His Webcam, a Boy Joins a Sordid Online World." *New York Times,* December 19, 2005.

[47] Cassidy, Michael, "To Surf and Protect: The Children's Internet Protection Act Polices Material Harmful to Minors and a Whole Lot More," 11 *Mich. Telecomm. Tech. L. Rev.* 437, 2005.

[48] Their website is http://www.fbi.gov/innocent.htm.

[49] US Customs Department Press Release, March 20, 2002. (Available http://www.usdoj.gov/criminal/ceos/Press%20Releases/PR-Artus.pdf.) See also Deutsche Welle, "Child-Porn Ring Busted," March 21, 2002. (Available at http://www.dw-world.de/dw/article/0,,481259,00.html.)

[50] FBI Press Release, March 18, 2002. (Available at: http://www.fbi.gov/pressrel/pressrel02/cm031802.htm.)

and England, including rock guitarist Pete Townshend.[51] (Numbers in the United States were reportedly in the area of 35,000.[52]) However, the UK investigation was flawed and a number of people arrested were released without facing criminal charges, including Townshend, who maintains that he was conducting research.[53] The number of people arrested in Operation Ore was so great that pedophile experts worried that they would put too great a strain on the criminal justice system.[54]

More recent operations have netted thousands of suspected pedophiles around the world, accusing them of producing and trading pictures of abused children through Internet chat rooms and running pornographic websites.[55] In February 2007, Austrian authorities discovered a Vienna computer that was accessed through a Russian website.[56] On the computer were depictions of rape and violent sexual abuse against young children (the oldest children were reportedly about 14 years old). More than 2,300 people tried to access the computer's images over the next 24 hours. Austrian law enforcement officials seized the materials and recorded the IP address, passing the information on to law enforcement officials throughout the world. (Approximately 600 people in the United States tried to access the site and their IP addresses were forwarded to the FBI.)

Like drug trafficking and terrorism, the international trade in child pornography over the Internet is an international problem requiring the cooperation of different police forces around the world. The Convention on the Rights of the Child (an international treaty to protect children from exploitation) has an optional protocol "on the sale of children, child prostitution and child pornography," which stipulates that all parties will prohibit the sale of such material. (The United States is a party to the protocol.) Interpol has also helped coordinate international law enforcement operations against pedophiles and has created a database to identify the victims portrayed in these images.

There are a number of law enforcement organizations as well as private groups that track down child pornographers and child predators online. The Innocent Images program, run by the FBI's cybercrime program, has begun to work with foreign law enforcement officers to combat the global distribution of child pornography.[57] Private groups like the Internet Watch Foundation in the UK[58] and the National Center for Missing and Exploited Children[59] help combat Internet child pornography worldwide.

---

[51] Lyall, Sarah, "Britain's Hunt for Child Pornography Users Nets Hundreds Besides Pete Townshend," *New York Times,* January 15, 2003, BBC News, "Operation Avalanche: Tracking child porn," November 11, 2002. (Available at http://news.bbc.co.uk/2/hi/uk_news/2445065.stm.)

[52] Quayle, Ethel, *Child Pornography: An Internet Crime,* New York, Routledge, 2003, p. 5.

[53] Hoge, Warren, "British Rock Star Receives Lesser Punishment in Internet Case," *New York Times,* May 8, 2003.

[54] BBC News, "Operation Ore: Can the UK cope?" January 13, 2003. (Available at http://news.bbc.co.uk/2/hi/uk_news/2652465.stm.)

[55] Bernstein, Richard, "Germany Says It Uncovered Huge Child Pornography Ring," *New York Times,* September 27, 2003.

[56] Smith, Craig S, "Child Pornography on Vienna Computer Prompts Worldwide Hunt," *New York Times,* February 8, 2007.

[57] http://www.fbi.gov/page2/feb06/innocentimages10years2.htm.

[58] http://www.iwf.org.uk/.

[59] http://www.missingkids.com/.

CONCLUSIONS

The technological innovations that have made globalization possible, particularly the innovations in computer technology and the creation of the Internet, have given birth to a whole new world of criminality. In cybercrime and intellectual property theft two very different worlds collide: the high-tech world of computer experts, usually highly educated and middle to upper middle class individuals not prone to crime or violence, becomes linked with the dangerous world of organized crime. While not usually violent, copyright pirates and cybercriminals sap a great deal of money from legitimate online and IP businesses and hinder the production of new films and music. Cybercrime, particularly electronic blackmail and the theft of confidential information, places an even greater burden on companies that require some level of trust on the part of their consumers. E-commerce requires companies to use consumers' financial data to sell goods and services online. In the end, these sorts of crimes represent a toxic dose of technology, expertise, and cross-border criminality.

Like other aspects of globalized crime, computer crime presents many challenges for the nations of the world, as well as for the nascent international criminal justice system. Not only are the criminals often more sophisticated than the government, law enforcement, or their victims, they are capable of using shrewd techniques to mask their identity and location from investigators. Even if they are located by police, they cannot necessarily be arrested and extradited as there is little harmony between the cybercrime laws of different states around the world. This means that many cybercrooks can make huge profits in relative safety and anonymity—and the international criminal justice system has only begun to respond this threat. As the world becomes even more closely interconnected by new technological innovations, the world's politicians and criminal justice professionals have only just begun to seriously confront the problems.

QUESTIONS

1. Do you believe that it is wrong for people to buy bootleg software or films? Do you believe that it is wrong to download music or movies off of the Internet? Do you think that these should be considered *crimes?* Why or why not?

2. How secure is your computer? Do you fear being a victim of cybercrime? Do you do anything to avoid being victimized by cybercriminals?

3. Is there a way to change a culture so that intellectual property laws would be better protected? How would you try to convince China to protect intellectual property?

READING AND RESOURCES

Two strong books on cybercrime, both of which touch on the global dimensions of cybercrime, are Newman, G. and Clarke, R. (2003) *Superhighway Robbery: Preventing E-Commerce Crime.* Portland: Willan Publishing and Grabosky, P., Smith, R., and Dempsey, G. (2001) *Electronic Theft: Unlawful Acquisition in Cyberspace.* Cambridge: Cambridge University Press. While both books are good introductions to the material, cybercrime is a very rapidly changing field and material can quickly become out of date.

The Cybercrime Research Center is a nonprofit organization that monitors cybercrime. Their website is http://www.crime-research.org/ and they publish the Cybercrime Law Report, a newsletter that monitors new developments in cybercrime (http://www. crime-research.org/library/cybercrime.pdf).

The Justice Department's Computer Crime & Intellectual Property Section (http://www. cybercrime.gov) has a number of valuable resources regarding IP theft and cyber-crime, including important legal cases and press releases on recent law enforcement operations.

The University of Dayton School of Law has a website that collects domestic and international information on cybercrime. Their website is http://www.cybercrimes.net/.

"The Scene" is an ongoing drama series broadcast on the Internet that deals with the warez scene. It is downloadable at http://www.welcometothescene.com/.

Choate, Pat (2005) *Hot Property: The Stealing of Ideas in an Age of Globalization.* New York: Knopf. A nice study of the various aspects of the global war against intellectual property theft.

Clifford, Ralph D. (ed.) (2006) *Cybercrime: The Investigation, Prosecution, and Defense of a Computer-Related Crime,* 2nd ed. Durham: Carolina Academic Press.

13

Conclusion: The Future
of International Criminal Justice

❖

Crime without Borders is meant as an introduction to international criminal justice. It is introductory in two senses. First, it is introductory because you, the reader, probably didn't know much about the international criminal justice system prior to reading it. Hopefully you have learned some of the basics of this fast-growing corner of the criminal justice world and will continue to study it and follow its developments. Second, it is introductory because much of international criminal justice is only at its beginning. A vast amount of international criminal justice has yet to take shape. This means that it will also probably be subject to dramatic transformations in the future. It is likely that later editions of this book will look very different from this one simply because the international criminal justice system itself will be very different. Already, I've had to go back and revise major portions of the manuscript as new and significant developments in international criminal justice have taken place just in the course of writing it. The institutions of criminal justice are never static but rather constantly change as a result of political, economic, and cultural shifts. As globalization rapidly changes the world we live in, international criminal justice will also transform in numerous ways.

One of the central themes of this text is that, like the rest of the economy, the underground criminal economy has globalized. Just as McDonald's, Coca-Cola, and Visa are a part of the new economic order, so are human smuggling, drug trafficking, terrorism, and cybercrime. And since globalization is an ongoing process, taking on new dimensions and new features, it is highly likely that international crime will act similarly. A businessman in the nineteenth century could not have predicted the existence of home computers, much less the invention of the Internet, and the next phase of globalization will be equally unpredictable. Thus, in this final chapter of the text, I will point to a few crucial issues that could influence the development of international crime and likewise will shape the development of the international criminal justices system. Some of these insights (along with your own theories, of course) may help you to examine current events related to international criminal justice.

In this chapter, we will do two things. First we will briefly look toward the future and talk about some developments that could impact on the future of international justice. Some of these are political or economic issues that depend on the wisdom of world leaders. How the United States sees itself in relation to the rest of the world will have a tremendous impact on the way that the international criminal justice system develops. Some of these changes will depend on the function of the global market. Where capital flows will affect where crime goes. Second, we will briefly examine some other important fields of international crime, subjects that you might want to research further.

THE CHANGING NATURE OF SOVEREIGNTY

As we discussed in Chapter 2, the concept of sovereignty has been the centerpiece of international politics since the Peace of Westphalia in 1648. Prior to the formation of the International Military Tribunal at Nuremberg in 1945, it was a central legal principle that leaders of sovereign states could do whatever they wanted *wherever they wanted* without having to be held criminally liable for their actions. One of the central features of twentieth-century international law in general and twentieth-century international criminal law in particular is that this principle has been seriously weakened. Sovereignty does not mean everything that it once did. Globalization has changed what it means to be a sovereign state and has tied the hands of political leaders in some important ways that we have studied here.

As we saw in relation to the ICC in Chapter 2, many in the U.S. government and in the American population at large are skeptical about the utility of international institutions and are fearful of surrendering aspects of American sovereignty to an international court. Thus, despite the strong American support for international institutions like the ICTY and the IMT, and despite America's strong efforts to fight crime abroad that impact on our citizens (such as their antiterrorism and antidrug efforts abroad), the United States has been bitterly opposed to many international institutions and has resisted scrutiny by the international community in its antiterrorism efforts. Clearly, this ambivalence to the globalization of criminal justice is important, and many other states have stood alongside the United States in fighting international efforts that they perceive as a threat to their national sovereignty. The belief that states are autonomous and independent entities that should be allowed to do what they wish remains a strongly held belief in the world, particularly among those with political power, and it is unlikely that the concept of sovereignty will completely disappear from the world any time in the near future.

Much of the future of international criminal justice will depend on the future of the role of sovereignty in international relations. If political and economic conditions weaken this concept, there is good reason to believe that parts of the international criminal justice system will be strengthened in turn. For example, if courts around the world accept principles of universal or extraterritorial jurisdiction and don't perceive them as a threat to their authority, it is likely that national governments will not have the final say regarding what happens in their own countries. Like in the *Pinochet* case discussed in Chapter 4, foreign states or international courts may usurp a state's right to deal with its own criminals on its own terms in certain cases. Similarly, if states allow countries like the United States to assert extraterritorial jurisdiction and prosecute people for crimes that are committed outside their borders, it is likely that a state will no longer have a monopoly on the legitimate use of force within its own borders. This means that in many ways the concept of a "state" as it has been understood for the last 350 years will be gone. Sovereignty will not disappear, but its contours, the meaning of the notion of sovereignty, will be quite different from those that were envisioned at the Peace of Westphalia.

On the other hand, if there is a backlash against these developments, one can expect the international criminal justice system to "retract" and institutions like the ICC to become less important to international affairs. States may grow wary of giving these institutions too much power and undermine the ICC's efforts to fight international crimes, or the court could bungle some important cases, throwing its usefulness into doubt. Governments could cut off their funding or refuse to provide political or institutional support for the court. In response to such developments, national criminal justice systems may be forced to take up the slack and expand their extraterritorial authority to deal with international crimes. Similarly, organizations like Interpol or Europol, institutions that do not enforce laws internationally (and thus do not directly threaten the sovereign powers of governments) but instead help coordinate national law enforcement organizations, will become more important. Limitations placed on the power of international criminal justice institutions would not remove the threat of international crime and so *somebody* would have to step up to help global society deal with it.

How sovereignty develops and changes will depend on a lot of different factors, only some of which have to do with criminal justice. As we saw when we discussed the ICC, much of the American criticism of the court has little to do with the court itself and more with traditions of American isolationism, American exceptionalism, and a general distrust of international institutions that is a part of modern American culture. If more countries adopt this American attitude toward international courts, the international criminal justice system will probably become weaker and have less influence on international crime. Political developments could likewise change the structures of international justice as different governments seek to influence the courts and exert control over the other institutions of international criminal justice. There is no crystal ball that would tell us what the future holds for international criminal justice institutions and any number of forces can strengthen or weaken it.

AMERICAN POWER

A second major influence on future developments in international criminal justice will be the role of America in the world. As we've seen, many developments in international criminal justice have been driven by American concerns and much of the current international criminal justice system reflects American approaches to criminal justice. At present, America is the global "hegemon"—an unrivaled world power that can do almost whatever it wishes in the world without fear of damaging repercussions. While America has been weakened by developments in Iraq and elsewhere, it is nonetheless still true that at present no state can compete with America for global economic, political, and military dominance. Like the Roman Empire in antiquity and the British Empire in the eighteenth century, there is no serious challenger to American power in the world, and, understandably, this has had a great influence on the international criminal justice system.

However, if this situation changes and America becomes weaker, or if another state begins to rival America (say, China, or a more unified Europe), the international criminal justice system could easily change in response to these developments. American interest in stopping the flow of drugs into the United States and in preventing future terrorist attacks has had a strong influence on the development of international criminal justice. Effectively, America has been in the driver's seat, directing the allocation of resources for international criminal justice, using this influence to help create treaties and other legal structures that create international criminal laws, as well as helping other countries to enforce these laws. Sometimes they do this through legal or law enforcement assistance, other times through threats of sanctions. While the United States hasn't been able to stop the ICC, it has played a role in limiting its authority and may have seriously hampered its ability to function effectively. However, other parts of the world may not be so concerned about drug trafficking or terrorism, preferring instead to expend their resources fighting other sorts of transnational and international crimes. If other states had a global influence comparable to America's, then national criminal justice systems as well as the international system would probably become interested in different things than those they presently focuses on. New treaties would be written, new laws enforced, and new policies developed to confront the problems that concern the leaders of these newly influential states. The concerns (drugs, terrorism) driving much of the current international criminal justice system would probably be very different in a world where America was not *the* world leader. Whether the system would be better or worse, stronger or weaker, however, are completely different matters.

THE SUCCESS OR FAILURE OF INTERNATIONAL CRIMINAL INSTITUTIONS

In some ways, the test of international criminal justice is the ability of these institutions to function effectively. Many international institutions are bloated with excess staff who draw massive salaries and are often slow to respond to new crises. Some are corrupt. If the ICC follows in their footsteps, it will only create further skepticism about international criminal justice. Skeptics, such as many in the United States, who are wary about the ICC will then use this as grounds for refusing to cooperate further with the ICC and its kindred organizations, which would undoubtedly cause them to "whither on the vine." Likewise, if the choice of cases that the ICC takes on seems biased or foolish, for example, if they only prosecuted crimes committed by weak states, but refuse to investigate crimes committed by citizens of powerful states, they will not receive support from smaller nations. (However, if they only prosecute citizens of strong states, they are likely to lose their much-needed support.) Finally, if the ICC's prosecutions only make conflicts worse than they might otherwise have been, by preventing peace talks from taking place because the relevant actors fear prosecution, even those who believe in the human rights principles that the ICC is designed to defend will turn away from them.

NEW INTERNATIONAL CRIMES

Perhaps most importantly, the international criminal justice system will have to respond to new types of criminal threats as they arise. Different sorts of crimes will require new ideas from the international criminal justice community. In this text we have looked at some of the most significant international crimes—terrorism, drug smuggling, human trafficking, and cybercrime—but most of these crimes are not very old and they have also changed significantly over their short lives. The Internet, the essential tool of cybercrime, is only a few decades old, and as we saw in Chapter 8, illegal drug trafficking has changed in many ways in the century that it has been in existence, as new markets develop and new drugs become popular. It seems as though the only thing that has remained constant in the world of international criminal justice is the fact that international crime is constantly changing.

Of course, governments and the international criminal justice system will have to change to confront these new threats. This might mean developing new treaties, laws, and courts to deal with special sorts of crimes or expanding the existing institutions to cover these crimes that are beyond their initial mandate. It has been suggested that the ICC, for example, could be used to prosecute drug traffickers or terrorists, two sorts of criminals who do not at present fall under its jurisdiction.

COSMOPOLITANISM

Finally, and most abstractly, the international criminal justice system will rise and fall depending on whether people believe that there is such a thing as an "international community" and an international criminal justice system. The global criminal justice system will flourish if humanity develops a cosmopolitan outlook, seeing all humans as connected to each other, believing that national and ethnic differences are not significant when compared to our commonalities. (The term *cosmopolitan* means literally, "a citizen of the world."[1]) Do people, not only politicians, government officials, and criminal justice professionals but also average citizens, believe that they are part of a single world with common interests and common goals, and, equally importantly, do they act accordingly? This cultural change will have a tremendous impact on international justice.

A lot of developments in international politics have taken place because grassroots activists, concerned about a particular cause, have pressed their governments to do something about it. Sometimes states and their leaders have opposed certain policies, but have bended to the will of popular opinion and supported important steps in the development of international criminal justice. Whether it is antislavery activism in the nineteenth century, antihuman trafficking activism in the twentieth, or efforts to prevent and punish genocide after World War II, committed individuals and groups without any government affiliation have changed the face of international justice. If more people promote the development of international criminal justice, it will undoubtedly shape the future of international justice.

This cosmopolitan worldview, the desire to see oneself not simply as a member of a particular country, religion, community, or ethnic group, is not universal and has not been

---

[1] See Appiah, Kwame, *Cosmopolitanism: Ethics in a World of Strangers,* New York, W. W. Norton, 2007.

a constant part of history. The reality is that, more often than not, other sorts of identities have been more important in defining ourselves than our common humanity. "Us" (our country, our tribe, our ethnic group) has usually been opposed to a "them" that is perceived as an enemy. If such "tribal" allegiances are valued more highly than our common humanity, then there is good reason to believe that many international criminal justice institutions will be weakened by a lack of support. If people continue to care about what happens elsewhere and support human rights both at home and abroad, than a legal system designed to defend these rights will undoubtedly be strengthened. These ideals will undoubtedly be affected by political and economic changes around the world and many of these forces lie far beyond the power of the international criminal justice system.

MORE RESEARCH

The topics covered in *Crimes without Borders* are not the only subjects of international crime and criminal justice. There is a *lot* more to study. If you are interested in further research, here are some brief descriptions of international crime issues that you might find interesting:

International Illegal Trade in Stolen Art and Antiquities

After the United States and its allies invaded Iraq in 2003, many of the country's collection of ancient artifacts were looted from museums or excavation sites. Eventually, most of these priceless pieces were sold to collectors on the international black market. However, this is only the most recent in a long series of thefts of cultural artifacts, stretching back to the days of European colonialism. There is a flourishing international market in stolen archaeological treasures and pilfered works of art. During World War II, Jews and others were robbed of their private art collections by Nazi occupiers throughout Europe—many of which have yet to be returned. States, along with UNESCO (the United Nations Educational, Scientific and Cultural Organization), have come together to create treaties to determine who rightfully owns what, but nonetheless, a good deal of allegedly stolen art and antiquities remain in dispute.[2] Lawyers and investigators have worked to track some of these pieces down and return them to their original owners. Other pieces sit in museums, their ownership debated between different governments, each claiming a right to the works.

International Trade in Stolen Goods

Drugs and human beings, the two major forms of smuggling that we've discussed in the text, are not the only things that are smuggled, of course. Thousands of other types of goods are illegally transported across borders, whether it is stolen automobiles transported to Eastern Europe or Mexico, or credit card information stolen from American consumers and transferred abroad. Rare or protected animals are either captured or killed by poachers in nature

---

[2] Two important treaties on the subject are the "Convention on the Means of Prohibiting and Preventing the Illicit Import, Export and Transfer of Ownership of Cultural Property" (1970) and the "UNIDROIT Convention on Stolen or Illegally Exported Cultural Objects" (1995).

preserves in Africa, Asia, and India, and taken abroad to collectors. Sometimes their body parts (such as ivory or tiger parts) are taken and sold in Asia or Europe, where they are valued for their medicinal properties. Smuggling is big money and wherever there are borders separating a consumer from a producer there will be people willing to break to law to fill the demand.

International Monetary Counterfeiting

Counterfeit currency has long been a problem for the international community. Sometimes foreign currency is counterfeited and distributed by criminal gangs and other times it has been done by governments who want to harm another state's economy. As the U.S. Treasury Department points out, "Counterfeiting U.S. currency is a lucrative and relatively low-risk criminal enterprise in many parts of the world. Since US dollars are widely held by foreign banks and are used as currency in many countries, counterfeiters have many opportunities to pass counterfeit dollars outside of the US."[3] During war, states will often counterfeit enemy currency in order to undermine the enemy's economy by inflating prices and undermining confidence in its economic system. Other times, organized criminals will counterfeit money to spend on goods abroad. Regardless, using advanced computer technology (scanners, expensive printers), counterfeiters can make millions of dollars of fake currency quickly and easily and pass them on to unsuspecting merchants or currency dealers around the globe.

Piracy on the High Seas

As we discussed in Chapter 2, international piracy has long been a problem for the international community. Before drugs, terrorism, and human smuggling became international problems, piracy was the primary impetus for the development of an international criminal justice system. It was the first example of an "international crime." Pirates still exist and they conduct operations throughout the world, seizing ships, and either holding their crews for ransom or killing them outright—selling the ship and its cargo on the black market. In November 2005, a group of pirates attacked a cruise liner off the coast of Somalia with automatic weapons and grenade launchers and were only beaten back by the crew when they tried to board the ship[4]. While modern pirates are not the romantic figures that prowled the Caribbean in the seventeenth century, they still menace sea trade throughout the world and international law enforcement officials are constantly seeking new ways to thwart them.

International Trafficking in Prescription Drugs

Given the high cost of prescription medication in the United States, many consumers have looked abroad to find affordable alternatives to what is available in America. In many parts of the world, drugs that would require a prescription and cost a great deal of money can be easily purchased over the counter for a small fraction of the price that they

---

[3] U.S. Treasury Department, "The Use and Counterfeiting of United States Currency Abroad, Part 2" http://www.treasury.gov/press/releases/docs/counterfeit.pdf.

[4] "Pirates Attack Liner off Coast of Somalia" *New York Times,* November 6, 2005.

cost here. This has led many Americans to turn to Canada or elsewhere to buy their prescription medications (and has led to an avalanche of spam offering discount medications such as Viagra and Cialis). Some of these sellers are legitimate, but many prescription drugs advertised on line are fakes, and some can be unsafe for consumers (either they don't do what they're supposed to do, causing people to continue suffering, or they have ingredients that cause their own damage).

Weapons Trafficking

Global networks of criminal gangs smuggle arms around the world. These weapons are used by guerilla organizations in the jungles of Africa, criminal gangs on the streets of Europe, and other unsavory characters throughout the globe. Criminal operatives like Viktor Bout,[5] Alexander Islamov,[6] and Louis Minin[7] sell weapons to the highest bidder, including governments that are the subject of international embargoes because of their human rights violations. Often operating out of countries with weaker arms regulations, many arms smugglers operate in a gray area, somewhere between legality and illegality. (Many governments like the money and jobs that their homegrown weapons industries generate while publicly deploring illegal sales.) They often deal in arms as part of a much broader import–export operation, mixing arms sales with diamonds and other illicit goods. Organizations like the Campaign against Arms Trafficking monitor weapons tracking operations and seek to reduce the influence of the global arms industry.[8]

International Trafficking in Nuclear Technology

Many international observers believe that the most dangerous man in the world is a Pakistani scientist named Abdul Qadeer ("A.Q.") Khan. Weapons experts believe that during the 1990s Khan ran a vast network of agents that sold nuclear information and nuclear technology to governments around the world, including Iran, North Korea, and Libya (considered by many to be dangerous states that actively sponsor terrorism). The International Atomic Energy Agency, the international organization that monitors nuclear developments around the world, has been investigating Khan's enterprise and Khan's associates have been prosecuted in Switzerland and Germany. Khan himself is a celebrity in his home country because he was instrumental in Pakistan's own efforts to develop nuclear weapons. Because of his fame, the Pakistani government has placed him under house arrest, but he remains unprosecuted at this time, and the Pakistani government has refused to hand him over for questioning. Clearly, one of the most dangerous aspects of globalization is the threat that people like Khan will pass along information that will provide dangerous people

---

[5] Landesman, Peter, "Arms and the Man," *New York Times,* August 17, 2003 and Farah Douglas and Braun, Stephen, "The Merchant of Death," *Foreign Policy,* November–December, 2006.
[6] United Nations, *Report of the Panel of Experts pursuant to Security Council resolution 1343 (2001), paragraph 19, concerning Liberia,* New York: United Nations, 2001, U.N. document S/2001/1015.
[7] Chivers, C. J. "Ill-Secured Soviet Arms Depots Tempting Rebels and Terrorists," *New York Times,* July 16, 2005 and Naim, Moses, *Illicit,* pp. 38–64.
[8] Their website is http://www.caat.org.uk/.

with access to nuclear weapons technology and organizations like the IAEA may be the only thing separating the world from nuclear holocaust at the hands of terrorists.

Similarly, after the collapse of the Soviet Union, Russia and the other former Soviet states have had a difficult time controlling the thousands of nuclear weapons that the USSR once commanded. Likewise, nuclear material such as warheads, uranium, and other related technology is a hot commodity for terrorists and others. A black market of "loose nukes" has sprung up and the governments of the world have rushed to keep these dangerous weapons out of the hands of terrorists and rogue governments that would love to use them to kill millions.

Soccer Hooligans

Unquestionably, the most popular sport in the world is soccer (or "football" as it is called outside of the United States). While many American sports teams have rabid fans, nothing in the United States compares to the behavior of some of the most devout soccer fans in Europe. Known as "hooligans," these fans, particularly those in England, but also in the rest of Europe, have become synonymous with violence and mayhem. Many of them are affiliated with right-wing, racist paramilitary organizations such as the National Front, others are flunkies of other political organizations serving as their muscle. Hooligans often try to set off riots and looting sprees during or after the games.[9] Of course, the vast majority of soccer fans want nothing to do with the violence and crime that the hooligans represent and the "corporate culture" of modern football clubs has stopped a lot of hooliganism; it has nonetheless been a continuing presence in European soccer.

The hooligan movement is international because soccer is an international sport. Hooligans travel around the globe, following their teams when they go abroad, causing destruction in the foreign cities they play in, and fighting with the fans of the other teams—many of which are more than eager to fight. They interact with each other online and share information and strategies and post movie clips of their activities. Rival hooligan gangs even interact with each other and arrange brawls at pubs or street corners near a soccer match or prowl the neighborhoods, looking for an unfortunate fan who operates alone. European police forces have sought to prevent hooligans from traveling abroad and frequently monitor the airports near games, and have coordinated antihooligan police tactics.

International Organized Crime

Of course, we've discussed international organized crime outfits throughout this text. Different international gangs from different regions around the globe are involved in drug smuggling, human trafficking, and terrorism along with many other international crimes. However, we have not discussed the nature of these organizations themselves in any depth. That is, we have not discussed these organizations independent of their roles in these types of criminal activities—we have not examined who, exactly, they are. The Japanese Yakuza, the Sicilian Mafia, the Russian and Israeli mobs, Chinese triads, and many other criminal organizations act in an international capacity, planning and running criminal enterprises throughout the world, including substantial operations within the United States.

---

[9] Buford, Bill, *Among the Thugs*, New York, Vintage Press, 1993.

Each of these gangs has their own history, their own structure, and their own ways of doing business, all of which make fascinating subjects for research.[10]

These topics, and the topics covered in-depth within the pages of this text, represent only the tip of the iceberg. On any given day, a glance at the newspapers will tell you something new about the role that international criminal justice professionals play in the world, and, unfortunately, a good deal about new forms of globalized crime. The world is only becoming more closely interconnected, a fact that criminals are well aware of. To a greater and greater extent, criminal justice professionals are becoming aware of it too.

---

[10] See: Grennan, Sean and Britz, Marjie, *Organized Crime: A Worldwide Perspective,* New York, Prentice Hall, 2006.

References

ACLU v. *NSA*, Case No: 06-CV-10204 (2004, November 30).

Afghan concern at opium spraying. *BBC News*. Available at http://news.bbc.co.uk/2/hi/south_asia/4054657.stm.

Alford, W. P. (1995). *To Steal a Book is an Elegant Offense: Intellectual Property Law in Chinese Civilization* (Studies in East Asian law). Stanford: Stanford University Press.

American Law Institute web site. Available at http://www.ali.org.

The American Society of International Law web site. Available at http://www.asil.org.

Amnesty International (2006). "So does it mean that we have the rights?" *Protecting the Human Rights of Women and Girls Trafficked for Forced Prostitution in Kosovo*. New York: Amnesty International. Available at http://www.amnestyusa.org/news/document.do?id=1391B6E5EE9C8A9780256E7E0041EE72.

Anderson, T. L. (forthcoming). A history of drug and alcohol abuse in America. In: Harrison, L., Anderson, T., Martin, S., & Robbins, C. (Eds.) *Drug and Alcohol Use in Social Context*. Belmont, CA: Wadsworth Publishing.

Animal Liberation web site. http://www.animalliberation.net/.

Anti-Slavery International web site. Available at http://www.antislavery.org/.

Appiah, K. A. (2006). *Cosmopolitanism: Ethics in a World of Strangers*. New York: Norton, W. W. & Company, Inc.

Arnold, G. T. (1995). Bordering on unreasonableness?: The third circuit again expands the border search exception in *United States* v. *Hyde*. *Villanova Law Review*, *40*, 835.

Associated Press. (2006). "Brothers who ran cartel plead guilty." *New York Times*, September 26.

Associated Press. (2007). "Klan loses suit over fire: Jury awards $37.8 million." July 25, 1998. "Australian Is Charged In Terror Case." *New York Times*, March 2.

The Avalon Project at Yale Law School; The Nuremberg War Crimes Trials. Available at http://www.yale.edu/lawweb/avalon/imt/imt.htm.

Baker, A. & Rashbaum, W. K. (2006). "Heroin implants turned Puppies into drug mules, U.S. says." *New York Times*, February 2.

Bales, K. (1999). *Disposable People: New Slavery in the Global Economy*. Berkeley: University of California Press.

Bales, K. (2005a). Human trafficking: A worldwide concern. In: Bales, K. *Understanding Global Slavery: A Reader*. Berkeley: University of California Press.

Bales, K. (2005b). *Understanding Global Slavery: A Reader*. Berkeley: University of California Press.

"Bali duo sentenced to death." *Sydney Morning Herald*, February 14, 2006.

Barford, P. & Yegneswaran, V. (2006). An inside look at Botnets. *Special Workshop on Malware Detection, Advances in Information Security*. New York: Springer Verlag.

Bass, G. (2001). *Stay the Hand of Vengeance; The Politics of War Crimes Tribunals.* Princeton: Princeton University Press.

Bassiouni, C. (1999). *Crimes against Humanity in International Criminal Law.* The Hague: Kluwer Law International.

Bassiouni, M. C. (1996). International crimes: Jus cogens and obligation erga omnes. *Law & Contemporary Problems*, 59(4), 63–74.

Bayer, I. & Ghodse, H. (1999). Evolution of international drug control, 1945–1995. *Bulletin on Narcotics*, *LI*(1–2).

Bederman, D. (2001a). *International Law Frameworks.* Eagan: West Publishing Company.

Bederman, D. (2001b). *International Law in Antiquity.* Cambridge: Cambridge University Press.

Bellia, Patricia L. (2001). Chasing bits across borders. *The University of Chicago Legal Forum*, 35–101.

Benjamin, D. & Simon, S. (2002). *The Age of Sacred Terror.* New York: Random House.

Berkowitz, P. (2005). *Terrorism, the Laws of War, and the Constitution.* Stanford: Hoover Press.

Bernstein, R. (2003). "Germany says it uncovered huge child pornography ring." *New York Times*, September 27.

Blakesley, C. L. (1982). Criminal Law: United States jurisdiction over extraterritorial crime. *Journal of Criminal Law and Criminology*, 73(3), 1109–1163.

Blashfield, J. (2004). *Interpol.* World Almanac Library. New York: Gareth Stevens Publishing.

Blodget, H. How to solve China's piracy problem. *Slate.com post*, Tuesday, April 12, 2005.

Blumenthal, R., Balleza, M. & Grossman, W. (2006) "Three more convicted in deaths of immigrants in a trailer." *New York Times*, February 9.

Boister, N. (2005). Transnational Criminal Law? *European Journal of International Law*, 14(5), 953–976.

Bonner, R. (2000). "Laundering of money seen as 'easy'." *New York Times*, November 29.

Boyd v. *United States*, 116 U.S. 616 (1886).

Brenner, S. W. & Koops, B. (2004). Approaches to cybercrime jurisdiction. *Journal of High Technology Law*, 4(1), 1–46.

Bresler, F. (2002). *Interpol.* London: Sinclair Stevenson.

Briggs, M. & Lehman, D. J. (1995). "Nigerian smugglers make Chicago a heroin hub." *Chicago Sun-Times*, April 3, 1.

Brinkley, J. (2005). "Anti-Drug gains in Colombia don't reduce flow to U.S." *New York Times*, April 28.

Brooke, J. (1993). "NOV. 28-DEC. 4: A gangster's death; End of the hunt: The king of cocaine goes down shooting." *New York Times*, December 5.

Brownlie, I. (2003). *Principles of Public International Law* (6th ed.). Oxford: Oxford University Press.

Buford, B. (1993). *Among the Thugs.* New York: Vintage Press.

Statement of President Bush, G. W. (2004). On the Al-Hurra station. MSNBC. May 5.

Cambanis, T. (2002). "Leader of software theft ring sentenced." *Boston Globe*, August 17, 1B.

Candes, M. R. (2001). Comment: The victims of trafficking and violence protection act of 2000: Will it become the thirteenth amendment of the twenty-first century? *The University of Miami Inter-American Law Review*, 32, 571–702.

Cane, A. (1985). "U.S. Court's Request for Documents Refused." *Financial Times*, March 7.

Cassese, A. (2003). *International Criminal Law.* Oxford: Oxford University Press.

Cassese, A. (2004). The role of internationalized courts and tribunals in the fight against international criminality. In: Romano et al. (Eds.) *Internationalized Criminal Courts.* Oxford: Oxford University Press.

Cassidy, M. B. (2005). To Surf and protect: The Children's Internet Protection Act polices material harmful to minors and a whole lot more. *Michigan Telecommunications Technology Law Review*, 11, 437–472.

The Center for Immigration Studies website. Available at http://www.cis.org/.

Cha, A. E. (2003). "A Tempting offer for Russian pair." *Washington Post*, May 19, A1.

"Cheney pushes senators for exemption to CIA torture ban." *USA Today*, November 4, 2005.

Chepesiuk, R. (1999). *Hard Target: The United States War against International Drug Trafficking: 1982–1997*. Jefferson: McFarland Press, 211–222.

Statement of Michael Chertoff, Assistant Attorney General Criminal Division, U.S. Department of Justice, Before the Subcommittee on Crime Committee on the Judiciary (2001). U.S. House of Representatives, June 12. Available at http://www.cybercrime.gov/cybercrime61201_MChertoff.htm.

"Child-Porn ring busted." *Deutsche Welle*, March 21, 2002. http://www.dw-world.de/dw/article/0481259,00.html.

Chin, K. (1997). Safe house or hell house? Experiences of newly arrived undocumented Chinese. In: Smith, P. J. (Ed.) *Human Smuggling*. New York: Center for Strategic & International Studies, 169–195.

Chin, K. (1999). *Smuggled Chinese: Clandestine Immigration to the United States*. Philadelphia: Temple University Press.

Choate, P. (2005). *Hot Property: The Stealing of Ideas in an Age of Globalization*. New York: Knopf.

CIA World Factbook; China. Updated September 19, 2006. Available at http://www.cia.gov/cia/publications/factbook/geos/ch.html.

Clarke, R. (2005). "Ten years later." *The Atlantic Monthly*.

Clausing, J. (1999). "A Challenge to Domain-Name Speculators." *New York Times*, April 5, C4.

Clawson, P. L. & Rensselaer, L. (1996). *The Andean Cocaine Industry*. New York: St. Martin's Press.

Clifford, R. D. (Ed.) (2006). *Cybercrime: The Investigation, Prosecution, and Defense of a Computer-Related Crime* (2nd ed.). Durham: Carolina Academic Press.

Coalition Against Trafficking in Women web site. Available at http://www.catwinternational.org/.

Cole, D. & Dempsey, J. (2002). *Terrorism and the Constitution*. New York: New Press.

Constructing the state extraterritorially: Jurisdictional discourse, the national interest, and transnational norms. *Harvard Law Review*, 103(6) (1990), 1273–1305.

Conway, M. (2004). Cyberterrorism: Media myth or clear and present danger? In: Jones, I. (Ed.) *War and Virtual War: The Challenges to Communities*. Amsterdam: Rodolpi, 79–98.

Costa, M. E. III. (2004). Note & Comment: Extraterritorial application of the Maritime Drug Law Enforcement Act in: *United States* v. *Suerte. Temple International and Comparative Law Journal*, 18, 131.

Council on Foreign Relations; A Nonpartisan Resource for Information and Analysis web site. Available at http://www.cfr.org/issue/135/.

Crandall, R. (2002). *Driven by Drugs: U.S. Policy Toward Colombia*. Boulder: Lynne Rienner Publishers.

Crank, J. P. & Gregor, P. (2004). *Counter-Terrorism after 9/11*. Newark: Lexis-Nexis.

The Crimes of War Project. Available at http://www.crimesofwar.org.

"Cubans who landed on piling sent back." *Seattle Times*, January 10, 2006.

Cutler, S. F. (1999). Building international cases: Tools for successful investigations. *FBI Law Enforcement Bulletin*, 12, 1–5.

Cybercrime Law Report, 3(8). Available at http://www.crime-research.org/library/cybercrime.pdf.

Daley, S. (2001) "Rights for Dutch prostitutes, but no gain." *New York Times*, August 12, A1.

David, E. (2004). *Code de Droit International penal*. Paris: Bruylant.

"Defendant indicted for cam cording films in movie theaters, distributing the films on computer networks." *U.S. Newswire*, August 4, 2005.

Deflem, M. (2002). *Policing World Society: Historical Foundations of International Police Cooperation*. Oxford: Oxford University Press.

Democratic Republic of the Congo v. *Belgium*, Judgment 14, February 2002.

Denning, D. (2002). Activism, hacktivism, and cyberterrorism. In: Ermann, D. M. & Shauf, M. S. (Eds.) *Computers, Ethics, and Society*. Oxford: Oxford University Press.

Dershowitz, A. (2002). *Why Terrorism Works*. New Haven: Yale University Press.

Di Nicola, A. (2004). Trafficking in human beings and the smuggling of migrants. In: Reichel, P. (Ed.) *Handbook of Transnational Crime and Justice*. New York: SAGE Publications, 181–203.

Dixon, M. (2006). "Migrants flock to Canaries." *BBC New*, October 26, Available at http://news.bbc.co.uk/2/hi/europe/3950701.stm.

Dixon, R. (2002). Rape as a Crime in International Humanitarian Law: Where to from Here? *European Journal of International Law*, 13(3), 697–719.

Dragoon, A. (2000). Interview: Peter Nevitt, The man from Interpol. *CIO Magazine*, June 15. Available at http://www.cio.com/archive/061500/interpol.html.

"Editorial: One drug lord dies." *New York Times*, December 4, 1993.

Eichenwald, K. (2005). "Through his webcam, a boy joins a sordid online world." *New York Times*, December 19, A1.

Erbschloe, M. (2006). "Socially responsible IT management." *Digital Press*, June 13.

Europol: European Police Office web site. Available at http://www.europol.eu.int.

Europol. Organized illegal immigration into the European Union. Available at: http://www.europol.eu.int/publications/SeriousCrimeOverviews/2005/organised%20illegal%20immigration2005.pdf.

Executive Summary (2001). Estimates of the unauthorized immigrant population residing in the United States: 1990 to 2000, January 13. Available at http://uscis.gov/graphics/shared/aboutus/statistics/2000ExecSumm.pdf.

Ex-King Farouk of Egypt v. *Christian Dior*, 84 Clunet 717, 24 I. L. R. 228, 229.

Faison, S. (1997). "Grim tales of want from the North Korean border." *New York Times*, April 27.

Falco, M. (1996). U.S. drug policy: Addicted to failure. *Foreign Policy*, 102(1), 120–133.

Farah, D. (1993). "Escobar killed in medellin." *The Washington Post*, December 3, A1.

Fatemi v. *United States*, 192 A.2d 525; (1963) D.C. App.

Federal Bureau of Investigation, Asian Criminal Enterprise Unit (1998). Trafficking in Asian Aliens. Cited in O'Neill, R. *International Trafficking in Women to the United States: A Contemporary Manifestation of Slavery and Organized Crime*. Center for the Study of Intelligence Monograph.

Federal Bureau of Investigation. Innocent Images National Initiative. Available at http://www.fbi.gov/innocent.htm.

Federal Bureau of Investigation. Legal Attache Offices. Available at http://www.fbi.gov/contact/legat/legat.htm.

Feinberg, K. R. (1981). Extraterritorial jurisdiction and the proposed federal criminal code. *Journal of Criminal Law and Criminology*, 72(2), 385–399.

Ferencz, B. B. (1973). A Proposed Definition of Aggression: By Compromise and Consensus. *The International and Comparative Law Quarterly*, 22(3), 407–433.

Festa, P. & Wilcox, J. (2000). "Experts estimate damages in the billions for bug." *CNET News.com*, May 5, Available at: http://news.cnet.com/news/01003-200-1814907.html.

"Fifty-three are accused of smuggling Kurds to Europe." *New York Times*, December 16, 2005.

Final Act of the United Nations Diplomatic Conference of Plenipotentiaries on the Establishment of an International Criminal Court, Annex I, Resolution E, adopted July 17, 1998, UN Doc. A/CONF.183/10.

Fisher, S. K. (1996). Occupation of the Womb: Forced Impregnation as Genocide. *Duke Law Journal*, 46(1), 91–133.

Flynn, L. (2005). "U.S. discloses moves to stop piracy of intellectual property." *New York Times*, September 22, C1.

Fooner, M. (1989). *Interpol*. New York: Plenum Publishing Company.

Forero, J. (2004a). "Congress approves doubling U.S. troops in Colombia to 800." *New York Times*, October 11.

Forero, J. (2004b). "Ex-Cali boss is sent to U.S. in drug case." *New York Times*, December 4.

Forero, J. (2004c). "Surge in extradition of Colombian drug suspects to U.S." *New York Times*, December 6.

Forero, J. (2006). "Bolivia's knot: No to cocaine, but yes to coca." *New York Times*, February 12, 4.

Forsythe, D. (2005). *The Humanitarian: The International Committee of the Red Cross*. Cambridge: Cambridge University Press.

Foster v. *Florida*, 537 US. (2002). (Thomas, concurring).

Fowler, G. A. (2005). "China's logo crackdown." *Wall Street Journal*, November 4, B1.

France v. *Turkey*, *The Lotus Case*, 1927 PCIJ, Ser. A, No. 10.

Freeh, L. J. (Former FBI Director) (2000). Statement before the Joint Intelligence Committees, October 19, Available at http://www.fas.org/irp/congress/2002_hr/100802freeh.pdf#search=%22 Freeh%2C%20Louis.%20October%2019%2C%202000%20Press%20Conference%22.

Friedman, T. (2005). *The World is Flat; A Brief History of the Twenty-first Century*. New York: Farrar, Straus, and Giroux.

Gall, C. (2004). "Afghan poppy farmers say mystery spraying killed crops." *New York Times*, December 5.

Gardiner, S. (2006). "That Darned Khat: In search of New York's Most Elusive Drug." *The Village Voice*, November 21.

Garrison, A. H. (2004). Defining terrorism: Philosophy of the bomb, propaganda by deed and change through fear and violence. *Criminal Justice Studies*, 17(3), 259–279.

Gartenstein-Ross, D. (2005). "The Peculiar alliance: Islamists and neo-Nazis find common ground by hating the Jews," *The Weekly Standard*, August 31.

Gellman, B. (2002). "Cyber-Attacks by Al Qaeda feared," *The Washington Post*, June 27, 2002, A1.

Gerspacher, N. (2005). The Roles of international police cooperation organizations. *European Journal of Crime, Criminal Law, and Criminal Justice*, 13(3), 413–434.

Gill, T. D. (1989). *Litigation Strategy at the International Court: A Case Study of the Nicaragua v. United States Dispute*. Amsterdam: Martinus Nijhoff.

Glaberson, W. (2003). "Three are accused of swindling visitors to internet sex sites." *New York Times*, March 19.

Gnatek, T. (2005). "Darknets: Virtual parties with a select group of invitees." *New York Times*, October 5.

Goldstein, A. (2004). "Paige calls NEA a 'Terrorist' group." *Washington Post*, February 24, A19.

Gouverneur, C. (2002). "Iran loses its drugs war." *Le Monde Diplomatique*, March.

Grabosky, P. (2001). Computer Crime in a Borderless World. *Annales Internationales de Criminologie*, 38(1/2), 67–92.

Grabosky, P. (2004). The global dimension of cybercrime. *Global Crime*, 6(1), 146–157.

Grabosky, P., Smith, R. & Dempsey, G. (2001). *Electronic Theft: Unlawful Acquisition in Cyberspace*. Cambridge: Cambridge University Press.

Greenhouse, L. (1986). "House approves measure to make computer fraud a federal crime." *New York Times*, June 4.

Grennan, S. & Britz, M. (2006). *Organized Crime: A Worldwide Perspective*. New York: Prentice Hall.

Guerette, R. T. & Clarke, R. V. (2005). Border enforcement, organized crime, and deaths of smuggled migrants on the United States – Mexico border. *European Journal on Criminal Policy and Research*, 11(2), 159–174.

Gutierrez, M. (2004). "Northern laundromats for southern fat cats." Inter-Press Service Agency, August 20.

Gyandoh, M. K. (2001). Notes & Comments: Foreign evidence gathering: What obstacles stand in the way of justice? *Temple International and Comparative Law Journal*, 15(1), 81–100.

Harel, A. & Hass, A. (2001). "Two versions in case of Palestinian deaths." *Haaretz*. January 10. Available at http://www.kavlaoved.org.il/katava_main.asp?news_id=58&sivug_id=4.

Harvard Law School Library; Nuremberg Trials Project, A Digital Document Collection. Available at http://nuremberg.law.harvard.edu/.

Hayner, P. (2001). *Unspeakable Truths*. New York: Routledge.

"Help for gulf child camel jockeys." *BBC News*. December 2, 2004. Available at http://news.bbc.co.uk/1/hi/world/middle_east/4063391.stm.

Henkin, L. (1979). *How Nations Behave*. New York: Columbia University Press.

Hiro, D. (2005). *The Iranian Labyrinth*. New York: Nation Books.

Hoffman, B. (2005). *Inside Terrorism*. New York: Columbia University Press.

Hoge, W. (2003). "British Rock Star Receives Lesser Punishment in Internet Case." *New York Times*, May 8.

Hughes, D. M. (2000). The "Natasha" trade: The transnational shadow market of trafficking in women. *Journal of International Affairs*. 53(2), 625–651.

Hughes, D. M. (2001). The "Natasha" trade: Transnational sex trafficking. *National Institute of Justice Journal*, 8–15.

Human Rights Watch Report (2002a). *The Invisible Exodus: North Koreans in the People's Republic of China*. New York: Human Rights Watch, November. Available at http://www.hrw.org/reports/2002/northkorea/.

Human Rights Watch Report (2002b). *Slavery and Slave Redemption in Sudan*. New York: Human Rights Watch, March. Available at http://www.hrw.org/backgrounder/africa/sudanupdate.htm.

The International Committee for the Red Cross website. Available at http://www.icrc.org.

International Copyright Piracy: A Growing Problem with Links to Organized Crime and Terrorism (2003). Hearing before the Subcommittee on Courts, the Internet, and Intellectual Property of the Committee on the Judiciary, US House of Representatives, March 13.

International Law Enforcement Academy in Budapest, Hungary web site. Available at http://www.ilea.hu/.

International Narcotics Control Board 2005 Report. Available at: http://www.incb.org/incb/annual_report_2005.html.

The International Organization for Migration Studies web site. Available at http://www.iom.net/.

International Organization for Migration (2001). New IOM figures on the global scale of trafficking. *Trafficking in Migrants, Quarterly Bulletin*, April. Available at http://www.iom.int//DOCUMENTS/PUBLICATION/EN/tm_23.pdf.

"Internet piracy trio sent to jail." *BBC News*. 6 May 2005. Available at http://news.bbc.co.uk/1/hi/technology/4518771.stm.

Interpol web site. Available at http://www.interpol.intl.

Interpol (2005). "Significant Cases," December 9. Available at: http://www.interpol.int/public/FinancialCrime/IntellectualProperty/Cases/.

Interpol (2006). "People Smuggling." July 26. Available at: http://www.interpol.int/Public/THB/PeopleSmuggling/Default.asp.

Israel, C. (U.S. Coordinator for International Intellectual Property Enforcement) (2006). *Piracy and Counterfeiting in China*. Testimony before the US-China Economic and Security Review Commission, July 7. Available at http://www.hongkong.usconsulate.gov/uscn/trade/ipr/2006/060701.htm.

Jacobs, C. (2001). Letter. *New York Times*, May 2.

Jamieson, A. (2001). Transnational organized crime: A European perspective. *Studies in Conflict & Terrorism,* 24(5), 377–387.

Janis, M. (2003). *An Introduction to International Law*. New York: Aspen Publishers.

Johnson, D. (1999). Trafficking of women into the European Union. *New England International and Comparative Law Annual,* 5.

Jones, J. C. (2004). Alternative development in the South American Andes: Report of findings, December. Available at: http://ciponline.org/colombia/0509jone02.pdf.

Department of Justice Press Release. (2005). *Justice Department announces international internet piracy sweep: "Operation Site Down" attacks organized piracy networks In 10 countries,* June 30. Available at: http://www.usdoj.gov/opa/pr/2005/June/05_crm_353.htm.

Kaplan, D. E. (1999). "The wiseguy regime." *U.S. News and World Report,* February 15, 37.

Katz v. *United States,* 389 U.S. 347, 362 (1967) (Harlan, J., concurring).

Kempadoo, K. (2005). *Trafficking and Prostitution Reconsidered,* Boulder: Paradigm Publishers.

Kempadoo, K. & Doezema, J. (Eds.) (1998). *Global Sex Workers: Rights, Resistance, and Redefinition.* New York: Routledge.

Kershaw, S. (2005). "Violent new front in drug war opens on the Canadian border." *New York Times,* March 5, A1.

Keung, C. (2000). Comments: supporting the snakeheads: Human smuggling from China and the 1996 amendment to the U.S. statutory definition of "Refugee." *The Journal of Criminal Law and Criminology,* 90(4), 1271–1316.

Kirk, M. (Producer) (2003). *Cyberwar.* (Television Broadcast), April 24. Boston: Public Broadcasting System.

Kissinger, H. A. (2001). The pitfalls of universal jurisdiction. *Foreign Affairs,* 80(4).

Koehler, S. A., Ladham, S., Rozin, L., Shakir, A., Omalu, B., Dominick, J., et al. (2005). The risk of body packing: a case of a fatal cocaine overdose. *Forensic Science International,* 151(1), 81–84.

Kouri, J. (2006). "Two men plead guilty to cigarette racketeering enterprise that funded Hezbollah." *American Chronicle,* July 12.

Krim, J. (2004). "Anti-Counterfeiting initiative launched; Four U.S. agencies team up for effort." *The Washington Post,* October 5, E5.

Kronenwetter, M. (2004). *Terrorism: A Guide to Events and Documents.* Westport: Greenwood Press.

Kyle, D. & Koslowski, R. (2001).*Global Human Smuggling: Comparative Perspectives.* Baltimore: Johns Hopkins University Press.

Lague, D. (2006). "China begins effort to curb piracy of computer software." *International Herald Tribune,* May 30.

Landesman, P. (2004). "The Girls Next Door." *New York Times,* January 25.

Layne, M. (2001). Final Conference Paper: Estimating the flow of illegal drugs through Ukraine. National Institute of Justice International; U.S. Research Partnership with Ukraine, September.

Lee, J. (2002). "Pirates on the web, spoils on the street." *New York Times,* July 11.

Lewis, J. F. (2004). Testimony before the Senate Judiciary Committee, May 18.

Lewis, P. (1999). "UN criticism angers charities buying Sudan slaves' release." *New York Times,* March 12.

Liptak, A. (2007). "Suspected Leader of 9/11 Attacks Is Said to Confess." *New York Times,* March 15.

Loader, B. & Douglas, T. (2000). *Cybercrime: Security and Surveillance in the Information Age.* New York: Routledge.

Lyall, S. (2003). "Britain's Hunt for Child Pornography Users Nets Hundreds Besides Pete Townshend." *New York Times,* January 15.

MacIntyre, B. (2000). "From Russia with menace: hacker." *The Australian,* January 12, 8.

Magner, T. (2004). A less than "Pacific" solution for asylum seekers in Australia. *International Journal of Refugee Law,* 16(1), 53–90.

Makarenko, T. (2001). Traffickers turn from Balkan conduit to "Northern" route. *Jane's Intelligence Review,* 13(8): 27–29.

Makarenko, T. (2002). Crime, terror and the central Asian drug trade. *Harvard Asia Quarterly*, 6(3).

Malanczuk, P. (1997). *Akehurst's Modern Introduction to International Law* (7th ed.). New York: Routledge.

Malarek, V. (2004). *The Natashas: Inside the New Global Sex Trade*. New York: Arcade Publishing.

Mameli, P. (2002). Stopping the illegal trafficking of human beings: How transnational police work can stem the flow of forced prostitution. *Crime, Law & Social Change*, 38(1), 67–80.

Markoff, J. (2000). "Thief reveals credit card data when web extortion plot fails." *New York Times*, January 10.

Martin, M. K. (1999). A one-way ticket back to the United States: The collision of international extradition law and the death penalty. *Capital Defense Journal*, 11, 243.

Mateen, S. A. (2002). Money laundering by U.S. banks. *Dawn*, March 25.

Mayer, J. (2005). Outsourcing torture. *The New Yorker*, February 14.

Mazer, R. A. (2001). From t-shirts to terrorism. *Washington Post*, September 30, B2.

Meeson, K. M. (Ed.) (1996). *Extraterritorial Jurisdiction in Theory and Practice*. London: Kluwer Law International Ltd.

Melwani, L. (2001). Bitter Chocolate. *India Today*, August 8.

Mendelson, S. E. (2005). Barracks and brothels: Peacekeepers and human trafficking in the Balkans. *Center for Strategic and International Studies Report*. Available at http://www.csis.org/ ruseura/humanrights/trafficking/#pubs.

Mermelstein, M. (2003). Features: Searching far and wide. *Los Angeles Lawyer*, 6, 33–41.

Merriam, M. J. (1995). Note: United States maritime drug trafficking search and seizure policy: An erosion of United States constitutional and international law principles. *Suffolk Transnational Law Review*, 19, 441–472.

Mertha, A. C. (2005). *The Politics of Piracy: Intellectual Property in Contemporary China*. Ithaca: Cornell University Press.

Miko, F. T. & Park, G. (2003). Report for Congress; "Trafficking in Women and Children: The U.S. and International Response." Congressional Research Service, The Library of Congress March 6.

Military and Paramilitary Activities in and Against Nicaragua (*Nicaragua* v. *US*) ICJ, Judgment of 26 November 1984.

Miller, J. (2006). Global Prostitution, Sex Tourism, and Trafficking. In Renzettie, C. M., Goodstein, L., & and Miller, S. (Eds.), *Rethinking Gender Crime, and Justice*. Boston: Roxbury Publishing, 139–154.

Miller, M. "Trafficking and Slavery (T/S) Systems and the European Union: A First Cut" (Unpublished Manuscript).

"Million Myanmar opium farmers face 'disaster' if crop eradicated: UN." Agence France-Presse, October 11, 2004.

Money Laundering Threat Assessment Group (2005). *U.S. Money Laundering Threat Assessment*. Available at http://www.treasury.gov/offices/enforcement/pdf/mlta.pdf.

Morris-Cotterill, N. (2001). Money Laundering. *Foreign Policy*, May/June.

Moseley, J. A. (2005). Note: The fourth amendment and remote searches: Balancing the protection of "the people" with the remote investigation of internet crimes. *Notre Dame Journal of Law, Ethics & Public Policy*, 19, 355–378.

Murray, A. (1998). Debt-bondage and trafficking: Don't believe the hype. In Kempadoo, K. & Doezema, J. (Eds.), *Global Sex Workers: Rights, Resistance, and Redefinition*. New York, Routledge. 1998, 51–64 Cited in: Miller, J. (2006) Global Prostitution, Sex Tourism, and Trafficking. In Renzettie, C. M., Goodstein, L., & and Miller, S. (Eds.) *Rethinking Gender Crime, and Justice*. Boston: Roxbury Publishing 139–154.

Musto, D. F. (1991). Drugs. In Foner, E. & Garraty, J. A. (Eds.). *The Reader's Companion to American History*. New York: Houghton Mifflin.

Mydans, S. (1990). "As sun sets, tempers rise at border." *New York Times*, June 22, A12.

Myers, W. H. (1996). The emerging threat of transnational organized crime from the East. *Crime, Law & Social Change*, 24(3), 181–222.

Nadelman, E. (1993). *Cops Across Borders: The Internationalization of U.S. Criminal Law Enforcement*. State College: Penn State Press.

National Criminal Justice Reference Service's (NCJRS). "In the Spotlight" website. Available at http://www.ncjrs.gov/spotlight/trafficking/publications.html.

Office of National Drug Control Policy; Executive Office of the President (2004). The National High Intensity Drug Trafficking Area Program: Annual Report, December. Available at: http://www.whitehousedrugpolicy.gov/publications/policy/hidta04/.

National Memorial Institute to Prevent Terrorism web site. Available at http://www.tkb.org/.

Newman, G. & Clarke, R. (2003). *Superhighway Robbery: Preventing E-Commerce Crime*. Portland: Willan Publishing.

Noble, R. K. (2003). *The Links between Intellectual Property Crime and Terrorist Financing*. Testimony before the United States House Committee on International Relations, July 16.

Noble, R. K. (2006). "Op-Ed: All terrorism is local, too." *New York Times*, Section 4, August 13, 11.

Nowak, P. (2005). "Lawsuits against pirates urged to test ruling; Cases will strengthen the system after disappointing judicial interpretation of copyright law, US trade official says." *South China Morning Post*, January 24, 4.

O'Brien, T. L. (2005). "King Kong vs. the pirates of the multiplex." *New York Times*, August 28.

Operation Avalanche: Tracking child porn. *BBC News*, 2002, November 11. Available at: http://news.bbc.co.uk/2/hi/uk_news/2445065.stm.

Operation Ore: Can the UK cope? *BBC News*, 2003, January 13. Available at: http://news.bbc.co.uk/2/hi/uk_news/2652465.stm.

"Operation Site Down indictment charges four defendants with copyright violations." *State News Service*, July 14, 2005.

Orton, I. (2006). The Investigation and prosecution of a cybercrime. In Clifford, R. D. (Ed.), *Cybercrime: The Investigation, Prosecution, and Defense of a Computer-related Crime* (2nd ed.). Durham: Carolina Academic Press.

The Paquete Habana, 175 US 677, 20 S.Ct. 290, 44 L. Ed. 320 (1900).

Paust, J. J. et al (Eds.) (2000a). *International Criminal Law*. Durham: Carolina Academic Press.

Paust, J. J. et al (Eds.) (2000b). *International Criminal Law: Cases and Materials*. Durham: Carolina Academic Press.

Perl, R. F. (2003). Drug trafficking and North Korea: Issues for U.S. policy. CRS Report for Congress, Congressional Research Service, December 5. Available at: http://fpc.state.gov/documents/organization/27529.pdf.

Perry, N. J. (2004). The numerous federal legal definitions of terrorism: The problem of too many grails. *Journal of Legislature*, 30, 249–274.

Pilch, F. (2003). "Rape as Genocide: The Legal Response to Sexual Violence." Unpublished manuscript.

"Pirates attack liner off coast of Somalia." *New York Times*, November, 2005.

Podgor, E. (2004). *Understanding International Criminal Law*. Newark: Lexis-Nexis.

The Polaris Project web site. Available at http://www.polarisproject.org/.

Podgor, E. S. (2003). "Defensive Territoriality": A new paradigm for the prosecution of extraterritorial business crimes. *Georgia Journal of International and Comparative Law*, 31(1), 1–30.

Podgor, E. S. (2004). Cybercrime: National, transitional, or international? *The Wayne Law Review*, 50, 97–108.

Pollitt, M. (2004). "The online mafia: Cyber gangsters are using computer networks to blackmail businesses." *The Independent* (London), Features, December 15, 11.

Powell, S. (2006). "I was forced to smuggle: Bali drug mule." *The Australian*, February 8, 6.

Power, S. (2002). *A Problem from Hell: America and the Age of Genocide.* New York: Basic Books.

Preston, J. (2006). "Ringleader gets 35-year term in smuggling of immigrants." *New York Times*, March 17, B5.

"Profile: Evo Morales." *BBC News*, 2005, December 14. Available at http://news.bbc.co.uk/1/hi/world/americas/3203752.stm.

"Profile: Gilberto Rodriguez Orejuela." *BBC News*, 2004, December 4. Available at http://news.bbc.co.uk/2/hi/americas/2417847.stm.

"Pro-Palestinian hackers hit Israeli sites." Al Jazeera Website, 2006, June 29. Available at: http://english.aljazeera.net/NR/exeres/84000EB1-908C-4A44-9B32-BFC0FE201B31.htm.

Quayle, E. (2003). *Child Pornography: An Internet Crime.* New York: Routledge.

Raghavan, S. & Chatterjee, S. (2001). "Slaves to chocolate: Children suffer to harvest a treat they rarely get to taste." *The Gazette* (Montreal, Quebec), June 23, B1.

Rashbaum, W. K. (2000). "Drug experts report a boom in ecstasy use." *New York Times*, February 26.

Ratner, S. & Abrams, J. (2001). *Accountability for Human Rights Atrocities in International Law: Beyond the Nuremberg Precedent.* Oxford: Oxford University Press.

Reich, W. (Ed.) (1998a). *Origins of Terrorism: Psychologies, Ideologies, Theologies, States of Mind.* Washington: Woodrow Wilson Center Press.

Reich, W. (1998b). Understanding terrorist behavior: The limits and opportunities of psychological inquiry. In Reich, Walter (Ed.), *Origins of Terrorism: Psychologies, Ideologies, Theologies, States of Mind.* Washington: Woodrow Wilson Center Press.

Reiman, J. H. (1998). *The Rich Get Richer and the Poor Get Prison: Ideology, Class, and Criminal Justice.* Boston: Allyn and Bacon.

Report of the Foreign Affairs Committee (1984). House of Commons, London, England, December 12.

Richards, D. G. (2004). *Intellectual Property Rights and Global Capitalism: The Political Economy of the Trips Agreement.* New York: ME Sharpe.

Richards, J. R. (1999). *Transnational Criminal Organizations, Cybercrime, and Money Laundering: A Handbook for Law Enforcement Officers, Auditors, and Financial Investigators.* Boca Raton: CRC Press.

Riding, A. (1987). "Cocaine billionaires; The men who hold Colombia hostage." *New York Times Magazine*, March 8.

Risen, J. & Lichtblau, E. (2005). "Bush lets U.S. spy on callers without courts." *New York Times*, December 16.

Robespierre, M. (1794). Report upon the principles of political morality which are to form the basis of the administration of the interior concerns of the Republic. Cited in Garrison, A. H. (2004). Defining terrorism: Philosophy of the bomb, propaganda by deed and change through fear and violence. *Criminal Justice Studies*, 17(3), 259–279.

Robinson, J. (1998). United States practice penalizing international terrorists needlessly undercuts its opposition to the passive personality principle. *Boston University International Law Journal*, 16, 487.

Romero, S. (2005). "Patrolling the border for migrants from Mexico, with a humanitarian goal." *New York Times*, July 20.

Roth, K. (2001). The case for universal jurisdiction. *Foreign Affairs*, 80(5).

"Russian hacker gets three years." *The Seattle Times*, 2003, October 5, B3.

Ryf, K. C. (2002). Notes: The first modern anti-slavery law: The trafficking victims protections act of 2000. *Case Western Reserve Journal of International Law*, 34(1), 45–71.

Sanger, D. E. (2005). "President imposes trade sanctions on Chinese goods." *New York Times*, February 5.

Scharf, M. P. & Corrin, M. K. (2001). On dangerous ground: Passive personality jurisdiction and the prohibition of internet gambling. *New England Journal of International and Comparative Law*, 8(1), 19–36.

Scheffer, D. (2006). How the Compromise Detainee Legislation Guts Common Article 3. *Jurist*, September 25. Available at: http://jurist.law.pitt.edu/forumy/2006/09/how-compromise-detainee-legislation.php.

Schmitt, E. (2002). "Four top officials on immigration are replaced." *New York Times*, March 16.

Sclafani, K. S. (2001). Comment: If the United States doesn't prosecute them, who will? The role of the United States as the "World's Police" and its jurisdiction over stateless vessels. *Tulane Maritime Law Journal*, 26, 373–397.

Sell, S. K. & Prakash, A. (2002). Globalization and governance: Examining the contest between business and NGO agendas in intellectual property rights. *The GW Center for the Study of Globalization Occasional Paper Series*, December 16.

Senlis Council (2006). Impact assessment of crop eradication in Afghanistan and lessons learned from Latin American and Southeast Asia, January. Available at http://www.senliscouncil.net/modules/publications/009_publication.

Sewell, S. & Kaysen, C. (Eds.) (2000). *The United States and the International Criminal Court.* Lanham: Rowan and Littlefield.

Shane, S. (2006). "Bin Laden Is Said to Talk Of Moussaoui." *New York Times*, May 24.

Shane, S. & Zarate, A. (2006). "F.B.I. killed plot in talking state, a top aide says." *New York Times*, June 24.

Shields, E. (2005). "US weighs costs of Plan Colombia." *BBC News*, July 5. Available at: http://news.bbc.co.uk/2/hi/americas/4627185.stm.

Shishkin, P. & Crawford, D. (2006). "In Afghanistan, heroin trade soars despite U.S. aid." *The Wall Street Journal.* January 18, 1A.

Smith, C. (2007) "Child Pornography on Vienna Computer Prompts Worldwide Hunt." *New York Times*, February 8.

Smith, G. D. (1991). Commentary No. 13: Terrorism and the rule of law: Dangerous compromise in Colombia. Canadian Security Intelligence Service web site. Available at: http://www.csis-scrs.gc.ca/en/publications/commentary/com13.asp.

Smith, P. J. (1997). Chinese migrant trafficking: A global challenge. In Smith, P. J. (Ed.) *Human Smuggling: Chinese Migrant Trafficking and the Challenge to America's Immigration Tradition.* The Center for Strategic and International Studies.

Smith, R. G. (2004). Impediments to the successful investigation of transnational high tech crime. *Trends & Issues in Crime and Criminal Justice. Australian Institute of Criminology.* Available at: http://www.crime-research.org/articles/trends-and-issues-in-criminal-justice/.

Sontag, D. (1997). "Poor and deaf from Mexico betrayed in their dreams." *New York Times*, July 25.

Spangenberg, M. (2002). "International Trafficking of Children to New York City for Sexual Purposes." New York: EPCAT USA. Available at http://www.ecpatusa.org/pdf/trafficking_report_final.pdf.

Speart, J. (1995). "The new drug mules." *New York Times Magazine*, June 11, 44.

Spenser, D. (1999). This coyote's life. *NACLA Report on the Americas*, 33(3) 22–23.

Spenser, D. (2001). Smuggling migrants through South Texas: Challenges posed by Operation Rio Grande. In Kyle, D. & Koslowski, R. (Eds.), *Global Human Smuggling: Comparative Perspective* (129–165). Baltimore: Johns Hopkins University Press.

Stone, J. (1977). Hopes and Loopholes in the 1974 Definition of Aggression. *The American Journal of International Law*, 71(2), 224–246.

Strassheim v. *Daily*, 221 U.S. 280 (1911).

Secretariat of the Budapest Group. (1999). "The Relationship between Organized Crime and Trafficking in Aliens." Vienna: International Center for Migration Policy Development. http://www.icmpd.org/uploadimg/OCandTR.pdf.

Tailby, R. (2001). *Organized Crime and People Smuggling/Trafficking into Australia*. Australian Institute of Criminology. Canberra, Australia. Retrieved from http://www.aic.gov.au/publications/tandi/ti208.pdf.

Thomas, D. (2006). "Websites face more attacks; BLACKMAIL: The number of sites being held to ransom is on the increase." *Financial Times* (London), May 31, 4.

Thomas, T. S. & Kiser, S. D. (2002). Lords of the silk route: Violent non-state actors in central Asia. *INSS Occasional Paper 43*, United States Air Force Institute for National Security Studies, USAF Academy, Colorado.

Thucydides. (1952). *History of the Peloponnesian War*. Warner, R. (trans.), New York: Penguin Press.

Tolerance.org, A web project of the Southern Poverty Law Center. Available at http://www.tolerance.org.

Treaster, J. (1992). "From Somalia to U.S. Khat Finds a Foothold." *New York Times*, December 14.

Treaster, J. B. (1989). "The cali cartel: Colombia's smoother drug gang." *The New York Times*, September 9.

Treaster, J. (1993). U.S. altering tactics in drug war. *New York Times*, September 17.

Tyldum, G. & Brunovskis, A. (2005). Describing the unobserved: Methodological challenges in empirical studies on human trafficking. *International Migration*, 43(1–2).

UN Special Tribunal for Sierra Leone web site. Available at http://www.sc-sl.org/.

United Nations Educational, Scientific and Cultural Organization. (1970). *Convention on the Means of Prohibiting and Preventing the Illicit Import, Export and Transfer of Ownership of Cultural Property*. New York: United Nations Educational, Scientific and Cultural Organization.

United Nations Office on Drugs and Crime web site. Available at http://www.unodc.org/

United Nations Office on Drugs and Crime. *Trafficking in Human Beings*. Available at http://www.unodc.org/unodc/en/trafficking_human_beings.html.

United Nations Office on Drugs and Crime (2003). *The Opium Economy in Afghanistan: An International Problem*. New York: United Nations.

UNODC press release, June 28, 2006. Available at http://www.unodc.org/unodc/press_release_2006_06_28.html.

US Customs Service Press Release (2002). *US Customs, 10 Foreign Countries, Serve Multiple Search Warrants on Internet Child Pornography Ring*. Washington: US Customs Service, March 20. Available http://www.usdoj.gov/criminal/ceos/Press%20Releases/PR-Artus.pdf.

US Immigration and Customs Enforcement web site. Available at http://www.ice.gov/.

US Department of Justice. National Drug Threat Assessment. Available at http://www.usdoj.gov/ndic/pubs11/13846/mdma.htm.

US Department of Justice. A History of Cocaine. Available at http://www.usdoj.gov/oig/special/9712/appc.htm#N_1_.

United States v. *Alvarez-Machain* (91–172), 504 U.S. 655 (1992).

United States v. *Fernandez-Caro*, 677 F.Supp. 893 (S.D. Tex. 1987).

United States v. *Maturo*, 982 F.2d 57 (2d Cir. 1992). Cited in Podgor, Ellen, *Understanding International Criminal Law*, 72.

United States v. *Ramsey*, 431 U.S. 606 (1977).

United States v. *Stephen A. Saccoccia*, Nos. 93-1618, 93-2208, 94-1506 58 F.3d 754; 1995 U.S. App. LEXIS 15956; 42 Fed. R. Evid. Serv. (Callaghan) 355 (June 28, 1995).

United States v. *Verdugo-Urquidez*, 58 USLW 4263, U.S., 108 L.Ed. 2d 222, 110 S.Ct. 1056 (1990).

United States v. *Yunis*, 681 F. Supp. 909 (D.C. Cir. 1988). Cited in Paust, J. J. (Ed.) (2000). *International Criminal Law*. Durham: Carolina Academic Press.

The University of Dayton School of Law. *Cybercrimes; Law on the Digital Frontier*. Available at http://www.cybercrimes.net/.

USA Patriot Act (2001). H.R. 3162. Available at http://thomas.loc.gov/cgi-bin/query/z?c107: H.R.3162.ENR:

US Department of Justice (2006a). National Strategy To Combat Identity Theft. Available at: http://www.cops.usdoj.gov/mime/open.pdf?Item=1732.

US Department of Justice (2006b). U.S. names intellectual property enforcement chief in Asia, January 5. Available at: http://usinfo.state.gov/ei/Archive/2006/Jan/10–176639.html.

US Department of Justice, Computer Crime & Intellectual Property Section web site. Available at http://www.cybercrime.gov.

US Department of Justice (2005). Cali cartel leader extradited to the United States to face drug trafficking charges, March 11. Available at http://www.usdoj.gov/opa/pr/2005/March/05_crm_118.htm.

US Department of Justice (2002). Department of Justice issues T visa to protect women, children, and all victims of human trafficking, January 24. Available at http://www.usdoj.gov/opa/pr/2002/January/02_crt_038.htm.

US Department of Justice. US National Central Bureau of web site. Available at http://www.usdoj.gov/usncb.

US Department of Justice. Foreign Corrupt Practices Act – International Agreements Relating to Bribery of Foreign Officials. Available at http://www.usdoj.gov/criminal/fraud/fcpa/intlagree.

US Department of Justice. Computer Crime and Intellectual Property Division. Illegal "warez" organizations and Internet piracy. Available at: http://www.usdoj.gov/criminal/cybercrime/ob/OBorg&pr.htm.

US Department of Justice (2006). Legal authorities supporting the activities of the National Security Agency described by the president, January 19.

US Department of Justice, US National Central Bureau of Interpol; Point of Contact for International Law Enforcement. Available at http://www.usdoj.gov/usncb/usncborg/pointinterlaw.html.

US Department of State. Distinctions Between Human Smuggling and Human Trafficking. Available at http://www.state.gov/p/inl/rls/fs/49768.htm.

US Department of State. Obtaining Evidence Abroad. Available at http://travel.state.gov/law/info/judicial/judicial_2514.html.

US Department of State. Office of Foreign Missions web site. Available at http://www.state.gov/ofm/.

US Department of State. Office to Monitor and Combat Trafficking in Persons. Available at http://www.state.gov/g/tip/.

US Department of State. Patterns of Global Terrorism. Available at http://www.state.gov/s/ct/rls/pgtrpt/.

US Department of State. Preparation of Letters Rogatory. Available at http://travel.state.gov/law/info/judicial/judicial_683.html.

US Department of State. Terrorist Groups. Available at http://www.state.gov/documents/organization/45323.pdf.

US Department of State (2005). *Trafficking in Persons Report*. US Department of State Publication 11252, June. Available at http://www.state.gov/documents/organization/47255.pdf.

US State Department (2006). *International Narcotics Strategy Report*. Available at: http://www.state.gov/p/inl/rls/nrcrpt/2006/vol1/html/62106.htm.

US Treasury Department. "What You Need to Know About U.S. Sanctions Against Drug Traffickers." Available at http://www.treasury.gov/offices/enforcement/ofac/programs/narco/drugs.pdf.

US Treasury Department (2003). *The Use and Counterfeiting of United States Currency Abroad, Part*, March. Available at http://www.treasury.gov/press/releases/docs/counterfeit.pdf.

US-UK Extradition Treaty. Cited in Martin, M. K. (1999). A one-way ticket back to the United States: The collision of international extradition law and the death penalty. *Capital Defense Journal*, 11, 243.

Varga, G. (2003). "Tapes of Beatles are recovered." *The San Diego Union-Tribune*, January 11, Jpg. A-1.

Veillette, C. (2005). Plan Colombia: A Progress Report. June 22. Available at http://www.fas.org/sgp/crs/row/RL32774.pdf.

Verton, D. (2003). *Black Ice: The Invisible Threat of Cyberterrorism*. New York: McGraw-Hill, 31–35.

Victims of Trafficking and Violence Protection Act of 2000 (2000) H.R. 3244, 106th Cong. § 112(a).

Wallace, M. R. (2002). NOTE: Voiceless victims: Sex slavery and trafficking of African women in Western Europe. *Georgia Journal of International & Comparative Law*, 30(3), 569–592.

Watson, G. R. (1993). The passive personality principle. *Texas International Law Journal*, 28(1), 1–23.

Weber, A. M. (2003). Annual Review of Law and Technology: VIII. Foreign and International Law: A. Cyberlaw: Cybercrime: The Council of Europe's convention on cybercrime. *Berkeley Technology Law Journal*, 18, 425–446.

Wedgewood, R. (2000). The Constitution of the ICC. In Sewell, S. & Kaysen, C. (Eds.). *The United States and the International Criminal Court*. Lanham: Rowan and Littlefield.

Weimann, G. (2004a). *Special Report: Cyberterrorism: How Real is the Threat?* Washington, DC: United States Institute of Peace Press.

Weimann, G. (2004b). www.terror.net, How modern terrorism uses the internet. United States Institute of Peace Special Report, March.

Weimann, G. (2006). *Terror on the Internet, the New Arena, the New Challenges*. Washington, DC: United States Institute of Peace Press.

Werke, G. (2005). *Principles of International Criminal Law*. The Hague: T.M.C. Asser Press.

White House Office of National Drug Control Policy, Fact Sheet. Available at http://www.whitehousedrugpolicy.gov/publications/pdf/ncj201387.pdf.

White House Fact Sheet. Overview of the Foriegn Narcotics Kingpin Designation Act Available at: http://www.whitehouse.gov/news/releases/2001/06/20010601–3.html.

White, N. R. (2004). *Defending the Homeland*. New York: Thompson Wadsworth.

Williams, P. (1993). The international drug trade: An industry analysis. *Low Intensity Conflict & Law Enforcement*, 2(3), 397–420.

Willoughby, R. (2003). Crouching fox, hidden eagle: Drug trafficking and transnational security – A perspective from the Tijuana-San Diego border. *Crime, Law and Social Change*, 40(1), 113–142.

Willoughby, W. W. (1925). *Opium as an International Problem*. Baltimore: The Johns Hopkins Press.

Wilson, R. (2006). *The Politics of Truth and Reconciliation in South Africa*. Cambridge: Cambridge University Press.

Wise, E. M., Podgor, E. S., & Clark, R. S. (2004). *International Criminal Law: Cases and Materials* (2nd edn). Newark: Lexis Nexis.

Wren, C. (2000). "U.N. forsakes effort to curb poppy growth by Afghans." *New York Times*, September 18.

Wren, C. S. (1996). "Business schemes change dynamics of the drug war." *New York Times*, May 5.

Wren, C. S. (1999). "Seizure of ecstasy at airport shows club drug's increase." *New York Times*, October 19.

Yacoubian, G. S. (2003). Should the subject matter jurisdiction of the International Criminal Court include drug trafficking? *International Journal of Comparative Criminology*, 3(2), 175–190.

Yoo, J. (2005). *The Powers of War and Peace: The Constitution and Foreign Affairs after 9/11*. Chicago: University of Chicago Press.

Young, S. (2004). *Verdugo* in cyberspace: Boundaries of fourth amendment rights for foreign nations in cybercrime cases. *Michigan Telecommunications and Technology Law Review*, 10(1), 139–174.

Youngstown Co. v. Sawyer, 343 U.S. 579 (1952). Justice Jackson, Concurring.

Zeller Jr., T. (2006). "Cyberthieves silently copy your passwords as you type." *New York Times*, February.

Zhang, S. & Chin, K. (2002). Enter the dragon: Inside Chinese human smuggling organizations. *Criminology*, 40(4), 737–768.

Index

❖